Asking Questions About

Cultural Anthropology

A CONCISE INTRODUCTION

Asking Questions About

Cultural Anthropology

A CONCISE INTRODUCTION

SECOND EDITION

Robert L. Welsch
FRANKLIN PIERCE UNIVERSITY

Luis A. Vivanco
UNIVERSITY OF VERMONT

New York   Oxford
OXFORD UNIVERSITY PRESS

Oxford University Press is a department of the University of Oxford. It furthers
the University's objective of excellence in research, scholarship, and education
by publishing worldwide. Oxford is a registered trade mark of Oxford University
Press in the UK and certain other countries.

Published in the United States of America by Oxford University Press
198 Madison Avenue, New York, NY 10016, United States of America.

For titles covered by Section 112 of the US Higher Education
Opportunity Act, please visit www.oup.com/us/he for the
latest information about pricing and alternate formats.

Library of Congress Cataloging-in-Publication Data
Names: Welsch, Robert Louis, 1950- author. | Vivanco, Luis Antonio, 1969-
author.
Title: Asking questions about Cultural Anthropology : a concise introduction
/ Robert L. Welsch, Franklin Pierce University, Luis A. Vivanco,
University of Vermont.
Description: Second Edition. | New York : Oxford University Press, [2018] |
"© 2019, 2016 by Oxford University Press"—T.p. verso. | Includes
bibliographical references and index.
Identifiers: LCCN 2018018213| ISBN 9780190878078 (Paperback : alk. paper) |
ISBN 9780190878108 (Ebook)
Subjects: LCSH: Ethnology.
Classification: LCC GN316 .W469 2018 | DDC 305.8—dc23 LC record available at
https://lccn.loc.gov/2018018213

9 8 7 6 5 4 3 2 1
Printed by LSC Communications, United States of America

Robert L. Welsch

To Sarah for her love and support, and to my students who have nudged me toward a broader and more complex view of the human condition and humanity's remarkable diversity.

Luis A. Vivanco

To Peggy, Isabel, Felipe, and Camila for their love and support, and to my students who have taught me much about the importance of inspired teaching and learning.

Contents in Brief

Contents

6 Sustainability

Environment and Foodways • 117

12 Religion
Ritual and Belief • 257

13 The Body

Biocultural Perspectives on Health and Illness • 279

Letter From the Authors

Dear Reader,

Imagine how people would react to you if the next time you went to the university bookstore you tried to haggle at the cash register for your textbooks. Or if the next time you caught a cold you explained to your friends that you were sick because a jealous person had hired a witch to cast a spell on you. In both cases, a lot of people would think you are crazy. But in many societies throughout the world, a lot of ordinary people would consider you crazy for *not* haggling or for *not* explaining your misfortunes as the workings of a witch.

Issues such as these raise some interesting questions. How do people come to believe such things? How are such beliefs reflected in and bolstered by individual behavior and social institutions in a society? Why do *we* believe and act in the ways we do? Such questions are at the core of the study of culture. The idea of culture is one of anthropology's most important contributions to knowledge.

The goal of our textbook is to help students develop the ability to pose good anthropological questions and begin answering them, our inspiration coming from the expression "99% of a good answer is a good question." In a deliberately concise way, we guide students through contemporary and provocative issues and then use theories, ethnographic case studies, and applied perspectives as ways of explaining how anthropologists have looked at these topics over time. Our approach emphasizes what is currently known within the study of cultural anthropology and issues that continue to challenge anthropologists.

Central to the plan of this book are three underlying principles that guide our approach to cultural anthropology:

- An emphasis on learning how to ask important and interesting anthropological questions.
- Applying anthropology to understand and solve human problems.
- Respecting tradition, with a contemporary perspective.

Every chapter, every feature of the book has been written with these principles in mind. We have written a book about anthropology that draws on insights anthropologists have learned during the twentieth century. At the same time, with its cutting-edge content and pedagogy, this is a textbook that provides what students need for the twenty-first century.

For most students, an introductory course in cultural anthropology is the only educational exposure they will have to anthropological thinking. Most readers are unlikely to see anthropological thinking as relevant to their own lives unless we find a way to make it so. This book represents our endeavor to do just that.

Here's wishing you greater appreciation of cultural anthropology and a lifetime of cultural revelations to come.

Sincerely,

Robert L. Welsch
Luis A. Vivanco

About the Authors

Robert L. Welsch currently teaches cultural anthropology at Franklin Pierce University and previously taught for many years at Dartmouth College. He was affiliated with the Field Museum in Chicago for more than two decades. Trained in the 1970s at the University of Washington, at a time when anthropologists still focused mainly on non-Western village-level societies, and when cultural materialist, Marxist, structuralist, and interpretive theories dominated the discipline, Welsch has focused his research on medical anthropology, religion, exchange, art, and museum studies in the classic anthropological settings of Papua New Guinea and Indonesia, and the history of anthropology as a professional discipline. He is Associate Professor of anthropology at Franklin Pierce University.

Luis A. Vivanco teaches cultural anthropology and global studies at the University of Vermont, where he has won several of the university's top teaching awards. He was trained at Princeton University in the 1990s, when post-structuralist perspectives and "studying up" (studying powerful institutions and bureaucracies, often in Western contexts) was becoming commonplace. Vivanco has worked in Costa Rica, Mexico, Colombia, and the United States, studying the culture and politics of environmentalist social movements, the media, science, ecotourism, and urban mobility with bicycles. He is Professor of anthropology and co-director of the Humanities Center at the University of Vermont.

Preface

What is cultural anthropology, and how is it relevant in today's world? Answering these core questions in a concise way is the underlying goal of this book.

Cultural anthropology is the study of the social lives of communities, their belief systems, languages, and social institutions, both past and present. It provides a framework to organize the complexity of human experience and comprehend global cultural processes and practices. The practice of cultural anthropology also provides knowledge that helps solve human problems today.

Unlike textbooks that emphasize the memorization of facts, *Asking Questions About Cultural Anthropology: A Concise Introduction* teaches students how to think anthropologically. This approach helps students view cultural issues as an anthropologist might. In this way, anthropological thinking is regarded as a tool for deciphering everyday experience.

❦ Organized Around Key Questions

Each chapter is built around key questions that can be answered by cultural anthropology. Through these unique chapter-opening and follow-up questions, students will see how classic anthropological concerns relate to contemporary situations.

❦ Solving Human Problems

At the heart of *Asking Questions About Cultural Anthropology: A Concise Introduction* is the belief that anthropology can make a difference in the world. We explain how anthropologists have looked at a wide range of human issues over time—mediating conflict, alleviating social problems, and contributing to new social policies—exploring examples but also explaining challenges that still remain.

❦ The Past Through a Contemporary Perspective

Asking Questions About Cultural Anthropology: A Concise Introduction represents our effort to close the gap between the realities of the discipline today and traditional views that are also taught at the introductory level. We believe that there is much to be gained, for ourselves and our students, by strengthening the dialogue between generations and subfields of anthropologists. We endeavor to bring classic anthropological examples, cases, and analyses to bear on contemporary questions.

An Active, Concise Approach

We recognize the appeal of a shorter introductory text that covers the essential concepts, terms, and history of cultural anthropology. Many instructors prefer such an efficient approach because it introduces students to the widely accepted fundamentals while permitting the complementary use of monographs, a reader, articles, lectures, field-based activities, and other kinds of supplements. In constructing this text we have aimed to balance concise coverage of fundamental content with a continued commitment to an active, learner-centered pedagogy that will also help students develop their anthropological IQ. For those instructors who prefer greater breadth and depth along with that active approach, we recommend our full-featured textbook *Cultural Anthropology: Asking Questions About Humanity*.

Why We Wrote This Book

In view of how most academic work and life is organized and practiced today, our co-authorship is a somewhat unlikely collaboration. We come from different generations of anthropological training, teach at different kinds of institutions, do our research in opposite corners of the world, and work on different topics. Given the pressures and realities of regional and topical specialization within the discipline, we might not even run into each other at conferences, much less have reason to work together.

But as teachers concerned with sharing the excitement of anthropological findings and thinking with our undergraduate students, we share a lot in common. For one, we believe that there is strength in diversity, and we think our differing backgrounds are more representative of the breadth of the discipline and who actually teaches introductory courses in cultural anthropology. Because both of us feel that anthropological thinking is for everyone, we wrote this textbook to appeal to instructors who blend traditional and contemporary views of anthropology and teach students of many cultural backgrounds. We do this by treating the learning experience as a process of actively asking questions about real-world problems and applying theoretical insights to understand them, as nearly all anthropologists actually do.

Guiding You Through the Book

Each chapter opens with a contemporary, real-life story introducing the theme of the chapter. The chapter-opening narrative concludes with the core questions at the heart of the chapter. Core questions posed at the beginning of the chapter are reflected in the titles of each major section in the chapter. Furthermore, the end of each section in a chapter is capped with a thought-provoking question in *Thinking Critically About Anthropology*, encouraging assimilation and application of key concepts.

Each chapter includes one of two types of boxed features. *Thinking Like an Anthropologist* boxes invite student to exercise their own anthropological IQ.

These features first present students with a concrete ethnographic situation and several questions for further inquiry, and then introduce another scenario that prompts students to formulate their own questions about this new but related subject matter. *Anthropologist as Problem Solver* boxes describe cases in which anthropologists have applied disciplinary insights and methods to help alleviate social problems, mediate conflicts, and (re)define policy debates. These cases also provide insights into careers that take advantage of an anthropology background.

At the end of each chapter is a table that summarizes key points about each section and highlights issues yet to be resolved. The goal here is to help students understand settled knowledge and the findings of anthropology, as well as issues that continue to attract anthropological attention. These tables demonstrate that anthropology is a living and dynamic discipline.

❧ New in This Edition

Building on the successful approach established in the first edition, the second edition of *Asking Questions About Cultural Anthropology* features a number of changes designed to keep the material up to date, relevant, and engaging for students. The following are the most visible changes:

- **A new chapter**—"Race, Ethnicity, and Class" (Chapter 9)—that explores how culturally shaped ideas about race, ethnicity, and class shape people's lives and experiences. Taking a critical approach to common assumptions about the relationship between identity and inequality, this new chapter addresses the central question, *If differences of identity are not rooted in biology, why do they feel so real, powerful, and unchangeable?*

- **A thoroughly revised chapter**—"Materiality" (Chapter 14)—on material culture. Expanding on the discussion of material objects in the first edition, this chapter explores how and why objects have meaning and power to us in various cultural contexts, and it examines issues related to the ownership of artifacts from other cultures.

- **New thematic boxes.** New boxes draw students' attention to a wide variety of concerns that are important to anthropologists today, including the social impacts of anthropological research (Chapter 1), the preservation of endangered languages (Chapter 4), food insecurity among migrant workers (Chapter 6), holistic approaches to fighting poverty (Chapter 7), counting and classifying race in the American census (Chapter 9), (non)acceptance of trans people in America (Chapter 10), identifying and addressing health concerns (Chapter 13), and building and maintaining relationships with peoples whose cultural objects are on display in Western museums (Chapter 14).

- **New chapter-opening stories drawn from real life.** New case studies exploring the Syrian refugee crisis (Chapter 5), responses to climate change in the Marshall Islands (Chapter 6), the importance of social networks to entrepreneurs in China (Chapter 7), the 2014 Ebola outbreak in West Africa and the fear of the disease becoming widespread in the United States (Chapter 13), and the controversy surrounding the *Into the Heart of Africa* art exhibit in Canada (Chapter 14) help students relate major themes in each chapter to people's real-world experiences.

- **A new epilogue.** The final section in this book draws together important themes that run throughout the chapters—including the importance of appreciating human diversity, embracing a holistic perspective, and rejecting ethnocentrism—to help students recognize the many ways in which studying cultural anthropology can enrich their understanding of their world.

In addition to these changes, we have added new coverage of key topics in various chapters to ensure students receive a well-rounded introduction to cultural anthropology. These additions include the following:

- Chapter 1 features an expanded discussion of ethical obligations anthropologists must consider when conducting their research and sharing their findings.
- Chapter 2 provides a revised definition of culture.
- Chapter 4 contains new sections on how anthropologists study language.
- Chapter 5 provides new coverage of the cultures of migration.
- Chapter 6 includes a new discussion of anthropologists' interest in the social dimensions of climate change.
- Chapter 7 features new explorations of cross-cultural perspectives on the significance of debt and the concepts of property and ownership.
- Chapter 10 features a revised approach to gender, sex, and sexuality, focusing on the fluidity of maleness and femaleness.
- Chapter 11 includes new material on the study of cultural patterns in child-rearing, and on international adoptions and the problem of cultural identity.
- Chapter 12 provides an in-depth analysis of the issues surrounding the 2015 attack on the offices of Charlie Hebdo in Paris, pointing out that such attacks are not merely the result of a "clash of civilizations."

❦ Ensuring Student Success

Oxford University Press offers students and instructors a comprehensive ancillary package for *Asking Questions About Cultural Anthropology*.

For Students

Asking Questions About Cultural Anthropology is accompanied by an extensive **companion website** (www.oup.com/us/welsch), which includes materials to help students with every aspect of the course. For each chapter, you will find:

- Chapter outlines
- Flashcards
- Self-grading quizzes
- Activities

- Links to online resources
- Access to the **OUP Anthropology Video Library** (see below for more information)

❦ For Instructors

Instructors who adopt *Asking Questions About Cultural Anthropology* will have access to a truly exemplary set of ancillary materials to enhance teaching and support students' learning.

The **Ancillary Resource Center (ARC)** at www.oup-arc.com is a convenient, instructor-focused single destination for resources to accompany *Asking Questions About Cultural Anthropology*. Accessed online through individual user accounts, the ARC provides instructors with access to up-to-date ancillaries while guaranteeing the security of grade-significant resources. In addition, it allows OUP to keep instructors informed when new content becomes available.

The ARC for Asking Questions About Cultural Anthropology includes:

- A digital copy of the **Instructor's Manual**, which includes:
  - A comprehensive introduction written by the authors describing their pedagogical vision and offering advice on how to promote active learning in the classroom
  - Chapter outlines
  - Learning objectives
  - Discussion of key controversies that expand on chapter review tables in the book
  - Key terms and definitions and summaries
  - PowerPoint slides
  - Web links
  - In-class activities and project assignments
  - Suggestions for class discussion
  - Additional readings
  - An image bank
- A **Test Bank** written by the authors and organized around principles from Bloom's Taxonomy for cognitive learning, including:
  - Multiple-choice questions
  - True/false questions
  - Fill-in-the-blank questions
  - Essay prompts
- Access to the **OUP Anthropology Video Library,** containing video clips intended to complement the OUP suite of titles that are published for cultural anthropology and general anthropology courses. The library features excerpts of ethnographic films from Documentary Educational Resources. The clips are organized by topic for easy reference. Each clip features a brief description, a discussion about why the clip is important, and questions for reflection and discussion.

Acknowledgments

The authors would like to thank the many individuals who have supported this project from its inception to the final stages of production. The impetus for this book lies with Kevin Witt, who had an inspired vision for a new kind of anthropology textbook and the foresight to identify and support the team to write it. In its early stages, while this project was with McGraw-Hill, development editors Pam Gordon, Nanette Giles, Susan Messer, and Phil Herbst each played an important role in shaping the manuscript.

At Oxford University Press, Sherith Pankratz, our acquisitions editor, and our two development editors, Thom Holmes (first edition) and Janice Evans (second edition), have managed this project and helped us further refine our vision with exceptional care and expertise. We would also like to thank associate editor Meredith Keffer for her support, especially with the visual program. In addition, we would like to thank assistant editor Larissa Albright, advertising and promotion product associate Marissa Dadiw, associate editor Andrew Heaton, assistant editor Jacqueline Levine, and assistant editor Paul Longo for their helpful feedback on the headings. We would also like to thank permissions coordinator Cailen Swain. In production, we would like to thank designer Michele Laseau, production editor Keith Faivre, and copy editor Wendy Walker. And last, but by no means least, we would like to acknowledge and thank our marketing team, including Tony Mathias, Frank Mortimer, Jordan Wright, and the other hardworking men and women who are marketing this book and getting it into the hands of the students for whom we wrote it.

It is important to acknowledge and thank Agustín Fuentes of the University of Notre Dame, co-author of our general anthropology textbook, *Anthropology: Asking Questions About Human Origins, Diversity, and Culture* (published by OUP), who has helped shape our thinking on numerous dimensions of cultural anthropology.

We are grateful to Franklin Pierce University, the University of Vermont, Dartmouth College, the Hood Museum of Art, the Field Museum, the U.S. National Museum of Natural History (a branch of the Smithsonian Institution), the American Museum of Natural History in New York, the University of Costa Rica, and the National University of Colombia, all of whom have provided support in diverse ways. In particular we appreciate the support and encouragement of Kim Mooney, President of Franklin Pierce University; James Dumond, Provost of Franklin Pierce; Kerry McKeever and Paul Kotila, Academic Deans at Franklin

Pierce; and Jean Dawson and John Villemaire, Division Chairs of the Social and Behavioral Sciences at Franklin Pierce. At the University of Vermont the Provost's Office and the Office of the Dean of the College of Arts and Sciences have provided important institutional support for this project.

Numerous librarians aided the development of this project at various stages, including Paul Campbell, Amy Horton, Leslie Inglis, Paul Jenkins, Gladys Nielson, Wendy O'Brien, Eric Shannon, Melissa Stearns, Lisa Wiley, and Jill Wixom at Frank S. DiPietro Library at Franklin Pierce University in Rindge, New Hampshire; Laurie Kutner at Bailey-Howe Library at the University of Vermont; Amy Witzel, Fran Oscadal, and John Cocklin, at Baker Library at Dartmouth College; and the staff of Alden Library at Ohio University in Athens, Ohio.

We want to especially thank our colleagues Kirk M. and Karen Endicott, Robert G. Goodby, Debra S. Picchi, Douglas Challenger, John Villemaire, John E. Terrell, Robert J. Gordon, and Richard Robbins, all of whom have offered support, encouragement, and insights throughout the various phases of writing this book. Many other colleagues have contributed to this project in direct and indirect ways, including shaping our thinking about various anthropological topics, sparking ideas and being a sounding board about matters of content and pedagogy, and reading and responding to draft chapters. These colleagues include, at Dartmouth College, Hoyt Alverson, Sienna R. Craig, Brian Didier, Nathaniel Dominy, Seth Dobson, Dale F. Eickelman, Kathy Hart, Sergei Kan, Brian Kennedy, Kenneth Korey, Joel Levine, Deborah Nichols, and John Watanabe; and at the University of Vermont, Ben Eastman, Scott Van Keuren, Cameron Wesson, Brian Gilley, Jennifer Dickinson, Teresa Mares, Amy Trubek, Scott Matter, Deborah Blom, and the late Jim Petersen.

Several students at Franklin Pierce, the University of Vermont, and Dartmouth College have helped with research during the various stages of writing and rewriting. These include Kristin Amato, Cory Atkinson, D. Wes Beattie, Chris Boyce, Kyle Brooks, Justyn Christophers, Michael Crossman, Matthew Dee, Brian Dunleavy, Catherine Durickas, Nathan Hedges, Elizabeth Jurgilewicz, Kelsey Keegan, Saige Kemelis, Brian Kirn, Cooper Leatherwood, Adam Levine, Kevin Mooiman, Taber Morrell, Rebecca Nystrom, Shannon Perry, Keenan Phillips Adam Slutsky, Scott Spolidoro, and Michael Surrett.

We want to thank our students at Franklin Pierce University and the University of Vermont who have test-driven various early drafts of this book as well as the first edition. Their feedback and insights have been invaluable. But in particular we want to thank Courtney Cummings, Kimberly Dupuis, John M. Gass, Kendra Lajoie, Holly Martz, Scott M. McDonald, Lindsay Mullen, and Nick Rodriguez, all of whom were students in AN400 at Franklin Pierce during the fall semester of 2012. Having used drafts of the text in their "Introduction to Cultural Anthropology" class, they reviewed all of the chapters in the book in focus-group fashion and offered useful insights about examples and writing in each chapter.

Last but certainly not least, we would like to thank our families for all the critical emotional and logistical support they have provided over the years to ensure the success of this project. Luis's children Isabel, Felipe, and Camila have aided us in various ways, from prodding questions about the book and anthropology to, at times, comic relief when we needed it. Our wives, Sarah L. Welsch and Peggy O'Neill-Vivanco, deserve our deepest gratitude for all their wise counsel over the many years this book was in development, and their ongoing support as we continue to improve it.

☙ Manuscript Reviewers

In creating this second edition, we have greatly benefited from the perceptive comments and suggestions of many talented scholars and instructors. Their insight and suggestions were immensely helpful.

Chris Baker
Walters State Community College

Beverly Bennett
Wright College

Alice Baldwin-Jones
LaGuardia Community College

Noor Borbieva
Indiana University-Purdue University Fort Wayne

Keri A. Canada
Colorado State University

Kimberly Cavanagh
University of South Carolina Beaufort

Elizabeth Higgs
University of Houston

Akbar Keshodkar
Moravian College

Kimora
John Jay College of Criminal Justice

Alice Kingsnorth
American River College

Denise Knisely
Northern Kentucky University

Pamela A. Maack
San Jacinto College

Sarah Martin
Spokane Falls Community College

Amy Nichols-Belo
Mercer University

Scott Sernau
Indiana University South Bend

Phillips Stevens, Jr.
University at Buffalo, SUNY

Brian Stokes
Allan Hancock College

In addition, we would like to thank the reviewers whose thoughtful comments helped to shape the first edition: Augustine Agwuele, Texas State University; Data D. Barata, California State University, Sacramento; O. Hugo Benavides, Fordham University; Keri Brondo, University of Memphis; Leslie G. Cecil, Stephen F. Austin State University; Carolyn Coulter, Atlantic Cape Community College; Matthew Dalstrom, Rockford University; Joanna Davidson, Boston University; Henri Gooren, Oakland University; Liza Grandia, Clark University; Ulrike M. Green, Orange Coast College; Shawn Dead Haley, Columbia College; Douglas Hume, Northern Kentucky University; Su Il Kim, Metropolitan State

College of Denver/Pikes Peak Community College; Diane E. King, University of Kentucky; Frances Kostarelos, Governors State University; J. Christopher Kovats-Bernat, Muhlenberg College; Kuinera de Kramer-Lynch, University of Delaware; Scott M. Lacy, Fairfield University; Louis Herns Marcelin, University of Miami; Linda Matthei, Texas A&M University, Commerce; Faidra Papavasil-iou, Georgia State University; Mark Allen Peterson, Miami University; Harry Sanabria, University of Pittsburgh; Elizabeth A. Scharf, University of North Dakota; Rocky L. Sexton, Ball State University; Carolyn Smith-Morris, Southern Methodist University; Victor D. Thompson, University of Georgia; James E. Todd, Modesto Junior College/California State University, Stanislaus; Susan R. Trencher, George Mason University; Neeraj Vedwan, Montclair State University; Jennifer R. Wies, Eastern Kentucky University; and Cherra Wyllie, University of Hartford.

Ancillary Co-Authors

Our sincere thanks to the scholars and instructors who aided in the creation of the ancillary materials. Along with the textbook co-authors, they helped create high-quality additional resources specifically for this text:

Mark Anthony Arceño
The Ohio State University
(PowerPoint slides)

Meryl Lodge
University of Minnesota
(Instructor's Manual, Test Bank, student resources)

1

Anthropology

Asking Questions About Humanity

Human beings are one of the world's most adaptable animals. Evolutionary history has endowed our species with certain common physical characteristics, instincts, and practices that have helped us to survive, even thrive, in every conceivable terrestrial environment. Yet no group of people is exactly like another, and as a species we exhibit tremendous variations across groups—variations in our adaptations to the environment, physical appearance, language, beliefs, and social organization.

Humans have always encountered groups of people who look different, speak unfamiliar languages, and behave in unexpected or unpredictable ways. Although

Intercultural Interactions. In 1767, Captain Samuel Wallis and his crew were the first Westerners to reach Tahiti. Their first interactions were peaceful and included an exchange of gifts between Wallis and Queen Oberea. The cultural differences between the Tahitians and the English raised many important questions about human differences and similarities, for both parties—the kinds of dynamics that interest anthropologists today.

sometimes hostility and wars break out between groups because of such differences, usually people have found ways to get along, often through trade and alliances. To be effective at establishing strong social and political bonds in spite of human differences has always required that people have a practical understanding of human variation.

Some of history's great travelers and explorers developed that practical understanding, among them the Venetian merchant Marco Polo (1254–1324), the Norman cleric Gerald of Wales (1146–1223), the Flemish Franciscan missionary William of Rubruck (1220–1293), the Moroccan traveler Ibn Batuta (1304–1368), and the Chinese admiral Zheng He (1371–1433). These individuals were all deeply interested in other peoples, and their writings express sophisticated understandings of how and why the groups they encountered looked, acted, worshiped, and spoke as they did (Bartlett 1982; Larner 1999; Menzies 2002; Dreyer 2007; Harvey 2007; Khanmohamadi 2008; Fazioli 2014). Similarly, there is a rich historical legacy of intellectual thought about human variation. The great Chinese philosopher Confucius (551–479 BCE) wrote in two of his *Analects* some principles for establishing relationships with *yi* [yee], meaning cultural and ethnic outsiders. A generation later, the Greek historian Herodotus (484–425 BCE), in his multi-volume *Histories* , described the diverse peoples and societies he encountered during his travels in Africa, Southwestern Asia, and India, offering a number of possible explanations for the variations he observed across groups.

While all of these individuals were curious about other peoples and at times were quite rigorous in their ways of thinking about human variation, they were not anthropologists as we think of them today. Still, their various studies show that getting along with peoples from different cultures has always been important.

These points lead us to our first question, the question at the heart of this chapter: *What is anthropology, and how is it relevant in today's world?* Embedded in this broader question are the following problems, around which this chapter is organized:

How did anthropology begin?
What do the four subfields of anthropology have in common?
How do anthropologists know what they know?
How do anthropologists put their knowledge to work in the world?
What ethical obligations do anthropologists have?

Anthropology is the study of human beings, their biology, their prehistory and histories, and their dynamic languages, cultures, and social institutions. Anthropology provides a framework for asking questions about and grasping the complexity of human experience, both past and present. Anthropology is about where humans have been, but it also provides knowledge that helps solve human problems today.

❦ How Did Anthropology Begin?

During the nineteenth century, **anthropology** emerged in Europe and North America as an academic discipline devoted to the systematic observation and analysis of human variation. Three key concerns began to emerge by the 1850s that would shape professional anthropology. These were (1) the disruptions of industrialization in Europe and America, (2) the rise of evolutionary theories, and (3) the growing importance of Europe's far-flung colonies and the vast American West with their large indigenous populations whose land, mineral wealth, and labor Europeans and Americans wanted to control.

The Disruptions of Industrialization

Industrialization refers to the economic process of shifting from an agricultural economy to a factory-based one. Industrialization disrupted American and European societies by bringing large numbers of rural people into towns and cities to work in factories. These disruptions raised questions that motivated great social thinkers who later influenced the rise of anthropology as a social scientific discipline, in particular German political economists Karl Marx (1818–1883) and Max Weber (1864–1920) and French anthropologist-sociologist Émile Durkheim (1858–1917).

At the beginning of the nineteenth century, most people in Western countries were rural farmers. The rise of factory economies changed such basic aspects of life as the range of people individuals encountered and might marry, the activities they spent their days doing, and the role of religion in their lives. In the midst of these upheavals, anthropology developed as a discipline that sought to understand and explain how people organize their communities and how those communities change. It also led scholars to consider how industrialization affected peoples in European colonies in Africa, Asia, Latin America, and the Pacific Islands. Important new questions were posed: Why did these diverse societies organize their lives in the ways they did? Why had the civilizations of China, India, and the Arab world developed social, political, and economic patterns so different from those of Europeans? Asking about how European villages and cities were structured and how they perpetuated their cultures ultimately led to questions about how all sorts of non-Western societies worked as well.

The Theory of Evolution

Evolution refers to the adaptive biological changes organisms make across generations. English naturalist Charles Darwin (1809–1882) developed a theory of how different species of plants and animals had evolved from earlier forms. The key mechanism of his evolutionary theory was what he called "natural selection," a process through which certain inheritable traits are passed along to offspring because they are better suited to the environment.

For Darwin, the question of the origin of species was not a religious one (as many people in his time believed) but an **empirical** one, best answered by observing whether species had changed and whether new species had emerged over time.

Thanks to contemporary geologists, Darwin knew that many early species such as the dinosaurs had suddenly arisen in the geological record, flourished, and then died out. For him, such changes were evidence that the natural environment had selected some species for survival and that extinction was the outcome for those not well suited to changing environments. When Darwin published his groundbreaking work, *On the Origin of Species*, in 1859, he experienced a backlash, and rather few scientists accepted Darwin's ideas immediately. But as the century progressed, more and more scholars came to accept the idea of evolution. Today, scientists no longer view biological evolution as controversial, and nearly all anthropologists and biologists accept evolution as the only way to explain the relationship among animal and plant species or why humans have certain physical abilities and characteristics.

Colonial Origins of Cultural Anthropology

Colonialism is the historical practice of more powerful countries claiming possession of less powerful ones. American seizure and domination of Indian lands is a form of colonialism. Overseas, the colonial period flourished from the 1870s until the 1960s, and whites established mines, fisheries, plantations, and other enterprises using local peoples as inexpensive labor. Colonies enriched the mother countries, often impoverishing the indigenous inhabitants.

Colonized peoples everywhere had different cultures and customs, and their actions often seemed baffling to white administrators, a fact that these officials chalked up to their primitive or savage nature. Colonialists justified their actions—both politically and morally—through the **othering** of non-Western peoples, that is, defining colonized peoples as different from, and subordinate to, Europeans in terms of their social, moral, and physical norms (Said 1978). At the same time, early anthropologists were developing new social scientific methods of studying non-Western societies, primarily to inform colonial officials how to govern and control such different peoples.

Figure 1.1   The Salvage Paradigm. Efforts to document indigenous cultures "before they disappeared" motivated anthropologists and others—including well-known American photographer Edward S. Curtis, who took this picture of an Apsaroke mother and child in 1908—to record the ways of traditional people.

Most Europeans and Americans expected their colonial subjects to die out, leading to the urgent collection of information about tribal societies before it was too late. Well into the 1920s, anthropologists pursued an approach known as the **salvage paradigm**, which held that it was important to observe indigenous ways of life, interview elders, and assemble collections of objects made and used by indigenous peoples because their traditions would soon disappear (Figure 1.1). Of course, today we know that while some Indian tribes, especially along the East Coast of North America, largely died out, many other groups have survived and grown in population. But these Native American cultures have had to adjust and adapt to the changing American landscape.

Anthropology as a Global Discipline

By the end of the nineteenth century, anthropology was an international discipline, whose practitioners were mainly based in Western Europe and the United States. Although they had some shared concerns, anthropologists in particular countries developed specific national traditions, studying distinct problems and developing their own styles of thought. Throughout the twentieth century, anthropology began to emerge in many other non-European countries as well. Many students in colonial territories had attended European and American universities, where they learned anthropology, and in many cases these students brought anthropology back home. In these countries, anthropology often focuses on practical problems of national development and on documenting the minority societies found within the country's borders. Today, anthropology is a global discipline with practitioners in dozens of countries asking many different kinds of questions about humanity.

THINKING CRITICALLY ABOUT ANTHROPOLOGY

Can you think of something you do at your college or university that feels "natural" but is probably done somewhat differently at another college? Consider, for example, how your experiences in high school classes may have led you to expect something different from your college classes.

⍋ What Do the Four Subfields of Anthropology Have in Common?

Anthropology has traditionally been divided into four subfields: cultural anthropology, archaeology, biological anthropology, and linguistic anthropology (Figure 1.2).

Cultural anthropology focuses on the social lives of living communities. Until the 1970s, most cultural anthropologists conducted research in

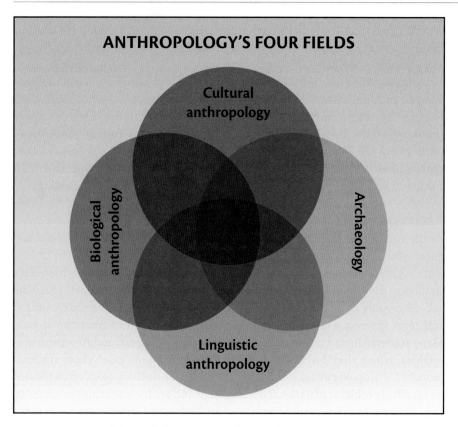

Figure 1.2   Anthropology's Four Fields.

non-Western communities, spending a year or two of fieldwork observing social life. They learned the local language and studied broad aspects of the community, such as people's economic transactions, religious rituals, political organization, and families, seeking to understand how these distinct domains influenced each other. In recent decades, they have come to focus on more specific issues in the communities they study, such as how and why religious conflicts occur, how environmental changes affect agricultural production, and how economic interactions create or maintain social inequalities. Today, anthropologists are as likely to study modern institutions, occupational groups, ethnic minorities, or the role of computer technology or advertising in their own cultures as they are to study cultures outside their own.

Archaeology studies past cultures by excavating sites where people lived, worked, farmed, or conducted some other activity. Prehistoric archaeologists study prehistory (life before written records), trying to understand how people lived before they had domesticated plants and animals, as well as patterns of trade and warfare between ancient settlements. Prehistoric archaeologists are especially interested in the transition from hunting and gathering to agriculture, and the rise of cities and states. Another branch of archaeology is *historical archaeology*, which studies the material remains of societies that also left behind written and oral histories. Focusing primarily on the past 500 years, historical archaeology supplements what we know about a community or society with studies of recent historical migrations and cultural shifts.

Biological anthropology (also called physical anthropology) focuses on the biological aspects of the human species, past and present, along with those of our closest relatives, the nonhuman primates (apes, monkeys, and related species). A mainstay of biological anthropology has been the attempt to uncover human fossils and reconstruct the pathways of human evolution. By the 1950s and 1960s, biological anthropologists expanded into the study of human health and disease and began to look at the nonhuman primates (especially monkeys and apes) to determine what is part of our basic primate biology and what comes with culture. Biological anthropology is currently a field with many specializations; in addition to evolution, health and disease, and primate behavior, researchers also study human genetics, the impact of social stress on the body, and human diet and nutrition.

Linguistic anthropology studies how people communicate with one another through language, and how language use shapes group membership and identity. Linguistic anthropologists also look at how language helps people organize their cultural beliefs and ideologies. These anthropologists have traditionally studied the categories that indigenous people use in their own languages, attempting to understand how they classify parts of their social and natural worlds in unique ways.

Anthropology is by nature an interdisciplinary discipline. Its subfields cross into many other academic disciplines across the social and natural sciences. Cultural anthropologists, for example, often draw on sociological and psychological approaches, as well as historical and economic data. Most archaeologists need to understand the principles of geology, including how rock layers form over time and techniques used to date artifacts. Biological anthropology draws heavily on morphology (which deals with the form and structure of organisms), cellular biology, and genetics.

One thing that keeps such diverse subfields together is a shared history. In the early twentieth century, anthropology became organized into the four subfields we know today, from a shared evolutionary perspective. Archaeologists and cultural anthropologists, especially in North America, generally see themselves as asking similar kinds of questions about human cultures. Another reason for the persistence of the four-field approach is that anthropologists share certain fundamental approaches and concepts, which they agree are important for making sense of humanity's complexity. These include culture, cultural relativism, diversity, change, and holism.

Culture

Imagine how people would react to you if the next time you went to the university bookstore to buy your textbooks you tried to haggle at the cash register. Or if the next time you had a cold you explained to your friends that your sickness was caused by a witch's spell. In both cases most people would think you are crazy. But in many societies throughout Africa, Asia, Latin America, the Pacific, and other regions, a lot of ordinary people would think you are crazy for *not* haggling or for *not* explaining your misfortunes as the workings of a witch.

Every human group has particular rules of behavior and a common set of explanations about how the world works. Within the community, these behaviors and explanations feel totally natural, which is to say, self-evident and necessary. People who behave differently are strange, wrong, maybe even evil. Yet what feels natural to one group may seem totally arbitrary to another. In anthropology, the term **culture** refers to the taken-for-granted notions, rules, moralities, and behaviors within a social group that feel natural and suggest the way things should be. The idea of culture is one of anthropology's most important contributions to knowledge.

Anthropologists believe that people have culture in two senses: the general and the particular. Culture in the general sense refers to humans' possession of a generalized capacity, even necessity, to create, share, and pass on their understandings of things through culture. Culture in the particular sense refers to the fact that people live their lives within particular cultures, or ways of life. In Chapter 2, we explore the concept of culture more deeply, but here it is important to know that when anthropologists use the term *culture* they are nearly always referring to ideas about the world and ways of interacting in society or in the environment in predictable and expected ways.

Cultural Relativism

Anthropologists carry with them basic assumptions about how the world works and what is right or wrong, and these assumptions typically become apparent when one is studying a culture that makes completely different assumptions. One possible response to the gap in understanding that comes with being in another culture is **ethnocentrism**, assuming one's own way of doing things is correct, while simply dismissing other people's assumptions as wrong or ignorant. Such a position would render the attempt to understand other cultures meaningless, and it can lead to bigotry and intolerance. To avoid such negative outcomes, anthropologists have traditionally emphasized **cultural relativism**, the moral and intellectual principle that one should seek to understand cultures on their own terms and withhold judgment about seemingly strange or exotic beliefs and practices.

Human Diversity

Another of anthropology's major contributions to knowledge has been to describe and explain human **diversity**, the sheer variety of ways of being human around the world. When anthropologists talk about diversity, they mean something different from the popular usage of the term in the United States, which typically refers to different kinds of art, cuisine, dress, or dance, as well as to differences among various racial and ethnic groups.

Defined anthropologically, *diversity* refers to multiplicity and variety, which is not the same as mere difference. Within multiplicity and variety, there is both difference *and* similarity. This idea of diversity-as-multiplicity can shed light on the cultural effects of globalization. People now drink Coca-Cola, wear Levi's jeans, and watch CNN all over the world, leading many observers to believe that the diversity of human cultures is in decline because more people are participating in a global economy. Yet cultural differences do not just disappear. In fact, globalization creates many new opportunities for cultural diversity—differences *and* similarities—to thrive.

An example drawn from the southern Mexican state of Chiapas illustrates this point (Figure 1.3). In Chiapas, some indigenous people have adapted Coca-Cola for use in their religious and community ceremonies. For many generations Tzotzil Mayas [**tso**-tseel **my**-ahs] in the community of San Juan Chamula used alcoholic drinks, particularly fermented corn drinks and distilled sugar cane liquor, in their public and religious rites (Nash 2007). To create these rites, traditional Mayan religious leaders blended Catholic and indigenous traditions, combining Catholicism's celebration of saints' days with the Mayan belief that consuming intoxicating spirits helps individuals access sacred powers. Alcoholism, however, became a severe problem, and beginning in the 1940s many Mayas began converting to Protestant sects that ban alcohol, eroding the power of traditional religious leaders. In the 1980s these leaders began substituting Coca-Cola for alcoholic drinks in ceremonies. Some leaders gained great personal wealth as distributors of Coca-Cola, deepening socioeconomic class divisions in the community (Nash 2007). But community members incorporated Coca-Cola into their ritual lives easily, accepting the notion that the soft drink's bubbles have powers once associated with alcohol, for example, the ability to help individuals belch out bad spirits residing in their bodies (M. Thomas 2008).

Here is a powerful example of diversity-as-multiplicity: globalization has brought changes to San Juan Chamula that resemble conditions in many other places around the globe, but Mayas have imposed their own meanings on the soft drink, using it in ways that reinforce some of their own distinctive cultural traditions.

Figure 1.3   A Coca-Cola Distributor in San Juan Chamula, Chiapas, Mexico.

Change

As the previous example about globalization and Coca-Cola demonstrates, our world is dynamic and constantly changing. Anthropologists in each subfield are specialists in studying human change. For example:

- *Cultural anthropologists* study topics as diverse as how and why religious change happens; what happens when a dominant economic system like capitalism is incorporated into a traditional economy; and how and why political violence can erupt in societies experiencing rapid social change.
- *Archaeologists* study the effects of environmental change on past societies; how changes in material culture reflect ongoing social, economic, and political changes; and how complex state societies were formed and disintegrated.
- *Biological anthropologists* study the processes of human evolution, and how our bodies and genetic make-up change in relation to environmental changes, migration, diseases, and other dynamics.
- *Linguistic anthropologists* study how new languages are formed when different languages come together, and how social changes, such as changes in gender relations, are reflected in and emerge from how people communicate with each other.

Some of these changes, particularly changes in cultural practices, can emerge over a few years or a generation or two. Others, like changes in human biology, can take many generations and are imperceptible to most living observers. Americans, for example, have gotten considerably taller than we were in colonial times, probably because of changes in diet. But this fact is largely unnoticed by modern Americans unless we tour colonial houses from the 1700s, where the doors are not nearly as tall as those of today.

Anthropology also mirrors the changing world in which it is practiced. As new topics, issues, and problems emerge, anthropologists study things they would not have studied several decades before. Today, for example, archaeologists may study municipal garbage dumps to understand what people actually consume and throw away. Cultural and linguistic anthropologists may explore how people create new forms of communication and community in cyberspace. Biological anthropologists specializing in primate behaviors may design studies to aid wildlife conservation officials.

Moreover, the face of anthropology has changed in recent decades. Once a discipline dominated by white European and American men, anthropology is increasingly practiced by women and members of many ethnic and racial minority groups. In the United States today, in fact, women constitute the majority of professional anthropologists. Around the world, decolonization has brought once excluded indigenous peoples and minorities into universities, where many have studied anthropology, further expanding the kinds of backgrounds and perspectives represented in the global discipline.

Holism

In bringing together the study of human biology, prehistory, language, and social life under one disciplinary roof, anthropology offers powerful conceptual tools for understanding the entire context of human experience. The effort to synthesize these distinct approaches and findings into a single comprehensive explanation is called **holism**. American anthropology has strived to be the most holistic, a legacy of German-born Franz Boas, long considered the founder of American anthropology.

In the discipline's early years, it was possible for individuals like Boas and his students to work in all four subfields, because the body of anthropological knowledge was so small. But within several decades, the expansion of the discipline and increasing specialization within its branches forced anthropologists to concentrate on a single subfield and topics within subfields, a continuing trend today. In the face of specialization, anthropology has struggled to retain its holistic focus.

And yet many anthropologists are deeply dedicated to holism, citing its ability to explain complex issues that no single subfield, much less any other social science, could explain as effectively (Parkin and Ulijaszek 2007). But how do anthropologists actually come to know what they know? We turn to this issue in the next section.

THINKING CRITICALLY ABOUT ANTHROPOLOGY

Can you suggest ways that you may learn how people in your town or city view college students from your campus?

❧ How Do Anthropologists Know What They Know?

Anthropology employs a wide variety of methodologies, or systematic strategies for collecting and analyzing data. Some of these methodologies are similar to those found in other natural and social sciences, including methods that involve the creation of statistics and even the use of mathematical models to explain things. Other methods aimed at describing different cultures are more closely allied with the humanities.

The Scientific Method in Anthropology

Anthropology often uses the **scientific method**, the most basic pattern of scientific research. The scientific method starts with the observation of a fact, a verifiable truth. Next follows the construction of a hypothesis, which is a testable explanation for the fact. Then that hypothesis is tested with experiments, further observations, or measurements. If the data (the information the tests produce) show that the hypothesis is wrong, the scientist develops a new hypothesis and then tests it. If the new tests and the data they produce seem to support the hypothesis, the scientist writes up a description of what he or she did and found, and shares it with other scientists. Other scientists then attempt to reproduce those tests or devise new ones, with a goal of disproving the hypothesis (Figure 1.4).

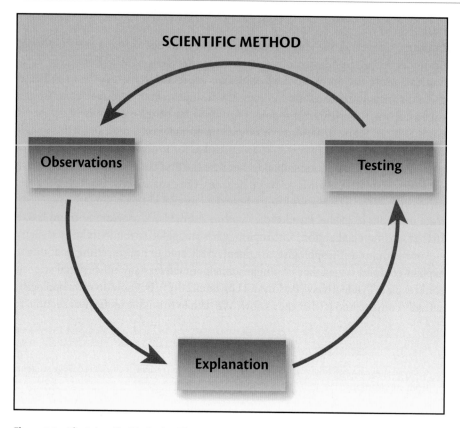

Figure 1.4   The Scientific Method.   The process is circular, not linear.

Note that this way of doing things is a method, not the pursuit of ultimate truths. Its goal is to devise, test, and disprove hypotheses. Life's big questions—"Why are we here?"—are *not* the goal of science. At best, science can provide a reasonable degree of certainty only about more limited questions—"How did our species develop the traits we now have?" Scientists regularly disagree among themselves. Researchers with differing backgrounds and orientations ask different types of questions and look at data in different ways. Scientists tend to see such debates as beneficial to the practice of science because the more questions asked, the more observations made, and the more tests conducted, the more knowledge is produced.

THEORIES GUIDE RESEARCH

Theories, which are tested and repeatedly supported hypotheses, are key elements of the scientific method. A **theory** not only explains things, it also helps guide research by focusing the researcher's questions and making the findings meaningful. While many Americans assume that a theory is some wild hunch or guess, when scientists use the term *theory*, they mean a carefully constructed hypothesis that has repeatedly been tested and retested. There is rarely any guessing involved.

QUANTITATIVE DATA COLLECTION

Building and testing hypotheses and theories require data. Anthropology's subfields employ a number of techniques for gathering and processing data. Some of these techniques use **quantitative methods**, which classify features of a phenomenon, count or measure them, and construct mathematical and statistical models to explain what is observed. Most quantitative research takes place in the subfields of biological anthropology and archaeology, although some cultural and linguistic anthropologists use quantitative techniques as well.

As an illustration of quantitative research, consider the work of Agustín Fuentes, a biological anthropologist at the University of Notre Dame with whom we have co-authored another book (Welsch, Vivanco, and Fuentes 2017). His research examines the nature of human–monkey interactions, and how, when, and why diseases get passed between these species. Fuentes and his team observe monkeys and humans interacting in Bali, Singapore, and Gibraltar. In each location they record quantitative details about the interactions and people's rates of contact with monkeys. They take blood or fecal samples from both the monkeys and the humans, analyzing them for pathogens and parasites. All these variables are considered independently and then compared statistically to see what patterns emerge. Fuentes has discovered that human–monkey interactions vary depending on the species of monkey, human cultural patterns, gender differences in humans, and sex differences in the monkeys (Fuentes 2007).

QUALITATIVE DATA COLLECTION

Anthropologists also employ **qualitative methods**, in which the aim is to produce an in-depth and detailed description of social behaviors and beliefs. Qualitative research involves interviews with and observations of people. Research data come in the form of words, images, or objects. In contrast with quantitative methods, qualitative research does not typically use research instruments like surveys or questionnaires. The research instrument is the researcher himself or herself, whose subjective perceptions and impressions of the subject matter also become the basis for knowledge. The **ethnographic method**, which involves prolonged and intensive observation of and participation in the life of a community, is a qualitative methodology and is a hallmark of cultural anthropology.

Luis Vivanco, one of this book's authors, is a cultural anthropologist who uses qualitative methods to ask how global environmentalism changes people's relationships with nature in Latin America. In one of his projects, he conducted more than twenty months of research in Monteverde, Costa Rica, a rural community bordering a tropical cloud forest and renowned worldwide as a site of conservation and ecotourism. He interviewed and observed local farmers, environmental activists, ecotourists, and scientists, usually on multiple occasions and in public

Figure 1.5   Monteverde Bus.   In his research on environmentalism in Costa Rica, Luis Vivanco explored the social dynamics of ecotourism. This focus led him to spend a lot of time among ecotourists, such as the ones shown here arriving in Monteverde by bus.

settings (Figure 1.5). He collected newspaper clippings and reports from local environmental groups and took pictures of people doing things. His fieldnotes, recordings, images, documents, and personal experiences with environmentalists and farmers have helped him understand environmentalism to be a complex arena of social conflict where people struggle not just over how to protect nature, but also over how to deal with rapid social changes caused by globalization (Vivanco 2006).

THE COMPARATIVE METHOD

Unlike other scientists, anthropologists do not conduct experiments or make predictions. Instead, anthropologists use the **comparative method** (Kaplan and Manners 1972:42–43). The comparative method allows anthropologists to derive insights from careful comparisons of two or more cultures or societies.

The research of this book's other author, cultural anthropologist Robert Welsch, illustrates how anthropologists can use the comparative method. Welsch has conducted extended ethnographic research both in Papua New Guinea and in Indonesia (Welsch 2006). One of his projects made use of comparative research strategies to understand the social and religious meanings of masks and carved objects in three societies along the Papuan Gulf of New Guinea. To conduct his comparative study, Welsch studied museum collections, pored over published and unpublished accounts of the people who collected the masks, and interviewed older villagers about their traditional practices.

He learned that although these three societies used the same kinds of objects, their differing decorative styles expressed differences in the social purposes for which each society used these same objects.

When Anthropology Is Not a Science: Interpreting Cultures

Not all anthropologists characterize what they do as science. Describing other people and interpreting their actions require an understanding of their inner lives and beliefs that no scientific methodology can grasp.

These days most cultural anthropologists disregard the scientific ideal of the researcher's detachment from his or her subject of study: the belief that researchers should not talk about what they feel and experience, or how their emotions and experiences influence what they learn (Fabian 2001). The work of American anthropologist Renato Rosaldo (b. 1941), who studied head-hunting in a Filipino society called the Ilongot [Ill-**lahn**-goht], illustrates this point of view. When Rosaldo (1989) asked the Ilongots to explain why they take heads, they said that when a loved one dies, their grief turns to rage, and the only way to vent that rage and get on with life is to take the head of a traditional enemy. Rosaldo initially dismissed this explanation, assuming there had to be a "deeper" purpose, such as creating group cohesion or allowing young men to prove their worthiness for marriage by showing they could kill an enemy.

Then Rosaldo's wife, Shelly, also an anthropologist, died in an accident during fieldwork in the Philippines, and his own devastating loss generated a similar combination of grief and rage. While he was adjusting to Shelly's death, Rosaldo could grasp emotionally what the Ilongot were getting at. Dealing with the death opened his eyes to the force of emotions in social life, something he and most other anthropologists had never really considered. Rosaldo (1989) realized that his training as an anthropologist, which emphasized scientific detachment, accounted for his initial dismissal of Ilongot notions of head-hunting. He concluded that his other interpretations of head-hunting were not wrong, they just gave him an incomplete picture of why the Ilongot did it. He also concluded that ethnographic knowledge is an open-ended process; as the ethnographer's own life experiences and knowledge change, so do his or her insights into other cultures.

But anthropologists do not just try to understand the world of culture and other human concerns, they also intervene in it in practical ways, which is an issue we explore next.

THINKING CRITICALLY ABOUT ANTHROPOLOGY

How might you use a comparative perspective when visiting another country while on vacation? Consider the cultural contexts you have experienced and how these might provide a comparative framework for experiencing a novel society and culture.

✿ How Do Anthropologists Put Their Knowledge to Work in the World?

Anthropological research is relevant and useful for addressing many social problems. At some point in their careers, most anthropologists get involved in work with practical, real-world concerns, applying their research skills and knowledge to the creation or implementation of policies, the management of social programs, the conduct of legal proceedings, or even the design of consumer products.

Applied and Practicing Anthropology

Practical applications are such an important component of anthropology that some anthropologists consider them the "fifth subfield." These practical applications include those of **applied anthropology**, anthropological research commissioned to serve an organization's needs, and those of **practicing anthropology**, the broadest category of anthropological work, in which the anthropologist not only performs research but also gets involved in the design, implementation, and management of some organization, process, or product. Under both labels, anthropologists have effectively put their discipline to work addressing difficult social, health, and educational problems, as the following snapshots demonstrate.

MARY AMUYUNZU-NYAMONGO: BRINGING CULTURAL KNOWLEDGE TO HEALTH PROGRAMS IN KENYA

Like many other anthropologists, Kenyan anthropologist Mary Amuyunzu-Nyamongo (Figure 1.6) works on pressing social and health problems confronting her country. One of the many problems she has studied is the lack of detailed knowledge of local communities that is necessary to make health programs work. Amuyunzu-Nyamongo collected local knowledge from insights about people's health beliefs and practices through qualitative research. For example, during a campaign to control mosquito-borne illness in a coastal village,

Figure 1.6 Cultural Anthropologist Mary Amuyunzu-Nyamongo.

government officials wanted to conduct blood screenings to identify levels of infection. They told school children to tell their parents to get screened, which failed. Amuyunzu-Nyamongo knew that in this culture, male heads of households control decision-making. She organized a meeting where the issue of screenings was introduced to them. Once these men became involved, the screenings became successful (Amuyunzu-Nyamongo 2006).

DAVINA TWO BEARS: APPLIED ARCHAEOLOGY ON THE NAVAJO RESERVATION

Because archaeologists often encounter burials when they excavate prehistoric Indian sites, American Indian communities have often found themselves at odds with archaeologists over the question of what to do with the human remains uncovered. Some Indians object to any excavation at all. But the work of Navajo archaeologist Davina Two Bears (2006; Figure 1.7) runs counter to the expectations many people may have about the inherent tensions between Indians and archaeologists. For several years now, she has worked with the Navajo Nation Archaeology Department, which emerged in 1988 from the Navajo Nation Cultural Resource Management Program. As both an archaeologist and a cultural resource management professional for the Navajo tribe, she advises on potential damage to archaeological sites that might be caused by road construction or building projects. Two Bears uses her archaeological training to prevent damage to ancient sites, which many Navajo people view as deserving great respect. Two Bears identifies and records the locations and characteristics of sites. When proposed projects would damage archaeological sites, Two Bears and her colleagues try to identify alternative locations. She feels that although she has been professionally trained, her work is more an extension of what Navajos have always done in protecting their ancestors and their ancestors' special sites.

Figure 1.7   Archaeologist Davina Two Bears.

JAMES MCKENNA: THE NATURALNESS OF CO-SLEEPING

In much of the Western world, it is considered "healthy" for an infant to sleep in a crib, alone, for long stretches during the night. When a baby wakes frequently or wants to sleep alongside the parents, many see the child as too dependent. In our society we also have many deaths from sudden infant death syndrome

Figure 1.8   Biological Anthropologist James McKenna.

(SIDS) in which infants die in the night for unknown reasons. Biological anthropologist James McKenna (1996; Figure 1.8) and his colleagues developed an explanation for how and why many SIDS deaths occur in the United States. Through intensive studies of sleeping mothers and infants around the planet, McKenna found that the frequent stirring of young infants, nursing, and the carbon dioxide and oxygen mix created by bodies close together are important aspects of the healthy development of human babies. His work shows that co-sleeping assists the infant's development and dramatically reduces the risk of SIDS.

MARYBETH NEVINS: SUPPORTING THE SUSTAINABILITY OF ENDANGERED LANGUAGES

There are an estimated 6,800 languages spoken in the world today, but many experts expect a great number of them to be gone within the next century. Many

Figure 1.9   Linguistic Anthropologist Marybeth Nevins.

linguistic anthropologists have begun to work directly in efforts to protect and maintain endangered languages. One of those is Marybeth Nevins (Figure 1.9), who conducts research in Arizona on the Fort Apache reservation and with the Susanville Indian Rancheria in California. Nevins observes that there is no "proper" way of preserving something as complex as a language, and she suggests that linguists should approach their efforts as open-ended exchanges with members of a language community. The goal is not to come in as "superheroes" to save a language, but to support efforts that keep the language in use and relevant to community life. This approach is driven by the value of "sustainability" as opposed to "revitalization" or "preservation."

These snapshots offer a small sample of the range of ways anthropologists put their discipline to work. As we discuss in the next section, anthropology—whether practical or academic in its orientation—raises important ethical issues.

THINKING CRITICALLY ABOUT ANTHROPOLOGY

Compare how an anthropologist and an engineer might each approach a problem involving where to situate a bridge or highway in a heavily populated area.

What Ethical Obligations Do Anthropologists Have?

Issues of **ethics**—moral questions about right and wrong and standards of appropriate behavior—are at the heart of anthropology, in two senses. First, anthropologists learn about how and why people in other cultures think and act as they do by researching their moral standards. Anthropologists often find these things out by adjusting themselves to that culture's rules of ethical behavior. Second, doing anthropology itself involves ethical relationships between researchers and others, raising many important and complex issues about the ethical conduct of anthropological research and practice. Ethics in anthropology—the moral principles that guide anthropological conduct—are not just a list of "dos and don'ts." Ethics is organically connected to what it means to be a good anthropologist (Fluehr-Lobban 2003). Here we consider three issues of common ethical concern for all anthropologists: doing no harm, taking responsibility for one's work, and sharing one's findings.

Do No Harm

The Nuremberg trials after World War II revealed that Nazi scientists had conducted harmful experiments on people in concentration camps. Scientists responded by establishing informal ethical codes for dealing with research subjects. But in 1974 abuse of medical research subjects in the United States led Congress to pass a law intended to prevent unethical research with human subjects (Figure 1.10). This new law required all research institutes and universities where research was conducted to establish an Institutional Review Board (IRB) to monitor all human subjects–based research. Medical, scientific, and social science organizations, including anthropological organizations, published codes of ethics that emphasized avoiding harm for people and animals who are the subjects of research.

"Do no harm" continues to be a bedrock principle in anthropology's primary code of ethics, the American Anthropological Association's Principles of Professional Responsibility (see inside front cover). Anthropologists routinely explain to people involved in their research any risks their participation might carry, and

Figure 1.10   Scandal at Tuskegee.   Between 1932 and 1972, the U.S. Public Health Service studied syphilis among white and black men. When scientists learned they could treat syphilis with penicillin, they gave the drug to the white men, but not the black men. This abuse precipitated reform in the use of humans as research subjects in the United States.

obtain their "informed consent" to participate. Anthropological publications avoid sharing confidential information and commonly disguise informants' identities, in case those individuals could be targeted for harm because of what they say.

Take Responsibility for Your Work

The primary ethical responsibility of anthropologists is to the people, species, or artifacts they study. Whether it is a pottery shard, a baboon, or a person, anthropologists are expected to side with their subjects. This does not mean an archaeologist is expected to throw himself or herself in front of a bulldozer to prevent an archaeological site from being destroyed, or that a cultural anthropologist should take up arms in defense of informants threatened by the police or the military. Rather, it means that anthropologists should take whatever action is possible when their subjects are threatened, short of doing something illegal or that would seriously harm themselves or others. Such action might include helping prepare legal paperwork to stop a bulldozer and conserve artifacts.

What complicates this principle is that anthropologists are also responsible to other parties. For example, anthropologists also have responsibilities to inform the public and to the sponsors who fund their research. In "Thinking Like an Anthropologist: Should Anthropologists Take Responsibility for the Influences They Have on the Societies They Study?" we examine yet another dimension of anthropological responsibility.

Thinking Like an Anthropologist
Should Anthropologists Take Responsibility for the Influences They Have on the Societies They Study?

Anthropologists begin their research by asking questions. In this box, we want you to learn how to ask questions as an anthropological researcher. Part One describes a situation and follows up with questions we would ask. Part Two asks you to formulate your own questions based on a different situation.

PART ONE: THE SOCIAL IMPACTS OF ANTHROPOLOGICAL RESEARCH

One of the biggest controversies to rock anthropology in recent decades focused on the work of American anthropologist Napoleon Chagnon with an Amazonian tribe called the Yanomami. Thanks to books and films Chagnon made about them during the 1970s and 1980s, the Yanomami are among the world's best-known tribal people, and Chagnon himself became somewhat of an academic celebrity. Generations of college students have learned about the aggressive dynamics of Yanomami life, due to Chagnon's depiction of them as the "fierce people" (Chagnon 1968). But Chagnon's work has come under intense scrutiny because of claims that it seriously harmed the Yanomami.

The scrutiny began with the work of an investigative journalist named Patrick Tierney who claimed that Western scientists, anthropologists, and medical researchers had abused the Yanomami. In a high-profile book published in 2000—*Darkness in El Dorado: How Scientists and Journalists Devastated the Amazon*—Tierney described how Chagnon had treated the Yanomami in an unethical

manner and distorted his findings about them. Some of Tierney's claims were proven to be unfounded, but others remain difficult to dismiss. One enduring claim is that Chagnon's image of the Yanomami as fierce and violent is a crude misrepresentation, more a reflection of Chagnon's confrontational personal style and belief in the innateness of violence in humans than an accurate representation of the Yanomami. A second is that Chagnon manipulated his data to prove that more violent men had more offspring, which could support his claim that

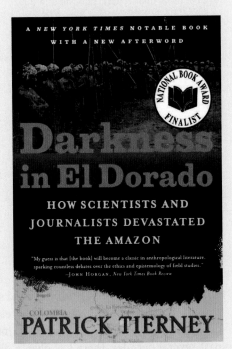

Tierney's *Darkness in El Dorado*.

continues

Thinking Like an Anthropologist *continued*

violence was genetically programmed. A third is that Chagnon actually exacerbated conflicts by giving away machetes to his friends, provoking even greater violence. Further, according to Tierney, when gold was discovered on Yanomami lands, Chagnon never publicly objected to the use of his work to justify violence against the Yanomami by goldminers.

The American Anthropological Association (AAA) responded to these allegations by setting up a task force to examine them, exposing deep divisions among anthropologists. Some anthropologists defended Chagnon, while others feared that Chagnon's unethical research practices and misrepresentations had compromised the integrity of the discipline. In its final report, published in 2002, the AAA task force asserted that Chagnon had indeed represented the Yanomami in harmful ways, and that he had not received informed consent or government permission to do some of his work. In 2005, however, the AAA voted to rescind its previous acceptance of the report, not because of anything in the report itself, but because the AAA had violated its own policy prohibiting the adjudication of ethics violations by getting involved in the first place. Concerns over the lasting impacts of these allegations on the integrity of the discipline persist even today.

What questions does this situation raise for anthropological researchers?

1. Are anthropologists responsible for how others use their research?
2. Should anthropologists place the welfare of their subjects over the success of their research?
3. Are anthropologists responsible for the negative social impacts of their fieldwork practices and findings?
4. Are there ways of doing research that are mutually beneficial to the anthropologist and the subjects of the research?

PART TWO: ANTHROPOLOGY STUDENTS AND ETHICAL RESPONSIBILITIES

As a student of anthropology, you may be confronted with ethical dilemmas about your conflicting responsibilities and the effects of your work. For example, it is possible that you will be asked to conduct basic research, such as studying a club or fraternity on campus, or a social setting or group in the community. You may witness illegal activities—such as alcohol use by a minor, drug dealing, or vandalism. What questions would you ask about this situation as an anthropological researcher? (Sample questions can be found at the end of this chapter.)

Share Your Findings

Historically, anthropologists took blood samples, did long-term ethnographic research, and excavated archaeological sites with little concern for those who might object to these activities, especially in indigenous communities. But during the past several decades, there has been a global sea change in favor of indigenous rights, and nowadays researchers routinely collaborate with native communities affected by their research.

An important ethical question now is who should control anthropological data and knowledge. For cultural anthropologists, the issue of control often relates to questions about who should define the research problem and preserve the data—the anthropologist or the subjects of research. Traditionally, the anthropologist has controlled those things, but communities have increasingly challenged anthropologists to provide them with research skills and information produced by research so they can continue to use them for their benefit after the anthropologist leaves.

THINKING CRITICALLY ABOUT ANTHROPOLOGY

If you were studying a local Head Start program and observed problems with local funding for the facility, what are ways you might suggest for anthropologists to get involved in helping the organization?

Conclusion

Since the 1850s, anthropologists have been asking questions about and developing perspectives on human societies past and present. Their expertise is on culture, diversity, how and why social change happens, the dynamics of human biology, and the ways people communicate with each other. The four subfields of anthropology—cultural anthropology, archaeology, biological anthropology, and linguistic anthropology—sometimes come together to offer powerful conceptual tools for understanding the whole context of human experience, an approach called holism. Featuring a range of methodological tools—sophistication with theory, quantitative methods, qualitative methods, and the comparative method—anthropology offers highly relevant insight into today's complex world.

But because anthropology deals with people, their bodies, and cultural artifacts that are meaningful to people, nearly everything anthropologists study invokes ethical concerns. Therefore, throughout this book we consider the ethics and application of anthropology research. But let us begin our journey toward an understanding of anthropology with a fuller discussion of the concept of culture.

Key Terms

Anthropology   p. 3
Applied anthropology   p. 16
Archaeology   p. 6
Biological anthropology   p. 7

Colonialism   p. 4
Comparative method   p. 14
Cultural anthropology   p. 5
Cultural relativism   p. 8

Culture   p. 8
Diversity   p. 8
Empirical   p. 3
Ethics   p. 19

Reviewing the Chapter

CHAPTER SECTION	WHAT WE KNOW	TO BE RESOLVED
How did anthropology begin?	During the nineteenth century, industrialization, evolutionary theory, and colonial contact led to the discipline of understanding how cultures operate and interact.	Anthropologists are still fascinated—and challenged—by the contrasts and changes in culture worldwide as a result of globalization.
What do the four subfields of anthropology have in common?	Anthropologists in all subfields share certain fundamental approaches and concepts, including culture, cultural relativism, diversity, change, and holism.	Some anthropologists continue to debate the idea that the subfields, with their distinct methods and specialized research interests, belong together in the same discipline.
How do anthropologists know what they know?	Anthropology has a strong relationship with the scientific method; all anthropologists use theories, collect data, and analyze those data.	While most cultural anthropologists reject the possibility of a completely objective analysis of human culture, archaeologists and biological anthropologists are thoroughly committed to the scientific method.
How do anthropologists put their knowledge to work in the world?	All four of the subfields have both theoretical and applied aspects. Applied research uses the insights of anthropological theory to solve problems.	Anthropologists continue to disagree about how best to apply their understanding of people from different backgrounds to address human problems.
What ethical obligations do anthropologists have?	Issues of ethics—moral questions about right and wrong and standards of appropriate behavior—are at the heart of anthropology.	Certain ethical issues have no easy resolution, such as what it means to do no harm; how to resolve conflicting responsibilities; or how and with whom to share findings.

SUGGESTED ANSWERS TO "THINKING LIKE AN ANTHROPOLOGIST"

Use these examples as a guide to answering questions for other "Thinking Like an Anthropologist" boxes in the book.

1. Does withholding information about illegal activities compromise the integrity of the discipline?
2. Would you be obliged to tell your professor everything you've found out through research, or can and should some information be held back?
3. Should loyalty to one's peer group transcend loyalty to one's university, or the discipline of anthropology?
4. How could you protect the identity of your informants?

2

Culture

Giving Meaning to Human Lives

In 2005, the National Collegiate Athletic Association (NCAA), the body that governs intercollegiate sports in the United States, banned teams with American Indian names and mascots from competing in its postseason tournaments. Clarifying the ruling, an official stated, "Colleges and universities may adopt any mascot that they wish. . . . But as a national association, we believe that mascots, nicknames, or images deemed hostile or abusive in terms of race, ethnicity or national origin should not be visible at the championship events that we control" (NCAA 2005). The ruling affected a number of schools with competitive sports programs, including Florida State ("Seminoles"), University of North Dakota ("Fighting Sioux"), and University of Illinois ("Fighting Illini").

The ruling concluded decades of pressure from American Indians, students, and others who have argued that these mascots stereotype and denigrate Indian

Mascot Chief Illiniwek. Chief Illiniwek performs during a University of Illinois football game. In 2007, after a long controversy, the university retired the mascot.

traditions. As one Oneida woman expressed, "We experience it as no less than a mockery of our cultures. We see objects sacred to us—such as the drum, eagle feathers, face painting, and traditional dress—being used, not in sacred ceremony, or in any cultural setting, but in another culture's game" (Munson 1999:14). To Indians, the mascots seem to be just another attack on Indian cultures by non-Indians—attacks they have endured for several centuries.

Outraged students, alumni, and political commentators have countered that these mascots honor Indian traditions, pointing to the strength and bravery of Native Americans, which they hope to emulate in their teams. They also point out that the mascots are part of venerable traditions, part of the living cultures of their universities. Abandoning their mascots is like turning their backs on a part of their own cultural heritage.

This battle of words over college mascots has brewed for decades, with participants on both sides making claims, sometimes exaggerated, about the other side's motivations or intentions. Yet each side in the controversy calls into play an issue of deep concern to them that divides the participants into two opposed groups, each with a radically different interpretation of the issue that often views the opposing point of view as irrational or wrong. In that respect, it is a cultural conflict.

The concept of culture is at the heart of anthropology. *Culture*, as anthropologists use the term, refers to the perspectives and actions that a group of people consider natural, self-evident, and appropriate. These perspectives and actions are rooted in shared meanings and the ways people act in social groups. Culture is a uniquely human capacity that helps us confront the common problems that face all humans, such as communicating with each other, organizing ourselves to get things done, making life predictable and meaningful, and dealing with conflict and change.

The culture concept provides a powerful lens for making sense of what people do, why they do it, and the differences and similarities across and within societies, a point that leads to a key question: *How does the culture concept help explain the differences and similarities in people's ways of life?* Embedded in this broader question are the following problems, around which this chapter is organized:

What is culture?
If culture is always changing, why does it feel so stable?
How do social institutions express culture?
Can anybody own culture?

In this chapter, we present an overview of how anthropologists approach culture and explain why it is so relevant to understanding human beliefs and actions. We also offer a definition of culture that informs and shapes the rest of this textbook. We start with the key elements that all anthropologists accept as central to any definition of culture.

❧ What Is Culture?

Culture has been defined in many ways by anthropologists, and there are nearly as many approaches to studying it as there are anthropologists. This lack of agreement does not frustrate or paralyze anthropologists. In fact, most anthropologists see this diversity of perspective as the sign of a vibrant discipline. A striking fact about this diversity is that most of these definitions emphasize a number of common features.

Elements of Culture

English scholar Sir Edward B. Tylor (1832–1917) was a founding figure of cultural anthropology. He offered the first justification for using the word *culture* to understand differences and similarities among groups of people. He defined culture as "that complex whole which includes knowledge, belief, art, morals, law, custom, and any other capabilities and habits acquired by man as a member of society" (1871:1). Two aspects of Tylor's definition, especially that culture is *acquired* (today we say *learned*) and that culture is a "complex whole," have been especially influential.

Since Tylor's time, anthropologists have developed many theories of culture, the most prominent of which are summarized in Table 2.1. We discuss many of these theories in later chapters, exploring in more detail how they have changed over time. One of the most important changes in cultural theory is that early anthropologists tended to see cultures in societies with simple technologies as more fixed and stable than anyone does today. Nevertheless, across all these theories, there are seven basic elements that anthropologists agree are critical to any theory of culture.

TABLE 2.1   PROMINENT ANTHROPOLOGICAL THEORIES OF CULTURE

Theory	Period	Major Figures	Definition
Social evolutionism	1870s–1910s	Edward B. Tylor (1871), Herbert Spencer (1874), Lewis Henry Morgan (1877)	All societies pass through stages, from primitive state to complex civilization. Cultural differences are the result of different evolutionary stages.
Historical particularism	1910s–1930s	Franz Boas (1940), Alfred Kroeber (1923), Edward Sapir (1921)	Individual societies develop particular cultural traits and undergo unique processes of change. Culture traits diffuse from one culture to another.
Functionalism	1920s–1960s	Bronislaw Malinowski (1922)	Cultural practices, beliefs, and institutions fulfill psychological and social needs.
Structural-functionalism	1920s–1960s	A. R. Radcliffe-Brown (1952)	Culture is systematic, its pieces working together in a balanced fashion to keep the whole society functioning smoothly.
Neo-evolutionism	1940s–1970s	Leslie White (1949), Julian Steward (1955)	Cultures evolve from simple to complex by harnessing nature's energy through technology and the influence of particular culture-specific processes.

Cultural materialism	1960s–1970s	Marvin Harris (1979)	The material world, especially economic and ecological conditions, shapes people's customs and beliefs.
Cognitive anthropology	1950s–1970s	Ward Goodenough (1965), Roy D'Andrade (1995)	Culture operates through mental models and logical systems.
Structuralism	1960s–1970s	Claude Lévi-Strauss (1949/1969, 1961)	People make sense of their worlds through binary oppositions like hot–cold, culture–nature, male–female, and raw–cooked. These binaries are expressed in social institutions and cultural practices like kinship, myth, and language.
Interpretive anthropology	1970s–present	Clifford Geertz (1973), Victor Turner (1967), Mary Douglas (1966), Roy Wagner (1975)	Culture is a shared system of meaning. People make sense of their worlds through the use of symbols and symbolic activities like myth and ritual.
Post-structuralism	1980s–present	Pierre Bourdieu (1977), Renato Rosaldo (1989), James Clifford, George Marcus, and Michael M. J. Fischer (Clifford and Marcus 1986, Marcus and Fischer 1986)	Not a single school of thought, but a set of theoretical positions that rejects the idea that there are underlying structures that explain culture. It embraces the idea that cultural processes are dynamic, and that the observer of cultural processes can never see culture completely objectively.

CULTURE IS LEARNED

Although all human beings are born with the ability to learn culture, nobody is born as a fully formed cultural being. The process of learning a culture begins at birth, and that is partly why our beliefs and conduct seem so natural: we have been doing and thinking in certain ways since we were young. For example, the Onge [ahn-**gay**], an indigenous group who live in the Andaman Islands in the Indian Ocean, learn from a very early age that ancestors cause periodic earthquakes and tidal waves. When these natural events occur, Onge have a ready-made explanation for how the world works, guiding their responses so that they do not have to learn how to deal with these things anew every time they occur. Anthropologists call this process of learning the cultural rules and logic of a society **enculturation**.

Enculturation happens both explicitly and implicitly. Your student experience illustrates how both processes have shaped you. Throughout your schooling, your teachers have explicitly taught you many things you need to know to be a productive member of society: to write, to analyze a text, to do mathematics, and so on (Figure 2.1). But you have also learned many other things that are more implicit, or not clearly expressed. These lessons include obedience to authority and respect for social hierarchy, learned for example from sitting in class facing forward in rows so the teacher can control your attention and movement. Bells and announcements over the loudspeakers also regulate your activities and the flow

Figure 2.1 Do You Get It? You were enculturated to read from left to right. But when speakers of Hebrew language are taught to read, such as those who might read this cartoon from a Hebrew language newspaper, they begin on the right and move left.

of your day. By the time you reach college, these patterns are so ingrained that you know more or less exactly what to do when you walk into the classroom without thinking about it. Enculturation hasn't stopped, though: it continues throughout your life. You might notice that you are also involved in enculturation, explicit and implicit, as a student at your college, as you learn its specific traditions and develop loyalty to certain mascots and other school symbols.

CULTURE USES SYMBOLS

Clifford Geertz (1926–2006) was one of the best-known American anthropologists in recent times. He proposed that culture is a system of symbols—a **symbol** being something that conventionally stands for something else—through which people make sense of the world. Symbols may be verbal or non-verbal. Symbols are things that people in a given culture associate with something else, often something intangible, such as motherhood, family, God, or country. To illustrate this point, Geertz posed an interesting question: How do we know the difference between a wink and a twitch (1973:6–7)?

As movements of the eye, winks and twitches are identical. But the difference between them is enormous, as anyone who has experienced the embarrassment of taking one for the other can attest. A twitch is an involuntary blink, and generally speaking carries no symbolic significance. A wink, however, communicates a particular message to a particular someone. Telling the difference and understanding what, if anything, the action is meant to communicate takes a lot of implicit knowledge. In an instant, we must consider a number of questions: Is there intent? What is the intent—conspiracy, flirtation, parody, ridicule, or something else? Would it be socially appropriate for this person to wink at me, and under what conditions? Underlying our considerations is a shared system of meaning in which we (and the winker) participate that helps us communicate with and understand each other. What sounds like a complex computational process actually comes quite naturally to the human mind. This is because of the human capacity for learning with symbols and signs that otherwise have little meaning outside a given culture.

Geertz's concept of culture, often called the **interpretive theory of culture**, is the idea that culture is embodied and transmitted through symbols. This fundamental concept helped anthropologists clarify the symbolic basis of culture, something virtually all anthropologists take for granted today. Because culture is implicit in how people think and act, they express culture in *everything* they do—playing games, speaking a language, building houses, growing food, making love, raising children, and so on (Figure 2.2). The meanings of these things—and the symbols that underlie those meanings—differ from group to group, and, as a result, people do things and organize themselves differently around the world. These differing meanings are what make the Balinese Balinese, Zapotecs Zapotecs, and Americans Americans.

Figure 2.2   It's Like Getting a Joke.   When a popular comedian like Trevor Noah tells a funny joke, most of us barely think about what makes it so funny. Like other examples of culture Geertz discussed, we just "get it."

CULTURES ARE DYNAMIC, ALWAYS ADAPTING AND CHANGING

In a globalized world with high levels of migration across cultural borders, communication flowing in all directions, and social and ethnic mixing, it is often impossible to say with any certainty where one culture or social group ends and another begins. As a result, many anthropologists today talk less about culture as a totally coherent and static *system* of meaning and more about the *processes* through which social meanings are constructed and shared.

Culture is a *dynamic* process. It is adaptive, helping people adjust to the changing worlds in which they live. At the same time, social groups are not uniform or homogeneous, because not everybody interprets the events of everyday life in the same way, nor do they blindly act out scripts already laid out for them to perform. So cultural processes are emergent, fluid, and marked by creativity, uncertainty, differing individual meaning, and social conflict. Relations of power and inequality routinely permeate these cultural processes.

CULTURE IS INTEGRATED WITH DAILY EXPERIENCE

As cultural beings, how we relate to the world seems natural to us, transparent, obvious, inevitable, and necessary. Our sense of passing time, for example, might contrast sharply with that of people in other cultures. In Western cultures, we think of time as an entity that moves from past to present to future. This concept—an element of culture—organizes and regulates our activities every day. It also motivates us to make plans, since this concept of time leads us to believe that time must be used or it will be lost.

Understanding that culture comprises a dynamic and interrelated set of social, economic, and belief structures is a key to understanding how the whole of culture operates. The integration of culture across these domains leads to expectations that are specific to a given social group. For example, most white middle-class American parents think it is "natural" for their babies to sleep in single beds, often in their own rooms (Small 1998:116–18). They believe that sleeping with their babies creates emotional dependence. In our society, which prizes personal independence and self-reliance, such dependence seems damaging to the child. Other societies find these ideas strange and exotic. The Gusii of Kenya, for example, think it is "natural" to sleep with their babies, not to mention holding them constantly during waking hours, precisely because they *want* them to grow up to be dependent on others. For them, proper human behavior means constantly relying on other people.

Figure 2.3   Yummy . . . Or Not. A meal of insect larvae might make some Americans vomit or retch, which shows how powerful cultural beliefs are: they actually provoke a biological response to something that is perfectly digestible, if not healthy and delicious.

How we sleep also demonstrates that activities you might think of as "natural"—that is, biologically based, as sleeping is, and therefore universally the same for all humans—are actually culturally patterned. Culture helps shape the basic things all humans must do for biological survival, like eating, sleeping, drinking, defecating, and having sex. There is no better illustration of this fact than food preferences. As omnivores, humans can eat an enormous range of foods. But many Americans' stomachs churn at the thought of eating delicacies like rotten shark flesh (Iceland), buffalo penis stew (Thailand), or dogs (East Asia) (Figure 2.3).

No other animal so thoroughly dwells in artificial worlds of its own creation. Anthropologists stress that a **cross-cultural perspective** (analyzing a human social phenomenon by comparing that phenomenon in different cultures) is necessary to appreciate just how "artificial" are our beliefs and actions.

CULTURE SHAPES EVERYBODY'S LIFE

White middle-class North Americans tend to believe they have no culture, in the same way that most people feel they have no accent. But the other side of the coin is the tendency to view minorities, immigrants, and others who differ from white middle-class norms as "people with culture," as compared to people who have what they understand as a fairly general American culture. In the United States, these ideas are tied to social and institutional power: the more "culture," in this sense of the term, one appears to have, the less power one wields; the more power one has, the less one appears to have culture (Rosaldo 1989). This power of mainstream culture over ethnic cultures is about the relationships of power and inequality mentioned earlier. In fact, by differing from mainstream patterns, a group's culture becomes more visible to everyone. It is in this sense that groups with the most obvious cultures tend to be the least powerful. Nevertheless, *all* people's lives are embedded in and shaped by culture.

CULTURE IS SHARED

The notion that culture is shared refers to the idea that people make sense of their worlds and order their lives through their participation in social groups. Culture does not emerge from, and is not reducible to, individual psychology or biology. Anthropologists generally accept that purely psychological and biological explanations of human experience are inadequate.

An individual's comprehension of anything is always based on what his or her group deems collectively as proper and improper. Anthropologists commonly refer to such definitions as **cultural constructions**, which refers to the fact that people collectively "build" meanings through common experience and negotiation. In the debate over college mascots, for example, both sides collectively "constructed" the significance of these images and symbols for both Indians and colleges through their debates, protests, and discussions. A "construction" derives from past collective experiences in a community, as well as people talking about, thinking about, and acting in response to a common set of goals and problems.

CULTURAL UNDERSTANDING INVOLVES OVERCOMING ETHNOCENTRISM

One of the key aspects of culture is that it makes us feel that we are "right" and everybody else thinks and does things wrongly. As we mentioned in the previous chapter, this phenomenon is called *ethnocentrism*. For anthropologists, overcoming ethnocentrism is the first step to understanding other cultures. If we are constantly judging another society and how it does things by our own goals, morals, and understandings, we cannot ever understand that society in its own terms. From the beginning of cultural anthropology in America, anthropologists have argued that the only way to understand other cultures is in terms of that other culture's own goals, ideas, assumptions, values, and beliefs, which is the concept of *cultural relativism*. A relativistic perspective is a central tool for overcoming ethnocentrism, and it is a major feature of the anthropological perspective on culture.

Importantly, understanding another culture in its own terms does not mean that anthropologists necessarily accept and defend all the things people do. Even though the job of an anthropologist is not to judge other cultures but to learn to understand how and why other peoples do things as they do, anthropologists still carry basic values as individuals and as members of a particular society.

A number of anthropologists, in fact, advocate "critical relativism," or taking a stance on a practice or belief only after trying to understand it in its cultural and historical context. Critical relativism also holds that no group of people is homogeneous, so it is impossible to judge an entire culture based on the actions or beliefs of a few (Merry 2003). For example, many North Americans practice male circumcision, which other societies consider abhorrent, including people in the German city of Cologne, who banned circumcision in 2012 as a human rights abuse. There is even a small but growing social movement in the United States that condemns the practice along similar lines. But to criticize this practice is not to condemn the entire culture.

Another reason for advocating critical relativism is that, in an extreme form, cultural relativism can be a difficult position to uphold. It can lead to **cultural determinism**, the idea that *all* human actions are the product of culture, which denies the influence of other factors like physical environment and human biology on human action. Some critics also argue that extreme relativism can justify atrocities like genocide, human rights abuses, and other horrific things humans do to one another.

Defining Culture in This Book

Although all anthropologists agree that these seven elements of culture are critical to any definition, in their research different anthropologists emphasize or interpret these elements differently, which contributes to the diversity of culture theories expressed in Table 2.1. So while we, too, accept the importance of these key elements to any definition, we do approach culture throughout this book in a particular way. Building on the more general definition provided in Chapter 1, we define culture as *those collective processes through which people in social groups construct and naturalize certain meanings and actions as normal and even necessary.* In whatever manner any group of people does something, their way seems like the only sensible and obvious way to people in that community—it seems natural, obvious, and appropriate—even though other people might only scratch their heads, perplexed. No matter how much our culture changes during our lifetimes, our reactions to the people and things around us always seem normal or natural.

This definition emphasizes that culture is not a static set of rules, or a totally coherent system of symbolic beliefs that people "have" or "carry" like a toolbox that gets passed down from generation to generation, which have been rather common views of culture among anthropologists. Culture is more dynamic than these ideas allow, as cultures intermingle due to cross-border interconnections such as migration, global media, and economic globalization. Moreover, culture is emergent and even unstable, responding to innovation, creativity, and struggles over meaning. The power of this definition is that by presenting culture as a dynamic and emergent process based on social relationships, it leads anthropologists to study the ways cultures are created and re-created constantly in people's lives.

Throughout this chapter and in subsequent chapters we illustrate how our definition of culture works. But this definition does raise an immediate question: If culture is a dynamic process, why doesn't it always feel that way to people? We deal with this question in the next section.

THINKING CRITICALLY ABOUT CULTURE

How can an understanding of the complexities of culture help us make sense of the day-to-day world in which we live? Give an example from your life to illustrate your answer.

If Culture Is Always Changing, Why Does It Feel So Stable?

Imagine how chaotic life would be if you could not expect the same rules and processes for interacting with others from one week to the next. If we always had to stop and think about changes in the rules of social interaction, we could not function in our society. The very power of culture is that its processes feel totally natural and simultaneously predictable. Yet the previous section defined culture in a way that emphasizes its processes as dynamic and emergent. So how does something feel stable if it is so dynamic?

The concept of enculturation—the idea that people have been doing or believing things for much of their lives—only partly explains why culture feels so stable. There are a number of other features of culture—symbols, values, norms, and traditions— that help explain the sense of stability that people feel about it.

Symbols

One way of approaching the issue of cultural stability and change is by examining symbols (Sahlins 1999). A symbol, as we have already noted, is something that conventionally stands for something else. The relationship between the symbol and what it refers to is arbitrary, based on no particular rhyme or reason (Figure 2.4). Symbols can be more than just images or concepts, however; people also use their bodies as symbols. In Japan, for example, bowing is a form of greeting, but depending on how low one bows, it may also symbolize respect, apology, gratitude, sincerity, remorse, superiority, or humility.

Figure 2.4   Love, Affection . . . and Toilets.   Symbols are arbitrary. In the United States and several other countries, the heart conventionally symbolizes love and affection. But in rural Sweden and other parts of Scandinavia, people also associate the heart with outhouses, or rustic toilets (Lonely Planet 2014).

A society will store its conventional meanings in symbols because their meanings tend to be stable. But symbols and their meanings can and do change, sometimes dramatically. For example, during the Spanish conquest of the Peruvian Andes in the sixteenth century, the Spaniards carried banners of their patron saint, Santiago Matamoros, to ensure victory over the Indians. The Indians quickly absorbed Santiago into their native religion. They identified Santiago as their own god of thunder and lightning, Illapa, who they believed changes forms. To the Indians, Santiago symbolized the power of their own mountain gods and later encouraged resistance against the Spaniards (Silverblatt 1988).

Values

Studying values also helps us to understand how change and stability are so closely related. **Values** are symbolic expressions of intrinsically desirable principles or qualities. They refer to that which is moral and true for a particular group of people. For example, "Mom and apple pie" symbolize American core values (values that express the most basic qualities central to a culture), such as patriotism or loyalty to country. In the United States, "Mom" expresses the purity of selfless sacrifice for the greater good. "Apple pie," a common food since colonial times, expresses Americans' shared heritage. Of course, not everybody eats apple pie and not every mother is loyal to her family, much less sacrifices herself for the greater good. The point is not that these ideals reflect what actually happens in the real world. Rather, they orient thinking about one's obligations as a citizen, like putting aside differences with other Americans and being willing to sacrifice oneself for love of family and country.

Values are conservative in that they conserve prevailing ideas about social relations and morality. Yet, this does not mean that a community's values do not change. Nor does it mean that within a society or community, people will not have opposing values. It is not even uncommon for people to hold conflicting values simultaneously.

Norms

While values provide a general orientation for social relations, norms are more closely related to actual behavior. **Norms** are typical patterns of behavior, often viewed by participants as the rules of how things should be done. In our society, for example, it would be unimaginable to try to haggle over the price of toothpaste at the grocery store because everyone expects you to pay the listed price. But in many other societies, especially in the Arab world and in Indonesia, the norm is just the opposite: no matter how small the item, it is considered rude to *not* haggle. In such places, taking the first asking price disrespects the seller. For more expensive items, such as a digital camera, buyers and sellers may expect to haggle over the price for an hour.

Norms are stable because people learn them from an early age and because of the social pressure to conform. Norms also tend to be invisible (we're usually not conscious of them) until they are broken, as visitors to a different society or even city often find when they do things the "wrong" way. The scowls or expressions of disapproval you might get provide a **social sanction**, a reaction or measure intended to enforce norms and punish their violation. Long-established norms may eventually become **customs**, which have a codified and lawlike aspect.

Traditions

Tradition usually refers to the most enduring and ritualized aspects of a culture. People often feel their traditions are very old, which justifies actions that make no logical sense in contemporary times. With such justifications, individuals and groups go to great lengths to protect their traditions. The controversy between Indians and NCAA schools over mascots illustrates how powerful such traditions can be.

But anthropologists are aware that where traditions are concerned, appearances can be deceiving (Hobsbawn and Ranger 1983). For example, Scottish people often celebrate their identity with bagpipes and kilts made from tartans, plaid textiles that comprise stripes of different widths and colors that identify the wearers' clans. But these traditions, while indeed venerable, are not actually ancient. As a matter of fact, these objects, and the sense of a distinctive tradition they symbolize, emerged only during the eighteenth and nineteenth centuries (Trevor-Roper 1983). An English iron industrialist designed the kilt as we know it for his workers in the late 1700s. As the kilt caught on in the Scottish highlands, textile manufacturers began producing distinctive plaids to expand sales and found willing buyers among clan chiefs. The chiefs wanted to distinguish themselves and their ancestry as unique, so they adopted particular designs. When England's King George IV made a state visit to Scotland in 1822, the organizers heavily promoted the use of kilts and tartans to enhance the pageantry of the visit. This occasion legitimized highlands culture and established the look as a national institution. The power of tartans comes not from their antiquity, but from their association with the clans that have long been central to Scottish highlander social life. Of course, knowing that a particular tradition may be a recent invention does not mean people are any less protective of it (Figure 2.5).

Figure 2.5   Sumo Wrestling in Japan.   Like the use of tartans in Scotland, Sumo wrestling in Japan feels ancient, although key features of it—such as the practice of awarding one person the championship—are less than 100 years old.

Historically, anthropologists have emphasized that culture is "shared" among a group of people, implying a kind of uniformity and stability in culture. Clearly, people need a relatively stable and common base of information and knowledge in order to live together. But these different aspects of culture—symbols, values, norms, and traditions—are features that seem stable and common, even though they may not be shared by everybody in a society. There is another reason culture feels stable. It is that culture is expressed through social institutions, a theme we turn to next.

THINKING CRITICALLY ABOUT CULTURE

Most students think it is easy to identify the symbols, values, norms, and traditions that support other people's practices. But they find it more difficult to think about their own daily practices in the same terms. Use any of your own daily practices to illustrate how these four features of culture reinforce your own behavior.

❦ How Do Social Institutions Express Culture?

The **social institutions** of any society are the organized sets of social relationships that link individuals to each other in a structured way in that society. These institutions include patterns of kinship and marriage (domestic arrangements, the organization of sex and reproduction, raising children, etc.), economic activities (farming, herding, manufacturing, and trade), religious institutions (rituals, religious organizations, etc.), and political forms for controlling power. Each culture has its norms, values, and traditions for how each of these activities should be organized, and in each case they can vary greatly from one society to another due to cultural differences. Here we consider how mid-twentieth-century anthropologists approached culture's relationship to social institutions; we then turn to examine how changes in these institutions can shape cultural patterns, which ultimately transform the social institutions themselves.

Culture and Social Institutions

From the 1920s to the 1960s, many anthropologists understood culture as the glue that holds people together in ordered social relationships. Associated with British anthropologists Bronislaw Malinowski and A. R. Radcliffe-Brown, this theory, known as **functionalism**, holds that cultural practices and beliefs serve important purposes for society, such as explaining how the world works and organizing people into roles so they can get things done. Functionalists emphasize that social institutions function together in an integrated and balanced fashion to keep the whole society functioning smoothly and to minimize social change.

As an illustration of functional analysis, think back to the case of the Onge, the people who believe their ancestors make earthquakes and tidal waves. A functionalist would focus on how Onge beliefs about their ancestors explain how the natural world works, and on how these beliefs in turn help shape and are shaped by their migratory hunting-and-gathering existence. Working together with other structures of Onge society, such as political organization, economics, and kinship, these beliefs contribute to the maintenance of an ordered society.

For functionalists, cultures were closed, autonomous systems. But even at the height of its influence, critics insisted that functionalism's vision of culture was *too* stable. Not all societies function smoothly, and functionalism's static view of culture could not explain history and social change. One of Britain's most prominent anthropologists, E. E. Evans-Pritchard, famously broke with functionalists in 1961 when he said that anthropology should not model itself on the natural sciences but on humanistic disciplines, especially history with its processual focus.

In spite of its shortcomings, functionalism has left us an important legacy: the **holistic perspective**, a perspective that aims to identify and understand the whole—that is, the systematic connections between individual cultural beliefs, practices, and social institutions—rather than the individual parts. This does not mean that contemporary anthropologists still see a society as wholly integrated and balanced. Rather, the holistic perspective is a methodological tool that helps show the interrelationships among different domains of a society—domains that include environmental context, history, social and political organization, economics, values, and spiritual life. Thus, the life of a community becomes expressed through the social relationships among its members, organized as they are through their social institutions. To understand how changes in cultural values can lead to changes in social institutions, consider the relationship between diet, industrialization, and sexual deviance in America.

American Culture Expressed Through Breakfast Cereals and Sexuality

Let us begin by posing a simple question: Why do so many Americans prefer cereal for breakfast? Most of us do because it is part of a "healthy and nutritious diet" (the standard industry line) or because of its convenience. In any event, eating cereal for breakfast has become a social norm for a majority of Americans. It builds on positive cultural values attributed to health and on the symbolism of "healthy food = a healthy body." But corn flakes began in the nineteenth century as a cure for sexual deviance, masturbation being the most worrisome.

Nineteenth-century religious leaders considered masturbation an abomination, and the emerging scientific disciplines of psychiatry and surgery claimed that masturbation caused shyness, hairy palms, jaundice, insanity, cancer, and murderous behaviors (Figure 2.6). From 1861 to 1932, the U.S. Patent Office issued some two dozen patents on antimasturbation devices to prevent boys from masturbating, among them a safety pin to close the foreskin of the penis, various kinds of male chastity belts, and an electric bell attached to the penis that would notify parents if their son got an erection during the night. As recently as 1918, a U.S. government brochure advised new parents to prevent their babies from masturbating by tying their hands and legs to the sides of their cribs. Circumcision became the most commonly performed surgery in the United States based on the view that it prevented masturbation.

John Harvey Kellogg (1852–1943), the inventor of corn flakes, was a physician from Battle Creek, Michigan. He was a follower of the health food movement of vegetarian and dietary reformer Sylvester Graham (1794–1851), who had developed graham flour used in graham crackers. When Kellogg became director of a Seventh-day Adventist sanitarium in Battle Creek, he built on Graham's ideas, inventing corn flakes and various granolas as food for his patients. Both men were concerned with health

Figure 2.6   The Effects of Masturbation, Circa 1853. This image comes from a book called *The Silent Friend* about the "horrors of masturbation." At the time, common wisdom held that masturbation would lead to insanity.

and sexuality—they especially abhorred masturbation, which they attributed to animalistic passions that were enhanced by a rich, meaty, or spicy diet. Both believed that bland but healthy foods were the way to soothe these volatile and unhealthy sexual urges (Money 1985).

Eating cereal has never prevented masturbation, of course, and no one today would argue that it does. Over time, the meaning of both cereal and masturbation have shifted. In fact, these days, an increasing number of medical professionals embrace masturbation as good for mental health. But the initial assumptions that masturbation was abhorrent and that bland food could curb sexual impulses were enough to create corn flakes.

During the nineteenth century, the American breakfast, like the rest of the diet, was a hearty meal of meat, eggs, fish, biscuits, gravy, jams, and butter. Although farmers worked off the calories in their fields, as America became more urban such rich meals became a sign of prosperity, just as the ideal body type was full-bodied for both men and women. But as American culture began to value healthy eating early in the twentieth century, industrial cereal makers, like C. W. Post and Kellogg's brother William, took advantage of this connection between cereals and good health to market their creations as nutritious foods. By the 1920s the American diet had shifted dramatically, and the ideal body type became much thinner. The result was an increased demand from consumers for convenient and tasty breakfast cereals, spawning a giant breakfast cereal industry associated with good taste and health rather than with preventing sexual deviance.

In answering our initial question about why many Americans prefer cereal for breakfast, we see interrelationships between separate domains like beliefs (about sexual morality, good health), social institutions and power (expert knowledge, medical practices), and daily life (changes in labor organization and economic life, dietary preferences). This is the holistic perspective.

This example also shows the integration of specific domains. For instance, beliefs about sexual morality are intertwined with institutions of social authority, such as sanitariums, and medical disciplines like psychiatry and surgery, and those institutions in turn regulate people's sexual relationships. Similarly, changes in people's economic relationships and work habits help shape and are shaped by their ideas about what is good to eat. At any historical moment, these domains feel stable because they are reflected in the other domains, even though some may be highly transitory and dynamic. The values, norms, and traditions in one domain are buttressed and supported by values, norms, and traditions in many other domains.

And herein lies the power of a cultural analysis: it shows how doing something that feels totally "natural" (eating cereal in the morning) is really the product of intertwined cultural processes and meanings. In "Thinking Like an Anthropologist: Understanding Holism" we present a scenario to illustrate how simple innovations can lead to changes in social institutions.

Thinking Like an Anthropologist
Understanding Holism

Anthropologists begin their research by asking questions. In this box, we want you to learn how to ask questions as an anthropological researcher. Part One describes a situation and follows up with questions we would ask. Part Two asks you to formulate your own questions based on a different situation.

PART ONE: INTRODUCING CASH CROPS TO HIGHLAND NEW GUINEANS

When anthropologist Ben Finney (1973) studied coffee as a cash crop in the Eastern Highlands of Papua New Guinea, he observed that some younger men planted large fields in coffee and some had become coffee buyers. Many of these men eventually became very successful coffee planters and buyers, acquiring whole fleets of trucks, which they used to bring coffee beans to local warehouses and to coastal cities (Westermark 1998).

Women process coffee in a local factory in Highland Papua New Guinea.   Although men initially planted coffee as a cash crop, as the economy has begun to modernize, some farmers have built factories for roasting and bagging the roasted coffee as we see here.

On the face of it, this program was dramatically successful in introducing a valuable cash crop to a region that had known only subsistence horticulture. But a holistic approach illustrates that coffee also brought important social consequences for Highland communities.

In the 1950s an Australian colonial ban on tribal warfare opened up large tracts of no-man's-land between formerly hostile groups. Colonial officers brought coffee seedlings for villagers to plant in this formerly useless land. Some highlanders planted coffee; others rejected the whole idea, saying "what good is coffee, you can't eat it and pigs can't eat it either," pigs being an especially important form of wealth in Highlanders' political and economic lives. Most of the village leaders and prominent elders continued planting sweet potatoes and tending pigs as they always had. The pigs ate surplus sweet potatoes and were used in feasts and ceremonial exchanges with friends and rivals in other villages. Men with extensive exchange networks became village leaders called "big men." Big men achieved prominence and influence over others from their own hard work, assisted by the hard work of their wives and female relatives in the gardens. Traditional subsistence farmers made fun of their coffee-planting neighbors.

But after seven years, the coffee trees began to bear fruit, and the officers showed the coffee planters how to pick, process, and sell the beans. The young coffee planters now had larger sums of cash than people had ever seen. Coffee profits increased as the trees matured. Unexpectedly, younger men found themselves with money that they would have had to work for months or years on a coastal plantation to earn.

These young coffee growers used this money to achieve social status because they, unlike the older men, had access to all sorts of imported goods in the stores. In some cases, the prestige of these new big men was even greater than that of the older big men. Suddenly, everyone wanted to become a coffee planter, but after seven or eight years nearly all of the open land was already planted in coffee.

Elimination of tribal warfare and the introduction of coffee did not eliminate the big man political system or the cultural logic upon which it is based. But a holistic perspective shows that it did have important ramifications throughout the society.

What questions does this situation raise for anthropological researchers?

1. How did Highland society change as a result of coffee?

2. What were the unexpected effects of introducing coffee on this small-scale egalitarian society?

3. Which effects were positive? For whom were they positive? Who experienced negative consequences from the introduction of coffee?

PART TWO: INTRODUCING SMARTPHONES TO AMERICAN COLLEGE STUDENTS

Consider the relatively recent rise in the use of smartphones by high school and college students. As little as fifteen years ago, most students were forced to use a telephone land line if they wanted to talk to their friends, which usually meant that they were calling from home. With their mobility, texting ability, and access to the Internet, smartphones have brought lifestyle changes for young people that nobody anticipated. Using a holistic approach, what questions would you ask about this situation as an anthropological researcher? (Sample questions can be found at the end of this chapter.)

THINKING CRITICALLY ABOUT CULTURE

Anthropologists feel that holism is important because it links together lots of things that people in other disciplines do not routinely think about. Use an example of an object in daily life (e.g., a book or laptop you use in class) to show how it is holistically linked to other aspects of American life.

🌱 Can Anybody Own Culture?

As we have defined culture, the question of owning culture may appear to make little sense. How can somebody own the collective processes through which people construct and naturalize certain meanings and actions as appropriate and necessary? For the most part, owning culture is about power relations between people who control resources and (typically) minority communities who have been kept outside the mainstream. Nobody can really own culture, but many will claim the exclusive right to the symbols that give it power and meaning.

The debate over sports teams' Indian mascots is only one example of a conflict over who has the right to use, control, even "own" symbols, objects, and cultural processes. This conflict is related to the phenomenon of **cultural appropriation**, the unilateral decision of one social group to take control over the symbols, practices, or objects of another. Cultural appropriation is as old as humanity itself. The fact that people adopt ideas, practices, and technologies from other societies demonstrates the fluidity of social boundaries and partly explains why societies and cultures are changing all the time.

Yet cultural appropriation also often involves relationships of domination and subordination between social groups. For American Indians, for example, the pressure to assimilate into dominant white Euro-American society has coincided with the dominant society's appropriation of Indian cultural symbols. That appropriation goes beyond the use of Indian images as sports mascots and includes, among others, kids "playing Indian," New Age religion's imitation of Indian spirituality and rituals, Hollywood movies about Indians, and even the use of the Zia Pueblo sun symbol on the New Mexico state flag (Strong 1996; Brown 2003). While some Indians do not mind, others find these uses of Indian symbolism degrading and simplistic, because they ignore the realities of Indian communities and traditions, or because nobody asked permission to use their culturally meaningful objects and symbols. For example, Zia Pueblo brought a lawsuit against the state of New Mexico in 1994, formally demanding reparations for the use of the Zia sun symbol in the state flag (Figure 2.7).

Figure 2.7 The Cause of Indigenous Rights. Indigenous groups forced the United Nations to establish the Permanent Forum on Indigenous Issues in 2000. The Forum's goal is to address the human, cultural, and territorial rights of indigenous peoples around the world.

Anthropologists have not escaped indigenous scrutiny and criticism for claiming expertise about native cultures. Anthropologist Kay Warren (1998), for example, studied the rise of the Pan-Maya ethnic movement in Guatemala. When she gave an academic presentation on Maya political activism, Maya intellectuals and political leaders in attendance responded by challenging the right of foreign anthropologists even to study Maya culture. As Warren points out, indigenous movements like Pan-Mayanism reject the idea that anthropological knowledge is neutral or objective. They insist that doing anthropology raises important political and ethical questions: Who should benefit from anthropological research? Why do the people studied by anthropologists not get an opportunity to help define and evaluate research projects?

Responding to such questions, a number of anthropologists like Warren have modified how they do cultural research, including inviting the subjects of their research to be collaborators in all stages of the research, from the definition of the study all the way through to publication.

THINKING CRITICALLY ABOUT CULTURE

Discuss whether people from one culture could "own" a dance—like the samba from Brazil—that originated with people from another ethnic group. Could anyone own a style of pop music?

Conclusion

At the heart of all anthropological discussions of culture is the idea that culture helps people understand and respond to a constantly changing world. As we have defined it, culture consists of the collective processes through which people construct and naturalize certain meanings and actions as appropriate and even necessary. Based on symbols and expressed through values, norms, and traditions, culture offers a relatively stable and common base of information and knowledge so that people can live together in groups. A holistic perspective on culture illustrates how different domains of a society interrelate. But culture is also dynamic, responding to innovation, creativity, and struggles over meaning.

In spite of the many difficulties involved in studying culture, it is more important than ever to understand culture, what it is, and how cultural processes work. The big and urgent matters of our time have cultural causes and consequences. These matters range from the problems posed by development and change for indigenous groups and heated conflicts about social identity over mascots and traditions on college campuses, to others like terrorism, environmental degradation and sustainability, ethnic diversity and racial conflict, religious intolerance, globalization, and healthcare. As you read this book, you will learn how anthropologists use cultural perspectives to understand, explain, and even contribute to resolving problems related to these matters.

Key Terms

Cross-cultural
  perspective   p. 32
Cultural appropriation   p. 44
Cultural construction   p. 33
Cultural determinism   p. 34
Customs   p. 37

Enculturation   p. 29
Functionalism   p. 39
Holistic perspective   p. 39
Interpretive theory of
  culture   p. 31
Norms   p. 36

Social institutions   p. 38
Social sanction   p. 38
Symbol   p. 30
Tradition   p. 37
Values   p. 36

Reviewing the Chapter

CHAPTER SECTION	WHAT WE KNOW	TO BE RESOLVED
What is culture?	Culture is a central component of what it means to be human. Culture involves the processes through which people comprehend, shape, and act in the world around them.	Although most definitions of culture emphasize common themes, anthropologists have never agreed on a single definition of culture.
If culture is always changing, why does it feel so stable?	Cultural processes are emergent, fluid, and marked by creativity, uncertainty, differing individual meaning, and social conflict. Yet culture is also remarkably stable.	Anthropologists continue to debate which is more important—dynamism or stability—in explaining how culture works in people's lives.
How do social institutions express culture?	A holistic perspective enables anthropologists to understand how different social institutions and domains of a society are interrelated.	Anthropologists continue to debate how and why social institutions in any society change.
Can anybody own culture?	The phenomenon of cultural appropriation illustrates the tensions between cultural change and stability, and raises important ethical and political questions about anthropological knowledge itself.	Anthropologists continue to debate over which research and collaborative strategies are most effective to respond to the ethical and political issues raised by the creation of anthropological knowledge about culture.

Suggested Answers To "Thinking Like An Anthropologst"

Use these examples as a guide to answering questions for other "Thinking Like an Anthropologist" boxes in the book.
1. How has cultural life on campus changed because of smartphones?
2. Are there unexpected effects of introducing smartphones into college life?
3. How has the proliferation of smartphones changed college students' patterns of communication with their parents and friends?
4. Are people more connected socially than they were before?
5. Are there ways that people are less connected socially?
6. Does smartphone use have any impact on how college classrooms operate?

3

Ethnography

Studying Culture

You don't have to travel far and wide to study culture, and anthropologists have long studied the social lives of people in their home countries and communities. One such study was conducted during the 1980s and 1990s in East Harlem, a neighborhood in New York City, by American anthropologist Philippe Bourgois. East Harlem was and continues to be largely cut off from mainstream America, if not from the very city in which it exists. Its residents, who are still largely Puerto Rican, were isolated because of language and educational barriers, unemployment, poverty, and ethnic segregation. Bourgois lived in East Harlem to study how people experience this marginalization and how they make a living in an economy that does not seem to want them.

Life in Spanish Harlem. Ethnographic methods have been used to study the lives of many distinct societies and communities, including communities within the United States. For example, ethnographers have studied the lives of residents of East Harlem, New York City, such as those pictured here playing dominoes on the sidewalk.

Bourgois soon discovered that the neighborhood was saturated with crack co-caine, which came to the market in the 1980s. Over the next four years he spent hundreds of nights on the street and in crack houses, building trust with deal-ers and addicts. He tape-recorded and carefully transcribed many of his conver-sations with them, recorded their life histories, and visited with their families. He heard many stories about being excluded from mainstream jobs in midtown Manhattan, and thus falling back on crack as dealers or users. He documented the many self-destructive behaviors that so often accompany addictions. At times, the research was dangerous for Bourgois.

Bourgois found that census records and other official documents gave an in-accurate picture about wealth and poverty in East Harlem, because they did not account for the thriving underground drug economy. Studies by other social sci-entists were no more helpful, because they typically confirmed the stereotype that poor people in the inner city deserve their poverty, in large part because of their drug-related illegal activities. But during his conversations and interviews, Bourgois was stunned to learn that people who run crack houses work much like any business owner pursuing the American dream. As he wrote, "They are ag-gressively pursuing careers as private entrepreneurs; they take risks, work hard, and pray for good luck. They are the ultimate rugged individualists braving an unpredictable frontier where fortune, fame, and destruction are all just around the corner" (Bourgois 1995:326).

Such insights came to Bourgois only because, as an ethnographic fieldworker, he participated in the lives of the crack dealers over a long period. Never a crack user himself, Bourgois got to know dealers and users personally in ways that almost no one who sets American policy about poverty and drug use does. And he came away with an appreciation of the community's all-too-American aspir-ations, even when mainstream opportunities and employment had been denied to them.

For those of you accustomed to stereotypes of anthropologists working in far-flung corners of the world with non-Western people, Bourgois's research might seem surprising. In fact, until the 1970s, the typical path of the anthropologist was to seek an out-of-the-way place where cultural differences appear most pro-nounced. Today, cultural anthropologists are as likely to do fieldwork among advertising executives, factory workers, transnational migrants—or, in this case, urban drug dealers and users—as we are to live in villages in remote settings. Bourgois's five years of research involved a longer stay in "the field" than most anthropologists spend. But the distinctive methods he used were essentially the same as those of any cultural anthropologist fifty years ago who was studying people's lives in small villages in Africa, Latin America, or Oceania. At the heart of all of these research projects is a central goal: to learn about people who live in cultural circumstances different from our own. It leads us to ask: *How do anthro-pologists learn about other ways of life?* Embedded within this question are several more specific questions around which this chapter is organized:

What distinguishes ethnographic fieldwork from other types of social research?
How do anthropologists actually do ethnographic fieldwork?
What other methods do cultural anthropologists use?
What unique ethical dilemmas do ethnographers face?

Ethnographic research methods have been around for the better part of a century because they have proven to be an effective tool for helping anthropologists gather the kind of information they require to understand social complexities and the inner lives and beliefs of people. We begin by examining what traditional ethnographic research is all about.

What Distinguishes Ethnographic Fieldwork from Other Types of Social Research?

In popular culture, an aura of mystery has long surrounded the question of what cultural anthropologists do. In part, this is because anthropology is generally less well known than other social scientific fields such as economics, psychology, or political science. But even anthropologists can sometimes find it difficult to define precisely how they collect and produce data. Cultural anthropologists do research by building personal relationships over a long period, and it is difficult to tell a student exactly how to do that with people who are culturally different. Thus, although cultural anthropology shares some methods with other social sciences, it also has its own distinctive and effective methodological tools.

Social scientists gather data or information about human beings and the social, economic, political, and psychological worlds they inhabit. Their methods are either quantitative (e.g., statistical) or qualitative (e.g., descriptive and interpretive). Although most anthropologists use quantitative data, cultural anthropology is the most qualitative of the social sciences. Anthropological methods also emphasize holism, or paying systematic attention to all aspects of social life simultaneously, not simply a single dimension of people's lives, such as economic, political, psychological, or religious dimensions. Also important are long-term immersion and participation in a community (for a year or more), as well as an open mind, which yield insights we would never achieve had we started with preconceived ideas about the relationships among social, economic, political, and religious institutions.

Fieldwork

We call this long-term immersion in a community **fieldwork**. It is *the* defining methodology of the discipline. During fieldwork, anthropologists become involved in people's daily lives, observe and ask questions about what they are doing, and record those observations. Long-term immersion is critical to the method, generating insights we would not have if we simply visited the community a few hours a day, to administer a survey or questionnaire, or to conduct a brief interview. As virtually every anthropologist will tell you, people may say one thing but then go and do something completely different. Sticking around helps us put what people say in context.

Fieldwork also helps us decipher the implicit assumptions people make and the tacit rules they live by, which Clifford Geertz (1973) once described as "the informal logic of everyday life." Most Americans, for example, assume that drug dealers have a set of values that differs from their own, but Bourgois's long-term involvement with them suggests otherwise, even if their style of talking and their way of interacting with one another differ from those of other Americans. By participating directly in community activities, we can observe what is important to the community, what community members discuss among themselves, and how these matters intertwine with social institutions. This approach yields insights about people's behaviors, actions, and ideas that they themselves might not notice or understand, as we explore in "Thinking Like an Anthropologist: Fieldwork in an American Mall."

Seeing the World from "the Native's Point of View"

The decision to live for a long period of time in an unfamiliar community in order to observe and record cultural differences emerged after 1914 and led to profoundly new kinds of understandings of native peoples. It had become clear that living in the community did not guarantee cultural relativism—that is, understanding a native culture on its own terms—nor did it promise that the researcher could overcome his or her ethnocentrism and cultural bias. But it increased the likelihood that the anthropologist could get some sense of the world in terms that local people themselves understood.

Of course, nobody ever gets into another person's mind or shares another person's exact thoughts. Moreover, even when we think we understand how someone thinks, a similar but new situation often produces a different and unexpected reaction. Two seemingly different reactions are often triggered by different conditions or contexts. For example, when there is a political scandal, politicians are quick to criticize the other party but rarely make a fuss when their own is involved. Their moral outrage is situational, conditioned by the context of who is involved, how well they know them, and perhaps how much impact the incident might have on a party's outcome in the next election.

Now, put yourself in an anthropologist's shoes. As an outsider you might initially think that your informants can be similarly paradoxical. But after some time and effort to see things in terms of local context, things people say and do begin to make sense, and you are likely to feel generally that you are beginning to move beyond what anthropologists call an **etic perspective** (an outside observer's view on a culture) and see the world from an **emic perspective** (an insider's view

Thinking Like an Anthropologist
Fieldwork in an American Mall

Anthropologists begin their research by asking questions. In this box, we want you to learn how to ask questions as an anthropological researcher. Part One describes a situation and follows up with questions we would ask. Part Two asks you to formulate your own questions based on a different situation.

PART ONE: OBSERVING THE USE OF SPACE IN THE AMERICAN SHOPPING MALL

We've all been to a shopping mall, but have you ever stopped to consider how people actually use malls? Anthropologist Paco Underhill (2005) has spent his career studying the American shopping mall and advising retail businesses on how to use space to sell products to the American consumer. From his observations, it is clear that visiting a mall is a socially patterned experience, although visitors may not realize how their actions are being shaped by others.

Underhill begins his research on a mall in the parking lot. There, he observes the possible entrances to the mall and the fact that, from the outside, the shopper can see little of what is inside. Landscaping is minimal, as is any other attraction that might keep the would-be shopper outside, so visitors stream into the building. The goal of the mall, Underhill infers, is to get people inside to begin spending money.

Once people enter, Underhill observes, they need time to slow down and adjust to the space of the mall, so shops are rarely placed at the entrances; instead, these spaces are rented to doctors, accounting firms, and other businesses whose customers require appointments. After leaving this "decompression area," visitors come

to the excitement of the mall proper: shop after shop with brightly colored merchandise pouring out into the hallways to attract attention.

Unlike the halls of a hospital or an office building, those at the mall are extra wide. Underhill seeks to understand what goes on in these spaces that requires room for two broad lanes of foot traffic, often separated by stalls, carts, and tables filled with merchandise. While most people pop in and out of the many shops, others stop to look at the shop windows and the merchandise that lies on tables or hangs along the way. Still others—particularly during cold or stormy weather—power-walk alone or in pairs, getting exercise.

Underhill pays close attention to the people in these hallways and what they do, taking careful notes of his observations. He notes their ages and sexes, whether they walk by themselves or with others, who those others might be (children? parents? friends?), and whether these patterns change by day of the week and time of day. Entering the food court, Underhill observes the types of restaurants, the ways people interact with those restaurants, the kinds of shops

Inside an American Shopping Mall

continues

Thinking Like an Anthropologist *continued*

near them, and how long people linger before returning to shopping. Underhill then turns his attention to the restrooms, observing where they are located, which is often hidden away in distant corners and corridors, intended not to affect the shopping experience negatively.

As Underhill wanders in and out of the large anchor stores, he makes other observations. Merchandise is piled up in the entryways, some on sale, some seasonal. He observes what grabs people's attention, getting them to slow down and pause. He observes how and where stores place different kinds of products, which influences how people move through the store and what they are likely to see (and possibly purchase even though they did not come to buy that particular thing).

Underhill's research shows that by looking at the architecture and observing closely the flow of shoppers through it, we can sense what kinds of behavior the store managers had hoped to encourage, what behaviors they might have hoped to discourage, and how people actually make use of these semi-public spaces.

The experience of walking through a mall with Paco Underhill raises important questions for anthropological researchers, such as the following:

1. What might an anthropologist learn about the use of space from watching and observing what people do as opposed to interviewing them?
2. How can an anthropologist check the inferences he or she might make about the goals of store managers?
3. What should a fieldworker focus on when making observations?

PART TWO: OBSERVING THE USE OF SPACE IN THE COLLEGE LIBRARY

Consider the library at your college or university. Most libraries have a variety of tables, desks, and study carrels. The stacks may be open, or students may need to show their ID cards to get inside. Audiovisual materials may be accessible to everyone in the student body, or professors may put some videos or DVDs on reserve. Modeling your work on Paco Underhill's, what kinds of questions would you pose to orient your observations of a college library?

of his or her culture). Long before these terms came to be used, anthropologist Bronislaw Malinowski referred to the emic perspective as "the native's point of view" and asserted that it lay at the heart of the ethnographic method he claimed to have invented when he famously pitched his tent on the beach near the houses of Trobriand Islanders (Figure 3.1).

Avoiding Cultural "Tunnel Vision"

When approaching a different culture, we may find that much of what members of that culture do seems exotic and strange, and that our own cultural "tunnel vision"—unquestioned tacit meanings and perspectives drawn from our own culture that prevent us from seeing and thinking in terms of another culture's tacit meanings and perspectives—can lead to ethnocentrism. With effort and time, however, these people's actions seem less puzzling, even reasonable. We do not usually start thinking the way they do, and we will often continue to feel that their way of doing things is peculiar or even wrong, but we will gradually come to accept their reactions as making sense in terms of the local culture.

Figure 3.1 "The Native's Point of View." Bronislaw Malinowski's tent on the beach of Nu'agasi, Trobriand Islands.

Of course, people in other societies are ethnocentric as well. They feel that their way of doing things and their ways of thinking about the world are correct, while everyone else's are flawed. In other words, they have their own tunnel vision. When anthropologists attempt to see the world "from the native's point of view" we are not claiming that the other culture's way of thinking is necessarily better than our own. But by understanding the native's point of view we are attempting to unravel the cultural logic within which actions that might be unthinkable in our own society become commonplace.

For example, when Philippe Bourgois (1995) studied the lives of crack dealers in East Harlem, he did not condone using crack. But to understand the lives of his informants, he had to suspend his tunnel vision—that is, the perspectives and judgments that so many Americans make about those who sell and use crack cocaine. Fieldwork, the focus of our next section, was key to this understanding.

THINKING CRITICALLY ABOUT ETHNOGRAPHY

Just spending time in the field and speaking with locals are not enough to shake an anthropologist out of his or her own cultural tunnel vision. Why not? What are some other ways you can think of for an anthropologist to avoid cultural tunnel vision?

How Do Anthropologists Actually Do Ethnographic Fieldwork?

In cultural anthropology, fieldwork is more than a matter of simply collecting data. It is a core practice that integrates the primary philosophical elements of the discipline—especially a commitment to holism, cultural relativism, and ethical behavior—into a single frame of inquiry. Fieldwork relies less on a set of prescribed technical procedures or formulas than it does on a range of skills and techniques an anthropologist can draw on, depending on the context. At the heart of this approach to creating data and knowledge are participant observation, interviews, and note-taking.

Participant Observation: Disciplined "Hanging Out"

Participant observation is a key element of anthropological fieldwork. It is a systematic research strategy that is, in some respects, a matter of hanging out. One of the things that distinguishes anthropologists from college students—who also do a lot of hanging out—is that anthropologists record much of what transpires while we are hanging out. In the field, we are also in a social position that is very different from what we are normally accustomed to, and we must work hard to build rapport and friendships in a community where we have no friends (Figure 3.2). Establishing rapport requires a lot of discipline, as well as acceptance of local customs and practices, however peculiar, unfamiliar, or uncomfortable.

Participant observation makes the anthropologist a professional stranger, and is neither pure observation nor pure participation (Delaney 1988). As observers, anthropologists cannot remove themselves from the action. Yet giving in to participation too easily prevents one from noticing subtleties of behavior

Figure 3.2   Building Rapport in the Field.   Finding ways to "fit in" is always a key concern of anthropologists, and sometimes wearing appropriate clothing helps. In addition, an anthropologist can build rapport by demonstrating that he or she respects local customs and culture. Here co-author Robert L. Welsch wears traditional Mandarese clothing including a silk sarong, batik shirt, and cap to attend a wedding reception near Majene on the island of Sulawesi in Indonesia.

and learning to intuit their significance. Too much participation is sometimes referred to as "going native," because the researcher stops being an engaged observer and starts to become a member of the community.

Some years ago, anthropologist Johannes Fabian (1971) suggested that any notion that an anthropologist in the field is collecting "objective" data misses the point of the discipline. The data anthropologists bring home in their field notebooks were not out there to be gathered like blackberries; they were actively created through the relationships between an anthropologist and the people with whom he or she interacts. The anthropologist observes things in the field setting, observes them a second or third time, and later inquires about them, gradually pulling together an enriched sense of what he or she has observed. For Fabian such observations and understanding are neither objective nor subjective but the product of **intersubjectivity**, which means that they emerge out of relationships individuals have with each other.

The traditional term for the people from whom an anthropologist gets information is **informants**. But this term does not necessarily capture the subtlety of Fabian's point, and may describe only one kind of relationship an anthropologist has in a community. Some anthropologists find other terms more appropriate, including "collaborators" (evoking a shared enterprise in exploring culture), "interlocutor" (evoking ongoing conversations), and "consultants" (evoking advice shared by experts).

Interviews: Asking and Listening

Participant observation gives us many insights about how social life in another society is organized, but it is up to us as anthropologists to find systematic evidence for our perceptions. So another key goal of fieldwork is to flesh out our insights and gain new perspectives from **interviews**, or systematic conversations with informants, to collect data.

There are many kinds of interviews, ranging from highly structured, formal ones that follow a set script to unstructured, casual conversations (Table 3.1). Anthropologists use surveys and structured interviews to elicit specific kinds of information, such as terms for biological species, details about the proceedings of a village court case, or the meaning of symbols and behavior in rituals (Figure 3.3). In an **open-ended interview**, or unstructured interview, informants discuss a topic and in the process make connections with other issues. Open-ended questions usually encourage informants to discuss things the anthropologist wants to hear about, or that informants find especially meaningful.

The questions an anthropologist asks during an interview depend on the situation and the information he or she is seeking. Researchers often draw questions from theories and background literature, from an advisor or other colleague, or from simple curiosity. These questions change during fieldwork with new experiences and as we confront new cultural realities. A solid education prepares us to ask insightful questions. As the expression goes, "99% of a good answer is a good question." For example, anthropologists find that questions posed to elicit a "yes"

TABLE 3.1

CHARACTERISTICS AND NATURE OF DIFFERENT KINDS OF INTERVIEWS

Kinds of Interviews	Nature of Interview	Clear Focus for Interview	Kind of Fieldnotes
Interview schedule	Questions are read from a printed script exactly as written. Often used for survey data collection.	Yes	Interview schedule form
Formal/structured interview	Interviewer has decided ahead of time what is important to ask and writes down the informant's answers or tape-records the interview. Often used for survey data collection.	Yes	Transcript of answers or of questions and answers.
Informal/open-ended interview	Interviewer has a general focus for the interview but may not have a clear goal of what information he or she wants. New questions emerge as the interview proceeds. A notebook may be present, but most of the time is spent in conversation rather than writing notes.	Sometimes	Preliminary notes that outline the discussion, later used to write up a full description of the context and content of the discussion.
Conversation	Resembles an ordinary conversation, and notebooks are not present. The anthropologist might ask certain questions, but the flow is very conversational. Afterward the anthropologist takes a few jot notes so he or she can remember the topics discussed or goes somewhere private to write up more detailed raw notes that can be fleshed out later.	Sometimes	Headnotes and jot notes, later used to write up a full description of the context and content of the discussion. Notes often include topics to follow up on in future interviews or conversations.
Hanging out (participant observation)	Involves spending time with members of the community in gender- and age-appropriate ways. It may involve helping with fishing, cooking, or planting; playing in some pickup sport; or hanging out in a coffee shop, diner, bar, or work environment. Anthropologists may occasionally make jot notes, but most of the time they record details in their notes later, when people are not around.	No	Headnotes and jot notes, later used to write up a full description of the context and content of the discussion. Notes often include topics to follow up on in future interviews or conversations.

or "no" answer are almost always unproductive. The goal is, quite simply, to get people talking, not to get them to provide simple, short answers. The more they talk, the more people reveal the cultural logic they use in their daily lives that they may not even be conscious of.

Taking Fieldnotes

Much of the time in the field is spent scribbling **fieldnotes**, which are written records of information the anthropologist collects. Some of this scribbling

Figure 3.3 Interviews in the Field. Interviews take place in all kinds of settings, from the most formal and sterile, such as an office, to informal settings like this one, in which co-author Luis Vivanco (left, holding plants) interviews an environmental activist in rural Costa Rica who is showing him an agricultural demonstration project.

happens in the ebb and flow of everyday life, as anthropologists jot down notes in conversation with others, or when a festival, ritual, or some other activity is taking place. Usually these scribbles are only shorthand notes made in small, unobtrusive notebooks (Figure 3.4). Unlike your professors, most people in the world are not comfortable when somebody opens a notebook and starts writing notes. But with time and plenty of explanation about what the anthropologist plans to do with the information, people become accustomed to it. Anthropologists have an ethical commitment to share their reasons for doing research with their informants openly, and explaining their goals often helps build rapport.

Many anthropologists bring out a notebook only when they are conducting structured interviews and surveys. They also write down many details after the fact, or after they have had a chance to reflect more deeply on something. It is simply too difficult to capture everything taking place or being said in the moment. Every day they write up the details about what they did, whom they spoke with, what struck them as odd or puzzling, and the context in which they saw or heard about certain things. A lot of them keep diaries where they express personal frustrations and keep what anthropologist Simon Ottenberg referred to as **headnotes**, which are the mental notes made while in the field (Sanjek 1990:93–95), all of which can prove to be useful later.

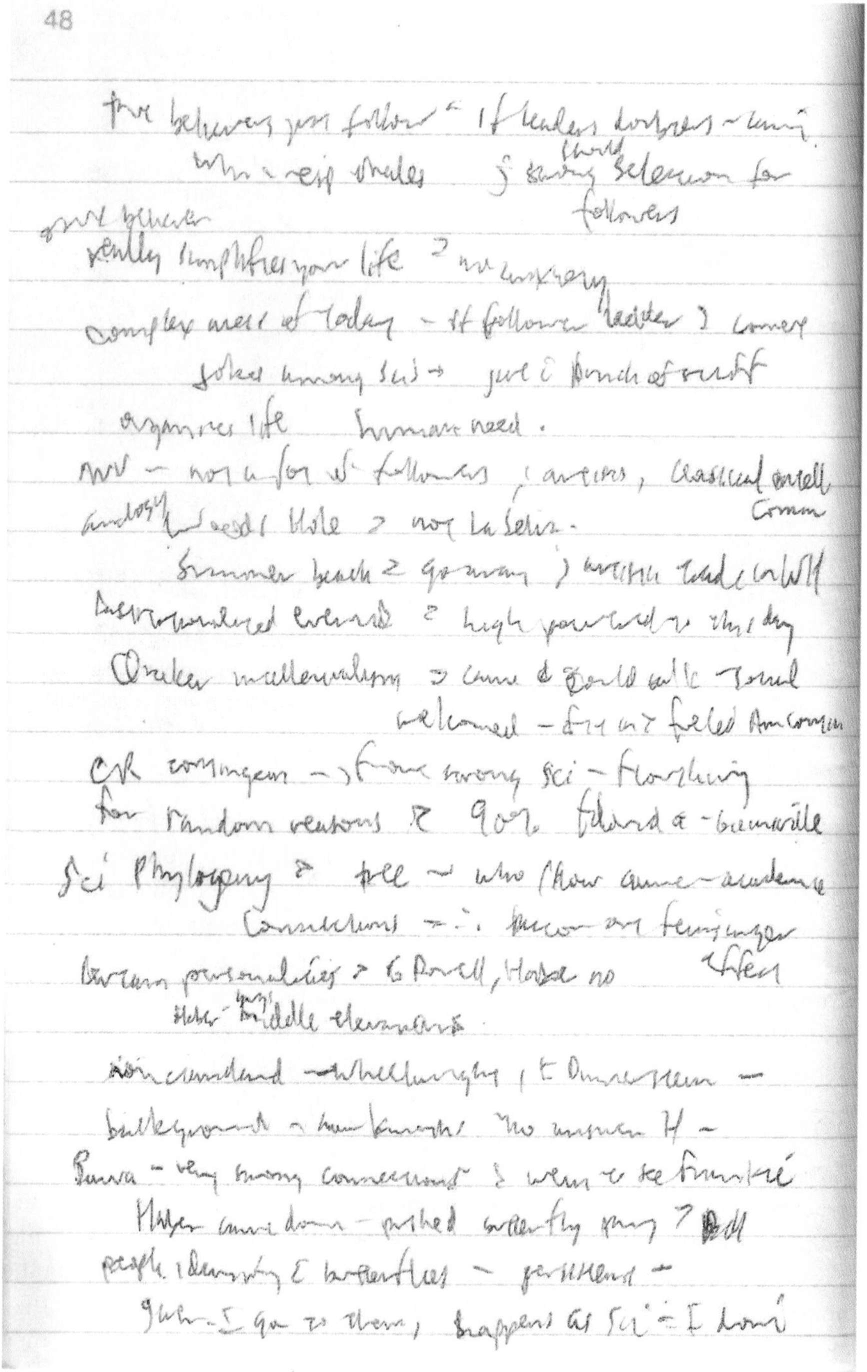

Figure 3.4 An Anthropologist's Fieldnotes. Pictured here is a page of fieldnotes from Luis Vivanco's fieldwork in Costa Rica during the 1990s and early 2000s. Every anthropologist develops his or her own particular way of taking notes.

Writing fieldnotes takes great discipline. It is also absolutely essential because, as one anthropologist has noted, "if it's not written down, it didn't happen" (Sanjek 1990). Think about it. You are in the field for at least a year. Once you get back home, settle in, organize and analyze all your fieldnotes, think about what you want to write, think about it again, and then write it, *several years* may have passed.

These techniques—of becoming involved in people's lives, getting them to talk, and taking notes about it—enable anthropologists to pursue a major goal of fieldwork, which is to see the world from the point of view of the people who are the subjects of research. Importantly, not every ethnographer will necessarily experience and record the same things, even in the same community. Fieldworkers have differences in background, personality, social identity, theoretical inclination, and perception that affect what they will observe, how people in a community will interact with them, and how they will interpret the data they collect. Every fieldwork project is, to a high degree, a very unique and individual experience. In the next section, we explore the other methods anthropologists use.

THINKING CRITICALLY ABOUT ETHNOGRAPHY

Fieldwork can be conducted in any social setting in which people are doing things and interacting with each other. Can you identify three social settings or communities in your "backyard" (e.g., your campus or city) in which you would like to conduct fieldwork? Why do those interest you?

🌱 What Other Methods Do Cultural Anthropologists Use?

Although participant observation and unstructured, open-ended interviews are the core research methods for cultural anthropologists, some projects require additional strategies to understand social complexity and the native's point of view. Some of the most important of these methods include the ones we review here: the comparative method; the genealogical method; life histories; ethnohistory; rapid appraisals; action research; anthropology at a distance; and analyzing secondary materials. While these methods were largely developed to help anthropologists gain insight into cultures very different from their own, they can also be useful to researchers studying their own societies. As we will see, however, anthropologists working in familiar settings must make an extra effort to approach those settings from a fresh perspective.

Comparative Method

Since the beginning of the discipline, anthropologists have used the comparative method, which involves systematic comparison of data from two or more societies (see Chapter 1). The first American anthropologist, Lewis Henry Morgan, for example, sent letters to people all over the world requesting lists of kinship terms in local languages. From these scattered reports he conducted a comparative study of kinship terminologies around the world, which he published as *Systems of Consanguinity and Affinity of the Human Family* (1871). Early anthropologists also used comparative data to establish models of how they believed the cultures of modern Europe had evolved from so-called primitive societies.

The comparative method is still relevant in anthropology today. For example, anthropologists studying globalization use a version of the comparative method called multi-sited ethnography, which involves conducting participant observation research in many different social settings. Another kind of comparative research strategy is exhibited by the **Human Relations Area Files** (HRAF), a database that collects and finely indexes ethnographic accounts of several hundred societies from all parts of the world (Figure 3.5). Each paragraph in the database has been subject-indexed for a wide variety of topics such as type of kinship system and trading practices. This indexing allows researchers to conduct statistical analyses about whether particular traits appear to be randomly associated or whether they are regularly found together in human cultures.

Genealogical Method

The **genealogical method** was developed by English anthropologist William H. R. Rivers in 1898 during the Cambridge Anthropological Expedition to the Torres Strait Islands, which lie between Australia and New Guinea (Figure 3.6). Rivers was studying visual perception among the Torres Strait Islanders and observed that they had an unusually high incidence of mild color blindness. To understand whether color blindness was genetically passed only in certain families or was a more generalized trait, Rivers needed to discern the relationships between the islanders.

The task was at first confusing, because Torres Strait Islanders used terms that Rivers interpreted as "mother," "brother," and "grandfather" for a much wider variety of people than just the relatives Euro-Americans refer to with these terms. Rivers (1906) developed a simple but systematic way of classifying all kin according to their

Figure 3.5   Opening Page of HRAF's Website.

relationship to his informants—for example, using MBD to refer to the mother's brother's daughter. This methodology was widely used during the past century and became a key tool for understanding all sorts of relationships in non-industrial societies, where political, economic, and social institutions are based on kin relationships. It is increasingly used in hospitals today to understand patients' genetic predisposition to certain diseases, such as breast and ovarian cancers.

Life Histories

Understanding the **life histories** of informants has been an important tool for anthropologists in understanding past social institutions and how they have changed. During the 1920s, American anthropologists developed life histories as part of their fieldwork on Indian reservations, because the questions they were studying had to do with the American Indian societies before they had been profoundly transformed by

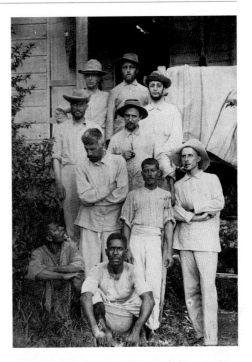

Figure 3.6 Members of the Cambridge Anthropological Expedition to the Torres Strait Islands. W. H. R. Rivers (standing left, wearing glasses), A. C. Haddon (standing in front of Rivers, looking down), C. G. Seligman (top right, with a pipe and glasses), linguist Sidney Ray (standing center, holding a pipe), and Charles Wilkin (standing front right). Each studied different aspects of life on the Torres Strait Islands, but their conversations provided a holistic view of the culture.

contact with white American society. Anthropologists quickly recognized that by interviewing elders about their lives, they could get an understanding of how life was before contact.

Life histories reveal important aspects of social life, such as whether or not the society being studied has changed dramatically. As people develop, become adults, mature, and grow old, they take on different roles in society and in its social institutions. By recording the life histories of a number of individuals, the anthropologist can build an image of how a person's age influences his or her role in the community and how typical social roles unfold over a lifetime.

Ethnohistory

Ethnohistory combines historical and ethnographic approaches to understand social and cultural change. The approach has been most important in studying non-literate communities, where few written historical documents exist, and those documents that do exist can be enhanced with archaeological and ethnographic data. In some cases, museum collections can provide valuable data about historic conditions.

Ethnohistorians are also interested in how societies understand and recount the past. The concepts of history and how to tell it may differ from one society to another. Western history is linear, reflecting a view of time as marching through past and present straight toward the future. But Mayan societies, for example, view time as cyclical, which is to say repeating itself during regular periodic cycles, so their notion of history is different from that in the Western world.

Rapid Appraisals

While typical anthropological studies involve an extended stay of a year or two in the field community, some field projects—including many applied anthropological studies—require answers to focused research questions within a month or two. One solution is a focused research strategy known as a **rapid appraisal**, sometimes jocularly referred to as "parachute ethnography," because the researcher drops in for a few weeks to collect data. Such focused fieldwork requires a general knowledge of both the region and the topic under investigation. This kind of research requires that the anthropologist have considerable field experience to begin with, so she or he knows to focus on the features that distinguish the community under study from other similar ones (Figure 3.7).

Action Research

One criticism of all social scientific research—not just ethnography—is that it often benefits the researcher more than the subjects of research. Even if the researcher publishes a study at the end, it may advance his or her career more than it improves the conditions of the people being studied. This problem is especially acute for disenfranchised communities, where the gap between a community's needs and a researcher's own personal interests may be greatest.

In the 1950s, prominent American anthropologist Sol Tax began advocating **action anthropology**, or research committed to making social change. He encouraged anthropologists

Figure 3.7 Short-Term Ethnography. Some projects have no time for long-term field research. Applied anthropologist Anthony Oliver-Smith investigates the impact of an earthquake in Peru.

to offer voluntary help to disenfranchised communities in airing their grievances and solving their collective problems. Tax believed in the importance of inserting one's political values into anthropological research and of treating research subjects as equal partners (Bennett 1996). Today, some anthropologists use a variant of action research methods by promoting the involvement of community members in formulating the research questions, collecting data, and analyzing the data. Often called **participatory action research**, it is based on the idea that marginalized people can and should do much of their own investigation, analysis, and planning (Chambers 1997). This approach not only aims to place the researcher and subjects on a more even plane; it also encourages researchers to share their methods so people can act to improve their own social, economic, and political conditions.

Anthropology at a Distance

At times anthropologists have no way of getting into the field at all. In times of war or political repression, for example, an anthropologist may be unable to conduct fieldwork in a particular setting. Instead, the researcher may conduct interviews with people who are from the community but who live elsewhere. Such studies can be thought of as anthropology at a distance.

One famous example is Ruth Benedict's research on Japanese society and culture during World War II, *The Chrysanthemum and the Sword* (1946). Because the United States was at war with Japan, Benedict could not visit Japan, so she interviewed Japanese living in the United States and read widely in the published literature about that country and its customs. The result was a solid account of Japanese culture as it was in the 1890s when most of her Japanese informants had left Japan.

Analyzing Secondary Materials

Anthropologists also use both published and unpublished materials to learn about other people's lives. For example, we can learn a great deal from media clippings, government reports, scientific studies, institutional memos and correspondence, and newsletters. These materials, called **secondary materials** because they are not **primary materials** (such as fieldnotes) from someone with direct personal knowledge of the people, provide yet another level of context for what we observe and learn in interviews. Like historians, though, anthropologists must read documents critically, paying attention to who wrote them, what their author's motivations (thus biases) might have been, and any other factors that may have influenced the writing and distribution of the document.

Special Issues Facing Anthropologists Studying Their Own Societies

An important reason anthropologists can understand other cultures is that when we go overseas or work with a community different from our own, the differences between our culture and theirs are immediately obvious. The effect of being a proverbial "fish out of water," struggling to make sense of seemingly senseless actions, heightens our sensitivities to the other society's culture. These sensitivities allow us to ask questions and eventually understand what seems obvious to members of the other community. What happens if we try to do this work within our own society?

When we understand the language and already have well-formed views about people's behavior and attitudes, being a "professional stranger" becomes more difficult. A common technique for gaining new insight under these circumstances is to study social conflicts, because when people are complaining or making allegations against others, their informal logic emerges quite clearly. For example, when anthropologist Laura Nader wanted to understand how American culture deals with relatively minor injustices—such as when a product breaks and consumers have a difficult time getting it fixed—she studied hundreds of consumer complaint letters received by her brother, the nationally prominent consumer rights activist Ralph Nader. In these letters, Laura Nader found people asserting their basic values about fairness and accountability (Nader and Rockefeller 1981).

It is important to remember as well that anthropology has always been an international discipline, conducted by people from many different countries outside Europe and North America. In non-industrialized countries where poor and/or indigenous populations are common, the goals of anthropology have often been closely aligned with national development needs, such as researching the health conditions of rural and poor people to improve government programs. Some anthropologists have also taken an activist stance such as fighting for minority rights (Ramos 1990, 2000).

Indigenous people also practice anthropology themselves. As one Maya ethnolinguist has observed, indigenous peoples often conduct anthropological research as a way of speaking not just *about* their own societies, but *for* their societies: "Our dominators, by means of anthropological discourse, have reserved for themselves the almost exclusive right to speak for us. Only very recently have we begun to have access to this field of knowledge and to express our own world" (Alonso Camal 1997:320). For example, the Pan-Maya ethnic movement in Guatemala, which is led by linguists (like the one just mentioned) who have studied anthropological theory and methods, aims to assert a research agenda and methods derived from and relevant to Maya social interactions and worldviews. This anthropology is often in direct tension with that of other national and foreign anthropologists, because one of its central goals is to support the political claims and self-determination of a particular indigenous group (Warren 1998).

Although issues like indigenous rights are highly political, for anthropologists what often underlies their involvement is the feeling of an ethical commitment to a certain group or issue. In our last section, we explore in more detail the ethical issues facing ethnographers.

❦ What Unique Ethical Dilemmas Do Ethnographers Face?

When Philippe Bourgois decided to conduct research among crack dealers and users in East Harlem, he knowingly entered a situation in which he would witness illegal activities that could put him and his informants at great risk. One central ethical dilemma he confronted was ensuring that he did not betray the people who trusted him. His commitment to protecting their interests was tested every day, since the dealers and users he interviewed would be subject to arrest, prosecution, and prison if he revealed their identities to authorities (Figure 3.8).

Unlike Bourgois, most anthropologists do not set out to study illegal activities. But all anthropologists, nevertheless, face certain common ethical dilemmas, no matter where they conduct their research. These dilemmas often arise in relation to anthropologists' commitment to do no harm, considerations about to whom anthropologists are responsible, and questions about and who should control anthropology's findings (see Chapter 1). Here we explore how such issues play out in the specific context of ethnographic research.

Protecting Informant Identity

Social research can impact its subjects in powerful ways. For example, when living in a community, anthropologists often learn about matters that their informants would prefer to keep secret from other members of their community. Disclosure of these secrets may lead to social

Figure 3.8   Philippe Bourgois in East Harlem. Bourgois's research with crack dealers and users required great sensitivity to the interests of his informants, most of whom were engaged from time to time in illegal activities. But his presence in a predominantly Puerto Rican community led police to stop him frequently on the street because they assumed that the only reason a young white man would be in East Harlem was to buy drugs.

isolation of an informant, contention in the community, or even criminal investigation. For example, many communities around the world stigmatize HIV/AIDS, alcohol use, and certain sexual practices. In some settings, such as in countries with repressive governments, simply talking with a foreign researcher may harm an informant by casting doubt on his or her loyalty or patriotism.

In order to do no harm, anthropologists need to conceal the identities of everyone they have interviewed and, sometimes, conceal content. Typically we use pseudonyms for informants in published accounts, but we might also change details to further disguise an informant's identity. In her monograph on Samoa, for example, Margaret Mead (1928) changed details about characteristics of the adolescent girls she interviewed so nobody, even within the small community she studied, could identify the girls. She was especially concerned about informants who had admitted to having had premarital sex, which Mead knew some older Samoans would disapprove of.

THE LIMITS OF ANTHROPOLOGY'S FIRST AMENDMENT PROTECTIONS

Anthropological fieldwork resembles the work of journalists in that we interview people to learn what is happening in a community. But anthropologists differ from journalists in several important ways. First, anthropologists tend to stay in a community gathering field data for a long time, and most anthropological data come directly from participant observation and interviews with informants. In contrast, journalists often get their information secondhand and rarely stay on assignment for more than a few days or weeks.

Second, unlike reporters in the United States, anthropologists have no constitutional protections that allow them to conceal their informants or the sources of their data. This means that while anthropologists are obligated to protect their informants, their fieldnotes, tape recordings, and photographs are nevertheless subject to a subpoena from a court should the police or some similar legal authority show cause that one should be issued.

WHO SHOULD HAVE ACCESS TO FIELDNOTES?

Generally anthropologists work hard to protect their fieldnotes from scrutiny, because they inevitably contain information that was given in confidence. When anthropologists publish excerpts, they do so in short passages that give the flavor of the field experience or of an interview. The purpose is not to reveal an informant's secrets. Most of us feel that our fieldnotes are too personal and private for public dissemination. In cases where fieldnotes have been published, they have nearly always been heavily edited.

In some communities, informants insist they should have access to and control of anthropological fieldnotes, since they helped create the data and should benefit from it (Brown 2003). This situation can create a dilemma for the anthropologist. On the one hand, many anthropologists share the sentiment that their research should benefit the community. On the other hand, they know that many communities are divided into factions and so raw data turned over to the community can benefit some and harm others. In situations where an anthropologist agrees to share fieldnotes, he or she must negotiate with community members what will be shared.

Anthropology, Spying, and War

Anthropologists ask prying questions and seem to stick their noses into many aspects of people's lives, which has led many anthropologists to be accused of spying. Anthropological research does bear some similarities to the work of spies, since spying is often a kind of participant observation. When anthropologists conduct participant observation, however, we are ethically obligated to let our informants know from the outset that we are researchers. As researchers, our primary responsibility is to our informants, not government agencies or the military.

Yet many anthropologists have used their anthropological skills in service to their countries. For example, during World War II a number of anthropologists assisted with the war effort. Ruth Benedict studied Japanese culture from interviews with Japanese people living in the United States. Sir Edmund Leach assisted the British government in Burma, and E. E. Evans-Pritchard used his knowledge of the Sudan to mobilize the war effort against Germany there (Geertz 1988). David Price (2002) has explored American anthropologist Gregory Bateson's wartime work with the OSS—the predecessor to the CIA. Bateson willingly used his anthropological insights about how to influence tribal peoples in order to ensure they sided with the Allies. In later years Bateson came to view his wartime service with regret because he had inadvertently assisted in the ill treatment, manipulation, and disempowerment of native peoples.

More recently, controversy swirled around the use of anthropological researchers in the U.S. wars in Iraq and Afghanistan. A U.S. military program called the Human Terrain System (2007 to 2014) placed non-combatant social scientists, some of them anthropologists, with combat units to aid officers in gathering information and working with local communities. This program was based on the reasonable assumption that the U.S. military had little knowledge or experience in these foreign cultures, and that military success required the insights provided by cross-cultural research (McFate 2005). But the American Anthropological Association—with the strong support of the vast majority of its members—condemned this program and its use of anthropology, recognizing the dilemma that Bateson's experience suggests, that anthropologists may end up helping the state act against vulnerable groups by providing cultural insights that can harm or disadvantage members of those groups. The deeper obligation of anthropology, some have asserted, is to reveal to the public the oversimplified images of the enemy offered by politicians and the media (Price 2002). Others have worried that the military use of anthropology in one place might undermine the trust between local communities and anthropological researchers in other places, compromising the trust and rapport all anthropologists strive to create with their informants.

THINKING CRITICALLY ABOUT ETHNOGRAPHY

In addition to disguising the identity of specific informants, anthropologists often disguise the identity of a village or a community to protect it from scrutiny by outsiders. But individuals and communities sometimes object to anthropologists' efforts to maintain their anonymity. How do you think an anthropologist should act in such a situation?

Conclusion

Anthropologists have used the ethnographic methods of participant observation and open-ended interviews for about a century and have developed systematic ways to get holistic data that are accessible to few other social scientists. Such methods were tested and developed as research strategies in remote, non-Western communities. But for the past thirty years anthropologists have shown that the same methods are effective for studying modern American culture.

Participant observation provides rich insights because it emphasizes a holistic perspective, direct experience, long-term participation in people's lives, and responsiveness to unexpected events. And, as Bourgois has shown, the insights that come from living in a community and participating in its daily life often yield unexpected and startling findings. For example, many other social scientists have studied the problem of drug use in urban minority neighborhoods. Few, however, have recognized, as Bourgois did, that although most drug dealers lack the benefits that many college students take for granted, many still pursue the American dream as active and energetic entrepreneurs.

Anthropologists use other methods besides participant observation and interviews, including the comparative method, the genealogical method, collecting life histories, ethnohistory, and rapid appraisal. Each of these research strategies is effective in tackling different research questions where participant observation may not be possible. And, as always, cultural anthropologists have an ethical responsibility to protect their informants from coming to any harm as a consequence of their research.

KEY TERMS

Action anthropology   p. 62

Emic perspective   p. 50

Ethnohistory   p. 61

Etic perspective   p. 50

Fieldnotes   p. 56

Fieldwork   p. 49

Genealogical method   p. 60

Headnotes   p. 57

Human Relations Area Files
   (HRAF)   p. 60

Informant   p. 55

Intersubjectivity   p. 55

Interview   p. 55

Life history   p. 61

Open-ended interview   p. 55

Participant observation   p. 54

Participatory action
   research   p. 63

Primary materials   p. 63

Rapid appraisal   p. 62

Secondary materials   p. 63

Reviewing the Chapter

CHAPTER SECTION	WHAT WE KNOW	TO BE RESOLVED
What distinguishes ethnographic fieldwork from other types of social research?	Ethnographic fieldwork requires anthropologists to live in the communities of the peoples they are studying for long periods of time. Fieldwork provides rich and nuanced insights about the cultural logic of social life and cultural practices because it offers the researcher a chance to see what people do, not just what they say.	Although nearly all anthropologists accept that immersive fieldwork is a reliable research method, scholars in other disciplines, particularly economics, political science, and psychology, do not accept it as reliable because it seems to them subjective.
How do anthropologists actually do ethnographic fieldwork?	Becoming involved in people's lives through participant observation, asking people questions through interviews, and then taking notes about it all are the ethnographer's most important research techniques.	No two ethnographers are likely to produce the same interpretation of any culture. Fieldworkers have distinct individual backgrounds that affect their interpretations, as well as how others in a community might interact with them.
What other methods do cultural anthropologists use?	Anthropologists draw on the comparative method, the genealogical method, life histories, ethnohistory, rapid appraisals, action research, anthropology at a distance, and the analysis of secondary materials. The choice of method depends on the context, the research questions, and the community under study.	Anthropologists still prioritize ethnographic fieldwork, and when anthropologists use other methods they can sometimes struggle to define what is uniquely "anthropological" about their work.
What unique ethical dilemmas do ethnographers face?	In the past few decades, anthropologists have increasingly attempted to help their study communities by assisting with locally defined goals or standing up for the rights of individuals in these communities. Anthropologists' primary ethical obligation is to protect the interests of informants.	While anthropologists increasingly take on dual roles as academic and applied anthropologists, many disagree about whether they can do both simultaneously. Efforts to protect informants are now well established, but questions still persist as to who owns ethnographic data.

4

Linguistic Anthropology

Relating Language and Culture

In her well-known book *You Just Don't Understand: Women and Men in Conversation*, linguist Deborah Tannen (1990) describes the tensions that arise between young couples because of the different ways women and men use language. Consider the case of Josh, a college student who has been dating his girlfriend, Linda, for more than a year. One day, he received a text from a close friend who was coming to town. Josh invited him to spend the weekend and to go see a baseball game. That evening, when Josh was over at Linda's he told her he was going to have a houseguest and wouldn't be able to see the film he had told her they would see on the day of the game. Linda became upset. Linda would never make such plans without talking about it with Josh first. In fact, she liked being able to say to her friends, "I'll have to check with Josh," because it showed how close they were. Josh's failure to check with her suggested to Linda a lack of intimacy in their relationship.

Talking Past Each Other? Men and women in the United States are socialized to communicate in different ways, which can produce tensions when one party doesn't recognize or appreciate differences in the other's approach to using language.

Josh was equally upset by Linda's reaction, although for different reasons. When Linda asked him why he did not consult her first, he replied, "I can't say to my friend, 'I have to ask my girlfriend for permission!'" For Josh, checking with Linda would make him feel subordinate to her, or worse, like a child. He felt Linda was trying to limit his freedom as an adult and as a man.

Josh and Linda speak the same language, yet they were clearly talking past one another. In their case, the same words—"I'll have to check with Josh (or Linda)"—meant very different things to each person. What explains the miscommunication? While the expression "Women are from Venus and men are from Mars" overstates the situation, in American culture, men and women do live in somewhat different worlds. We have different expectations of each other, expectations that help shape how we use language. If Linda were more direct, people would consider her harsh, aggressive, and unladylike. Josh's directness, however, would typically be seen as a sign of his strength, independence, and maturity, the supposed ideal for a man in American culture. Taking this a step further, we can see how American patterns of gender inequality are built into how we use language. In some settings—the workplace, say—Linda's concern for preserving good social relationships could appear as a sign of weakness, dependence, and uncertainty, limiting her ability to climb the corporate ladder.

This perspective on language leads us to ask a question at the heart of anthropology's interest in language: *How do the ways people talk reflect and create their cultural similarities, differences, and social positions?* Embedded within this larger question are the following problems, around which this chapter is organized:

How do anthropologists study language?
Where does language come from?
How does language actually work?
Does language shape how we experience the world?
If language is always changing, why does it seem so stable?
How does language relate to social power and inequality?

Language is one of the most rule-bound and structured aspects of human culture. Yet, ironically, language is also one of the least conscious and most dynamic aspects of culture. Language helps us make sense of the world around us, and our use of language both marks and reinforces social hierarchies and gender differences within a society. Before we get into these kinds of subtleties, however, it is important to understand how anthropologists approach the study of language, as well as where language comes from in the first place.

❦ How Do Anthropologists Study Language?

Linguistic anthropologists, like cultural anthropologists, work directly with their informants. Thus, much of their research involves fieldwork, building rapport with informants, and long periods of immersion in another culture. But the specific field strategy that a linguistic anthropologist adopts will depend on the kind of question he or she is asking about the use of language in a particular culture.

In the early decades of the twentieth century, anthropologists saw language as central to understanding culture. Franz Boas (1911) and his team of researchers who were studying the tribes of the Northwest Coast of North America in the late 1890s published many texts transcribed in their original Indian languages along with English translations. They insisted that the categories and concepts encoded in Native American myths and stories were distinctive to local cultures. They pioneered a tradition—expanded by Boas's student Edward Sapir—that has come to be called **anthropological linguistics**, the branch of linguistics that later influenced the development of linguistic anthropology. Anthropological linguists of this period conducted systematic analyses of languages, for example examining how verbs are constructed and inflected, how words are formed, and the range of meaning for particular words, using methods of descriptive linguistics. Later linguistic anthropologists developed a different set of methods called sociolinguistics, paying closer attention to the use of language in social contexts. We discuss both below.

THINKING CRITICALLY ABOUT LANGUAGE

Why do you think most people are unaware of how they actually use language? If you listen carefully to the patterns of speech of your friends, can you identify how they say commonplace things differently from one another? From your professors?

❦ Where Does Language Come From?

A **language** is a system of communication consisting of sounds, words, and grammar. This simple definition emphasizes three features: (a) language consists of sounds organized into words according to some sort of grammar, (b) language is used to communicate, and (c) language is systematic. But where does language come from? We can begin to answer this question in two ways: one is evolutionary—having to do with our biological heritage—and the other is historical, related to how languages have developed over time.

Evolutionary Perspectives on Language

The simple fact that we are able to make sounds and put them into meaningful sequences suggests two different biological abilities. First is the ability to make linguistic sounds using the mouth and larynx. Second is the ability to reproduce these sounds in an infinite variety of ways to produce a diverse range of thoughts. To what extent do we share these capabilities with other animals?

CALL SYSTEMS AND GESTURES

Most animals cannot talk because they do not have a larynx. Yet most animals use sounds, gestures, and movements of the body to communicate. Anthropological linguists refer to these sounds and movements as **call systems**, which are patterned forms of communication that express meaning. But this sort of communication is not considered to be language. Why? There are four major reasons:

1. *Animal call systems are limited in what and how much they can communicate.* Calls are restricted largely to emotions or bits of information about what is currently present in the environment, while language has few limitations on kind or amount of information it can transmit.
2. *Call systems are stimuli-dependent, which means an animal can communicate only in response to a real-world stimulus.* In contrast, humans can talk about things that are not currently happening in the real world, including things and events in the past or future.
3. *Among animals each call is distinct, and these calls are never combined to produce a call with a different meaning.* In contrast, the sounds in any language can be combined in limitless ways to produce new meaningful utterances.
4. *Animal call systems tend to be nearly the same within a species, with only minor differences between call systems used in widely separated regions.* In contrast, different members of our species speak between 5,000 and 6,000 different languages, each with its own complex patterns.

Humans are evolutionarily distinct from other animals in that we developed not just the biological capacity to speak through a larynx but the brain capacity to combine sounds to create infinite symbolic meanings. Both abilities form the basis of human language.

TEACHING APES TO USE SIGN LANGUAGE

It is clear that some apes have the ability to communicate, beyond the limits of a call system, as researchers who have attempted to teach American Sign Language (ASL) to apes demonstrate. A well-known example is a chimp named Washo, who learned over 100 signs that had English equivalents. Even more striking, she was able to combine as many as five signs to form complete, if simple, sentences (Gardner, Gardner, and Van Cantfort 1989). Similarly, Penny Patterson (2003) worked with a female gorilla named Koko, who before her death in 2018 at age 46 learned to use more than 2,000 signs and also combined them in short sentences (Figure 4.1).

Chimpanzees and gorillas clearly have the cognitive ability to associate signs with concepts and then to combine them in original ways. Such capabilities are not

Figure 4.1   Koko with Penny Patterson.

surprising among our nearest relatives in the animal kingdom, since the human capacity for language had to begin somewhere, and we would expect other advanced primates to have some limited abilities.

Historical Linguistics: Studying Language Origins and Change

Historical linguistics focuses on how and where the languages people speak today emerged. This approach uses historical analysis of long-term language change. The approach began in the eighteenth century as **philology**, which is the comparative study of ancient texts and documents. Philologists like the German Jacob Grimm (1822), best known for his collections of fairy tales, observed that there were regular, patterned differences from one European language to another. To explain these patterns he hypothesized that English, German, Latin, Greek, Slavic, and Sanskrit all came from a common ancestor. As speakers of languages became isolated from one another—perhaps because of migration and geographic isolation— the consonants in the original language shifted one way in Sanskrit, another way in Greek and Slavic languages, in a different direction in Germanic and English, and yet another way in Latin and the Romance languages, all of which came to be known as Grimm's Law. The supposed common ancestor language, which became extinct after these divergences took place, is called a **proto-language**.

GENETIC MODELS OF LANGUAGE CHANGE

Contemporary historical linguists call Grimm's approach "genetic," since it explores how modern languages derived from an ancestral language. To identify languages that have a common ancestry, historical linguists identify **cognate words**, which are words in two or more languages that may sound somewhat different today but would have changed systematically from the same word (Table 4.1). As groups of speakers became isolated from one another for geographic, political, or cultural reasons, consonants, vowels, and pronunciation diverged and eventually resulted in new, mutually unintelligible languages. For example, German, Dutch, and English are descended from the same proto-Germanic language, but speakers of these three languages cannot usually understand each other unless they have studied the other language.

TABLE 4.1

EXAMPLES OF COGNATE WORDS IN INDO-EUROPEAN LANGUAGES

English	Dutch	German	Norwegian	Italian	Spanish	French	Greek	Sanskrit
three	drei	drei	tre	tre	tres	trois	tri	treis
mother	moeder	mutter	mor	madre	madre	mère	meter	matar
brother	broeder	bruder	mror	fra	hermano	frère	phrater	bhrator

NON-GENETIC MODELS OF LINGUISTIC CHANGE: LANGUAGES IN CONTACT
Languages also change by being in contact with another language, which is a "non-genetic" model of change. Such change generally takes place where people routinely speak more than one language. In the speech of multilingual persons, the use of one of the languages is subtly influenced by the other language's sounds, syntax, grammar, and vocabulary. Evidence of this process can be seen in the use of the flapped and trilled *r* in Europe. In southern parts of Western Europe, the trilled *r* is typical, but this pronunciation seems to have given way in the north of France to a flapped *r* as is common in German and Dutch. In this process, distinctive pronunciations move across language boundaries from community to community like a wave.

Now that we have some understanding about the emergence of language, we can consider how language actually works.

THINKING CRITICALLY ABOUT LANGUAGE

How would you respond to a friend who claims that his or her dog understands English because it responds to English words in regular and predictable ways? What do examples like this tell us about language generally?

❧ How Does Language Actually Work?

Over the past century, linguists and linguistic anthropologists have studied the majority of the world's languages and found that each is highly structured. Moreover, most people are largely unaware of the structure of their language until someone makes a mistake. Even then, they do not always know what is wrong, they just know the sentence sounded wrong.

To explain such reactions, the Swiss linguist Ferdinand de Saussure (1916, 1986) suggested a distinction between the structure, or formal rules, of a language (*langue*) and the way in which people actually speak a language (*parole*). Distinguishing *langue* ("language") and *parole* ("speech") allows linguists to separate the rules and expected usage of language from what people actually say. The distinction is useful because it helps us realize that the rules we use to produce the sounds, word formation, and grammar as native speakers of a language can differ from how we actually speak, which is as much a social and cultural phenomenon as it is a function of language's structure. Here we explore first how language is formally structured, which is the field of descriptive linguistics, and then the social contexts of language use, which is the focus of sociolinguistics.

Descriptive Linguistics

The study of *langue,* or the formal structure of language, is called **descriptive linguistics**, which refers to the systematic analysis and description of a language's sound system and grammar. Linguists distinguish three types of structure in language: (a) **phonology,** the structure of speech sounds; (b) **morphology,** how words are formed into meaningful units; and (c) **syntax,** how words are strung together to form sentences and more complex utterances, such as paragraphs. (High school grammar classes mostly focus on morphology and syntax.) All languages have predictable phonological, morphological, and syntactic structures. Below we take a closer look at phonology and morphology.

PHONOLOGY: SOUNDS OF LANGUAGE

Linguists typically identify the distinct sounds of a language by marking systematic contrasts between pairs or groups of sounds. The majority of both these sounds and the contrasts appear in many of the world's languages, and yet each language has its own unique pattern of sounds. When linguists listen to natural language, such as when people talk un-self-consciously in ordinary conversations, they identify minimal pairs, which are pairs of words that differ only in a single sound contrast. Consider, for example, the initial sounds in the English words "pan," "ban," and "man." Three sounds, [p], [b], and [m], distinguish these three words, while the other sounds in these words are the same. Thus [p], [b], and [m] are considered to be distinct sounds in English.

Linguists often group distinct sounds based on how they are formed. For example, the consonant sounds [b], [d], [g], [p], [t], and [k] are known as stops because they are all made by an occlusion, or stopping, of the airstream though the oral cavity or mouth. In addition, [b], [d], and [g] are distinguished from [p], [t], and [k] in that they are voiced, or formed by the vibration of the vocal cords (glottis) at the Adam's apple. Similarly, the voiced consonants [m], [n], and [ng] are grouped together into the category of nasals because they are all formed by allowing air to pass through the nasal cavity.

Mind you, these are examples of sounds that occur in English. Other languages have different sounds. One of the most distinct, from our language's point of view, is the click (!) sound used by southern African peoples like the !Kung. While most speakers of any language are not fully aware of how they form the different sounds they use when speaking, linguists recognize that sound systems are surprisingly systematic.

Another interesting way to think about phonology is to consider **accents** and **dialects**, which are regional or social variations of a single language. Sometimes the variation occurs between generations or among people of different social classes. Part of the distinctive sound of these forms of speech results from differences in intonation, the pattern of rising and falling pitch, but usually careful analysis of the sounds shows that accents and dialects also have systematic differences in their respective sound systems.

Up to the 1970s linguists assumed that American English was becoming increasingly homogeneous. It seemed that, owing to schools or to national broadcasts on television and radio where the accent is standardized, regional dialects would disappear. In fact, variation in sound systems across America seems to be greater now than ever before. The sociolinguist William Labov (1990; Labov, Ash, and Boberg 2006) observed in the 1980s that language change in the sound system of American English was concentrated in the cities, and that it was most pronounced between generations in the same communities. Such findings suggest a much stronger role for peer groups in the transmission of linguistic forms than linguists had previously noticed.

MORPHOLOGY: GRAMMATICAL CATEGORIES

The elements of grammar—tense, word order, which genders are marked, and so on—are also structured. Just like cultural patterns, grammatical patterns learned during childhood feel extremely natural to native speakers in any language, even though the same forms and structures would seem quite unnatural to speakers of most other languages. A couple of examples—the first looking at tenses, the second at pronouns—will illustrate how varied even the most basic grammatical categories can be.

English speakers tend to assume that there are only three natural tenses: past, present, and future. But not all languages use this same set of tenses, and some languages do not even require that tense be unambiguously marked in any particular sentence. For example, the Ningerum language of Papua New Guinea uses five tenses: present, future, today-past, yesterday-past, and a-long-time-ago-past. Events that happened earlier in the day receive a different tense marking from those that happened yesterday or the day before. Similarly, events that happened several weeks, months, or years ago take a different tense marking. In contrast, Indonesian has no regular tense marking in its verbs but uses adverbs or other time references to emphasize when something has happened or will happen.

American English has fewer pronouns than many other languages do. We distinguish between singular and plural, among three persons (first person, second person, and third person), and among three cases (subjective, objective, and possessive). If we consider only person and number, we have six basic pronouns, plus two extra pronouns for gender marking in the third person singular (*he, she,* and *it*). This set of pronouns does not even begin to exhaust the possible pronoun distinctions that could be used. In French, for example, the second person singular pronoun ("you") takes two forms: *tu* (an informal form) and *vous* (a formal form). The Awin language of Papua New Guinea has singular, dual, and plural forms of its pronouns, meaning "you" (one person), "you two," and "you" (more than two).

Figure 4.2   One of the Most Common Signs in American Life. Even without words on it, we all know the meaning of this sign.

Figure 4.3   The Productive Use of Signs Around the World. The image of a red circle with a line crossing through it is recognized in many cultures as signifying "no." On this notice board in front of a business in Papua New Guinea, the "no" sign is placed over an image of a betel nut to communicate a ban on the sale of betel nut. When chewing betel nut, a common practice in Papua New Guinea, one needs to spit out bright red spittle frequently.

These basic examples illustrate some of the wide range of possibilities that arise in natural languages. Each configuration suggests certain distinctions that represent meaning encoded in the language's grammar. But such patterns do not alone create meaning.

Sociolinguistics

Sociolinguistics is the study of how sociocultural context and norms shape language use and the effects of language use on society. Sociolinguists accept whatever form of language a community uses—which de Saussure referred to as *parole*—as the form of language they should study.

When one examines the actual speech (*parole*) used in any community, one often finds that different people may use the same grammar and sound system (*langue*), but the actual sentences they make (*parole*) often carry different assumptions and connotations. This is because meaning emerges from conversation and social interaction, not just the formal underlying rules of language. We can see how sociocultural context shapes meaning by looking at signs, symbols, and metaphors.

SIGNS

Signs are words or objects that stand for something else, usually as a kind of shorthand (Figures 4.2 and 4.3). They are the most basic way to convey meaning. A simple example is the ordinary traffic sign that tells motorists to stop at an intersection. The colors, shapes, and designs used in such signs are largely arbitrary; when highway signs were invented early in the twentieth century, engineers could have selected any shape or color for the stop sign. The choice was not totally arbitrary, however, because Americans feel red is more dramatic than yellow or blue, and it may well have been associated with fire departments before the automobile.

SYMBOLS

Symbols, which we introduced in Chapter 2, are basically elaborations on signs. When a sign becomes a symbol it usually takes on a much wider range of meanings than it may have had as a sign. For example, most colleges and universities in America have mascots and colors associated with their football teams. A mascot, such as a wildcat or panther, is a sign of the team, but mascots also readily become a symbol for the whole school, so that the wildcat represents all of the distinctive features of the institution and its people. But note that symbols work because signs themselves are productive, capable of being combined in innovative and meaningful ways.

Anthropologist Sherry Ortner (1971) distinguished three kinds of culturally powerful symbols: summarizing symbols, elaborating symbols, and key scenarios.

Summarizing symbols sum up a variety of meanings and experiences and link them to a single symbol. An example is the American flag, which many Americans see as summarizing everything good about America, especially such things as "democracy, free enterprise, hard work, competition, progress, national superiority, and freedom" (Figure 4.4).

Elaborating symbols explain and clarify complex relationships through a single symbol or set of symbols. Elaborating symbols work in exactly the opposite way from summarizing symbols, because they help us sort out complex feelings and relationships. For example, the cow is an elaborating symbol among the Nuer and Dinka peoples of South Sudan. For these herding groups, cows are used for bride wealth, and people spend an extraordinary amount of time thinking about their cows, their

Figure 4.4 Making Use of a Summarizing Symbol. The Marine Corps War Memorial in Arlington, Virginia, pictured here is based on the famous photograph "Raising the Flag on Iwo Jima" by Joe Rosenthal. The image of Marines raising the flag has become a symbol of the American struggle for freedom.

Figure 4.5   An Elaborating Symbol to Make Sense of Social Relations.   Dinka cattle have various kinds of markings and colors, which the Dinka use to make sense of social differences in their community.

coloration, their body parts, and the like. The Nuer and Dinka think of the cow as resembling the body of society with its varied and interlinked parts. By talking about cows, they can talk about social relations within the community (Figure 4.5).

The key scenario differs from the other two kinds of symbols because it implies how people should act. A common American key scenario is the Horatio Alger myth. In Horatio Alger's many novels, this scenario often involves a young boy from a poor family, who works hard to become rich and powerful. It does not matter that most of us will not become these things; the scenario has meaning for how we feel about and evaluate hard work and persistence.

METAPHORS

Metaphors are implicit comparisons of words or things that emphasize the similarities between them, allowing people to make sense of complex social relations around them. For example, in our culture we metaphorize ideas as food, as in "this textbook gives you *food* for thought, and some things to *chew* over, although you probably can't *stomach* everything we tell you here." Another example is how we metaphorize love as a disease, as in "he got over her, but she's got it bad for him, and it broke her heart" (Sheridan 2006:54).

Through signs, symbols, and metaphors, language reinforces cultural values that are already present in the community. Simultaneously cultural norms and values reinforce the symbols that give language its power to convey meaning. Such relationships between language and culture raise a very interesting and old question: Do speakers of different languages see the world differently, just as people from different cultures might? We turn to this issue in the next section.

THINKING CRITICALLY ABOUT LANGUAGE

How might paying attention to the metaphors and symbols we use in our daily language allow us to frame important issues in more or less appealing ways? Consider, as an example, the use of the term *downsizing* rather than *firing* in employment contexts.

❦ Does Language Shape How We Experience the World?

Most Americans generally assume that the world is what it is, and our experience of it is shaped by whatever is actually happening around us. But as we saw in Chapter 2, our culture predisposes us to presume some features of the world, while other people's culture leads them to assume something different. For many decades anthropologists and linguists have been debating a similar point in relation to language: Does the language we speak shape the way that we perceive the physical world? According to the Sapir-Whorf hypothesis, which we examine next, it does.

The Sapir-Whorf Hypothesis

In the 1920s, the linguistic anthropologist Edward Sapir (1929) urged cultural anthropologists to pay close attention to language during field research. Recognizing that most non-European languages organized tense, number, adjectives, color terms, and vocabulary in ways different from English, French, or German, he argued that a language inclines its speakers to think about the world in certain ways because of its specific grammatical categories. It is anthropology's first expression of **linguistic relativity**, which is the idea that people speaking different languages perceive or interpret the world differently because of differences in their languages.

Sapir's student Benjamin Lee Whorf (1956) expanded on Sapir's work. Whorf had studied the language of the Hopi Indians and found that his knowledge of the grammars of European languages was little help in understanding Hopi grammar. He concluded that people who speak different languages actually do—are not just "inclined to," as his teacher Sapir would have said—perceive and experience the world differently. By the 1950s, linguistic anthropologists saw the ideas of Sapir and Whorf as related and began referring to them as the "Sapir-Whorf hypothesis." Let us illustrate the hypothesis with one of Whorf's best examples, the lack of tenses in Hopi.

Hopi Notions of Time

Whorf studied Hopi language and concluded that it lacked tenses like those we have in English. Hopi uses a distinction not expressed grammatically in European languages, which he called "assertion categories." These include (1) statements that report some fact (e.g., "he is running" or "he ran"), (2) declaration of an expectation, whether current or past (e.g., "he is going to eat" or "he was going to run away"), and (3) statements of some general truth (e.g., "rain comes from the clouds" or "he drinks only iced tea"). These three assertion categories do not overlap and are mutually exclusive. When translating these Hopi concepts into English, most people will use our tenses (past, present, and future), partly because we have to express tense in English to make a sentence, and partly because this is the only convenient way to express these different types of assertions in English.

Whorf argued that the structure of the Hopi language suggested different ideas to Hopi than translations of that language would to English speakers. He also linked these grammatical categories to Hopi "preparing" activities that

Figure 4.6   A Hopi Ceremony of Regeneration.   Tendencies in language are reflected in and reinforced by social action, such as this ritual that emphasizes regeneration and the recycling nature of the world.

surrounded certain rituals and ceremonies, arguing that "To the Hopi, for whom time is not a motion but a 'getting later' of everything that has ever been done, unvarying repetition is not wasted but accumulated" (1956). Americans, in contrast, might see repetitive actions before a celebration as a sapping of effort or as inefficiency (Figure 4.6).

Since Whorf's death in 1941, several linguists have challenged his interpretation of Hopi grammar. Malotki (1983), for example, argues that Hopi does, in fact, have tenses that resemble English tenses. Malotki's claims have not gone unchallenged, but if true, such a finding would call Whorf's example into question, although not necessarily his theory of the relationship between language and culture. Moreover, in the time between Whorf's and Malotki's research, Hopi have become more knowledgeable and conversant in English, suggesting that if the Hopi language now has tenses, these may be evidence of language change since the 1930s.

Ethnoscience and Color Terms

In the 1960s anthropologists began to explore how different peoples classified the world around them, focusing on how people conceptually group species of plants and animals or other domains, such as planets or colors. The study of how people classify things in the world became known as **ethnoscience** (see also Chapter 6). These studies began with a set of assumptions about the relationship between language and culture very different from those accepted by Sapir and Whorf. These scholars assumed that the natural world was a given, and that all human beings perceived it in the same way. Differences in classification were simply different ways of mapping categories onto empirical reality.

For example, anthropologists Brent Berlin and Paul Kay (1969) analyzed the color terms of more than 100 languages and found that basic color terms are consistent across languages. For example, if a language has only two basic color terms, they are terms for dark (black) and light (white). But if a language has three terms, they are black, white, and red. The third term is never green, blue, purple, or orange. An example of a language with three basic color terms is Lamnso, spoken in the Central African country of Cameroon (Figure 4.7). If a fourth color is present, then the terms are black, white, red, and blue/green. Some anthropologists suspect that these patterns are universal and may have to do with the way our optic nerve responds to light of different wavelengths.

This universal pattern does not disprove the Sapir-Whorf hypothesis, but it suggests that there are limits on the extent to which language shapes our experience of the world. Indeed, other studies have shown that when informants with limited numbers of basic color terms are given paint chips displaying a wide range of colors, they can distinguish among the different colors, but they classify the chips into groups that correspond to their basic color categories. Thus it seems that people who speak different languages do not actually see colors differently, they just classified them differently.

Is the Sapir-Whorf Hypothesis Correct?
By the late 1960s ethnoscience had largely dismissed the Sapir-Whorf hypothesis as having no significance for understanding human cognition. Today most

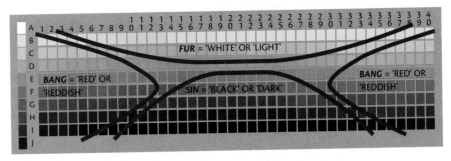

Figure 4.7   The Munsell Color Chart.   The Cameroon language of Lamnso has three basic color terms: *sin, fur,* and *bang,* which we would gloss as *black* (or *dark*), *white* (or *light*), and *red* (or *reddish*), respectively. But as we can see from the plot of these three color terms on a standard Munsell color chart, our sense of black, white, and red is not at all typical of the range of colors included in each of these Lamnso terms.

anthropologists accept what has come to be called the weak or non-deterministic version of the linguistic relativity argument, which suggests (much as Sapir wrote) that the language habits of a community lead people to think about the world in certain ways and not others. Such a reading of the Sapir-Whorf hypothesis supports the idea that some ways of thinking are guided by the language we use while others are not.

There are implications here for language change. Over the long term such suggested ways of thinking would lead to a preference in each language for some kinds of linguistic change over others. If we take a rather static view of language, this issue might lead us to believe that languages are very stable, slow to change; and yet throughout this chapter we have suggested that language is dynamic. Let us now consider how language can constantly be changing, yet seem so stable.

THINKING CRITICALLY ABOUT LANGUAGE

How might the coarse slang used in daily conversations by college and university students be interpreted differently by parents or grandparents?

If Language Is Always Changing, Why Does It Seem So Stable?

A striking paradox in linguistics is that, like culture, language constantly changes, yet most people experience their own language as stable and unchanging. We tend to notice the changes only when we hear other people in our communities using words, pronunciations, or grammatical forms that differ from our own. Usually national policies come into play to enforce or support the use and stabilization of certain linguistic forms over others, leading to language change within a strong framework of stability.

Linguistic Change, Stability, and National Policy

The increase of commerce, communication, and migration around the world over the past few centuries has produced new environments for language change. Colonial powers such as Great Britain, France, and Spain learned about new plants, peoples, and ways of living in their far-flung colonies. In the Americas, these powers also introduced slave labor from Africa, resulting in the blending of diverse African cultures, which were also blending with Native American cultures. These societies developed dynamic new languages, such as creole and pidgin languages, and implemented national language policies, in some cases to stabilize rapid linguistic change.

CREOLE AND PIDGIN LANGUAGES

In the Americas, local colonized societies developed hybrid languages that linguists call **creole languages**, languages of mixed origin that developed from a complex blending of two parent languages. A prominent example is the language commonly spoken in Haiti that combines several African languages with Spanish, Taíno (the language of Caribbean native peoples), English, and French.

In Asia and the Pacific, these hybrid forms have generally been called **pidgin languages**, which refers to a mixed language with a simplified grammar that people rarely use as a mother tongue, but to conduct business and trade. In the independent Melanesian countries of Vanuatu, the Solomon Islands, and Papua New Guinea, for example, local forms of Pidgin that combine various local languages and English have become national languages along with the colonial languages of English or French. In all three countries, the ability to speak Pidgin has positive social status.

NATIONAL LANGUAGE POLICIES

Different countries have tried to control language change through the creation of national language policies. Short of making one particular regional dialect the national language, however, countries have found it nearly impossible to dictate what language or what form of the national language the public will speak. Two examples—taken from the Netherlands and Quebec (Canada)—demonstrate different approaches to controlling processes of language change.

In the Netherlands during the twentieth century, Dutch linguists recognized that pronunciation and vocabulary had changed so much that spelling no longer reflected how people pronounced words. Dutch linguists recommended that spelling be changed to keep up with changing language use, and twice in the twentieth century the ruling monarchs, Queen Wilhelmina and Queen Juliana, issued royal decrees changing the official spelling of Dutch words to parallel actual use. The Dutch approach is quite tolerant of changing language.

French Canadians in the province of Quebec have been less tolerant of language change, successfully preserving Quebecois (the form of French spoken in Quebec) against the pressure of English-speaking Canadians, who have historically considered English to be the superior language. Although government officials throughout Canada must be bilingual in English and French, the province of Quebec conducts all government business primarily in French. To stem the tide of Anglicization (the creeping influence of English), the provincial parliament

Figure 4.8   Defending Quebecois from Anglicization.   In Quebec, store signs must display French, and any English they contain must not be more prominent than the French.

passed laws that require signs in public places to be in French. If English is also used, the English text cannot be longer or larger than the French translation (Figure 4.8). In this case, language use coupled with nationalist control of the provincial parliament has encouraged the use of French throughout the population of Quebec.

Language Stability Parallels Cultural Stability

As the situation of language use in Quebec demonstrates, the potential loss of a native language can be a critical issue for a group of people. In such cases, people view the use of a particular language not just as a means of communication but as integral to their cultural identities and worldviews. As a result, the preservation of language and culture are often seen to go hand in hand.

The connection between cultural stability and the ongoing use of language is an especially critical one for many indigenous peoples around the world, who are striving to protect their languages and distinctive ways of life in the face of rapid social change. As a result, many indigenous groups are facing what scholars call "language death," referring to the dying out of many minority languages. Some linguists argue that nearly half of the world's 5,000 or 6,000 languages are in jeopardy of dying out within a century (Hale 1992).

Many scholars believe that these dramatic losses will have considerable impact on the world's linguistic diversity, even as new languages are created all the time. And because of the close relationship between language and culture, the world's cultural diversity will suffer as well. As our discussion of the Sapir-Whorf hypothesis suggests, language is the primary medium through which people experience the richness of their culture, and loss of language suggests a genuine loss of a culture's fullness. In response to such concerns, many linguistic anthropologists have turned their attention to helping indigenous communities save their traditional languages; in "Anthropologist as Problem Solver: Helping Communities Preserve Endangered Languages," we examine an example from Papua New Guinea.

Anthropologist as Problem Solver
Helping Communities Preserve Endangered Languages

With about 1,000 different languages—roughly one sixth of all known languages—the island of New Guinea is one of the most linguistically diverse regions on earth. The vast majority of the island's distinct languages have very small numbers of speakers, often fewer than two or three hundred, which is not enough to protect these languages from extinction.

Linguistic anthropologist Lise Dobrin (2008) conducted fieldwork among the Mountain Arapesh in the Sepik region of Papua New Guinea, where a small community she calls Apakibur was attempting to preserve their language. In particular, community members were concerned because most of their youth were learning Tok Pisin, one of the country's four official languages, as their primary language. Dobrin notes that the language of daily life is no longer one of the Arapesh dialects, as it would have been in the 1930s when Margaret Mead conducted research in the same region. Today, the youngest fluent speakers of Arapesh are in their fifties, while everyone speaks Tok Pisin.

Describing the Arapesh as an "importing culture," Margaret Mead (1938:159–160) had noted that villages in the Sepik region might change languages within a generation or two. Other researchers have observed the sort of language shift predicted by Mead across the region, including in some coastal Arapesh villages that were abandoning Arapesh in favor of one of the unrelated Austronesian languages (Welsch 2013).

Like many American anthropologists, Dobrin did not want to impose her own views about the value of the indigenous Arapesh language or whether it should be saved. She recognized that the language people spoke should be up to them, not an anthropologist on a year's field visit. She also recognized that for communities to maintain their endangered languages, they needed to feel empowered, but she found that the Arapesh speakers she worked with, like most Papua New Guineans, felt their communities were the "last place" when viewed from the perspective of global wealth and power. How was it possible to feel empowered when all of the forces with either wealth or power who had so much gave so little to them and expected villagers to empower themselves? The symbolic message was that the Arapesh were unworthy.

The Arapesh people of Apakibur welcomed Dobrin's participation in a school program they had established to help their children learn Arapesh. Part of their excitement about the school program was its potential to draw interest from outsiders. Dobrin understood that helping the community with their

Preserving an Endangered Language. Linguistic anthropologist Lise Dobrin works with language teacher Matthew Rahiria to transcribe a recording of the Arapesh language.

continues

Anthropologist as Problem Solver *continued*

language would encourage a sense of reciprocal exchange that required both her and the
community to maintain efforts to keep the
program going. She argues that in Melanesia, outsider engagement in such programs is
not a reimposition of colonial control, but a
productive engagement built on an intercultural moral exchange that is highly valued in
Melanesian cultures. By participating as an
outsider, she was adding to the excitement
and interest of the language program for Arapesh youth. Reflecting on her experiences,
Dobrin encourages all anthropologists and
linguists to "embrace opportunities to participate in culturally appropriate relationships of
exchange" as a way of addressing the growing problem of language extinctions (Dobrin
2008:317–8).

QUESTIONS FOR REFLECTION

1. Why would an anthropologist's involvement in a program to preserve an endangered language not be seen by Arapesh as a
   reimposition of colonialist control?

2. What significance should we give to the fact
   that people throughout much of Melanesia
   seek, rather than reject, involvement with
   the West?

3. Do anthropologists and linguists have a
   responsibility to leave their study communities unchanged? Do they have an obligation to participate in the affairs of their host
   community?

As we have seen in this section, issues of language stability and change are
closely tied to questions of domination, control, and resistance, a theme we explore in more detail in our final section.

THINKING CRITICALLY ABOUT LANGUAGE

What is it about our language that makes it feel so personal and so much a part of us? How
is it that our language actually changes so seamlessly as we hear and adopt new words and
expressions?

🌱 How Does Language Relate to Social Power and Inequality?

Anthropological linguists established long ago that language use influences the
cultural context and social relationships of its speakers. But in recent years, they
have become especially attuned to issues of power and inequality in language use,
specifically how language can become an instrument of control and domination.
We explore these issues here by introducing the concept of language ideology.

Language Ideology

The concept of **language ideology** refers to the ideologies people have about the superiority of one dialect or language and the inferiority of others. A language ideology links language use with identity, morality, and aesthetics. It shapes our image of who we are as individuals, as members of social groups, and as participants in social institutions (Woolard 1998). Like all ideologies, language ideologies are deeply felt beliefs that are considered truths. In turn, these truths are reflected in social relationships, as one group's unquestioned beliefs about the superiority of its language justifies the power of one group or class of people over others (Spitulnik 1998:154).

Gendered Language Styles

Despite what your high school English teachers may have told you, there is no "proper" way to speak English or any other language. From the anthropological perspective of language ideology, there are only more and less privileged versions of language use. This is to say, language use either legitimates an individual or group as "normal" or even "upstanding" or defines that individual or group as socially inferior. Consider, for example, the findings of a classic study in sociolinguistics that explores how gendered expectations of how women speak English in our culture can reflect and reinforce the idea that women are inferior to men. In her research, Robin Lakoff (1975) described how "talking like a lady" involved the expectation that a woman's speech patterns should include such things as tag questions ("It's three o'clock, *isn't it?*"); intensifiers ("It's a *very* lovely hat!"); hedge ("I'm *pretty* sure"); or hesitation and the repetition of expressions, all of which can communicate uncertainty and were largely absent in expectations about men's speech. Lakoff argued that the social effects of speaking in this way can marginalize women's voices in contexts like a courtroom or a workplace, where speaking in a way that implies uncertainty— even if the speaker is not intentionally expressing uncertainty—can undermine a woman's testimony (as in a court of law) or trustworthiness (as in a workplace). Such situations, she suggested, are used to justify elevating men to positions of authority over women.

Lakoff herself recognized that some men may communicate in female-preferential ways, and not all women use the patterns just described, since language ideologies are not hard and fast for every speaker. Indeed, more recent research of email communications between men and women (Thomson, Murachver, and Green 2001) suggests that men and women can actually be quite flexible in their use of gendered language styles, changing these depending on who they are talking to. As a result, men may use female-preferential language when interacting with a woman, and women may use more typically male language patterns when interacting with a man, further suggesting that language ideologies do not always exercise total control over how people speak.

Language and the Legacy of Colonialism

In places like sub-Saharan Africa, nineteenth-century European colonial powers introduced their own language as the official language, in large part because they viewed indigenous languages as socially inferior to their European languages.

When the countries of this region acquired independence, many of these languages became one of several national languages. As a way of building a national identity, many newly independent nations have had to decide which of their many vernaculars to select as their official language or languages. In Zambia, for example, which gained independence from Great Britain in 1964, the government recognized seven of the most important of its seventy-three local languages, plus English, as national languages, since nearly everyone in Zambia knows one or another of these languages. In theory each is equal to the others, but in practice they are not, as listening to Zambian radio broadcasts reveals (Spitulnik 1998).

Although all eight of Zambia's official languages are given air time, English dominates the airwaves, both in the number of hours per week it is used and in having more sophisticated and cosmopolitan content. Certain of the more widely spoken indigenous local languages also get more air time than minority languages. Over the past decades, broadcasters have presented to their ethnically diverse listening public what they feel are appropriate topics in each of the different languages, such as themes related to subsistence farming for certain language groups considered less sophisticated, and themes related to business and politics for others deemed linguistically superior. These broadcasting decisions have shaped how the public evaluates each indigenous language, presenting some as more sophisticated than others, but all as less sophisticated than English. In this case, broadcasts not only become models of language hierarchy in Zambia but also reinforce hierarchical views of different languages and the ethnicities associated with them.

The broader point about language ideologies that comes across in each of our examples is that language can be used to exclude or marginalize some people in workplaces and social programs. Language routinely becomes a marker of position simultaneously in local, regional, national, and international contexts.

THINKING CRITICALLY ABOUT LANGUAGE

Students often feel they will never be able to participate in the professional lives of their advisors because their advisors and other professors seem to speak a language that many students do not understand. Of course, they are speaking English, but they use many complex words that few students know. How does language in this situation become a tool of control and power over students?

❦ Conclusion

The capacity for language is one of the central features that distinguish humans from other animals. Whatever the particular language being spoken, human languages are universally structured and rule-bound. But to end there—with the idea that language is something that all humans have access to and use in the same ways—misses the crucial facts that sociocultural context and norms shape language use and that the use of language has important impacts on everyday social relationships. To separate language from culture leads to an impoverished understanding of *both* language and culture.

This point, of course, is one that Sapir and Whorf made many decades ago when they advanced the idea that particular languages guide ways of thinking and acting. We can see a more updated illustration of the relationship between culture and language—and perhaps a more recognizable one to all of us—in the vignette that opens this chapter, in the different ways that Josh and Linda communicate with each other. Their particular miscommunication is not the result of a universal human situation in which women and men cannot understand each other, but the product of a particular culture that expects girls and women to speak in some ways, and boys and men in others.

We should not forget the social consequences of language use, especially when certain ways of talking and expression imply the correctness or superiority of one group, gender, or social class, and the incorrectness or inferiority of another. The broader point here is that language has great power to shape not just our meanings and comprehension of the world but our experiences as social beings as well.

Key Terms

Accent p. 76	Dialect p. 76	Phonology p. 76
Anthropological linguistics p. 72	Ethnoscience p. 82	Pidgin language p. 85
	Language p. 85	Proto-language p. 74
Call system p. 73	Language ideology p. 89	Sociolinguistics p. 78
Cognate words p. 74	Linguistic relativity p. 81	Syntax p. 76
Creole language p. 85	Morphology p. 76	
Descriptive linguistics p. 76	Philology p. 74	

Reviewing the Chapter

CHAPTER SECTION	WHAT WE KNOW	TO BE RESOLVED
How do anthropologists study language?	Linguistic anthropologists generally use participant observation to study how people use language in their everyday lives.	Some linguistic anthropologists disagree on how much emphasis should be placed on the study of paralinguistic cues such as pauses, changes in pitch and volume, and gestures.
Where does language come from?	Animals do not have language, but some primates have a rudimentary ability to use signs, which is a necessary but not sufficient condition for language to develop.	Although most linguistic anthropologists accept both genetic and non-genetic models, the relative importance of these models remains unclear, and we currently have no unified models that draw on both.

How does language actually work?	Language is systematic, but most descriptive linguistic models are static and do not express the dynamic nature of language.	By and large, linguistic anthropologists have not found historical models of language change to fully explain why particular sound systems or grammatical patterns have taken the forms they do.
Does language shape how we experience the world?	Meaning is conveyed through symbols, but particular meanings have their roots in the social processes of daily life.	Although the structures of language vary widely in different languages, anthropologists and linguists have never reached a consensus about whether the structure of language actually shapes the ways we perceive the world.
If language is always changing, why does it seem so stable?	Languages are always changing in small ways as sound systems gradually change and as new words are borrowed from other languages or created anew.	Although anthropologists recognize that languages change as cultures change, there is no current consensus about how these changes emerge.
How does language relate to social power and inequality?	A language ideology links language use with identity, morality, and aesthetics. It helps us imagine the very notion of who we are as individuals, as members of social groups and categories, and as participants in social institutions.	Anthropologists realize creole and pidgin languages are important, but they do not have a full understanding of the precise conditions under which these languages can assert their importance.

5

Globalization and Culture

Understanding Global Interconnections

During early September 2015, media outlets around the world fixated on the tragic image of a young boy whose body had washed up on a Mediterranean beach in Turkey. The boy was a Syrian refugee named Alan Kurdi, who drowned when the overcrowded boat he and his family were on capsized as they left Turkey for a nearby Greek island. His family had hoped that in Greece they might be able to gain visas that would allow them to resettle with relatives living in Canada. Although images and news stories of desperate refugees flooding into Europe had become increasingly common during the year—in 2015 alone, over 1.3 million people requested legal asylum in a European country—this particular image stood above the rest. It poignantly signaled that a full-blown humanitarian crisis was happening, the magnitude of which had not been seen in Europe since the Second World War.

An Influx of Refugees. Syrian refugees, such as those pictured here crammed on a boat, have been making harrowing trips across the Mediterranean to escape civil war in their country. These trips have taken many lives and sparked intense debate throughout Europe about how many refugees should be allowed to stay.

Taking stock of the European refugee situation, the leader of the International Rescue Committee, David Miliband, observed that large-scale displacement of people is a persistent feature of the contemporary world. As he told reporters, "This is not a blip. The forces that are driving more and more people from their homes—weak states, big tumults within the Islamic world, a divided international system. . . . None of these things are likely to abate soon" (Kambas and Bronic 2016). The plight confronting Syria, a mostly Arab country in the Middle East, is an especially acute illustration of these problems. What began as an internal conflict in 2011 between the government and pro-democracy protestors has escalated into a multi-sided war involving armed groups backed by Turkey, Russia, France, the United States, various Arab Gulf states, Iran, and militant Islamist groups that draw their fighters from many countries. The current war is also rooted in a century-long history in the Middle East in which armed conflict and foreign manipulation contribute to territorial disruption and the creation of refugees. As many as 11 million people, half of Syria's pre-war population, have been displaced by the current conflict.

Most people around the world have little direct knowledge of or connection to the Syrian conflict and its refugees. But globally circulating images of it have had powerful effects in distant places. The cross-border flow of people in and out of Syria and the role of foreign interests in shaping and responding to the refugee crisis also confirm that this story has complex globalized dimensions. These sorts of international connections influence more than just Middle Eastern wars and refugee crises, of course. Today, many aspects of people's lives everywhere are intertwined with globalization and cross-border interconnections.

Globalization raises compelling opportunities and dilemmas for anthropologists who have for so long studied culture as a local phenomenon. One question stands at the core of anthropological interest in globalization: *What do intensive global interconnections mean for understanding cultural processes in the contemporary world?* Embedded in this broader question are the following problems, around which this chapter is organized:

Is the world really getting smaller?
What are the outcomes of global integration?
Doesn't everyone want to be developed?
If the world is not becoming homogenized, what is actually happening?
How can anthropologists study global interconnections?

We aim to deepen your understanding of culture as a dynamic process by showing its importance for understanding contemporary global processes. For anthropologists, *globalization* illustrates how people create and change their cultures through interconnections with others. But not everybody participates equally in these diverse kinds of global connections, which means we also have to consider power relationships and social inequality.

❦ Is the World Really Getting Smaller?

Asian hip-hop in London, American retirement-fund investments in a South Korean steel conglomerate, Indian "Bollywood" movies in Nigeria, Mexican migrants cooking Thai food in a North Carolina restaurant—each of these situations confirms our sense that the world is getting smaller and cultural mixing is on the rise. This sense extends to anthropologists, who recognize that the people whose lives we study are often profoundly affected by global interconnections, migratory flows, and cultural mixing. During the past several decades, understanding how those processes of global interconnection affect culture has become an important issue for all anthropologists. For a discipline that has long tried to understand the differences and similarities between human groups and cultures, the idea that the world is getting smaller might suggest that the differences are melting away. But is the world really getting smaller? To answer this question, we first need to understand what globalization is.

Defining Globalization

Defining globalization is a challenge for two reasons. First, different academic disciplines define globalization differently because they study different things. Economists focus on investment and markets, political scientists on policies and interactions of nation-states, and sociologists on non-governmental organizations (NGOs) and other international social institutions. But there is a second problem. Is globalization a general *process* or a *trend* of growing worldwide interconnectedness? Is it a *system* of investment and trade? Is it the *explicit goal* of particular governments or international trade bodies that promote free trade? Or is it, as some say, "globaloney," something that does not actually exist at all (Veseth 2005)?

Anthropologists define **globalization** as the contemporary widening scale of cross-cultural interactions owing to the rapid movement of money, people, goods, images, and ideas within nations and across national boundaries (Kearney 1995; Inda and Rosaldo 2002). But we also recognize that social, economic, and political interconnection and mixing are nothing new for humanity. Archaeological and historical records show that humans have always moved around, establishing contacts with members of other groups, and that sharing or exchanging things, individuals, and ideas is deeply rooted in human evolutionary history.

Early American anthropologists also recognized these facts. Franz Boas and his students Alfred Kroeber and Ralph Linton developed a theory of culture that emphasized the interconnectedness of societies. The Boasians were **diffusionists**, emphasizing that cultural characteristics result from either internal historical dynamism or a spread (diffusion) of cultural attributes from one society to

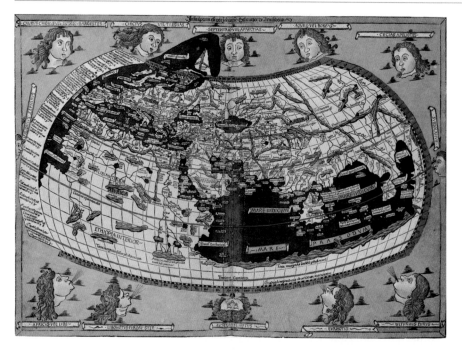

Figure 5.1   A Global Ecumene.   The Greeks referred to an ecumene as the inhabited earth, as this map shows. Much later, anthropologist Alfred Kroeber (1876–1960) used the term to describe a region of persistent cultural interaction. The term became current again in the 1980s and 1990s as anthropologists adopted it to describe interactions across the whole globe.

another (Figure 5.1). Later, beginning in the 1950s, Marxist anthropologists like Eric Wolf argued against the isolation of societies, suggesting that non-Western societies could not be understood without reference to their place within a global capitalist system.

And yet, until the 1980s, such themes of interconnectedness rarely interested most cultural anthropologists. Mainstream anthropology was locally focused, based on research in face-to-face village settings. But across the globe, nearly all societies were heavily engaged with neighboring communities, either as friends, economic partners, or hostile enemies. Today, anthropologists realize that paying attention only to local settings gives an incomplete understanding of people's lives. It also gives an incomplete understanding of the causes of cultural differences, which often emerge not in spite of, but *because of*, interconnections. While not every group participates at the same level in these broad regional or global connections, most communities are more interconnected than many researchers imagined as recently as twenty or thirty years ago.

The World We Live In

How do anthropologists characterize the world in which we live today? Several factors stand out, including the scale of human interconnections and a growing awareness of these interconnections (Nederveen Pieterse 2004). But these changes hardly mean that everybody is participating equally in the same globalizing processes. Further, the word *globalization*, unfortunately, tends to make us think of the entire globe, exaggerating the scale and expanse of financial and social interconnections, which, while great, are typically more limited and often more subtle than the word implies. Indeed some anthropologists prefer the term **transnational** in this context because it imagines relationships that extend beyond nations without assuming they cover the whole world (Basch, Schiller, and Blanc 1993). Whatever the case, it is useful to think of globalization as indicating persistent interactions across widening scales of social activity in areas such as communication, migration, and finances.

COMMUNICATION

At the heart of globalization are rapid increases in the scale and amount of communication taking place. With smartphones, the Internet, and email accessible in most parts of the world, it is clear that the scale of contact has made a quantum leap forward over the past generation. Such rapid and much more frequent communication means that people in very remote places can be in contact with others almost anywhere on the globe (Figure 5.2).

Figure 5.2   An Explosion in Mobile Phones.   Seven billion people, or 95% of the world's population, now live in an area covered by a mobile network. This connectivity, which was unimaginable even a generation ago, has had important consequences for people everywhere, including these young Aboriginals of the Taroqo tribe in Taiwan.

But access to these innovations is generally distributed unevenly. In 2016, for example, more than half the world's population (53%) did not use the Internet. Africa was the least connected, with 75% of that continent's people offline. In contrast, only 21% of Europeans were offline (ITU 2016). As a result, some observers—to highlight real inequalities of access—prefer to talk about the globalization of communication in terms of wealth and poverty.

MIGRATION

Another key feature of the changing scale of globalization is the mobility of people. Whether **migrants** (who leave their homes to live or work for a time in other regions or countries), or **immigrants** (who leave their countries with no expectation of ever returning), or **refugees** (who migrate because of political oppression or war, usually with legal permission to stay), or **exiles** (who are expelled by the authorities of their home countries) (Shorris 1992), people are on the move. According to the United Nations, the number of international migrants—people living in a country other than the one in which they were born—reached 244 million in 2015, which was a 41% increase from the year 2000 (UN 2016). Nearly two thirds of those international migrants live in Asia or Europe, but the United States is the single country with the largest number of international migrants (47 million) (Figure 5.3). These movements of people bring larger numbers of people in contact with one another, offering many possibilities for intercultural contact.

FINANCE

In the modern era, financial globalization involving the reduction or elimination of tariffs to promote trade across borders began in the 1870s. In recent decades, finance and the rapid movement of money across national boundaries have allowed corporations to move factories from one country to another. A generation ago, U.S. factories moved their operations to Mexico and China, but now many of these same factories have been shuttered and relocated to Honduras or Vietnam because of rising hourly labor costs in Mexico and China.

Under these conditions of globalized capital, many transnational corporations have accumulated vast assets. Currently, sixty-nine of the world's 100 largest economic entities are corporations, and the other thirty-one are countries. Walmart, the world's largest retailer, ranks as the tenth largest economic entity in the world, just behind Canada and ahead of Spain (Global Justice Now 2016). Because powerful corporate interests often influence the policies of governments, some see in this situation a movement of power away from nation-states (Korten 1995). But this economic growth and trade are also highly uneven. "Thinking Like an Anthropologist: Understanding Global Integration Through Commodities" explores the complexities of contemporary economic globalization.

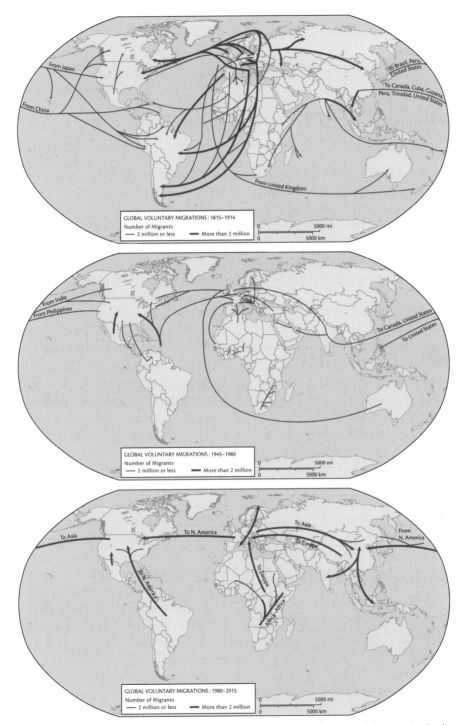

Figure 5.3 **Global Voluntary Migrations.** These three maps show dramatic differences in the directions of migratory flows. During the European colonial era, Europeans were motivated to migrate out of Europe because of opportunities in the colonies (top map). After the Second World War, decolonization saw a reversal in the flow, as non-Europeans and non-U.S. Americans began moving into Europe and the United States in search of new opportunities for themselves (middle map). Today, most migrants stay within the same major region of the world in which they are born (bottom map).

Thinking Like an Anthropologist
Understanding Global Integration Through Commodities

Anthropologists begin their research by asking questions. In this box, we want you to learn how to ask questions as an anthropological researcher. Part One describes a situation and follows up with questions we would ask. Part Two asks you to formulate your own questions based on a different situation.

PART ONE: THE T-SHIRT ON YOUR BACK

Concepts like the "global economy," "economic integration," even "globalization" are pretty abstract. Here, by considering the common T-shirt as a concrete example of economic globalization, we can show how your life is touched by seemingly remote and abstract economic, social, and political forces.

Let us begin with the tag on your shirt. Chances are pretty good it says "Made in . . ." followed by the name of some foreign nation: Bangladesh, Malawi, Malaysia, the Philippines, Mexico, or maybe China, which since 1993 has been the world's largest producer and exporter of clothing. Each year, Americans buy about

one billion garments from China, four for every U.S. citizen (Rivoli 2005:70).

To tell the full story of your T-shirt, though, we have to get the whole picture, which includes understanding the commodity chain, or the linked elements—labor, capital, raw materials, and so on—that contribute to the manufacture of a commodity. Quite likely, your T-shirt originated in a cotton field around Lubbock, Texas. The United States has dominated cotton production markets for two hundred years, thanks largely to our ability to be highly productive while controlling labor costs. Before the Civil War, slavery kept these costs down; now, tractors and government subsidies do. Raw cotton is then shipped off, quite likely to China, to be made into thread and cloth, and then, if it does not stay in China to be manufactured into a T-shirt, off to somewhere else to be cut and sewn. The manufacturer then sells the T-shirts to a distributor, probably a U.S.-based business, and maybe after changing hands once again for silk-screening, it goes to the retailer, who sells it to you.

But let's keep going. After you wear it for a while, you might toss it in the trash, where it finds its way into a landfill. Or you might donate it to a used clothing charity bin like those in the parking lots of some grocery stores. The charities themselves rarely handle your clothing, but in turn sell it to companies like Ragtex or Savers that sort, bundle, and ship used clothing in 1,000-pound bales to sub-Saharan Africa (the largest market for used U.S. clothing), Eastern Europe, East Asia, or Latin America. A whole new series of wholesalers and small traders take over from there (Veseth 2005).

Chinese Garment Factory. T-shirts are made in this garment factory.

In these markets, people rarely think of these clothes as castoffs or rags, as we do. For example, in Zambia, in southern Africa, where anthropologist Karen Tranberg Hansen (2000) has researched the local trade in used clothing, people call this clothing *salaula*, which means "opportunity," "choice," and "new chances." At the same time, the arrival of so many inexpensive T-shirts and other clothing to places like Zambia undermines the local clothing industry, which cannot compete with the low cost of these used items.

What questions does this situation raise for anthropological researchers?

1. Is the supply chain that created your T-shirt really "global"?
2. Why are T-shirt production facilities no longer in the United States, and why are these facilities in the places they are?
3. Who are the different actors who participate in the processes of manufacturing and using your T-shirt, both before and after you own it?
4. What are the consequences for local people of this global trade in T-shirts?

PART TWO: CHILEAN TABLE GRAPES
In industrialized economies like the United States and Europe, food is also quite likely to come from far away. This is especially true of fruits and vegetables, which can be harvested in the Southern Hemisphere during the North American winter, when domestic fruits and vegetables are not available in the United States. Chile is a major exporter of fruits to the United States and Europe, because its summer harvests coincide with the winter off-season in the Northern Hemisphere. If you wanted to understand global economic integration through table grapes such as those produced in Chile, what questions would you ask as an anthropological researcher?

Such analyses raise a key question: Who benefits from and who pays the costs of global interconnections? We turn to this important question in the next section.

THINKING CRITICALLY ABOUT GLOBALIZATION

Beyond communication, migration, and finance, what are some other culturally significant forces that make the world feel smaller?

⬩ What Are the Outcomes of Global Integration?

In public debates, the most common way of framing globalization's outcomes is in terms of winners and losers. Globalization's promoters focus on winners, arguing that greater economic integration brings unprecedented prosperity to millions. They cite evidence that the more open a country is to foreign trade, the more rapidly its economy grows (Norberg 2006). Critics focus on losers, invoking images of sweatshops and poverty. They offer evidence that the gap between rich countries and poor countries has actually widened, and we are witness to a "globalization of poverty" (Chossudovsky 1997). In recent years, a nationalist backlash has emerged, evident among some political leaders in the United States, Great Britain, France, and Russia who have argued that the real "losers" in globalization are the working classes in their countries whose jobs have been shipped overseas or "taken" by newer immigrants. In the face of such arguments, it is useful to remember that all sides are often discussing fairly narrow economic policy questions related to free trade, labor conditions, outsourcing of jobs, and so on. These are important issues, but they tend to ignore the cultural nuances of global interconnections, which include inequality, confrontation, domination, accommodation, and resistance.

Colonialism and World Systems Theory

For several decades, **world systems theory** has provided the social sciences with an important theoretical lens for understanding global inequality. Developed by economic historians André Gunder Frank and Immanuel Wallerstein, world systems theory rejects the idea that global interconnections are anything new, identifying the late fifteenth century as the beginning of a new capitalist world order that connected different parts of the world in new ways. During this historical period, according to world systems theory, the expansion of overseas European colonies was enabled by and rooted in the creation of a global capitalist market. This market was based on unequal exchange between a "core" (the home countries) and a "periphery" (the rest of the world). The core (the winners) developed its economy by exploiting the periphery (the losers), whose role was to provide labor and raw materials for the core's consumption. European colonial institutions and authority secured capitalism's ability to extract labor and natural resources from the periphery. The result is the periphery's long-term poverty, underdevelopment, and dependency on the core. In relation to these conditions, anthropologists have posed a question other social scientists have not: How has this world system affected the native peoples and cultural systems of the periphery?

In his influential book *Europe and the People Without History*, anthropologist Eric Wolf took on this question. Wolf argued that long-distance trade and cultural interaction were around long before the development of capitalism, but that the expansion of European colonialism and capitalism drew non-European people into a global market, in which, as producers of commodities, they were to serve the cause of capital accumulation as a subordinate working class (Wolf 1984:352–3). These processes disrupted, even destroyed, many societies (Bodley 1999).

But Wolf rejected the customary divisions we make between "West" and "non-West." He insisted that people in the periphery also have helped shape the world system because they have often resisted capitalist expansion. These are the common people usually ignored by the victorious elites when they wrote their histories. Wolf argued that we need to pay close attention to the peripheral people's active role in world history. His argument challenged not only popular stereotypes of indigenous people as isolated and passive, but also anthropology's bias toward the local—that is, the traditional ethnographic focus on villages and other small groups.

Because world systems theory focused on the rise of capitalism as a global system, this macro-level perspective did not readily lend itself to ethnographic research of smaller communities and non-global economics. But the theory helped anthropologists better explain the historical emergence and contemporary persistence of uneven development patterns around the world and has been of critical interest to scholars of **postcolonialism**, the field that studies the cultural legacies of colonialism and imperialism. It has also helped anthropologists understand the linkages between local social relations (families, kin networks, communities) and other levels of political-economic activity, like the regional, national, and transnational.

Cultures of Migration

One of world systems theory's key assertions is that the same conditions that produced an unbalanced world order have also generated territorial displacement and population flows, especially to supply labor for capitalist needs. Migratory flows involve structural **push-pull factors**. These factors include poverty, violent conflict, political uncertainties, and others that "push" individuals to migrate from their home countries, and factors like economic possibilities and social and political opportunities that "pull" them to host countries (Massey et al. 1993).

Anthropologists take such structural factors into account when studying migration. But detailed ethnographic studies of migrant-sending and migrant-receiving communities, as well as of migrants themselves, have revealed a greater level of complexity to these processes than a simple push-pull model allows (Brettell 2003). For example, when they migrate, individuals rarely act in social isolation. Their decision to migrate is often made by members of a household who consider its resources, the varying talents and abilities of its members, community traditions such as whether there is a history of migration, and the relative strength of opportunities in the destination (Kearney 1996; Cohen 2004). Not all individuals in a community have equal access to migration, either, because certain social groups—for example, relative economic elites, or members of a certain gender or ethnic group—sometimes have greater ability to be mobile than others.

Moreover, migrants typically move within and between social networks, made up of kin and other social connections, that shape their choice of destination. Reconnecting with those social networks is often a high priority for involuntary migrants, such as the Syrian refugees described at the outset of this chapter, especially since governments and bureaucracies that manage refugees often ignore the importance of these social ties in successful adaptation to a new place. Recognizing the simple anthropological insight that migrants want—at least initially—to maintain ties with people who speak their native language and understand their background can help immigrant groups adjust to life in their new country.

Cultural attitudes, perceptions, and symbolic values also shape migration, creating what anthropologists call a **culture of migration**. Through migration, people generate new meanings about the world, their home, and themselves. In many places where migration is prevalent, it is viewed as an important, even necessary, rite of passage into adulthood, a means to elevate or maintain social status, and an experience in which new social identities are formed (Nagengast and Kearney 1990).

Resistance at the Periphery

The expansion of the capitalist world system generated greater cross-border movement, but it also met with resistance from the peripheral peoples affected. Anthropologists have devoted considerable attention to this resistance, finding examples that range from open rebellion and mass mobilizations to more subtle forms of protest and opposition.

Many forms of resistance may not be obvious to us because they are rooted in culturally subtle forms of expression. For example, in one factory in Malaysia, spirit possession episodes have erupted, disrupting work and production goals (Ong 1988). According to the factory women of Malaysia, the facility violated two basic moral boundaries: close physical proximity of the sexes, and male managers' constant monitoring of female workers. Young female workers, who as Muslims are expected to be shy and deferential, believe that these two factors force them to violate cultural taboos that define social and bodily boundaries between men and women. They also believe that the construction of modern factories displaces and angers local spirits, who then haunt the toilets. For the women, these transgressions combine to provoke spirit possession, in which the women become violent and loud, disrupting work in the factory. Spirit possession episodes help the women regain a sense of control over both their bodies and social relations in the factory (Ong 1988:34). Such resistance interests anthropologists because it shows how people interpret and challenge global processes through local cultural idioms and beliefs.

Globalization *and* Localization

Greater global integration may also create opportunities for a phenomenon that some anthropologists call **localization**—the creation and assertion of highly particular, often place-based, identities and communities (Friedman 1994). Localization is evidenced by the recent rise of autonomy movements among Hawaiian separatists and other indigenous groups throughout the world that seek self-determination; nationalist and ethnic movements like that of the Basques in Europe; and other movements engaged in reinforcing local control, for example

by encouraging community-supported agriculture and the use of local curren-
cies (Friedman 1994). Each of these movements seeks to recuperate and protect
local identities and places in the face of greater economic and cultural integration
within a nation or a transnational network.

Other evidence of localization lies in people's patterns of consumption, which
is a common way that people express their local identities and ways of being. In
our own society, people choose certain clothing and shoe brands because they
believe it says something about them as individuals: their social status, lifestyle,
and outlook on the world, in particular. People in other countries do this too, but
because of local culture and history, patterns of consumption can communicate
very different things.

For example, among the Bakongo in the Republic of the Congo, a former French
colony in Central Africa, poor Bakongo youths in urban shantytowns of the capital city, Brazzaville, compete with each other to acquire famous French and Italian designer clothes (Figure 5.4). Calling themselves *sapeurs* (loosely translated
as "dandies"), the most ambitious and resourceful go to Europe, where they acquire fancy clothes by whatever means they can. By becoming hyper-consumers,
sapeurs are not merely imitating prosperous Europeans. Europeans may believe
that "clothes make the man," but Congolese believe that clothes reflect the degree
of "life force" possessed by the wearer (Friedman 1994:106). The *sapeur's* goal
is not to live a European lifestyle; his goal is to accumulate prestige by linking
himself to external forces of wealth, health, and political power. In highly ranked

Figure 5.4 Bakongo *Sapeur*. The *sapeur's* engagement in both transnational fashion worlds and
local processes of social stratification destabilizes any strong local–global dichotomy.

Congolese society, the poor Bakongo urbanite ranks lowest. By connecting to upscale European fashion trends, the *sapeur* represents an assault on the higher orders of Congolese society, who normally dismiss him as a barbarian.

People always define their identities locally. What is different today from previous generations, perhaps, is that people increasingly express their local identities through their interaction with transnational processes, such as communications, migration, or consumerism, and with institutions, such as transnational businesses. In today's world, people participate in global processes *and* local communities simultaneously. But they rarely participate in global processes on equal footing, because of their subordinate place in the world system or in their own countries. Nevertheless, many anthropologists feel that to identify them in stark terms as *either* winners *or* losers of global integration greatly simplifies the complexity of their simultaneous involvement in globalization and localization processes.

As these examples show, people can be accommodating to outside influences, even while maintaining culturally specific meanings and social relations, whether because of defiance or because they actively transform the alien into something more familiar (Piot 1999). In these circumstances, cultural differences exist not in spite of, but because of, interconnection. But it still seems difficult to deny that so many millions of people are striving to become developed and to pursue lifestyles similar to those of middle-class Americans.

THINKING CRITICALLY ABOUT GLOBALIZATION

Who should define who is a winner or loser in the processes of global integration? What kinds of criteria (financial, social, political, etc.) do you think are most appropriate for defining such a thing?

Doesn't Everyone Want to Be Developed?

Long before the current globalization craze, discussions about global integration were often framed as the problem of bringing "civilization" (Western, that is), and later economic development, to non-European societies. But the question we pose here—Doesn't everyone want to be developed?—has no easy answer. Ideas differ about what development is and how to achieve it, so first we must ask: What is development?

What Is Development?

In 1949, U.S. President Harry Truman gave his inaugural address in which he defined the role of the United States in the post–World War II world, when the West confronted the communist nations. He said, "We must embark on a new program for making the benefits of our scientific advances and industrial progress available for the improvement and growth of the underdeveloped areas"

(Truman 1949). He defined two thirds of the world as "underdeveloped" and one third as "developed." Truman believed that if poor people around the world participated in the "American dream" of a middle-class lifestyle, they would not turn toward communism (Esteva 1992).

The Cold War is over, but development is still with us. It is a worldwide enterprise that was never solely American. Many European nations give aid to their former colonies. The stated goals of this aid range from expanding capitalist markets through trade and the building of infrastructure to alleviating poverty, improving health, and conserving natural resources. Key actors include the United Nations, the government aid agencies of most industrialized countries, lending agencies like the World Bank, and non-governmental organizations (NGOs) like CARE International.

Contemporary international development still aims to bring people into the "modern" world and correct what it identifies as undesirable and undignified conditions like poverty and lack of modern conveniences. And, just as in the colonial era, "advanced" capitalist countries still provide the economic and social models for development.

But there is ambiguity to the concept of development. Is it a means to a particular end? Or is it the end itself? Who defines the shape and course of development? More important for our purposes, development has an ambiguous relationship with cultural diversity. Is its goal to foster the unfolding potential and purposeful improvement of people—from their own local cultural perspective? Or is it a program of forced change that is eliminating cultural diversity to create a world ordered on the universal principles of capitalist societies?

There are two distinct anthropological approaches to development: **development anthropology** and the **anthropology of development** (Gow 1993). While development anthropologists involve themselves in the theoretical and practical aspects of shaping and implementing development projects, anthropologists of development tend to study the cultural conditions for proper development, or, alternatively, the negative impacts of development projects. Often the two overlap, but at times they are in direct conflict.

Development Anthropology

Development anthropology is a branch of applied anthropology. It is a response to a simple fact: many development projects have failed because planners have not taken local culture into consideration. Planners often blame project failures on local peoples' supposed ignorance or stubbornness (Mamdani 1972). But it is often the planners themselves who are ignorant of local issues or set in their ways. Projects are more likely to meet their goals when they are fine-tuned to local needs, capacities, perspectives, and interests.

A classic example recognized by many anthropologists is the work of Gerald Murray on deforestation in Haiti. In the 1970s and 1980s, the U.S. Agency for

International Development (USAID) invested millions of dollars in Haitian re-forestation projects that consistently failed (Murray 1987). Poor farmers resisted reforestation because it encroached on valuable croplands. Worse yet, aid money directed to farmers kept disappearing in the corrupt Haitian bureaucracy. Murray saw that the planners misunderstood the attitudes and needs of local farmers, not to mention the most effective ways to get the resources to them. He suggested a different approach. Planners had conceived of this project as an environmental one. He convinced USAID instead to introduce it to farmers as planting a new cash crop, and to avoid involving the Haitian bureaucracy. Farmers would plant trees along the borders of their lands, allowing crops to continue to grow (Figure 5.5). After several years, they could harvest mature trees to sell as lumber. It was a very successful project: within four years, 75,000 farmers had planted 20 million trees, and many discovered the additional benefits of having trees on their land.

Development anthropologists often think of themselves as advocates for the people living at the grassroots—the poor, small farmers, women, and other marginalized people—who could be most affected, negatively or positively, by development but who lack the political influence to design and implement projects (Chambers 1997). Today, many anthropologists work in development agencies, both internationally (such as in USAID) and domestically (in community development organizations). The current president of the World Bank, the world's largest development bank, is an anthropologist, Dr. Jim Yong Kim (see Chapter 7). And yet there are limits to what anthropologists can do. Policy-makers and development institutions may not pay attention to their advice. Or the anthropologist may not have enough time to fully study a situation before having to make recommendations (Gow 1993).

Anthropology of Development

Other anthropologists have taken a more critical perspective. They argue that no matter how well intentioned, development is ethnocentric and paternalistic, and that the outcome of most projects is to give greater control over local people to outsiders, or to worsen existing inequalities as elites shape development projects to serve their own interests (Escobar 1991, 1995).

Anthropologist James Ferguson applied some of these perspectives in his study of the Thaba-Tseka Rural Development Project. This project was a World Bank and UN Food

Figure 5.5 Haitian Farmers Planting Saplings for Reforestation.

and Agriculture Organization (FAO) project that took place between 1975 and 1984 in the southern African country of Lesotho (J. Ferguson 1994). Its goal was to alleviate poverty and increase economic output in rural villages by building roads, providing fuel and construction materials, and improving water supply and sanitation. But the project failed to meet its goals.

Ferguson argued that intentional plans like this one never turn out the way their planners expect, because project planners begin with a distinctive way of reasoning and knowing that nearly always generates the same kinds of actions. In this case, planners believed that Lesotho's problems fit a general model: its residents are poor because they are subsistence farmers living in remote and isolated mountains, but they could develop further if they had technical improvements, especially roads, water, and sanitation.

According to Ferguson, this perspective has little understanding of on-the-ground realities. He noted that people in rural Lesotho have been marketing crops and livestock since the 1840s, so they have already been involved in a modern capitalist economy for a long time. They are also not isolated, since they send many migrants to and from South Africa for wage labor. In fact, most of the income for rural families comes from family members who have migrated to South Africa.

Ferguson argued that people in rural Lesotho are not poor because they live in a remote area and lack capitalism; they are poor because their labor is exploited in South Africa. By viewing poverty as a lack of technical improvements in the rural countryside, the project failed to address the socioeconomic inequalities and subordination that are the underlying causes of poverty in rural Lesotho. But the project did have a major unexpected consequence: the arrival of government development bureaucrats to put the development project's technologies in place undermined the power of traditional village chiefs. Ferguson concluded that development exists not to alleviate poverty, but to reinforce and expand bureaucratic state power over local communities.

Nevertheless, some anthropologists counter that we cannot sit on development's sidelines, that we have a moral obligation to apply our knowledge to protect the interests of the communities we study. Others insist that critics ignore the struggles within development institutions that indicate that there is not simply one discourse of development but a variety of perspectives among developers (Little and Painter 1995). Still others insist that development is less paternalistic and more accountable to local communities than it has ever been (Chambers 1997).

These debates remain unresolved, but now that we have some background, we can begin to answer the bigger question: Do people really want to be developed? The answer often depends on how much control over development processes people will have.

Change on Their Own Terms

In indigenous and poor communities around the world, it is not uncommon to hear variations on the following phrase, originally attributed to Lilla Watson, an

Australian Aboriginal woman: "If you have come here to help me, you are wasting your time. But if you have come here because your liberation is bound up with mine, then let us work together." According to this perspective, outside help is not automatically virtuous, and it can undermine self-determination. Some scholars view this basic desire—to negotiate change on one's own terms—as a fundamental challenge to development's real or perceived paternalism and negative effects on local culture (Rahnema and Bawtree 1997).

Understandably, in the face of forced change, people want to conserve the traditions and relationships that give their lives meaning. This point is one of the keys to understanding culture in the context of global change. Culture helps people make sense of and respond to constant changes in the world, and it is itself dynamic. But culture also has stable and conservative elements, and different societies have different levels of tolerance for change, both of which mean that cultural change is not a uniform process for every society. This situation of uneven change partly explains why we see the persistence of cultural diversity around the world in spite of predictions that it would disappear.

THINKING CRITICALLY ABOUT GLOBALIZATION

Are anthropologists ethically obligated to help communities develop if members of the community want their help?

✿ If the World Is Not Becoming Homogenized, What Is Actually Happening?

Like the previous question about whether everyone wants development, this one has no simple answer. Anthropologists are divided on this question. The interaction of culture with political, economic, and social processes is complex, and in many ways the world's material culture and associated technologies are becoming homogeneous. Anthropologists who study these processes pursue one or another form of cultural convergence theory. Other anthropologists see people all over the world using foreign cultural imports in their own ways and on their own terms. These scholars use an approach called hybridization theory. In this section we examine both theories.

Cultural Convergence Theories

In the 1960s the famous media scholar Marshall McLuhan suggested that the world was becoming a "global village" in which cultural diversity was in decline. Many social scientists agree. The British philosopher and social anthropologist Ernest Gellner, for example, believed the spread of industrial society created a common worldwide culture, based on similar conditions of work within the same industry. Making T-shirts in a factory is going to be similar whether situated in Honduras, Tanzania, or Vietnam. Gellner wrote that "the same technology canalizes people into the same type of activity and the same kinds of hierarchy, and that the same kind of leisure styles were also engendered by existing techniques and by the needs of productive life" (1983:116–7). Gellner's view was that local distinctions and traditions will gradually fade as Western ideas replace those in non-Western communities.

One variation on this theme imagines "Coca-Colonization," alternatively called Westernization or Americanization (Foster 2008). This model proposes that the powerful and culturally influential nations of the West (especially the United States) impose their products and beliefs on the less powerful nations of the world, creating what is known as **cultural imperialism**, or the promotion of one culture over others, through formal policy or less formal means, like the spread of technology and material culture.

The appeal of these theories is that they address the underlying causes of why the world feels smaller, as well as how rich societies systematically exploit poor societies by drawing them into a common political-economic system. They also appear to explain the appearance of a common **world culture**, based on norms and knowledge shared across national boundaries (Lechner and Boli 2005; Figure 5.6).

Figure 5.6   World Culture and the Olympic Games.   The Olympic Games is a quintessential global event: currently 205 countries participate in the Olympic Games, even more than are members of the United Nations. Drawing on certain core values—competitiveness, internationalism, amateurism, etc.—they foster an awareness of living in a single world culture.

But many anthropologists disagree with the basic assumptions that convergence theorists make about culture, and in fact most proponents of convergence are not anthropologists. The fact that people might consume the same goods, wear the same clothes, or eat the same foods does not necessarily mean that they begin to think and behave the same ways. A major limitation of convergence theories is that they underestimate variability and plasticity as key features of human culture and evolutionary history (J. Nash 1981).

Hybridization

An alternative theory that many anthropologists prefer is **hybridization**, which refers to open-ended and ongoing cultural intermingling and fusion. While the convergence theories imagine a world based on or moving toward cultural purities, hybridization emphasizes a world based on promiscuous mixing, border crossing, and persistent cultural diversity (García Canclini 1995; Piot 1999; Figure 5.7). Hybridization has several aliases, including syncretism and creolization. Anthropologists have usually applied the word *syncretism* to the fusion of religious systems; *creolization* is used to mean the intermingling of languages. In both cases, we see the synthesis of distinct elements to create new and unexpected possibilities.

Hybridization theory does have critics. Some argue that cultural mixing is merely a superficial phenomenon, the real underlying condition being convergence. Others charge that all the talk about boundary crossing and mixture ignores the fact that boundaries—national, social, ethnic, and so on—have not disappeared (Friedman 1999). At the heart of this criticism is the charge that hybridization theory ignores real political and economic power and inequalities. Others assert that these two approaches do not have to be mutually exclusive, but that convergence is happening in some places and hybridization is happening everywhere at the same time.

Figure 5.7   Hybridity and Warlpiri Media.   Warlpiri people of northern Australia have taken to watching and producing their own films. Their cinematic productions reflect particular social dynamics and perspectives, in the process hybridizing a Western technology and its practices.

Although these debates can be contentious, for a discipline historically accustomed to studying culture from a local vantage point (the stereotype of the anthropologist in a village), there is widespread consensus that taking on big questions like these opens up exciting new possibilities for research.

> ### THINKING CRITICALLY ABOUT GLOBALIZATION
>
> Can you identify any examples of cultural hybridization in your community? How does the example you came up with connect to transnational dynamics and processes?

❧ How Can Anthropologists Study Global Interconnections?

Today nearly every anthropologist accepts that it is impossible to make sense of local cultural realities without some understanding of the broader political, economic, and social conditions that also shape people's lives (Kearney 1995). The problem is that anthropologists have typically conducted their studies in a single field site (a village, community, tribe, or district), while the transnational or transregional connections may be very far away. So how can anthropologists simultaneously study a local phenomenon in a community and the national or international factors and forces shaping that community?

Defining an Object of Study

Some anthropologists, such as Eric Wolf, have defined their object of study as the world system itself, focusing on the role of culture in that system. Others who take a global system more or less for granted have focused on specific components within that system, especially objects, money, and ideas that "flow" and "circulate" around it (Appadurai 1996), or the "cosmopolitan" people (journalists, city people, world travelers) who move within and through it (Hannerz 1992). Still others contend that in a transient world, the migrant offers the most productive object of study (García Canclini 1995; Kearney 1995). Some reject the notion of a unified global system altogether and propose investigation of what Tsing (2000:348) describes as "interactions involving collaboration, misunderstanding, opposition, and dialogue" between transnational and local actors. A key component of this approach is learning how people find meaning in their places within broader political, economic, and cultural systems.

Each of these approaches raises questions about the adequacy of anthropology's most distinctive methodological tool, ethnographic research. Understood as intensive participation and observation in the everyday life of a single place over a long period of time, ethnographic research has yielded rich insights into how people live and make sense of their lives. But what if the community or the issues one wants to study extend beyond that place?

Multi-Sited Ethnography

One technique is to use **multi-sited ethnography**, which is a strategy of following connections, associations, and putative relationships from place to place (Marcus 1995). Its goal is not a holistic representation of the world system as a totality. Rather, it seeks to track cultural themes as they express themselves in distinct places and settings that are typically connected in some concrete way. Its goal is to describe relationships and connections between these different places. In this sense, multi-sited ethnography offers a comparative method by juxtaposing phenomena that were once thought "worlds apart" (Marcus 1995:102).

Multi-sited fieldwork has been productive for studying transnational phenomena like environmentalism and other social movements, the media, certain religious societies, and the spread of science and technology. As the object of anthropological research has expanded to include topics like these, more and more anthropologists are doing multi-sited research.

THINKING CRITICALLY ABOUT GLOBALIZATION

Can you identify any practical difficulties or ethical dilemmas involved in multi-sited research that might be different from those involved in traditional ethnographic research in a single community setting?

❧ Conclusion

No anthropologist can claim to have easy answers to the dilemmas, dislocations, and problems raised by globalization. But anthropological research can provide critical perspectives on how and why people relate to large-scale social, economic, and political changes in the ways they do.

As we have established in this chapter, culture helps people make sense of and respond to constant changes in the world, which is itself dynamic. But cultural change is not a uniform process. There are many reasons for this. Different societies have differing levels of tolerance toward change, and some are more protective of their cultural traditions than others. In addition, people can be open to outside influences even while maintaining culturally specific meanings and social relations. They do this by actively transforming the alien into something more familiar. Even more important, perhaps, is that not all people participate in global processes on equal terms. Their position within broader political-economic processes and regional dynamics helps shape their consciousness and their experience of global cultural integration. The complexities of migration demonstrate this point in general ways, and the crisis surrounding Syrian refugees described in the opening of this chapter does so in more specific ways.

The socioeconomic and political inequalities associated with globalization are one reason that cultural diversity continues to exist in the world. But there is another key reason. It is that cultures are created in connection with other cultures, not in isolation, as many anthropologists had previously thought. This is not to say that there are not certain elements that make the world feel smaller, including empirical changes in communications, migration, and finances. But does this mean we live in a global village, as Marshall McLuhan once claimed? Only if we think of a village as a place in which diversity, and not uniformity, is the defining feature of that village.

Key Terms

Anthropology of development p. 107

Cultural imperialism   p. 111

Culture of migration   p. 104

Development anthropology p. 107

Diffusionists   p. 95

Exiles   p. 98

Globalization   p. 95

Hybridization   p. 112

Immigrants   p. 98

Localization   p. 104

Migrants   p. 98

Multi-sited ethnography p. 114

Postcolonialism   p. 103

Push-pull factors   p. 103

Refugees   p. 98

Transnational   p. 97

World culture   p. 111

World systems theory   p. 102

Reviewing the Chapter

CHAPTER SECTION	WHAT WE KNOW	TO BE RESOLVED
Is the world really getting smaller?	It is impossible to make sense of local cultural realities without some understanding of the broader political, economic, and social conditions that also shape people's lives.	Anthropologists do not have easy answers for the cultural, economic, and political dilemmas raised by globalization.
What are the outcomes of global integration?	Not everybody participates equally in the diverse kinds of interconnections that make up globalization, and taking globalization seriously means taking power relationships and social inequality seriously.	While some anthropologists emphasize the destructive and dominating effects of global capitalism's spread for many non-Western societies, others have argued that expressions of resistance, creative localization, and migration are meaningful and important responses.

CHAPTER SECTION	WHAT WE KNOW	TO BE RESOLVED
Doesn't everyone want to be developed?	Development raises complex and politically charged issues about socioeconomic and cultural change for anthropologists and the indigenous and poor communities that are the target of development initiatives.	Anthropologists are deeply divided over the positive and negative impacts of development, and they continue to debate the merits and drawbacks of anthropological involvement in development and other projects that promote globalization.
If the world is not becoming homogenized, what is actually happening?	Globalization is a complicated matter that illustrates how people create and change their cultures not in isolation but through connections with others.	Although many anthropologists accept that globalization is a process primarily of hybridization, others argue that it is a process of cultural convergence.
How can anthropologists study global interconnections?	Multi-sited ethnography is one approach for tracking cultural themes as they express themselves in distinct places and settings, and it seeks to identify concrete connections between those places and settings.	Anthropologists continue to debate whether or not multi-sited research is as effective for understanding culture as traditional community-based ethnographic methods.

6

Sustainability

Environment and Foodways

Given current patterns of climate change, the Micronesian country of the Marshall Islands will probably be submerged by the end of this century. Consisting of five islands and twenty-nine coral atolls spread across 750,000 square miles of the western Pacific Ocean, all of the country's seventy square miles of land sit just a few feet above sea level. Consequently, rising seawaters represent an existential threat to the islands, adding another layer of woe in a region long fractured by the disruptions of European colonialism, the militarization of the Pacific during the Second World War, and U.S. nuclear and missile testing that has caused many environmental and health problems.

The Marshallese are already feeling the effects of climate change, including intensified drought and flooding. Climate change raises many pressing questions for the country's 53,000 people, the most obvious being where they will go as their

The Challenge of Climate Change in the Marshall Islands.   Climate change has intensified flooding in the low-lying Marshall Islands. In this instance, a king tide was energized by a storm surge, leading to the flooding of Majuro, the capital atoll.

homes disappear. Under current international law, they cannot gain status as refugees because the legal category "refugee" applies only to people displaced by persecution, not to those displaced by an environmental problem like climate change.

One of the ironies of this situation, at least from a Marshallese perspective, is that the environmental problems facing them are not of their making. Since about 2,000 BCE, islanders have developed strategies for living sustainably in a challenging environment where natural resources like fresh water, arable land, and fisheries are scarce and extreme weather events such as droughts, tsunamis, earthquakes, and hurricanes are common. Marshallese food production systems take these ecological conditions into account. One traditional practice is to grow taro, an important tuber in the Marshallese diet, in "humidity pockets" (pits dug in the ground and lined with layers of plants, organic mulch, and coral rubble), which reduces consumption of fresh water and increases food production in nutrient-deficient soils (Bridges and McClatchey 2009). Another is to prohibit or limit fish and crab harvests, for example, by designating a reef or an island, or parts of one, as *mo*, which means "prohibited" or "taboo" (Tibon n.d.). To distribute the environmental risks of island living, Marshallese have traditionally scattered food production sites and traded with other islands and atolls, using sophisticated seafaring knowledge to make long-distance voyages (Genz 2011).

But as a result of globalization processes, the Marshallese—like many other societies in the world today—do not manage their resources on their own terms. The dilemmas these processes create lead us to the question at the center of this chapter: *Why do some societies have sustainable relations with the natural world while others seem to be more destructive of their natural environments, and what sociocultural factors are driving environmental destruction in the contemporary world?* Embedded in this broader question are the following problems, around which this chapter is organized:

Do all people see nature in the same way?

How do people secure an adequate, meaningful, and environmentally sustainable food supply?

How does non-Western knowledge of nature and agriculture relate to science?

How are industrial agriculture and economic globalization linked to increasing environmental and health problems?

Are industrialized Western societies the only ones to conserve nature?

Different views of the natural world are closely related to distinct environmental management and food acquisition strategies. The environmental beliefs, knowledge, and practices of different societies, as well as their foodways, have long been major concerns at the heart of cultural anthropology. These issues have traditionally been studied in the settings of small-scale, non-Western societies where beliefs, knowledge, and practices differ markedly from Western views and practices. But in recent years, as global concern with environmental degradation, climate change, the loss of biodiversity, and industrializing foodways has mushroomed, anthropologists have also been paying close attention to the effects of global economic changes on human–nature relations and what sustainability means for different people. We begin by exploring how a people's environmental values and behaviors emerge from particular ways of thinking about the natural world.

❦ Do All People See Nature in the Same Way?

What nature means to people and how they see themselves in relation to it vary greatly around the world. Consider, for example, the relationships between indigenous settlement and natural ecosystems in southern Mexico and Central America (Figure 6.1). Some of these areas, such as the Yucatán Peninsula, the Petén

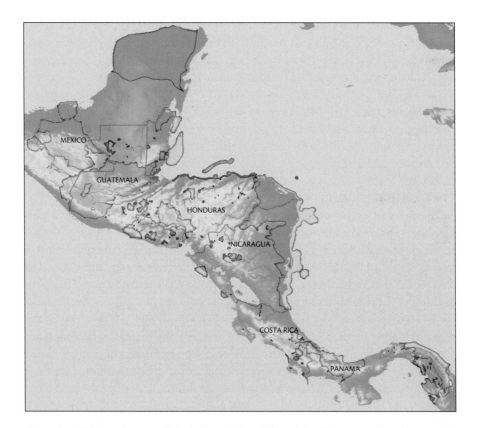

Figure 6.1   Linkages Between Biological and Cultural Diversity.   The areas outlined in red on this map mark zones where indigenous populations live and where intact biodiverse ecosystems can be found in Central America and Southern Mexico. This map is a simplified version of a map produced by the Center for the Support of Natives Lands and originally published in *National Geographic*, which superimposed the distribution of cultural diversity and the distribution of biological diversity in this area.

region of Guatemala, and the Miskito Coast of Nicaragua, have been inhabited for many centuries. After the arrival of the Spanish in the 1500s, they were safe areas for indigenous people because the Spanish conquerors found the tropical heat and diseases undesirable (Lovgren 2003). Why did the indigenous people not simply cut the forest down for fields, as European settlers did in other parts of the New World?

One reason was their low population density and subsistence economies based on swidden agriculture (see below) in which fields go back to forest to fallow after harvesting. But economic practices alone do not explain good stewardship; for that we need to understand the indigenous views of their environment. As Ken Rapp of the Center for the Support of Native Lands recently observed, "It's part of their belief system. They don't see a division between nature and man" (Lovgren 2003).

The Human–Nature Divide?

A good example of a group whose belief system fits with what Rapp described is the Itzaj, a Maya group that has lived in the Petén tropical lowlands of Guatemala since pre–Spanish contact times. According to Itzaj beliefs, humans and nature do not occupy separate realms; there is both real and symbolic reciprocity and communication between plants, animals, and humans. For example, forest spirits called *arux* ("masters of the wind") continually monitor people, and they play tricks on those who cut down too many trees or kill too many animals (Atran 2001:169). One effect is that Itzaj agricultural practices respect and preserve the forest.

The Cultural Landscape

Environmental anthropologists—practitioners of **environmental anthropology**, the subfield of anthropology that studies how different societies understand, interact with, and make changes to nature—have long insisted that it is important to understand the abstract ideas people have about landscapes and other ideas that influence people's behavior within those landscapes. One way to think of these abstract ideas is through the concept of a **cultural landscape**, which consists of the culturally specific images, knowledge, and concepts of the physical landscape that affect how people will actually interact with that landscape (Stoffle, Toupal, and Zedeño 2003:99). For example, the Itzaj consider nature to be an extension of their social world, full of spirits that influence their everyday lives. As a result they are less likely to wantonly destroy the landscape in which they live because doing so would equate to hurting themselves. Different social groups can also hold distinctly different and conflicting ideas of the same landscape.

Key to understanding the cultural landscape is the idea that people use metaphors to think about their natural environments, and these metaphors are

connected to social behavior, thought, and organization (Bird-David 1993:112).
For example, in many hunting and gathering societ-
ies, people use metaphors
of personal relatedness—
sexuality, marriage, or family
ties—to describe human–
nature relations (Figure 6.2).
Metaphors are always com-
plex, and different people
may not understand them
in the same ways. Never-
theless, metaphors offer insights into a community's
cultural landscapes that
symbolize the society's
feelings and values about
its environment. Whether a
society has sustainable relations with nature depends

Figure 6.2   Mother Nature as Metaphor. An example of
a metaphor of human–nature relatedness is "Mother Nature,"
a concept that is familiar in many cultures and that remains
popular in North America and Europe today. It represents
nature as a living force with feminine qualities of procreation
and nurturing, and it is an example of an "adult–child caring"
metaphor that exists in many societies (Bird-David 1993).

on many factors beyond how they conceptualize human–nature relations, a
theme we examine in the next section.

THINKING CRITICALLY ABOUT SUSTAINABILITY

People's images and metaphors of human–nature relatedness reflect and communicate their
attitudes toward nature and act as important guides to action. Besides "Mother Nature," can
you think of metaphors of human–nature relatedness in our society? How do you think those
metaphors relate to people's actual interactions with nature?

How Do People Secure an Adequate, Meaningful, and Environmentally Sustainable Food Supply?

How people think of their landscapes is also intertwined with how they actually
get their living from it—specifically, how a community gets and thinks about its
food. Anthropologists call the structured beliefs and behaviors surrounding the
production, distribution, and consumption of food **foodways**. There are important cross-cultural variations in foodways, which we explore here.

Modes of Subsistence

Anthropologists have long studied **modes of subsistence**, which refers to how people actually procure, produce, and distribute food. There are four major modes:

1. *Foraging,* or the search for edible things
2. *Horticulture,* or small-scale subsistence agriculture
3. *Pastoralism,* the raising of animal herds
4. *Intensive agriculture,* or large-scale, often commercial, agriculture.

For the past several thousand years, horticulture or more intensive agriculture has furnished most people with most of their food supplies. But societies are rarely committed to a single mode of subsistence, often combining two or more modes.

FORAGING

Foraging refers to searching for edible plant and animal foods without domesticating them. Hunter-gatherers, who obtain their subsistence through a combination of collecting foods and hunting prey, are called foragers. Most foragers live mobile lives, traveling to where the food happens to be, rather than moving the food to themselves (Bates 1998). Low population densities ensure that their impacts on the environment tend to be minimal.

A common stereotype about foraging is that it is a brutal struggle for existence. This stereotype is inaccurate, because in reality foragers tend to work less to procure their subsistence than people who pursue horticulture or pastoralism. For example, Richard Lee found that !Kung San (also known as Ju/'hoansi) hunter-gatherers of the Kalahari Desert in southern Africa spent less than twenty hours per week getting food (Lee 1969). Foragers also tend to view their environments not as harsh but as giving. It is easy to view foraging communities as a survival of our Paleolithic past since humans lived this way for 99% of our history. But contemporary foragers tend to inhabit extreme environments where horticulture or pastoralism are not feasible, such as the desert, the Arctic tundra, or certain rainforests.

HORTICULTURE

Horticulture is the cultivation of gardens or small fields to meet the basic needs of a household. It is sometimes referred to as subsistence agriculture, which refers to cultivation for purposes of household provisioning or small-scale trade, but not investment (Bates 1998). Horticulture emerged some 12,000 years ago with domestication, which gave humans selective control over animal and plant reproduction and increased the amount of reliable food energy available to them (Figure 6.3).

Horticultural farmers cultivate small plots and employ relatively simple technologies (hand tools like knives, axes, and digging sticks, for example) that have low impacts on the landscape. The most common form of horticulture in tropical regions is **swidden agriculture**, or slash-and-burn agriculture, in which cutting and burning vegetation improves nutrient-poor soils. A farmer can use a plot for several years, usually planting up to two dozen different crops that mature or ripen at different times. These garden plots often imitate the ecological diversity and structure of the rain forest itself, with some plants living in the understory shade, others in the partly shaded middle level, and others in the sunny top. By the time the crops are all harvested the soil is depleted, and the farmer will move to another plot to repeat the process. Old plots lie fallow, and if there are no other pressures on them, such as population growth or new settlers coming to the area, a farmer might not return to work one of these fallow plots for several decades.

Figure 6.3 Horticulture in Papua New Guinea. Mixed garden containing 23 species of cultivated plants enclosed in a fence in the lowland Ningerum area. Bananas planted outside are not of interest to wild pigs.

PASTORALISM

Pastoralism is the practice of **animal husbandry**, which is the breeding, care, and use of domesticated herding animals such as cattle, camels, goats, horses, llamas, reindeer, and yaks (Bates 1998). Rather than raising animals for butchering as food, pastoralists mainly consume their milk and blood and exploit their hair, wool, fur, and ability to pull or carry heavy loads. This approach allows them to get more out of the animal in the long run. Pastoralists typically occupy arid landscapes where agriculture is difficult or impossible (Figure 6.4).

Because a livestock herd can do quick, even irreparable, damage to vegetation in arid landscapes, this mode of subsistence requires the constant movement of herds (Igoe 2004). This movement is typically coordinated between herd-owning households. At the heart of this system is common ownership of land and social institutions that ensure herders do not sacrifice the fragile environment for short-term individual gains. These social institutions include livestock exchanges to redistribute and limit herd size, punishments for individuals who diverge from planned movement patterns, and the defense of rangeland boundaries to

Figure 6.4 Saami Reindeer Herder. The Saami, who live in northern Scandinavia, are pastoralists who live from reindeer herding.

ensure that neighboring pastoral groups cannot invade with their own livestock (McCabe 1990). When these institutions work successfully, pastoralism is a sustainable mode of subsistence, providing people with a stable source of nutritious foods without irreversibly destroying the fragile landscape.

INTENSIVE AGRICULTURE

While the goals of horticulture and pastoralism are to feed families, the goal of intensive agriculture is to increase yields to feed a larger community. Approaches to **intensification**, which refers to processes that increase yields (Bates 1998), include the following:

- *Preparing the soil*, with regular weeding, mulching, mounding, and fertilizers;
- *Using technology*, which can be simple, such as a harness or yoke that allows a farmer to use horses or oxen to plow a field; complex, such as a system of canals, dams, and water pumps that provide irrigation to an arid landscape; or very complex, like a combine harvester, a machine that harvests, threshes, and cleans grain plants like wheat, barley, and corn;
- *Using a larger labor force*, such as in Asian rice farming, which sustains the nutritional and energy needs of large populations, and provides many people with employment (Geertz 1963);

- *Managing water resources*, which can range from the practice of adding pebbles to fields to retain soil moisture (as ancient Pueblo dwellers of North America did), to the use of large-scale and sophisticated irrigation systems implemented by modern states;
- *Modifying plants and soils*, through selective breeding of plants to produce better yields, reduce the time needed to mature, or create a more edible product, as farmers have done for major grains like maize, rice, and wheat (Bates 1998).

Intensification carries certain tradeoffs. On the one hand, it solves an important problem, which is how to provide food for a large number of people, including those who do not work directly in food production. It also provides a relatively steady supply of food, though famines can still happen. On the other hand, by rearranging ecosystems to achieve greater control over nature, intensification can create environmental problems. For example, clearing a hillside to plant crops, build terraces, or install waterworks may increase productivity in the short run, but these can lead to the erosion of topsoils, the lowering of water tables, the concentration of salts in soils, the silting up of waterworks, and so on.

The most intensive form of agriculture is **industrial agriculture**, which applies industrial principles to farming. Key principles include specialization to produce a single crop, and the obtaining of land, labor, seeds, and water as commodities on the open market. Through the use of machines and other technology, industrial agriculture harnesses sources of energy such as steam power and petroleum, vastly increasing the scale of productivity, although those sources of energy are mostly nonrenewable. Technology-based farming has also redefined our notion of what agricultural work is. On some farms, such as those that produce grains like corn and wheat, farming now means tending to huge machines that provide nearly all the actual farm labor (Bates 1998). As a result of mechanization, a small rural labor force (in the United States, less than 2% of the total population) produces so much food that one of industrial agriculture's greatest economic problems is *over*production.

Food, Culture, and Meaning

As the variability in modes of subsistence demonstrates, the human species evolved to be adaptable to many different environments. The human diet also evolved to be flexible, and the range of things the human species can and does eat is tremendous. But our actual everyday diets usually involve a limited range of foods, determined by what is available, dietary restrictions, and what we have learned to prefer as members of a particular social community. Foodways are always culturally constructed, in that they are always surrounded by cultural beliefs and governed by systematic rules and etiquette particular to a social group. These cultural processes have implications for human sustainability because they also strongly shape how people think about and interact with landscapes through foodways.

For example, those of us who get our food from supermarkets tend to think of food as material, impersonal, and dissociated from the producer and its natural environment, reflecting a deeper view of nature as separate from the human domain. In contrast, the Hua, who live in the Eastern Highlands of Papua New Guinea, believe that food possesses mystical dynamism, vitality, and danger (Meigs 1997). For the Hua, the act of eating unites them with the individual who produced or shared food with them and invigorates them with the vital essences of the organisms they are consuming. They believe that because food is so spiritually powerful, humans are susceptible to its influences. To channel and protect these essences, the Hua have devised many rules governing who can grow, handle, share, and eat certain foods, as well as how those foods are grown.

FOODWAYS COMMUNICATE SYMBOLIC MEANING

In every society, food is a rich source of meaning, and people use it to communicate specific messages. Particular foods and meals can draw people together, especially when people share and consume foods that symbolize concepts like home, family, or conviviality. When you are homesick, the yearning for certain "comfort foods" is not just a desire for a familiar taste; it is a desire to feel connected to things that are symbolically important to you, such as your home and family. But food can just as easily communicate division and unequal power relations, as with so-called sumptuary laws that limit consumption of certain items along class lines (Figure 6.5).

The use of food as a form of symbolic communication is so pervasive that some anthropologists have suggested that food operates with logic similar to that of language. English anthropologist Mary Douglas, for example, observed that an English formal dinner takes on a certain precise order, just like a sentence: appetizers, soup, fish, and so on to dessert (Douglas 1966; Anderson 2005:110).

Figure 6.5 Sumptuary Laws, Circa 1500s England. These laws reflected and strengthened everyone's awareness of the advantaged position of aristocrats at a time when the European preference for meat eating allowed it to symbolize aristocracy.

FOODWAYS MARK SOCIAL BOUNDARIES AND IDENTITIES

Food preferences, etiquette, and taboos also mark social boundaries and identities. As anthropologist Carole Counihan (1999:8) has observed, "One's place in a social system is revealed by what, how, much, and with whom one eats." Eating practices might mark gender differences, as when men and women eat different foods. They might mark ethnic or regional differences, as when particular groups identify themselves closely with certain foods. Or they could mark profession or class status, as when certain individuals consume certain foods identified with their social station (Lentz 1999). These social markers are closely related to differing notions of **taste** that may exist between or within groups. *Taste* can refer to both the physical sensation on the tongue (as in "this crab cake tastes good") and social distinction and prestige (as in "her consumption of fine wine shows she has good taste") (MacBeth 1997).

Every society has a notion of the "perfect meal," which typically reflects people's culturally acquired tastes and is closely identified with their social identity and subsistence patterns as a group. For example, German anthropologist Gerd Spittler (1999) found that among the Kel Ewey Tuareg [kell **eh**-way **twar**-egg] nomads who live in the Sahara desert region in northern Mali, West Africa, the perfect meal is simple and always the same for everybody, regardless of their relative wealth. This meal includes cheese, dates, camel or goat milk, and the grain millet. Spittler theorizes that Tuareg prefer this meal because it identifies them as a people that provides a stable diet for all its members in a precariously dry environment. These Tuareg view variety in the diet—something that many of us take for granted—as a characteristic of people who must be so desperately poor and hungry they are forced to eat anything they can find.

FOODWAYS ARE DYNAMIC

Because foodways are so bound up with people's identities, it is easy to assume that people always hold on to them tightly. In some cases, foodways are remarkably persistent. For example, the diet in the region of Andalucía in southern Spain is about the same as it was during Roman times: crusty bread, olive oil, eggs, pork, wine, cabbage, herbs, onions, and garlic (Anderson 2005:163).

But foodways change for many reasons. Environmental changes, like overhunting or overfishing, change what is available. Or people begin to identify certain foods with good health, such as the reputation beef held among North Americans during the mid-twentieth century, but which in recent decades has given way to new ideas about the healthiness of a diet based on vegetables, soy products, and whole grains. Or formerly expensive foods, like white bread and processed sugar, become inexpensive because of new industrial processing techniques. Or changes in family dynamics force changes in eating habits, such as in North America, where women's increasing involvement in the workforce has helped fuel the rapid rise of convenience foods such as frozen dinners and takeout (Anderson 2005:165–8).

Although foodways are dynamic, people have a pretty stable concept of an appropriate diet that reflects their understanding of proper foods, good taste, and nutritional requirements. Underlying these facts is a simple logic: if a diet works, if it provides sustenance, meaning, and sustainable ecological relations, then people are unlikely to drop everything when something new comes along. People integrate new foods and cuisines into their existing dietary practices all the time, but since this logic of local foodways is also integrated into the production, preparation, and sharing of food, dramatic overnight change is unlikely. As we will see in the next section, the systematic ways people understand nature and sustainable management of it are also profoundly shaped by culture.

THINKING CRITICALLY ABOUT SUSTAINABILITY

Even though most of us probably get our food from a supermarket, can you identify examples of other modes of subsistence in our own society? How and why do these multiple modes of subsistence persist?

❦ How Does Non-Western Knowledge of Nature and Agriculture Relate to Science?

Anthropologists try to describe the traditional knowledge that different societies have of their natural environments, recognizing that all knowledge systems about nature, including science, are culturally based. This goal dates back to the beginnings of anthropology as a discipline. For example, during his years among the Trobriand Islanders (1915–18), Bronislaw Malinowski was keenly interested in people's knowledge of gardening, canoe building, and navigation. From observing these activities, he concluded that "primitive humanity was aware of the scientific laws of natural process" as well as magical processes, and went on to add that all people operate within the domains of magic, science, and religion (1948:196).

Do native knowledge systems have scientific validity? Malinowski reasoned that if knowledge is born of experience and reason, and if science is an activity characterized by rationality, then indigenous knowledge is part of humankind's scientific knowledge (Nader 1996:7). Since his time, anthropologists have demonstrated that scientific attitudes and methods of validation—close observation, experimentation, and analysis—are not unique to the West (1996:8). One key difference that distinguishes many non-Western knowledge systems from Western sciences, however, is that they are not necessarily viewed as distinct realms of knowledge, being integrated into people's spiritual beliefs and social practices, while in the West people tend to think of science as its own special domain of knowledge.

Ethnoscience

Early anthropological interest in knowledge systems of non-Western societies was called **ethnoscience** (see also Chapter 4, pp. 82–83). During the 1960s, when ethnoscience was at its peak influence, ethnoscientists aimed to describe and understand the conceptual models and rules with which a society operates, following Malinowski's call for anthropologists to see the world from "the native's point of view" (Sturtevant 1964:100). They began by comparing the systems of classification used by the different peoples they studied.

Classification systems are reference systems that group things or ideas with similar features. Examples include plant and animal taxonomies, kinship terminologies, color schemes, and medical diagnoses. Classification systems create a common intellectual framework that people use to work with the natural world and communicate with each other.

The Linnaean classification system is what the scientific discipline of biology uses to classify all living organisms into species. Closely related species belong to the same genus, and related genera (plural of genus) are grouped into families, and so on. Brent Berlin, who studied **ethnobiology** (indigenous ways of naming and codifying living things) of the Tzeltal Maya, has argued that the Tzeltal and most societies for whom we have data divide living things into groups based on shared morphological characteristics, as the Linnaean system does (Berlin 1973). Based on these findings, Berlin concluded that all human classification systems reflect a cognitive structure of the human brain that organizes information in systematic ways—in other words, that all human minds more or less think alike. But numerous challenges to Berlin's conclusions exist, based largely on the observation that some societies use non-morphological characteristics to classify plants and animals.

Traditional Ecological Knowledge

These days, anthropologists interested in themes related to ethnoscience tend to focus on **traditional ecological knowledge**, which consists of indigenous ecological knowledge and its relationship with resource management strategies. One of the more important findings of this field is that many ecological relations recognized by indigenous peoples are not known to Western science, because those relations involve species that are not found elsewhere, or because the knowledge resides in local languages, songs, or specialized ritual knowledge. Healers and shamans are important repositories of local plant knowledge and lore, and they may even keep their knowledge secret from other people in their own society. In recent years, controversy has erupted because pharmaceutical companies have been trying to gain access to the knowledge of traditional healers to identify plants that might be useful for developing new commercial drugs, sometimes without community consent (Brown 2003).

Because traditional ecological knowledge is customized to particular environments, it can also provide a highly effective basis for managing resources. For example, in the southern Mexican state of Oaxaca, Zapotec farmers have been growing maize on the same landscape for hundreds of years (Figure 6.6). Farmers have a highly systematic understanding of how soil qualities, weather patterns, lunar phases, plant–plant interactions, and plant–insect interactions affect maize harvests (Gonzalez 2001). Western scientists have discovered that Zapotec practices of intercropping (planting multiple crops together), building soil mounds for planting maize, letting the land lie fallow, and planting and harvesting by the phases of the moon all contribute to creating a highly productive and sustainable agricultural system (Gonzalez 2001).

Figure 6.6 Maize Biodiversity in Southern Mexico. Southern Mexico, where maize was domesticated some 8,000 years ago, has long been a hotspot of maize biodiversity. People like the Zapotec have developed tens of thousands of varieties of maize with different flavors, textures, adaptability to microclimates and soil conditions, and colors. Each variety reflects the highly specialized and customized knowledge of its farmers.

Some elements of Zapotec science do not correspond to Western science and beliefs about effective resource management, however. For example, ecological knowledge is not separate from other forms of knowledge, such as ideas about morally acceptable behavior. Zapotecs believe that maize has a soul that rewards people who share with others. As a result, they believe that the success of a harvest is directly related to the farmer's positive social relations with other members of the community.

The Zapotec case demonstrates that traditional ecological knowledge has allowed communities to thrive for a long time on a landscape without destroying it. Unlike Western sciences, which claim to have universal tools for understanding nature, the Zapotec knowledge of nature is rooted in local cultural traditions, beliefs, and landscapes. It is also not viewed as a separate domain of specialized knowledge but is integrated into people's daily lives, spiritual practices, and so on. In the contemporary world, such knowledge and practices are confronting new challenges related to the spread of industrial agriculture and economic globalization. In the next section, we examine how these challenges affect a community's environment and health.

THINKING CRITICALLY ABOUT SUSTAINABILITY

The idea that traditional ecological knowledge provides an effective basis for managing natural resources is often resisted most strongly by Western agricultural scientists, who often dismiss these knowledge systems as not scientific and rigorous. How should anthropologists respond to these kinds of claims?

❦ How Are Industrial Agriculture and Economic Globalization Linked to Increasing Environmental and Health Problems?

Industrial agriculture and economic globalization are fueling major changes around the world, creating environmental problems and challenging health and sustainability. In analyzing these problems, anthropologists have found that environmental degradation results from a complex interplay of social, cultural, natural, and political-economic factors that relate to two important questions: How do people consume natural resources in their lifestyles and foodways? And who pays the cost of that consumption? In beginning to address these questions it is important to examine one of the most common—yet simplistic—explanations for environmental problems, which is population growth.

Population and Environment

Eighteenth-century theologian Thomas Malthus argued that human population grows exponentially, quickly overwhelming a limited resource base and leading to famine. Some modern environmentalists have argued that the same is happening on a global scale in the world today. The problem seems self-evident: a small planet cannot indefinitely support a quickly expanding human population (now over seven billion), and ecological ruin awaits us if we do not limit our population growth.

There are several problems with this view. One is that social scientists have yet to identify any confirmed case of environmental and social collapse because of overpopulation or mass consumption (Tainter 2006). Another is that humans have tended to adapt to the land's **carrying capacity**, which is the population an area can support, by developing new technologies and intensifying agriculture, as discussed earlier. Sustainable social systems also often respond by adopting new cultural practices to cope with rapid ecological deterioration. In other words, they are resilient, able to absorb change by changing social practices.

Anthropologists have also shown that the environmental disruptions that lead to famines result from a complex interplay of natural conditions with existing patterns of social inequality. For example, during the 1985 Ethiopian famine, Western aid and relief agencies like the World Food Programme and the U.S. Agency for International Development argued that Ethiopia's population was too large, resulting in the overconsumption of natural resources, environmental collapse, and famine. Their solution was to implement programs of food relief and land reclamation projects to improve agricultural yield.

But these programs failed, because the experts who conceived them misunderstood the complex causes of the famine. The experts based their models on exaggerated data about land degradation and ignored other data, particularly the disastrous effects of the country's civil war and socialist government, which disrupted food distribution channels. Legal barriers that led to insecure access to land also discouraged farmers from investing in traditional soil conservation measures (Hoben 1995). This famine was not a consequence of overpopulation but the result of these other interrelated factors. No one of these factors by itself would have produced the famine and the environmental problems associated with it.

Ecological Footprint

In the Malthusian view, sustainability is a matter of controlling population where it seems to be growing most. But it does not address a simple fact: different societies, as well as people within those societies, consume differing amounts of resources. The concept of an **ecological footprint** addresses this issue by measuring what people consume and the waste they produce. It then calculates the amount of biologically productive land and water area needed to support them. As Figure 6.7 demonstrates, people in industrialized countries consume much more than people in non-industrialized countries (Wackernagel et al. 1997). Of course, these are just averages; some individuals consume more and others less, usually related to their relative wealth or poverty.

The distinction between the average Indian and the average North American as shown in the image is the latter's involvement in consumer capitalism. Consumer capitalism promotes the cultural ideal that people will never fully satisfy their needs, so they will continually buy more and more things in their pursuit of happiness. This cultural ideal has enormous consequences for sustainability. We see these consequences in the production of goods (the extraction of nonrenewable raw materials to make consumer products); the distribution of goods (the reliance on fossil fuels to transport goods to market); and the consumption of goods (the landfills that get filled with nonorganic trash). As a result, while Americans make up only about 5% of the world's population, they consume roughly 25% of its resources. Most Americans do not understand the destructiveness of consumer lifestyles, although signs of it are everywhere: urban sprawl, polluted air and waterways, acid rain, unhealthy forests, climate change, and environmental health problems linked to contamination.

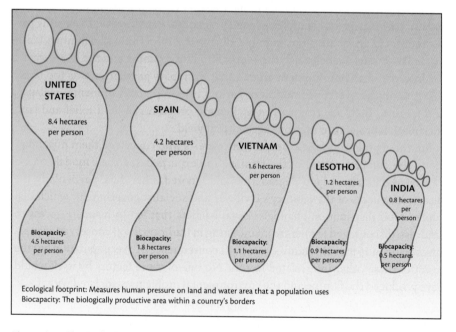

Figure 6.7   The Ecological Footprints of Five Countries.

In most regions of the world, industrial agriculture has particularly strong impacts on the landscape. In recent decades, thanks to the **Green Revolution**—the transformation in agriculture in the Third World through agricultural research, technology transfer, and infrastructure development—rural communities throughout the world have seen pressures to shift from traditional modes of subsistence and agriculture to industrialized agriculture. The goal is to enhance profitability and generate foreign revenue by exporting items that other countries do not have, so that the countries can make investments in domestic development and pay back loans to those international institutions.

For small-scale subsistence farmers in Honduras studied by anthropologist Susan Stonich, these pressures have generated important dilemmas. Since the 1950s, large commercial cotton plantations and cattle ranches have encroached on small farmers, pushing them into less productive land on mountain slopes. As commercial farms have gotten larger, the size of small farms has declined, causing many farmers to give up and migrate to the cities. Those who remain on their farms have shifted from subsistence agriculture to growing cash crops for export. The intense pressure to produce high yields has led them to deforest hillsides and abandon most soil conservation measures, both of which undermine the long-term fertility of their lands. Eventually farmers find themselves in a desperate situation in which they are aware that they are "destroying the land" (Stonich 1993).

Communities that have shifted from small-scale farming to producing cash crops for export often face another significant problem—lack of **food security** for local populations. Food security refers to access to sufficient nutritious food to sustain an active and healthy life. As we will see in "Anthropologist as Problem Solver: Teresa Mares and Migrant Farmworkers' Food Security in Vermont," concerns over food security have become an important area of anthropological research and application.

Analyses that focus on the linkages between political-economic power, social inequality, and ecological destruction are typical of the approach called **political ecology**. Many anthropologists who study environmental problems align themselves closely with political ecology, which rejects single-factor explanations, like overpopulation, ignorance, or poor land use, as explanations for environmental degradation, and focuses instead on the socioenvironmental impacts of industrial economies.

Industrial Foods, Sedentary Lives, and the Nutrition Transition

Even as they can provide a reliable source of food, industrialized foodways also have important consequences on people's health. One dimension of this problem is the role industrial foods have played in the dramatic global rise of people who are overnourished, as reflected in growing global rates of **obesity**, which is having excess body fat to the point of impairing bodily health and function, and of **overweight**, or having abnormally high accumulation of body fat. There are now more people in the world who are suffering the effects of overnourishment—estimated

Anthropologist as Problem Solver
Teresa Mares and Migrant Farmworkers' Food Security in Vermont

Known for its high-quality cheeses and as the home of the iconic ice cream brand Ben & Jerry's, Vermont has long enjoyed a reputation as an idyllic agrarian landscape full of milk cows. But dairy farming is a difficult, year-round job with unreliable financial returns due to fluctuations in the price of milk. The activity has shifted in the past sixty years from being managed primarily as small-scale family-run operations to what is now a highly mechanized industry made up of a small number of large farms. Not able to rely on locals, who no longer want to work on these farms, the Vermont dairy industry has increasingly staked its survival on the employment of low-wage migrant farmworkers, most of them undocumented laborers from southern Mexican states like Chiapas, Veracruz, and Oaxaca.

University of Vermont food anthropologist Teresa Mares, who studies how the diets and foodways of Latino/a immigrants change as a result of migration (Mares 2014), set out to research ethnographically what the lives of these farmworkers are like and how their dietary patterns have changed now that they work on dairy farms. She quickly found out through interviews with farmworkers and immigrants' rights advocates that working on a dairy farm in rural Vermont is a stressful and isolating experience. These farmworkers rarely get away from their places of work because they are afraid of being deported. Moreover, they have limited access to transportation to travel the long distances from the farms to the nearest towns.

Mares conducted a "Community Food Security Assessment" of these farmworkers, which is a U.S. Department of Agriculture survey that measures household access to food, food availability and affordability, and community food production resources. The results showed that something most of us take for granted—the ability to go to a supermarket to get nutritious food—is almost impossible for these farmworkers, who have to rely on others to do the shopping for them, usually their employer or someone else who lives on or near the farm. These trips are often irregular, and miscommunication between Spanish and English speakers is a common problem, resulting in hunger due to inconsistent access to any food, much less food that is culturally familiar and affordable.

Teresa Mares.

There are multiple ironies to this situation, the most obvious one being that the very people producing an iconic food product themselves suffer from food insecurity and hunger. Another irony is that most of these people left their homes in rural Mexico in the first place because of food insecurity brought on by the kinds of globalizing factors now opening jobs for them in Vermont's dairy industry. Among these factors is the 1994 North American Free Trade Agreement (NAFTA), which displaced southern Mexican farmers who could not compete with cheaper American imports of Midwestern corn and milk from various dairy states, including Vermont.

Recognizing an opportunity to address an acute problem and to create new opportunities for collaborative research with colleagues in other fields like agriculture and health, Mares worked with her university's extension office and community volunteers to create a program that would make seeds, tools, and technical guidance available to farmworkers so that they could plant their own vegetable and herb gardens on the dairy farms. Mares met regularly with farmworkers participating in the program, interviewing them at length about issues such as their knowledge about gardening techniques, what kinds of foods they liked to eat, their cooking patterns, and their household spending patterns. She also worked alongside them in gardens and kitchens—hoeing soils, transplanting seedlings, making meals, and so on—which are useful vantage points from which to observe their actual food practices.

This research has produced detailed ethnographic insights into how farmworkers cope with food insecurity and struggle to maintain food practices that are meaningful to them, as well as the successes the program has had in improving the farmworkers' food security. It has also been useful to the people who run the program, who have used Mares's data to assess the effectiveness of the program and to improve its delivery as they begin to address other issues of food insecurity in rural Vermont.

QUESTIONS FOR REFLECTION

1. Review the USDA's Community Food Security Assessment Toolkit (available online at https://www.ers.usda.gov/publications/pub-details/?pubid=43179). How do the data this toolkit elicits differ from the data one might gather from participant observation? In what ways do the two types of investigation complement each other?

2. What kinds of ethical dilemmas accompany research with a community like undocumented farmworkers?

at one billion overweight and 475 million obese people—than people classified as undernourished, estimated at 875 million (Food and Agriculture Organization of the United Nations [FAO] 2012; International Obesity Task Force 2013). Because obesity and overweight can cause chronic diseases—diabetes and heart disease among them—health officials and researchers consider them to be among the most serious public health crises facing the world.

Obesity is a complex metabolic syndrome, or combination of medical conditions. Smoking and insufficient nutrition during pregnancy, as well as certain environmental toxins that disrupt endocrine production, are related to obesity.

Some individuals may be genetically predisposed to gain weight more easily than others, but obesity tends to develop in a person who eats a lot of food while expending little energy (Ulijaszek and Lofink 2006).

Social factors influence how much food people eat and contribute directly to the production of obesity and overweight. These factors include the presence of other individuals at a meal, television viewing, portion size, cultural attitudes toward body fat, and learned preferences (Ulijaszek and Lofink 2006). Consider how powerful just one of these factors—television viewing—can be: in the United States during the 1990s, a child watched on average ten thousand television advertisements for food per year, with 95% of those foods being sugared cereal, sweets, fast food, and soft drinks, all of which are fattening (Brownell 2002).

The worldwide rise of obesity and overweight is also tied to a global **nutrition transition**, the combination of changes in diet toward energy-dense foods (high in calories, fat, and sugar) and declines in physical activity. These changes in diet are related to an abundant, secure, and inexpensive food supply, the very definition of success for industrial agriculture. But this success is double-edged, because the result is a food supply of relatively low nutritional quality, offering processed grains, fats, and refined sugars instead of fruits, vegetables, whole grains, and lean meats—the foods on which we thrive as a species. The other major change is the movement worldwide since the mid-nineteenth century of massive numbers of people away from rural areas, where they tend to lead physically active lives, to cities and suburbs, where they lead more sedentary lives and have more transportation options. For example, in 1900 only about 10% of the world population lived in cities. Today it is 50%, and rates of urbanization continue to be high around the world.

Both of these factors also explain why the problem of obesity is a problem not just in wealthy countries like the United States but also in poor countries. Because small-scale farms, which produce locally grown and nutrient-rich food, can rarely compete with the low-cost foods of transnational agribusinesses, many small-scale farms have shut down their operations. With fewer farms to support rural livelihoods, people then migrate to urban areas, where they tend to be less physically active.

Anthropology Confronts Climate Change

In recent years, anthropologists have also turned their attention to climate change, offering perspectives on the nexus of nature, culture, science, politics, and belief that shapes ideas about its causes, government policies related to it, and the diverse ways people make sense of it (Crate 2008; Barnes and Dove 2015). Anthropology's holistic perspective emphasizes climate change as one of a number of environmental influences on people's social lives, and not the single variable driving environmental change in the world today. This perspective also brings attention to the ways current patterns of industrial production and consumption related to climate change are already altering people's livelihood strategies and interactions with the economy and the environment (Crate 2008; Barnes and Dove 2015).

Anthropologists have studied the social dynamics, cultural patterns, and institutional processes that shape how problems of climate are framed, studied, and communicated in the world of science. Key to these social dynamics are tensions between scientific specialties that use different methods and theories, uncertainties in climate modeling, and funding patterns that prioritize the reductionist perspectives of scientific authorities over the holistic perspectives of social scientists in the construction of public knowledge and policy (Lahsen 2015; Moore, Mankin, and Becker 2015).

Human societies have long dealt with climate variability, and different societies have different ways of conceptualizing that variability (Orlove 2005; Crate 2008). For example, as Roderick McIntosh (2015) has described, the Mande people of arid West Africa have long grappled with unpredictable and abrupt changes in precipitation and river patterns. They have developed their own climate ethnoscience in which certain individuals—"weather machines"—study their society's knowledge of long-term weather patterns and have the cultural authority to help shape community responses, which can include migration, shifts between pastoral and horticultural economies, and modifications of agricultural practices. Flexibility and resilience lie at the heart of the Mande understandings of how to deal with climate variability and change, which suggest broader lessons for the rest of us as we begin to better understand the effects of climate change globally.

THINKING CRITICALLY ABOUT SUSTAINABILITY

There is perhaps no more consequential issue for the future of human environmental and bodily health than the changing dynamics of foodways in the contemporary world. What role do you think anthropologists should play in the issues of changing foodways? What specific kinds of knowledge or interventions do you think are most appropriate for anthropologists?

Are Industrialized Western Societies the Only Ones to Conserve Nature?

In 1872, the creation of the world's first national park, Yellowstone, ushered in a new era of modern nature conservation with global effects. Around the world today, hundreds of millions of acres of wilderness landscape and ocean are formally protected. In many cases, these efforts have stemmed the tide of near-certain destruction from extractive industries, settlement, or uncontrolled exploitation.

At the same time, the dominant cultural model for administering protected areas is based on the separation of humans and nature. It emphasizes that nature must be kept uninhabited by people, and it has led to forced evictions of indigenous peoples and generated significant social conflict (Colchester 2003; Chapin 2009).

Figure 6.8 Stereotypes of Green Indians. In 1971, the "Keep America Beautiful" campaign developed by the U.S. government aired an anti-pollution television ad featuring an American Indian (portrayed by an Italian-American actor with the stage name of Iron Eyes Cody) who sheds a tear because of pollution. There is usually a large gap between such romantic stereotypes and the real conditions in which indigenous groups relate to the environment.

Anthropologists have studied these dynamics closely, approaching the resulting conflicts as rooted in distinct cultural approaches toward nature's protection.

In exploring whether or not non-Western societies have had similar intentions to conserve and protect nature, it is necessary to overcome a powerful stereotype that native peoples are "natural environmentalists" always in tune with the natural world (Figure 6.8). Anthropologists have documented many examples of destructive indigenous relationships with nature, among them "aboriginal overkill" that led to human-caused extinctions of certain animals toward the end of the Pleistocene Era (Ice Age) (Krech 1999). The key to answering this section's question is to consider first how indigenous societies have created landscapes that either deliberately or unintentionally have the effect of protecting natural ecosystems and wildlife, and second the ways in which Western societies approach the same objective.

Anthropogenic Landscapes

Upon close examination, many landscapes that appear "natural" to Westerners—sometimes the very landscapes that Westerners want to conserve without people on them—are the result of human involvement and manipulation. In other words, they are **anthropogenic landscapes**, or landscapes modified by human action in the past or present.

An important example is the East African savannas of northern Tanzania and southern Kenya. The Maasai, who live there as pastoralists, have extensively modified the environment to support their cattle. They burn scrub brush to encourage the growth of nutritious pasture grass, an act that helps support wildlife biodiversity because these are the same nutritious pastures that the savanna's world-famous wildlife populations of zebras, wildebeest, and other large animals also eat (Igoe 2004). But today, some of these fragile scrublands are in crisis because Maasai pastoralists are overgrazing. To understand why they now overgraze, we must look at the clash between Western and Maasai notions of managing nature.

The Culture of Modern Nature Conservation

To prevent overgrazing and to conserve resources for themselves and wildlife populations, Maasai traditionally practiced a form of pastoralism called *transhumant pastoralism*, in which they range over large territories of commonly held property on regular paths and cycles. During drought years, when pastures are most susceptible to overgrazing, the Maasai would traditionally bring cattle to swamp areas and permanent waterholes. But during the twentieth century national parks and nature reserves were typically formed around these permanent wet areas (since a lot of wild animals congregate there, too), preventing Maasai access to them. Park administrators and scientists did not understand the delicate balance between people and wildlife that was sustained by the constant movement of people, their herds, and the wild animals. The result is that the Maasai were forced to overgraze areas outside the park during drought periods, producing resentment among the Maasai and conflicts with park officials (Igoe 2004).

These park officials practice what anthropologist Dan Brockington (2002) calls "Fortress Conservation," an approach to conservation that assumes that people are threatening to nature, and that for nature to be pristine the people who live there must be evicted. This approach was undergirded by the philosophical divide that Western cultures imposed between people and nature, and it was enabled by European and American colonial expansion, which commonly instituted controls on native people's use of natural resources (Grove 1995).

Environmentalism's Alternative Paradigms

Anthropologists recognize that the displacement of local people for the purposes of conserving nature can be counterproductive, producing exclusion, resistance, and social tension. But we also recognize that environmentalism has multiple expressions.

During the past several decades there have been a number of experiments in "co-management" between national or international conservation groups and indigenous people. In places like Nepal, Alaska, Canada, Panama, Brazil, and Australia, indigenous people have been allowed to continue living in protected areas and have some say in park management. This collaborative approach creates new kinds of opportunities for dialogue, power sharing, and relationship building between conservationists and indigenous communities (Natcher, Hickey, and Hickey 2005). But this approach can also create new dilemmas for indigenous communities; outside conservation groups still exercise considerable control, especially over funding, and scientists often disrespect indigenous knowledge about wildlife and landscape dynamics even though they are supposed to be "co-managing" the resources with the indigenous community (Igoe 2004:158; Nadasdy 2005).

At the heart of co-management is a move toward recognizing and redressing how social inequalities and injustices affect possibilities for conservation and environmental sustainability. An even stronger approach along these lines is the **environmental justice** movement, a social movement that addresses the linkages between racial discrimination and injustice, social equity, and environmental quality (Figure 6.9).

Figure 6.9   The Birth of Environmental Justice.   Environmental justice was born in the early 1980s, when a toxic waste dump was proposed in Warren County, North Carolina, the poorest county in the state and where 84% of residents were African American. Civil rights leaders organized a protest, arguing that these facts, not the ecological suitability of the site to store toxic waste, motivated the decision to build the waste dump in their county.

Environmental justice is now a global movement, and unlike environmentalism oriented toward creating nature preserves that tend to focus on scenic landscapes and biodiversity, it tends to be organized around the defense of a people's livelihood and social justice concerns (Guha 2000:105). Marshall Islanders, for example, have been active in this movement, framing their situation as rooted in problems related to outsider control and domination, including nuclear fallout, sea level rise, economic under-development, and poor public health, that undermine local self-determination and livelihoods.

THINKING CRITICALLY ABOUT SUSTAINABILITY

Americans often assume that people interested in conserving nature tend to be middle-class people who are able to make donations to environmental groups because they have money left over after meeting their basic needs. In other words, protecting nature is a luxury that poor people cannot afford. Based on what we have discussed in this section, why is this view skewed?

🌿 Conclusion

Anthropologists agree that we must pay close attention to the social practices and structures that shape how communities relate to their natural environments. When we do, we can see that non-industrialized people typically have a deep understanding of their environments, and they routinely understand the behaviors of animals and plants as well as, if not in some cases better than, scientists from other regions. In such communities, the cultural landscape envisions nature differently than do people in the West, often using metaphors that express people's reciprocal ties to the land, or as the Marshallese case that opened this chapter demonstrates, drawing on social, political, and spiritual strategies that protect ecosystems from exploitation.

The cultural landscape of human–nature separation that we see in modern conservation initiatives has only recently begun to appreciate these facts. Historically, Western industrialized countries have designed conservation programs that expel indigenous peoples from landscapes those peoples may have lived on sustainably for many years, even living in ways that support the biodiversity of other species, as is the case of the Maasai.

Anthropologists agree that careful use of natural resources is the basis of a sustainable society. As a result, it is important to look critically at the world's ecological crisis. But the causes of our current problems—as was the case in past ecological crises—cannot be reduced to any single cause. We have to consider factors like elite mismanagement of resources, government policy choices, inflexible responses to change, and consumption patterns that extract key resources, create waste, and contribute to changes in climate, ecosystem viability, and so on. We also have to consider who pays the cost of these patterns and realize that questions of unequal access to resources and social patterns of injustice are often at the heart of the world's key ecological crises.

Key Terms

Animal husbandry   p. 123
Anthropogenic landscapes
   p. 138
Carrying capacity   p. 131
Cultural landscape   p. 120
Ecological footprint   p. 132
Environmental
   anthropology   p. 120
Environmental justice   p. 139
Ethnobiology   p. 129

Ethnoscience   p. 128
Food security   p. 133
Foodways   p. 121
Foraging   p. 122
Green Revolution   p. 133
Horticulture   p. 122
Industrial agriculture   p. 125
Intensification   p. 124
Modes of subsistence   p. 122
Nutrition transition   p. 136

Obesity   p. 133
Overweight   p. 133
Pastoralism   p. 123
Political ecology   p. 133
Swidden agriculture   p. 123
Taste   p. 127
Traditional ecological
   knowledge   p. 129

Reviewing the Chapter

CHAPTER SECTION	WHAT WE KNOW	TO BE RESOLVED
Do all people see nature the same way?	Different cultures have different ways of conceptualizing the boundaries between humans and the natural world. Metaphors often play a major role in these conceptualizations.	Anthropologists continue to debate the extent to which general conceptual models and metaphors, or the material forces of nature itself, shape human relations with the environment.

CHAPTER SECTION	WHAT WE KNOW	TO BE RESOLVED
How do people secure an adequate, meaningful, and environmentally sustainable food supply?	Humans have developed four general modes of subsistence—foraging, horticulture, pastoralism, and intensive agriculture—each of which carries certain social and environmental tradeoffs and opportunities. Cultural meanings also play a central role in shaping how people acquire, share, and consume foods.	Although they are under great pressure in a world increasingly dominated by intensive agriculture, foragers, horticulturists, and pastoralists persist. Anthropologists are working to understand how and why they persist, as well as the pressures on these modes of subsistence. In addition, anthropologists continue to work through how cultural attitudes and social practices surrounding food relate to social categories and dynamics such as class, race, ethnicity, and gender.
How does non-Western knowledge of nature and agriculture relate to science?	Different societies have developed highly systematic and sophisticated knowledge systems for classifying the natural world, some of which closely resemble Western science. Unlike Western science, however, which views its methods and findings as universally applicable, these knowledge systems are often highly localized and customized to particular ecosystems and rooted in local moralities.	Anthropologists are still working to understand the specific ways in which traditional ecological knowledge shapes practices of ecological and agricultural management, as well as how it is changing to adapt to new challenges, such as climate change.
How are industrial agriculture and economic globalization linked to increasing environmental and health problems?	The ecological impact of a society depends on its ecological footprint, or the amount of natural resources people require to live their lifestyles. Industrial agriculture's rapid expansion around the globe is related closely to unequal political-economic relationships and creates new environmental and health risks.	Anthropologists are still identifying the conditions under which social groups can adopt new cultural ideas and practices that promote resilience and sustainability. Anthropologists are also relatively new to public health policy discussions about critical issues like food security and obesity, and have just begun to define the anthropological dimensions of these issues. One area where anthropological research has relevance is in studying how societies and social groups understand and adapt to climate change.
Are industrialized Western societies the only ones to conserve nature?	While Western conservation practice is based on the separation of humans and nature, the stewardship traditions of non-Western societies often start from principles that view humans as important actors in nature. Western nature conservation practices have often disrupted and marginalized local cultures, many of which have had highly successful adaptations to their environments.	As some conservationists have realized new opportunities of co-managing natural resources with indigenous communities, anthropologists are divided over whether these approaches actually benefit indigenous communities.

7

Economics

Working, Sharing, and Buying

After the death of Chairman Mao Tse-tung in 1976, Chinese state leaders began to rethink their policies of collectivization and centralized allocation of resources. Calling the new approach "Socialism with Chinese Characteristics," the state made bureaucratic changes to encourage private control of capital and goods (Osburg 2013). As a result of these changes, private entrepreneurs have begun to flourish, and some of them have created fortunes in real estate, manufacturing, construction, entertainment, and services. Entrepreneurs have also gained a new social profile as sought-after marriage partners and trendsetters in fashion and consumption (Osburg 2013). At the same time, many are seen as morally suspect profiteers and beneficiaries of illicit activities and corruption, because of close ties to government officials who provide them with contracts, licenses, and extralegal protections in exchange for bribes and kickbacks.

The Key to Business Success.　Luxurious nightclubs, such as the one pictured here in Beijing, are critical locations where Chinese businessmen and government officials cultivate *guanxi*, or social networks, and friendships rooted in sentimental bonds. These relationships are believed to be keys to business success.

This entrepreneurial sphere is a strongly masculine one, rooted in gendered forms of obligation and the creation of value (Osburg 2013). Well-connected male entrepreneurs spend a lot of time and money in luxurious clubs entertaining state officials, clients, and fellow businessmen through banqueting, drinking, gambling, and hiring sex workers (Osburg 2013). The goal of doing these things is to expand and strengthen *guanxi* [**gwahn**-shee], which are informal webs of social relationships individuals create and use to pursue their own ends. *Guanxi* can help get things done in the slow-moving bureaucracy or get new government contracts. Reciprocity, especially the give-and-take of favors, is a key element of a *guanxi* network, and individuals who can use *guanxi* to benefit others can gain important power and social prestige.

But these networks also involve sentimental ties associated with *renqing* [**wren**-cheeng], or affective interpersonal relationships, such as those between kin and close friends. Spending many hours together in leisure and entertainment—creating shared experiences of intimacy, vulnerability, and transgression—is one of the ways businessmen can transform the short-term interests of *guanxi* into the long-term bonds of *renqing* (Osburg 2013). Yet the pressure to spend so much time at clubs is exhausting and expensive, and it can generate feelings of being trapped in moral compromises and undesirable obligations (Osburg 2013).

Many Western observers have celebrated the rise of China's new entrepreneurial class as the vanguard of capitalist free enterprise and a liberal democratic opening. But this view misunderstands the complex mixture of capitalism and political authoritarianism that characterizes the Chinese economy, and the heavy dependence of private entrepreneurs on the state. More importantly, this economy is not a simple transplant of capitalistic practices and beliefs from the West; rather, it is shaped by and embedded in particular Chinese political structures, social relationships, and culturally defined yet dynamic patterns of masculinity, desire, and morality. In fact, *all* economies are shaped by such social and cultural particularities.

At the heart of anthropology's interest in economics is the following question: *How do cultural processes shape what people want and need to live, and how do they shape the work people do to get it?* Embedded in this broader question are the following issues, around which this chapter is organized:

Is money really the measure of all things?
How does culture shape the value and meaning of money?
Why is gift exchange such an important part of all societies?
What is the point of owning things?
Does capitalism have distinct cultures?

Anthropologists who study economies and economic activities are interested in how people satisfy their needs and why they want certain things in the first place. Although we have long debated the exact nature of the relationship between economy and culture, one cannot be fully understood without the other. We begin exploring this relationship by considering the nature of value.

❦ Is Money Really the Measure of All Things?

Many North Americans and Europeans are accustomed, if not also deeply committed, to the idea that money is the measure of all things. We hear all the time that everything has a price and that the price of an object reflects its real value. But what would be the price in dollars of the original Declaration of Independence of the United States? A favorite blanket you have had since child-

Figure 7.1   How Much Is Grandmother's Antique Battle-Axe Worth?   In the U.S. television show *Antiques Roadshow*, an expert evaluates the market value of household antiques. The popularity of the show, not to mention the motivation people have to go on it with their antiques, is ultimately less about the money than it is about other factors. What do you think those factors are?

hood? The Wailing Wall, Jerusalem's most sacred Jewish site? A gold wedding band that mothers have passed to their daughters for seven generations?

Somebody could try to set dollar values, or even try to buy or sell these things (Figure 7.1). But some objects and relationships carry such sacred or special qualities that they can never really be reduced to a monetary equivalent (Werner and Bell 2004). The awkwardness you might feel thinking about people doing so—as well as the controversies that erupt when someone tries to sell something such as human body parts, virginity, or Holocaust memorabilia—suggests that some deep set of processes defines what is an acceptable economic transaction and how we establish monetary values for things. Those processes are cultural. Culture—the processes through which people construct and naturalize certain meanings and actions as normal and even necessary—not only shapes what is acceptable to transact, but how and why the transaction will take place, and how the objects or services being exchanged are valued.

Culture, Economics, and Value

If money is not the measure of all things, where exactly within the processes of culture does **value**—the relative worth of an object or service—come from? **Economic anthropology**, the subdiscipline concerned with how people make, share, and buy things and services, has long considered this question. Economic anthropologists study the decisions people make about earning a living, what they do when they work, the social institutions that affect these activities, and how these three matters relate to the creation of value (M. E. Smith 2000; Wilk and Cliggett 2007).

Although both anthropologists and economists study the origins of value and how economies work, they generally have different goals. Economists typically try to understand and predict economic patterns, often with a practical goal of help-ing people hold on to and increase their wealth. Economists study communities in terms of economic statistics, and they assume that economic transactions in one community or country are like transactions in any other.

Anthropologists, on the other hand, do not assume that transactions are the same everywhere, as they recognize that culture shapes the character of any transaction. Furthermore, we tend to study how people lead their day-to-day economic lives by means of direct, long-term interaction with them. As a result, we tend to focus more than economists do on understanding the world's diversity of **economic systems**, the structured patterns and relationships through which people exchange goods and ser-vices, and making sense of how these systems reflect and shape particular ways of life.

Anthropologists rely on four major theoretical approaches to understanding how economies create value (Table 7.1). Three of these (neoclassical economics, substantivism, and Marxism) are traditional approaches within the social sci-ences, while the fourth (cultural economics) has been developed by anthropolo-gists. These approaches are discussed in more detail below.

TABLE 7.1   THEORIES OF CULTURE, ECONOMY, AND VALUE

Theoretical Approach	What Is the Economy?	How Does the Economic System Work?	How Is Value Created?
Neoclassical Economics	The economy is a division of labor and the exchange of goods and services in a market.	Workers cooperate in the division of labor to produce goods. The market brings together buyers and sellers to exchange those goods.	Value and wealth are created by competition between buyers and sellers.
Substantivism	The economy is the substance of the actual transactions people engage in to get what they need and want.	Economic processes are embedded in and shaped by non-market social institutions, such as the state, religious beliefs, and kinship relations.	Value is relative, created by particular cultures and social institutions.
Marxism	Capitalism, which is a type of economic system, is a system in which private ownership of the means of production and a division of labor produce wealth for a few, and inequality for the masses.	People participate in capitalism by selling their labor. That labor is appropriated by those holding the means of production.	Labor (especially the exploitation of others' labor) is a major source of value.
Cultural Economics	The economy is a category of culture, not a special arena governed by universal economic rationality.	Economic acts are guided by local beliefs and cultural models, which are closely tied to a community's values.	Value is created by the symbolic associations people make between an activity, good, or service and a community's moral norms.

The Neoclassical Perspective

Scottish moral philosopher Adam Smith wrote about the creation of value in his influential book *The Wealth of Nations* (1776/1976). Smith observed that in "primitive" societies individuals did a lot of different kinds of work—growing and preparing food, making their own clothing, building their own homes, and so forth—but in the "civilized" societies of eighteenth-century Europe, such jobs were done increasingly by "the joint labor of a great multitude of workmen." This change was due to the **division of labor**, the cooperative organization of work into specialized tasks and roles (A. Smith 1776/1976). Citing the example of sewing pins, Smith marveled at how dividing the process of making a sewing pin into distinct actions performed by different specialized laborers—one laborer to draw out the wire, a second to cut it, a third to straighten it, and so on—produced exponential growth in the number of pins that could be made in a day.

This change was revolutionary. Before the division of labor, Smith noted that a pin would take a lot of time and effort for an individual to make, and so the value of the pin lay in the amount of labor it took to make one. But with the division of labor reducing that time and effort, the value of the pin was now established by its **exchange** (the transfer of objects and services between social actors) in a **market**, a social institution in which people come together to buy and sell goods and services.

For Smith and the economists who follow him, market exchange reflects a natural human propensity to (as Smith famously said) "truck, barter, and exchange." It was also the most successful mechanism for determining value and making wealth possible. Within the market, individuals pursue their own self-interest, using their capacity for reason and calculation to maximize their individual satisfaction. The world has finite resources ("limited means"), but everybody has unlimited desires ("unlimited ends"), and the result is competition among individuals. Every person's struggle to get the most value theoretically keeps prices, costs of production, profits, and interest rates low while generating great wealth (Wilk and Cliggett 2007). This theory is the foundation of **neoclassical economics**, which studies how people make decisions to allocate resources like time, labor, and money in order to maximize their personal satisfaction.

Among anthropologists, this influential theory has provoked a long debate over the nature of the economy. It is, we will see, basically an unresolved debate, but exploring the positions illustrates how anthropologists interested in the relationship between culture, economics, and value have applied—and criticized—neoclassical thought.

The Substantivist–Formalist Debate

In 1944, the Hungarian-American economic historian Karl Polanyi published his book *The Great Transformation* to explain how modern **capitalism**—the economic system based on private ownership of the means of production, in which prices are set and goods distributed through a market—emerged in Europe

(Polanyi 1944/1975). Polanyi insisted that the rise of the market in Europe was not natural and inevitable, but a social process that both supported and was supported by the creation of modern nation-states.

In developing that argument, Polanyi proposed that studying economies involves making a distinction between "formal" and "substantive" economics. By **formal economics**, he meant the underlying ("formal") logic that shapes people's actions when they participate in an economy, as we see in the apparently self-interested and rational decision-makers of neoclassical economic theory. By **substantive economics**, he referred to the daily transactions people actually engage in to get what they need or desire, or the "substance" of the economy. These transactions are embedded in and inseparable from other social institutions, such as politics, religion, and kinship. Anthropologists found this distinction useful for describing issues they were studying in other societies.

THE SUBSTANTIVIST POSITION

Polanyi's own approach to economics was substantivist. Its primary goal was to describe how the production and **redistribution** of goods (collection of goods in a community and then redivision of those goods among members) were embedded in and shaped by non-market social institutions, such as the state, religious beliefs, and kinship relations. Substantivism held that societies have unique social institutions and processes that influence economics like other aspects of culture. From this perspective, the value of goods in an economic system is culturally relative, rooted in particular cultures and social institutions (Wilk and Cliggett 2007).

Substantivists felt that the concept of an "economy" did not do justice to how making a livelihood is inseparably interwoven with customs and social relations in other societies. They argued that research should focus on a broad field of social relations and institutions that provided people with what they needed to live, instead of any predetermined or limited notion of an economy centered on a market.

THE FORMALIST REACTION

By the 1960s, some anthropologists began to criticize substantivism's lack of attention to individual action and behavior, shifting their focus to formal economics. To formalists, people everywhere confront limited means and unlimited ends (wants), and therefore they make rational decisions that are appropriate to the satisfaction they desire (M. E. Smith 2000). Being anthropologists, the formalists understood that "satisfaction" could be culturally defined and variable but, they asserted, the decision-making processes people used to achieve satisfaction were basically the same everywhere (Wilk and Cliggett 2007).

By the late 1970s, the debate between substantivists and formalists had fizzled out with no clear winner. The main reason is that the two sides were essentially arguing past each other: one side was talking about societies and their institutions, while the other was talking about individuals, their rationality, and their market transactions.

The Marxist Perspective

The substantivist–formalist debate also fizzled because a number of anthropologists had begun to adopt Marxism, the political and economic theories associated with German political economist Karl Marx (1818–1883). In his analysis of British capitalism, Marx characterized the English system as pitting the conflicting interests of a wealthy class (who owned factories) against those of a poorer working class (laborers in the factories) (Marx 1867/1990). At the heart of this system, Marx argued, was a division of labor that produced inequality and conflict.

From the Marxist point of view, the substantivists and formalists had wasted their time debating the nature of exchange and redistribution, while the neoclassicists misunderstood economic activity as individual choice and decision-making. The real problem is explaining why and how the production and trade of goods enforces and maintains the social inequality.

Marxists use the concept of **surplus value**, which is the difference between what people produce and what they need to survive, to address this problem. In a capitalist society, workers create greater value than they receive for their labor, generating surplus value. For example, a worker in a widget factory might make $35 of widgets in an hour from $5 of materials and get paid $10 per hour. What happens to the $20 of surplus value? The owner of the factory, who controls the **means of production**—the machines and infrastructure required to produce the widget—appropriates it, the Marxists argue, thus exploiting the worker's productivity. This surplus value is the basis of private wealth, but it also creates permanent conflict between the worker and owner classes. The institution of private property and the state, through its social and economic policies, support this inequality.

Marxist analysis introduced issues of power, domination, and the unequal distribution of wealth into anthropology's discussions of culture and economy. But not all attempts to apply Marxist analysis to non-Western societies have been satisfying, because non-capitalist economies work so differently. In particular, such studies do not always adequately address the culturally specific symbolic and moral dimensions of economic interaction, to which we turn next.

The Cultural Economics Perspective

The idea that symbols and morals help shape a community's economy lies at the heart of **cultural economics**. Cultural economics views the economy as a category of culture, not a special arena governed by universal utilitarian or practical reason (Sahlins 1972, 1976). The roots of this approach lie in substantivism. The cultural economist's goal is to understand, from "the native's point of view," the local beliefs and cultural models that guide and shape economic activities (Gudeman 1986).

To the cultural economist, a close relationship exists between the words *value* (desirability) and *values* (moral norms). Both refer to the symbolic expression of intrinsically desirable principles or qualities. This relationship also implies that moral norms and economic activity influence each other (Sayer 2000).

Anthropologists working in this vein have been especially interested in **prestige economies**, economies in which people seek high social rank, prestige, and power instead of money and material wealth. In indigenous Maya communities of Guatemala and southern Mexico, for example, men have traditionally participated in the *Cofradía* [ko-fra-**dee**-ah] system, a hierarchical system dating from colonial times that combines civic leadership and Catholic religious authority (M. Nash 1958) (Figure 7.2). As they enter higher offices with greater responsibilities and power, these men also have the obligation to spend more of their personal wealth on community fiestas and infrastructure. Some will go broke or deep into debt doing so. Underlying this system is a moral philosophy emphasizing that the path to status and rank requires an individual to share generously with others whatever material wealth he has.

Recent studies in cultural economics have tended to focus on the dynamism of local economies, recognizing that one society may encompass several local economic models simultaneously, perhaps at different levels or among different institutions (Robben 1989; Gudeman 2001). Such a perspective can help us better understand how and why businessmen in China work so hard to build *guanxi* and *renqing* relationships with their business partners, mixing Chinese notions of appropriate and moral economic activity with capitalistic models of economic behavior.

Figure 7.2   Members of a *Cofradía* in Guatemala. *Cofradías*, which are Catholic civil-religious associations, are a classic example of a prestige economy since members gain social prestige and authority even as they may go deeply into financial debt to participate.

Returning to this section's broader focus on how value is created, it should be clear that none of these theoretical approaches—neoclassical economics, formalism, substantivism, Marxism, or cultural economics—accepts that money is the measure of all things. While the specifics of these theories differ, each nevertheless accepts, at least partially, that cultural processes and social relationships play a central role in establishing value, and that culture and economics are intertwined in complex ways.

THINKING CRITICALLY ABOUT ECONOMICS

Cultural economics argues that a single society can have multiple local cultural models of appropriate economic action and behavior circulating in it. For example, in the United States, even as dominant cultural models of economic behavior resemble Adam Smith's rational economic actors, some religious communities have certain expectations about appropriate economic behavior, such as saving a certain amount of money, donating a certain percentage to the religious institution, and so on, which make explicit connections between economic behavior and morality. Can you think of other cultural models of economic behavior in the United States?

❦ How Does Culture Shape the Value and Meaning of Money?

If value and its meanings are created through the processes of culture, then it stands to reason that the value and meanings of **money** itself—an object or substance that serves as a payment for a good or service—are also created through culture. Money provides a standard measure of value, allowing people to compare and trade goods and services. Anything durable and scarce can serve as money. Cowrie (a type of mollusk) shells, rings made of precious metals, and even enormous stone disks have been used as money. **Commodity money** has another value beyond itself, such as gold, which can be used as jewelry. **Fiat money** is created and guaranteed by a government, such as U.S. paper dollars. Money is not simply a medium of exchange; it has functions and implications beyond our economic lives, as we explore here.

The Types and Cultural Dimensions of Money

Across the world, money is many things to many people, and not everybody wants it for the same reasons. In market-based economies like that in the United States, people want money because it can be used to buy nearly any good or service. Anthropologists call this **general purpose money** because it is money that is used to buy almost anything. Portability and mobility are important features of general purpose money, as we see in our dollar bills, coins, credit cards, and electronic transfers.

Another type of money is **limited purpose money**, which refers to objects that can be exchanged only for certain things. For example, the pastoral Tiv people of

Nigeria traditionally could purchase cattle and pay bride price (things of value a groom gives to his bride's father) only with brass rods. The Tiv traditionally used money not for basic subsistence, but primarily to gain access to goods that give social respectability and prestige, such as a marriage partner, cattle, and other livestock (Bohannon and Bohannon 1968).

For the Tiv, powerful moral rules regulated the ways in which money was used. The Tiv traditionally had three separate **spheres of exchange**, or bounded orders of value in which certain goods can be exchanged only for others: ordinary subsistence goods, prestige goods, and rights in people, especially women and slaves (Bohannon and Bohannon 1968). The British colonial period in Nigeria (1900–1960) undermined this traditional system, because the British introduced general purpose money. Young Tiv men working as laborers and paid in British currency began using it to pay for prestige goods like cattle and bride price. The acquisition of cash value for prestige goods, Bohannon observed, was not just an economic problem: it was a moral problem since it disrupted Tiv notions about what money could be used for.

Even general purpose money has cultural and moral dimensions beyond its function as a medium of exchange (Parry and Bloch 1989). We all know, for example, that you cannot simply walk into your university's accounting office, pay a large sum of money, and receive a diploma. Our ideas about getting an education involve a moral obligation to work hard and apply oneself. Buying a diploma could even feel "dirty," contaminating the purity and goodness we associate with the process of education. An anthropological explanation for this situation lies in the concept of **transactional orders**, or realms of transactions a community uses, each with its own set of symbolic meanings and moral assumptions (Parry and Bloch 1989). The transactions involved in getting an education, which are steeped in long-term obligations and expectations, are morally distinct from other short-term transactions that have no special moral obligations, such as buying a magazine at your university bookstore (Figure 7.3).

Figure 7.3   "Dirty Money" and Transactional Orders. One of the reasons people involved in organized criminal enterprises launder money gained from illegal activities is to hide the origins of their wealth from the government. But these people are also moving this money from one symbolic realm or transactional order to another, so once it's been laundered it is symbolically "clean" and can be shared with intimates, including spouses and children who should be protected from the morally suspect activities through which it was gained. In this case, a Mexican drug cartel leader sought to launder his money through a racetrack in Oklahoma, which the FBI raided.

Money and the Distribution of Power

Different kinds of money reflect and shape the distribution of power in distinctive ways. In his book *Debt: The First 5,000 Years*, anthropologist David Graeber (2011) explores the historical relationship between money and debt cross-culturally. He observes that when we are in debt to others we feel great moral pressure to pay it off, even if it causes sacrifice and suffering.

Graeber writes that this situation began 5,000 years ago when states started creating new kinds of money to promote trade. Commodity money was historically common because it required no trust to exchange. Indebtedness and violence tend to grow with the rise of commodity money, however, because it is scarce, can be stolen, and is not easily traceable. As an alternative approach, governments have created fiat money to regulate and control the flow of money and intervene in creditor–debtor relations because political unrest grows with high levels of indebtedness. These different types of money are related to distinctive kinds of social dynamics and power relations, some of them quite violent and negative. But whatever the type of money, the broader pattern is one in which debtor–creditor relations are full of tension and conflict.

But being in debt to others is not universally viewed as a moral problem or characterized by conflict. In many societies with what Graeber calls "human" (as opposed to "commercial") economies—in which people's goal is not to acquire money but to create and maintain social relationships—credit and indebtedness is a sign of trust and solidarity. Money, which may take the form of yams, pigs, stones, or other objects, is used not to acquire goods or gain material wealth, but to provide a unit of account or measure for socially important things—for example, to arrange a marriage, prevent a feud, console mourners at a funeral, or seek forgiveness for a crime (Graeber 2011:130). Sometimes debts incurred in these processes remain unsettled because they are so important socially that they cannot be repaid using money. For much of history, most economies worked this way, and some still do, as we explore in the next section.

THINKING CRITICALLY ABOUT ECONOMICS

Do you feel a need to protect certain relationships from money? What relationships? What is the meaning of money for you in these situations?

Why Is Gift Exchange Such an Important Part of All Societies?

Exchange, which anthropologists understand as the transfer of things and gifts between social actors (Carrier 1996a:218), is a universal feature of human existence and relates to all aspects of life. In many societies, the exchange of gifts is the central defining feature of its economy.

Gift Exchange and Economy: Two Classic Approaches

It may sound strange to think of a gift exchange in economic terms. We tend to think of gifts as personal expressions of **reciprocity**, the give-and-take that builds and confirms relationships. For Americans the problem is that we distinguish the economy from gift-giving, while in the non-industrial societies anthropologists have traditionally studied, exchanging gifts is at the heart of the local economy. So how are gifts related to economy? Two classic approaches to this question date back to the 1920s.

MALINOWSKI AND THE KULA

The exchange of gifts is a central feature of life in Melanesian societies of the Southwest Pacific, a fact that Bronislaw Malinowski discovered while he was in the Trobriand Islands. He wrote that for Trobriand Islanders, "to possess is to give.... A man who owns a thing is expected to share it, to distribute it, to be its trustee and dispenser" (1922:97).

He found no better illustration of this phenomenon than the *Kula* [**koo**-la], an extensive inter-island system of exchange in which high-ranking men gave ornamental shell armbands (*mwali*) and necklaces (*soulava*) to lifelong exchange partners on other islands. In the highly structured *Kula*, armbands traveled in one direction and necklaces in the opposite direction (Figure 7.4). For Trobriand Islanders these shell valuables were about the most valuable things one could

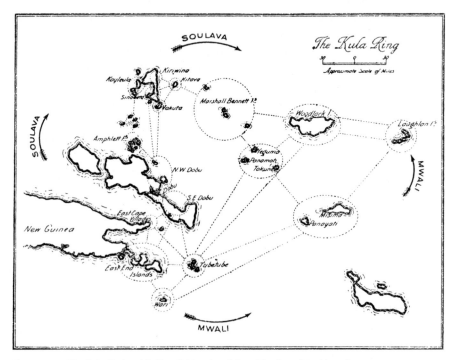

Figure 7.4   The *Kula* **Cycle with** *Mwali* **(Armbands) and** *Soulava* **(Necklaces).**

possess, even though men typically owned them for only a few months before they gave them to other partners (anthropologists call this **delayed reciprocity**, which means a long lag time between receiving a gift and paying it back). These shell valuables had no real function, as they were rarely worn, and had no other use. Their value came when they were given away because that is when they brought renown to the man who gave them away.

Malinowski also observed that when men sailed to visit their partners on another island, in addition to the armbands and necklaces, they always brought along many utilitarian goods, such as vegetables, fish, or pots to exchange on the side for things they could not get on their own island. Malinowski theorized that these ritualized *Kula* exchanges functioned to enhance the status of individual men and distribute goods people could not otherwise get on their home islands. *Kula* is such an important dimension of Trobriand society that colonialism did not undermine it. In fact, it has expanded in recent decades, involving more islands and lower-ranking individuals.

MAUSS AND THE SPIRIT OF THE GIFT

Marcel Mauss (1872–1950) was the founder of modern French anthropology. In 1924, he published his most influential work, *The Gift*, which compares gift exchange and its functions in a wide range of non-Western societies.

Unlike Malinowski, who viewed gift exchange primarily in terms of how it contributed to an individual's status and identity, Mauss viewed gift exchange in terms of how it builds group solidarity. Gift exchange, Mauss insisted, is steeped in morality and based on obligation, which has three dimensions: (1) *the obligation to give*, which establishes the giver as generous and worthy of respect; (2) *the obligation to receive*, which shows respect to the giver; and (3) *the obligation to return the gift in appropriate ways*, which demonstrates honor. It thus creates and maintains bonds of solidarity between people who would otherwise pursue their own personal interests (Mauss 1924/1954).

Later anthropologists have built on Mauss's insights into how gift exchange lies at the heart of human society. One of the most influential of these was Marshall Sahlins (1972), who argued that gift exchanges help manage group boundaries. Sahlins identified three types of reciprocity involved in gift exchange, each of which defines the social relationship between a giver and a receiver:

1. **Generalized reciprocity** refers to giving something without the expectation of return, at least not in the near future. It is uninhibited and generous giving, such as that which takes place between parents and children, married couples, or close-knit kin groups.
2. **Balanced reciprocity** occurs when a person gives something and expects the receiver to return an equivalent gift or favor at some point in the future. The *Kula* and American exchanges of birthday presents are examples.

3. **Negative reciprocity**, which economists call barter, is the attempt to haggle one's way into a favorable personal outcome. It exists between the most distant relations, such as between strangers or adversaries.

Sahlins's typology is useful because it suggests that social relationships shape the kinds of reciprocity that people practice. But recent studies of gift-giving have focused less on the objective types of reciprocity and more on how people interpret gift exchange.

Gift Exchange in Market-Based Economies

Although our cultural models dismiss its economic significance, gift exchange is important in American and European societies for a lot of the same reasons it is in other societies: it establishes social status, reaffirms relationships, and gives people access to the goods and sometimes influence that they want and need. As in any society, important implicit rules guide our gift exchange.

Figure 7.5   Marketing Celebrities to Sell Goods. Retailers try to help us overcome the impersonality of commodities by creating marketing campaigns that personalize their products. One strategy is to associate a product with a widely recognized celebrity, such as Beyoncé Knowles-Carter, pictured here. Celebrities can generate positive feelings about a product even if they don't actually say anything about its quality.

Even the gifts we give for holidays and birthdays follow implicit rules. Gifts between siblings or friends have to be repaid in equal value every bit as much as the *Kula* valuables do. Ideally, gifts should also be personal and embody the relationship between giver and receiver. Thus most Americans feel these gifts should not be cash, because it places a concrete value on the relationship. Somewhat less impersonal are **commodities** (mass-produced and impersonal goods with no meaning or history apart from themselves) bought at a mall. Yet in many ways commodities are equivalent to the money spent to buy them. One solution described by anthropologist James Carrier (1995) is to turn impersonal commodities into personal gifts by wrapping objects as personal presents, which symbolically distances the goods from an anonymous retail environment and suggests that the giver made a greater effort than simply going to a store (Figure 7.5).

Three points stand out here: (1) gift exchanges are deeply embedded in the social relations of every society; (2) by personalization we can transform impersonal commodities into personal gifts; and (3) we, like everyone else in the world, invest tremendous symbolic meaning in the things we give, receive, and consume. This third point has significant subtleties, which we explore in more detail in the next section.

THINKING CRITICALLY ABOUT ECONOMICS

According to anthropologists, "reciprocity," "exchange," and "sharing" each have different meanings. In what ways do you think these are different from each other?

⚘ What Is the Point of Owning Things?

People impose control and exclusive possession over objects, which raises the issue of ownership. As with all economic systems and transactions, questions about why people own things are best addressed through a cross-cultural lens.

Cross-Cultural Perspectives on Property

For anthropologists, ownership is about interactions between people. Two major issues characterize these interactions: (1) they are about the assertion and negotiation of rights in something, many of these rights being held not by individuals but by a group, and (2) they involve declarations and claims that are rooted in culturally specific forms of symbolic communication (Strang and Busse 2011:4).

For example, in societies where the kinds of gift-giving systems described in the previous section are pervasive, some objects cannot be given away. Annette Weiner (1992) calls these objects "inalienable possessions," and their inherent value transcends their exchange value. For example, the Maori "Sacred Cloak," made from the feathers of kiwis and other birds and worn traditionally by nobility, is understood to be a manifestation of a kin group's cosmological origins and historical continuity (Figure 7.6).

Figure 7.6   Maori Sacred Cloak.

It cannot be given away by any individual because rights in it are held by the kinship lineage.

Weiner observes that in some circumstances, inalienable possessions are transferred to others, but only as temporary loans. She contends that in an economy where the moral code is based on gift-giving, transferring such objects means that the giver/owner has rights over the receiver, thus creating status differences between people (Godelier 1999).

Appropriation and Consumption

So why do people come to want certain things in the first place? Sometimes it has to do with securing access to a critical resource, but often it also has to do with what a community considers "cool"—that is, impressive or trendy. But objects are not naturally "cool." Whatever symbolic distinctions or qualities they have are culturally constructed through the process of **consumption**, defined as the act of using and assigning meaning to a good, service, or relationship (see also Chapter 14). Through consumption people make cultural meaning, build social relationships, and create identities (Douglas and Isherwood 1978; Appadurai 1986). Every culture distinguishes between what is appropriate and what is inappropriate to consume, providing social avenues to consuming culturally accepted goods and limiting consumption of things considered inappropriate.

Consumption begins with an act of **appropriation**, which is a process of taking possession of the object and making it one's own (Miller 1995; Carrier 1996b). Consider, for example, the consumption of a smartphone. The initial act of appropriation takes place as you shop for it. Shopping entails narrowing your choices on the basis of price, size, look, brand, special features, and your sense of how you want to be seen by others, until you identify the device you want to buy. After paying for it, you continue the appropriation process by personalizing it—by downloading special apps, putting a particular case on it, and so on. These customizations, as well as how and when you use your smartphone, in turn reflect and define who you are as a person—for example, an informed techie who loves the latest gadgets or a social butterfly who is always networked—and your social position in society.

In societies where people still make many of the things they consume, people may be just as concerned with wanting "cool" things—things that identify the owner as worthy of respect—as many Americans are. Of course, other cultures' ideas of what "cool" is may differ greatly from ours. For instance, when people around Aitape on the North Coast of Papua New Guinea exchange food and other subsistence goods with their friends in neighboring villages, they also often give their partners handmade netted string bags with unique designs common to their home villages. String bags are a tangible manifestation of the trader's generosity and commitment to the social and economic relationship between the two exchange partners (Figure 7.7).

People are especially proud of the bags that come from very distant villages, because they indicate an extensive network of friends.

Returning to the situation that opens this chapter, it is clear that a shift toward a market economy in China made it possible for Chinese people to consume things they could not during the Maoist era. Consumerism itself was not new in China; many people had long been **consumers**, people who rely on goods and services not of their own making (Humphrey 2002:40). But consciousness of consumption changed. Now that the state no longer controls the production of many consumer goods, and foreign goods pour in, Chinese people have a bewildering array of choices about how and what to consume. The consumption patterns of new rich entrepreneurs—their choices of fashion, the cars they drive, the foods they eat, and so on—have become important because they help common Chinese people navigate through that variety and shape their sense of what objects and services carry symbolic prestige. The influx of new consumer goods is the grounds of creating new cultural meanings and social relationships in Chinese society.

Consumption is a key feature of capitalism, but if consumption varies around the globe, does the capitalist system also vary?

Figure 7.7 Prestige Goods. Although both of these bags are considered prestige goods in their specific cultures, a vast conceptual distance exists between how and why people consume them. String bags (top) represent an individual's wealth in social relationships, while Gucci bags (bottom) represent an individual's material wealth.

> **THINKING CRITICALLY ABOUT ECONOMICS**
>
> If it is true that changing consumption patterns are visible manifestations of broader cultural changes, what can the massive acquisition of cellular phones and smartphones by millions of people during the past decade tell us about changes in how people communicate?

❦ Does Capitalism Have Distinct Cultures?

For the better part of the twentieth century, capitalism and socialism existed as opposed forms of economic organization, an opposition that dominated global politics during the Cold War. After the collapse of the Soviet Union and Eastern Bloc regimes in 1989 and China's shift toward "Socialism with Chinese Characteristics," many economists and political leaders, especially in the United States, asserted that "capitalism won." But under the influence of local cultures, capitalism takes varied forms. As defined previously, capitalism is an economic system based on private ownership of the means of production, in which prices are set and goods distributed through a market. Beyond this generally accepted definition, theoretical approaches to capitalism vary depending on the researcher's philosophical approach (Blim 2000). For example, followers of influential sociologist Max Weber study the distinct types of capitalism that have existed in different times and places; formalists study capitalism through the actions of individuals and institutions; and Marxists study the changing nature of industrial production, the conditions of workers, and the connection between small-scale economic activities and broader global economic trends.

In spite of theoretical orientation, however, anthropologists view capitalism as a cultural phenomenon. In fact, its deepest assumptions are cultural: capitalism assumes certain values and ideals to be natural, in the sense that this is the way things really are. It seems inevitable that well-being can be achieved through consuming material things. But anthropologists also recognize that the cultural contexts and meanings of capitalist activities take diverse forms. Let us compare two examples—one drawn from Wall Street, the other from Malaysia—to illustrate how capitalist activities and meanings can vary across cultures.

Culture and Social Relations on Wall Street

Investment banks on Wall Street, site of the New York Stock Exchange and America's financial capital, are popularly seen as a bastion of individual entrepreneurialism and cold rationalism in pursuit of profits (Figure 7.8). But anthropologists have found that social relationships and cultural processes shape transactions on Wall Street in far more complex ways than our image of Wall Street may suggest.

What interests anthropologists is how people construct meanings in the context of such social relationships and how those meanings shape social action and individual conduct. For example, anthropologist Karen Ho (2009) studied investment banks and the international banking industry on Wall Street using participant observation and open-ended interviews. She reports that bankers and traders think

Figure 7.8   The New York Stock Exchange on Wall Street, the Heart of U.S. Capitalism.

of Wall Street as an entity that mediates vast and anonymous flows of capital throughout the world.

But Ho had conducted participant observation within these global networks as an investment banker herself, and she found that strong personal relationships were essential to successful transactions, precisely because the market was so vast and because the risks and strengths of any particular global segment were so difficult to decipher with assurance. As a result, bankers who told their clients they had "global reach" and coverage "everywhere in the world"—which was a central part of the image they promoted to convince investors to do business with them—were not being entirely honest. In reality, Ho found, most firms had minimal coverage in most parts of the world, often maintaining empty or barely staffed offices where they only occasionally did business. Their relationships with local banking firms and clients were nearly dormant, being reactivated only when new investment opportunities arose. Ho's point is that without the rich personal relationships and knowledge of local conditions and markets, these banks have almost no reach whatsoever, demonstrating that modern financial markets are every bit as dependent on social relationships and local knowledge as any daily transaction anthropologists might study in a rural village setting.

Entrepreneurial Capitalism Among Malays

The Southeast Asian nation of Malaysia provides an example of a very different culture of capitalism. During the past several decades, Malaysia has aggressively pursued economic growth through industrialization and the creation of investment opportunities. Malaysia is an Islamic country; the majority of the people are Muslim ethnic Malays. During British colonial times (early 1800s to the mid-1900s) the nation's Chinese minority dominated the economy and remained considerably better off than most of the Malay majority. Since the late 1960s the Malaysian government's goal for economic growth has been to reduce economic inequality between the country's ethnic Chinese and ethnic Malays by giving Malays preferential treatment and greater control over economic resources through set-aside provisions, government subsidies, special investment programs, and preferential opportunities for university education.

Anthropologist Patricia Sloane (1999) studied the impact of these policies on the culture of Malay entrepreneurs in urban Kuala Lumpur, Malaysia's capital. Few Malay capitalists in her study were extremely wealthy, but they were part of the growing Malaysian middle class. These Malay capitalists' aspirations are not "global" but self-consciously local. Their business ideology was embedded in local values and committed to promoting the economic interests and growth of the Malay ethnic group.

These processes have created a new class of Malay entrepreneurs who think of themselves as the cornerstone of a new, modernized Malaysia. They accept that capitalism is a self-interested enterprise, but they also feel bound by traditional Malay values, insisting on investment and development that serve traditional obligations to family, community, and other Malays. Their idea of capitalism is one in which wealth, social balance, and even salvation are the rewards for those who abide by the moral dictates of social responsibility and obligation. At the heart of these values lie Islamic economic principles—such as the prohibition on charging interest, prohibitions on exploitive or risky activities, and the obligation to share wealth after meeting one's family needs (Sloane 1999:73).

One effect of these ideals is that few enterprises are economically successful, so business failures are common. But Malays do not view these facts with embarrassment, because for many individuals the primary business goal is not to generate huge profits but to extend and deepen their social networks and to cultivate contacts with powerful people. Entrepreneurship is thus not simply about economic action and profit accumulation; it allows people to show how they are both fully engaged in the modern world of global capitalism and respectful of traditional Islamic and Malay obligations and values.

The challenge for Malays, in other words, has been to pursue a capitalist economy that both improves their material quality of life and conforms to their local cultural values, social practices, and on-the-ground realities. This challenge is not unique to Malaysia. In "Anthropologist as Problem Solver: Jim Yong Kim's Holistic, On-the-Ground Approach to Fighting Poverty," we consider how one anthropologist has sought to create capitalist development that is sensitive to local realities.

Anthropologist as Problem Solver
Jim Yong Kim's Holistic, On-the-Ground Approach to Fighting Poverty

When he became president of the World Bank in 2012, Jim Yong Kim was not just the first anthropologist and physician to hold such a high position in the world's largest development agency but was also the first leader to actually have direct work experience in the field of international development. Kim, who was raised in Iowa as the child of Korean War refugees, received an M.D. and a Ph.D. in medical anthropology from Harvard and is a co-founder of Partners in Health, a Massachusetts-based organization that provides high-quality health care for poor people in Haiti, Peru, Mexico, Russia, and parts of Africa. Within the World Bank, which had traditionally been led by economists or businessmen, there has been concern that someone whose career had focused so much on community-level health and humanitarian intervention is not an appropriate leader for an institution that lends money to Third World countries to promote capitalist economic development and fight poverty (Boseley 2012; Rice 2016).

But Kim has a different view on the matter. As an anthropologist, he understands that poor health is a symptom of—and a contributor to—deeper patterns of social inequality, poverty, and lack of economic opportunity. This understanding shaped the work he had done with Partners in Health, which was the first healthcare provider in Haiti to provide HIV and tuberculosis treatment for the poor. Kim and his colleagues approached community health as not just a matter of medical treatment, but as one that requires a holistic and on-the-ground approach working to remove the causes of poor health in the first place. There are many factors at work, including specific cultural patterns of disease transmission, dirty water, lack of food, political disempowerment, and weak access to jobs and economic opportunity. Partners in Health worked on all these issues, and many of them are the same ones the World Bank works on. But the World Bank addresses these things from a very different and abstract vantage point, one that involves looking at balance sheets, budget documents, and economic models and charts.

Jim Yong Kim.

continues

Anthropologist as Problem Solver *continued*

As a profit-driven development bank, the World Bank is a very different kind of institution than Partners in Health. Its lending practices and policies have long been criticized for deepening poverty and human suffering. But in the past couple of decades the World Bank has been changing, for example by introducing social and environmental safeguards into projects it funds. Kim, who had been a staunch critic of the bank, saw an opportunity to help further its evolution.

His presidency has brought a new sensibility to bank leadership informed by his holistic, on-the-ground anthropological background. This sensibility involves a greater appreciation of local development priorities, a deeper understanding of the actual impacts of economic policies on people's lives, and a stronger humanitarian orientation.

QUESTION FOR REFLECTION

1. What differences do you think exist between economists and anthropologists in terms of how they think about economic development?
2. What do you think are the advantages and disadvantages of Kim's holistic, on-the-ground perspective for determining economic development plans?

THINKING CRITICALLY ABOUT ECONOMICS

If capitalism can vary across cultures, do you think models of capitalist behavior and thought can also differ within a society? Can you think of any examples drawn from what you know about the different kinds of industries and businesses you would find in the American capitalist economic system? How can you explain the variability of capitalism within a single society?

✴ Conclusion

Most North Americans assume that the best way to get the things we need and want is to get a job and begin getting a paycheck. But this is definitely not how people do it everywhere in the world. Whether they are Chinese businessmen gaining access to business opportunities through the cultivation of *guanxi* and *renqing*, Trobriand Islanders trading for goods on other islands, or Malaysian entrepreneurs pursuing business practices informed by Islamic values, people differ in their cultural strategies and ideas about how to conduct their economic lives. And, when we step back and look at our own economic lives in a consumer capitalist society, we can see that we too have developed distinctive strategies for exchanging goods and money, such as when we symbolically transform commodities into personalized gifts or possessions.

Economic ideas and behaviors never exist independently of culture, morality, and social relationships. Culture shapes what is acceptable to transact, how and why a transaction occurs, and how the goods and services being exchanged are valued. This point is especially important for understanding the complexities of contemporary global economic changes. In an economically interconnected world, the creation of new markets and economic relationships has an impact on whether and how people in a particular place will be able to acquire certain goods and services. But these processes never occur in a cultural and social vacuum, which is why economic processes continue to play out in distinct ways in communities around the world.

Key Terms

Appropriation   p. 158
Balanced reciprocity   p. 155
Capitalism   p. 147
Commodities   p. 156
Commodity money   p. 151
Consumers   p. 159
Consumption   p. 158
Cultural economics   p. 149
Delayed reciprocity   p. 155
Division of labor   p. 147
Economic anthropology   p. 145

Economic system   p. 146
Exchange   p. 147
Fiat money   p. 151
Formal economics   p. 148
General purpose money   p. 151
Generalized reciprocity   p. 155
Limited purpose money   p. 151
Market   p. 147
Means of production   p. 149
Money   p. 151
Negative reciprocity   p. 156

Neoclassical economics   p. 147
Prestige economies   p. 150
Reciprocity   p. 154
Redistribution   p. 148
Spheres of exchange   p. 152
Substantive economics   p. 148
Surplus value   p. 149
Transactional orders   p. 152
Value   p. 145

Reviewing the Chapter

CHAPTER SECTION	WHAT WE KNOW	TO BE RESOLVED
Is money really the measure of all things?	Economies never exist independently of already existing social relationships and culture. Culture shapes what is acceptable to transact, how and why transactions take place, and how the goods or services being exchanged are valued.	Still unresolved is the issue of how to define the category "economic." Is it a particular logic and decision-making process? Or is it the substance of the economy, meaning how we provision ourselves through the daily transactions of goods and services?
How does culture shape the value and meaning of money?	People's relationships and attitudes toward money depend on factors such as whether their society uses general purpose money and/or limited purpose money; whether it uses commodity money or fiat money; spheres of exchange; and cultural distinctions between transactional orders.	Anthropologists are still working through the diverse cultural meanings of money, especially the ways money circulates and shifts meanings through distinct transactional orders.

CHAPTER SECTION	WHAT WE KNOW	TO BE RESOLVED
Why is gift exchange such an important part of all societies?	The exchange of things is a universal feature of human existence. Many societies have met people's material and social necessities through highly organized and principled gift exchanges, but rich subtleties and cross-cultural variations exist in how, when, what, and why people engage in gift exchange.	Although anthropologists accept the central importance of gift exchange in all societies, they continue to embrace distinct theoretical models concerning reciprocity and gift exchange, and debates persist over whether these models adequately capture the complexity of other cultures' approaches to reciprocity.
What is the point of owning things?	Anthropologists approach ownership and property not as static legal categories but as culturally variable matters of social interaction and as bundles of rights. People often want to own things they think are "cool," but the symbolic distinctions and qualities that make objects cool and worthy of respect are always culturally constructed.	People's relationships with objects are more complicated than economic perspectives on consumption suggest. Anthropologists are still documenting and seeking to understand those complexities.
Does capitalism have distinct cultures?	Capitalism is as much an economic system as it is a cultural phenomenon, whose actual practices and cultural models vary across and within cultures.	The idea that capitalism is not a monolithic economic structure but a variable culturally diverse set of practices is not universally accepted in anthropology, especially by Marxist anthropologists.

Politics

Cooperation, Conflict, and Power Relations

If you follow the news, you'll know that reporting about politics is a major focus of any newspaper or news website. Stories about what the president recently said, conflicts between political parties, or scandals involving local political figures tend to dominate the headlines. But even as these kinds of stories are the lifeblood of public discourse in any country, they offer a fairly narrow view of what politics actually is. Why do we not find stories like the following?

- In Papua New Guinea, a young woman commits suicide in protest of being abused by a man, to motivate her male relatives to seek justice and reparations.
- In a village in the Venezuelan Amazon, a Yanomami headman scrapes the ground with a machete to shame others to join him in cleaning the village before a feast.

Revenge Suicide as Politics. This painting (detail) represents a suicide performed as a revenge against wrongdoing in Papua New Guinea, by native artist Apa Hugo. See page 176 for a discussion of the complete image.

- In 1930s Italy, government officials concerned with the problem of declining fertility among the Italian people introduce a census, social insurance programs, housing projects, and social work to support an increase in the size, growth rate, and "vitality" of the population.
- In Cameroon, high-ranking government officials use sorcery to undermine their rivals and impress villagers with their immunity from occult forces.
- In Hawaii, a community leader guides disputing adversaries and family members through a healing process in which everyone is expected to share their feelings and grievances openly.

Of course, one reason we do not find such reporting about politics in U.S. news is that these events have little or no bearing on the lives of most of us. But it is easy to come to the conclusion that politics is simply what politicians or political parties said and did in the latest news cycle. Anthropologists take a wider view of **politics**, understanding it to be those relationships and processes of cooperation, conflict, social control, and power that are fundamental aspects of human life.

The preceding list also suggests that people exert power in diverse ways. Some of these are formal and fairly stable, through institutions and procedures—government offices, armies, codified laws, rituals, or legal proceedings—that are easily identifiable elements of most societies. Others are less formal and more fleeting, such as the creation of alliances, or acts of protest, accusation, sorcery, and shame. Techniques include coercion, oppression, persuasion, and influence, as well as truth-seeking, the collection and sharing of information, and the desire to know intimate details about people's lives.

This approach to politics moves beyond the idea that modern states, which function through elections, bureaucracies, and so on, should be the sole focus of anthropological interest. Just as important is the diversity in how people around the world manage power relations at all levels of social life, from the interpersonal to the national and transnational. We can hardly begin to understand this diversity if we focus exclusively on the formal institutions of modern states, because that approach misses the fact that cooperation, conflict, social control, and power are rooted in and emerge from people's everyday social interactions, belief systems, and cultural practices.

At the heart of anthropology's approach to politics is a key question: *How is power acquired and transmitted in a society?* Embedded in this broader question are the following problems, around which this chapter is organized:

Does every society have a government?

What is political power?

Why do some societies seem more violent than others?

How do people avoid aggression, brutality, and war?

For anthropologists, politics is about how people manage their everyday social relationships through force, influence, persuasion, and control over resources. But before we understand how these processes work in different societies, we need to address the opportunities and pitfalls of thinking about politics solely in terms of how formal political systems work.

✿ Does Every Society Have a Government?

This question might seem strange because the answer seems so obvious. Our society has **government** (a separate legal and constitutional domain that is the source of law, order, and legitimate force) from the federal level down to the most local. We may assume other societies must have something similar. Otherwise, wouldn't they be in the throes of anarchy? Not necessarily. Consider the !Kung San (also known as Ju/'hoansi), a hunter-gatherer society in the Kalahari Desert of southern Africa. !Kung have historically lived in egalitarian bands of fifteen to twenty people and are an **acephalous society**—that is, they have no governmental head or hierarchical structure. Until they were brought under the control of the Namibian and South African governments, !Kung did not even have a notion of a distinct political sphere, and important band decisions were made by group consensus. Leadership was informal, life was organized around sharing food, and those who did not share were taunted and shamed mercilessly, or even pushed out of the band (Figure 8.1).

Figure 8.1   The Power of Sharing.   In many hunter-gatherer societies, such as the !Kung San pictured here, individuals are obligated to share their goods, especially food. This obligation represents a powerful force for ensuring social stability.

The emphasis on sharing and egalitarianism kept people more or less in line without the need for government or **laws**, which are a set of rules established by some formal authority.

If governments are not a universal feature of human existence, why do we tend to think of politics primarily in terms of how formal governments work? Part of the reason is historical, the other part philosophical.

The Idea of "Politics" and the Problem of Order

Our modern notion of politics emerged during the Enlightenment (1650–1800), a period of social upheaval in Western Europe in which the rise of industrial capitalism and revolutionary democracies challenged the existing social and political order. Two of the major figures concerned with the problem of disorder caused by these changes were the English philosophers Thomas Hobbes (1588–1679) and John Locke (1632–1704). Hobbes believed that humans are naturally selfish, competitive, and warlike, leading to violence and a chaotic free-for-all as people pursue their own personal interests, a condition avoided only by the absolute rule of a monarch (Hobbes 1909). Locke disagreed, arguing that chaos was avoidable by creating a more limited government based on a "social contract" in which certain basic individual rights are recognized (Locke 2003). This is our modern idea—and justification—for democratic government, and it is what modern politicians refer to when they talk about the "rule of law."

Structural-Functionalist Models of Political Stability

During the early twentieth century, the global expansion of British colonialism helped fuel the rise of British anthropology. Colonial authorities often turned to anthropologists to help them make sense of the foreign societies now under British control. This situation presented British anthropologists with important opportunities to study the maintenance of order in societies without formal governments and political leaders. The theory they used was **structural-functionalism**, which held that the different structures of a society (religion, politics, kinship, etc.) functioned in an integrated way to maintain social order and control.

In Africa, structural-functionalists identified numerous ways in which societies maintained order and social control without formal political institutions (Radcliffe-Brown 1952). For example, kinship could work, as it did among the Nuer pastoralists of Sudan, to organize men into lineages that normally live separately but would come together to meet external threats. The division of men from different families into associations like **age-grades** (groupings of age-mates who are initiated into adulthood together), such as among the Maasai of Kenya and Tanzania, could work as a rudimentary political system (Kurtz 2001). Beliefs in witchcraft or sorcery can also promote order. Throughout Africa, for example, people who do not behave according to community norms are identified and punished as witches. Without formal courts, structural-functionalists insisted, such practices maintained social control and operated as a criminal justice system (Gledhill 2000).

Neo-Evolutionary Models of Political Organization: Bands, Tribes, Chiefdoms, and States

In the 1940s and 1950s, as political anthropology was taking shape in the United States, American anthropologists called neo-evolutionists sought to classify the world's diversity of political systems and explain how complex political systems, especially states, had evolved from simpler forms of social and political organization. Anthropologists Marshall Sahlins and Elman Service (1960) suggested a typology of societies with different forms of political and economic organization. By considering who controls food and other resources in any given society, they defined four types of society: **bands, tribes, chiefdoms**, and **states**. This typology was intended both to describe different kinds of society as well as to explain how more complex political forms had developed from simpler ones.

Bands and tribes in this scheme were examples of **non-centralized political systems**, in which power and control over resources are dispersed among members of the society. Chiefdoms and states were examples of **centralized political systems**, in which certain individuals and institutions hold power and control over resources. Table 8.1 outlines how this classification incorporates politics, economy, size, and population density.

Challenges to Traditional Political Anthropology

Political anthropology's early focus on political systems was valuable for describing the diverse ways in which humans create and maintain social order, with or without formal governments. But reality hardly ever corresponds to these simple theoretical models. A major problem with the bands–tribes–chiefdoms–states typology is that many cases blur the boundaries between types. For example, a society might have tribe-like qualities, as is the case with the Nuer, but because it has a population of 1.8 million people, it does not have the same kinds of social relations as a "tribe" of 500 people.

The emphasis on static political systems and order came at the expense of understanding the historical and dynamic nature of political processes, characterized by conflict, intrigue, manipulation, and other techniques of control. As the British anthropologist Lucy Mair (1969) pointed out, political structures only provide individuals with roles. Within a role, individuals make choices and decisions, manipulate others, and strategize, all in the pursuit of power. From this point of view, the proper focus of political anthropology is political power, an issue we turn to next.

TABLE 8.1

A NEO-EVOLUTIONARY TYPOLOGY OF POLITICAL ORGANIZATION

	NON-CENTRALIZED		CENTRALIZED	
	Band	**Tribe**	**Chiefdom**	**State**
Type of subsistence	Foraging	Horticulture and pastoralism	Extensive agriculture, intensive fishing	Intensive agriculture
Population density	Low	Low to medium	Medium	High
Type of economic exchange	Reciprocity	Reciprocity and trade	Redistribution through chief, reciprocity at lower levels	Markets and trade; redistribution through state based on taxation
Social stratification	Egalitarian	Egalitarian	Ranked	Social classes
Ownership of property	Little or no sense of personal ownership	Lineage or clan ownership of land and livestock	Lineage or clan ownership of land, but with strong sense of personal ownership	Private and state ownership of land
Type of leadership	Informal and situational; headman	Charismatic headman with some authority group decision-making	Charismatic chief with limited power, usually based on giving benefits to followers	Sovereign leader supported by aristocratic bureaucracy
Law and legitimate control of force	No formal laws or punishments; right to use force is communal	No formal laws or punishments; right to use force is held by lineage, clan, or association	May have informal laws and specified punishments; chief has limited access to coercion	Formal laws and punishments; state holds all access to use of physical force
Some examples	!Kung San (southern Africa); Inuit (Canada, Alaska); Batek (Malaysia)	Yanomami (South America); Nuer (South Sudan); Cheyenne (United States)	Kwakiutl (Canada, Alaska); precolonial Hawaii	Aztec (Mexico); Inca (Peru); Euro-American monarchies and representative democracies

Source: Adapted from Lewellen (1983:20–21).

THINKING CRITICALLY ABOUT POLITICS

A complex institution like your college or university has many ways of governing the faculty, staff, and student body. These include formal institutions of governance, such as a faculty senate or president's office, as well as less formal associations and belief structures that help maintain order. What are some of these less formal forms of governance, and how do they contribute to the maintenance of order?

⚘ What Is Political Power?

The shift from viewing politics as a problem of order to viewing it as a problem of how people gain and wield power began to flourish in the 1960s and continues to the present. Power is typically considered to be the ability to make people think or act in certain ways, through physical coercion or through more symbolic means, such as persuasion (Kingsolver 1996). Beyond this very general definition, however, there are many nuances to political power.

Defining Political Power

Whether it is an exchange of goods, a religious ceremony, or a conversation between a man and a woman, practically all aspects of human existence are imbued with power. But not all power is *political*. For anthropologists, **political power** refers to how power is created and enacted to attain goals that are presumed to be for the good of a community, the common good (Kurtz 2001:21).

The exercise of political power requires legitimacy. Legitimacy can come from an independent source—a source outside the individuals that make up a community—such as gods or ancestors, inheritance, some high office, the ability to cure an illness, or the outcome of some legal process, such as an election. Or it can come from a dependent source—that is, power given by other social actors: *granted* from one leader to another, *delegated* from a leader to a follower for a specific purpose, or *allocated* by the community to a leader (Kurtz 2001:26).

In addition, political power is tied to control over material resources (territory, money, or other culturally defined goods); human resources (willing followers and supporters); and symbolic resources (flags, uniforms, badges of rank, or other objects that give meaning to political action) (Figure 8.2). There are other important dimensions to political power.

Political Power Is Action-Oriented

People everywhere gain and manage political power through a combination of decision-making, cooperation, opportunism, compromise, collusion, charm, gamesmanship, strategic alliance, factionalism, resistance, conflict, and other processes. A focus on these processes was central to **action theory**, an approach that emerged in the 1960s. Action theorists closely followed the daily activities and decision-making processes of individual political leaders like chiefs in African villages or headmen in Amazonian settlements. They argue that politics is a dynamic and competitive field of social relations in which people are constantly managing their ability to exercise power over others (Vincent 1978). In other words, it is not enough to *be* president of the United States; one has to *act* as the president.

To follow political action, one must be familiar with a society's specific rules and codes about who gets to exercise power and under what conditions. Anthropologist F. G. Bailey (1969) compared these codes to those of playing a game. In politics, as in a game, there are *normative rules*, fairly stable and explicit ethical

Figure 8.2   The Symbolism of Trump's Baseball Cap.   As candidate for president of the United States, Donald Trump wore baseball caps bearing his "Make America Great Again" campaign slogan. The message it conveyed was fittingly patriotic, but more importantly, its presence on a common baseball cap allowed the billionaire Trump to portray himself to his core white, working-class followers as a "man of the people" and thus an appropriate candidate to represent them.

norms by which players must abide, such as honesty, fairness, and so on. There are also *pragmatic rules*, which are the creative manipulations necessary to win the game itself. For example, in U.S. politics, normative rules require political actors to be open, fair, and honest. But we know, based on reading the political news in the newspaper, that there are also the pragmatic rules of gaining and holding on to power, which often involve favoritism and even outright lying (Lewellen 2003).

Political Power Is Structural

It became clear to political anthropologists by the 1980s and 1990s that certain power relationships transcend any individual. Political anthropologists began to refer to such power as **structural power**, which is power that not only operates within settings but also organizes and orchestrates the settings in which social and individual action take place (Wolf 2001:384). "Structure" here means something very different from how the early structural-functionalists understood it. They were interested in social institutions ("structures," as a noun), while this newer perspective focuses on the mix of social processes, relationships, and institutions that shape or "structure" (as a verb) social action.

In this view, power does not lie in a group or individual's exercise of will over others through domination or manipulation, but is dispersed in many shapes and forms, produced and reproduced through the combined actions of important social institutions, science and other knowledge producers, and people living their everyday lives (Foucault 1978). Anthropologist David Horn (1994) used this approach to study how and why Italians of today accept state intervention in their lives. He traces their acceptance to the rise of social thought, planning, and research around the reproductive health of Italian families after World War I. During this period, the Italian government instituted a census and other programs to measure statistically the population's size, growth rate, and health conditions. Using this information, they instituted new policies of hygiene and family management, including a 1927 tax on bachelorhood and efforts to eliminate contraception and abortion. Although many of these policies failed, Horn observes that these changes had an important effect on Italians, in that they came to accept the idea that the body is not simply the domain of a private individual, but a social problem that requires scientific and state intervention. As a result they began to willingly accept that they should share intimate details about their reproductive lives with the state and that the state has the right to issue directives intended to manage citizens' lives—all of which are ideas that Italians take for granted today.

Political Power Is Gendered

During the past forty years, feminist anthropologists have observed that while men tend to dominate formal political processes in most societies, relationships between men and women intersect with political power in complex ways. In a number of societies, women exercise formal leadership and political power. In other settings, women may have very little formal power, but they can mobilize to assert power in response to events.

In many societies, women may be so disempowered politically and socially that their ability to take direct action lies only in the most dramatic action of all, taking one's own life. For example, on the island of New Britain in Papua New Guinea, some women commit "revenge suicide" in response to abuse or shame (Figure 8.3). Here young women are powerless figures. But a woman's act of suicide shifts the burden of shame to her tormentor (often a husband), and it can even mobilize her own male relatives and other community members to acknowledge the injustice, forcing them to seek accountability from the offending party (Counts 1980). Although taking such actions may be difficult for many Westerners to comprehend, this situation suggests we must consider forms of political power that are available to those we do not conventionally understand to be "powerful."

Political Power in Non-State Societies

To some extent, the exercise of political power differs between state and non-state societies. For example, in non-state societies such as tribal societies of South America and Melanesia, power tends to be temporary and episodic, emerging from personal charisma, not from elections or inheritance from a powerful parent. The Amazon headman, for example, is "a first among equals." He assumes

Figure 8.3 Revenge Suicide in New Guinea. This painting by contemporary Papua New Guinea artist Apa Hugo from 2003 illustrates how suicide can be used as a weapon of the weak. The caption written on the painting in Pidgin English means: "A man fights with his wife and the wife commits suicide. Her parents are distraught and cry in mourning" (*Man krosim meri na—meri i wari na i go sua sait. Na papa mama i wari na karai i stap*).

his status as leader by being able to persuade followers, not because he controls power or resources on his own. Such leaders, who are sometimes called Big Men, cannot transfer their status and power through inheritance when they die. A Big Man cannot force others to do anything, but he gains influence and authority by giving away wealth and shrewdly persuading others, through a combination of smooth talk and peer pressure, to produce goods they will provide him, which he can then redistribute. In their 1970 documentary film *The Feast*, filmmaker Timothy Asch and anthropologist Napoleon Chagnon (1997) show how a Yanomami headman in southern Venezuela sponsors a feast aimed at building an alliance with another community with which his own community had recently been at war. As headman he could not force anyone to help clear the plaza or cook the plantain soup that would be the centerpiece of the feast. His loud haranguing did little to motivate his fellow clan members, but when he led by example his clansmen started helping and made it a successful feast, forming a new alliance. Persuasion was his most valuable tool.

In contrast to the status leadership of a Big Man, the kind of political power your hometown mayor has is a quintessential expression of how political power works in a state society. Your mayor is an officeholder, a person who gets power from his or her elected or appointed office. In state societies and chiefdoms, power and authority reside in offices and institutions. Formal rules dictate who can gain an office and the conditions under which it can be gained. Officeholders usually have greater access to resources, such as money from taxes and a bureaucracy that can exercise social control over a community. Like Big Men, however, mayors and other American officials often draw on their personal connections to achieve things.

The Political Power of the Contemporary Nation-State

Modern states are typically called **nation-states**, independent states recognized by other states and composed of people who share a single national identity. A nation is a population who thinks of itself as "a people" based on sharing—or imagining that they share—a common culture, language, heritage, identity, or commitment to particular political institutions (Robbins 2001:82). The political form of the nation-state originated in Europe several hundred years ago, but it has become so common that now all the world's territory falls under the control of one or another nation-state.

Contrary to Locke's idealizations of the "social contract," membership in a nation-state is not typically voluntary. For many of the world's peoples, conquest and colonialism forced them into nation-states. Leaders of nation-states exercise various forms of political power to assert social control over non-state societies and to ensure the conformity of all their citizens.

These forms of social control include promoting a sense of unity by drawing symbolic lines between those who are included—often it is some version of the "chosen people"—and those who are excluded. Excluded groups may be defined as enemies (citizens of competing nation-states, or non-state actors such as "terrorists") or as inferior because of racial or ethnic differences. Nation-states exercise power over their citizens by creating and managing information about them using institutionalized surveillance, through means such as issuing national identity cards, distributing censuses, monitoring social media, wiretapping, and hacking computers. Surveillance secures and expands leaders' power and authority, by identifying potential opposition or non-conformism threatening their authority. Many nation-states also use prisons, torture, and violence against citizens who do not conform to dominant values or identities (Figure 8.4).

People around the world have long understood the tradeoffs of living within nation-states, and not surprisingly, many have resisted and evaded their absorption and assimilation by states. Political scientist and anthropologist James Scott (2009) has described how, for two thousand years, disparate groups of people

Figure 8.4   Trail of Tears.   The 1830 Indian Removal Act in the United States forcibly moved Indians from Georgia, Alabama, Mississippi, and Florida to Indian Territory (now Oklahoma). This state-sponsored policy cleared Indians from lands desired by whites, leading to the deaths of thousands of Indians.

have been living in upland Southeast Asia in basically stateless societies. The region, known as Zomia, is a rugged and remote mountainous region the size of Europe that consists of parts of seven contemporary nation-states, extending from India and Myanmar in the west through China and into Vietnam, Laos, Cambodia, and Thailand in the east. The 100 million or so people who live in this highly ethnically and linguistically diverse region have historically avoided the control of lowland states by living in dispersed, autonomous communities. According to Scott, over time these groups came to the highlands fleeing slavery, conscription, taxes, epidemics, and warfare in the lowlands. They have histori-cally been mobile, avoiding persecution by pushing deeper into the highlands and developing subsistence patterns, such as foraging and shifting cultivation (see Chapter 6), that enable regular movement. Their identities are also flexible, rooted in the maintenance of oral traditions and the reinvention of kinship gene-alogies as groups move around from country to country. Scott suggests that this long history of autonomy may be coming to an end as contemporary nation-states have begun to assert greater control in these remote areas with the aid of what he calls "distance-demolishing" technologies, such as roads, bridges, airplanes, modern weapons systems, and global positioning systems (Scott 2009:11).

Although nation-states introduce new political dynamics—especially for-malized political parties and bureaucratized elections—it is important to stress that the political mechanisms that we have explored in non-state societies can also operate in state settings. There is no absolute separation between state and non-state political organization. One illustration is that in a number of West

Anthropologist as Problem Solver
Maxwell Owusu and Democracy in Ghana

Since its independence from Britain in 1957, the West African country of Ghana has alternated between civilian- and military-controlled national governments. When the most recent military government (1981–1992) allowed elections in 1992, the Fourth Republic of Ghana emerged, based on a new constitution with a foundation in democratic principles.

An influential actor in that process was Ghanaian-born political anthropologist Maxwell Owusu of the University of Michigan. Owusu served as a consulting member of the Constitutional Experts Committee, which drafted the 1992 constitution proposals. Owusu has been a staunch critic of autocratic and repressive leadership in post-independence Ghana and other African nation-states. He is an advocate of popular participatory democracy. But as an anthropologist he understood the problems of imposing foreign political models—such as Western-style democracy with competing political parties—on African societies with different histories and indigenous political traditions. As he has written (Owusu 1992:384), "African

democracy may require the integration of indigenous methods of village co-operation with innovative forms of government, combining the power of universal rights with the uniqueness of each district's or nation's own customs and respected traditions."

A viable solution, Owusu insisted, is to create a decentralized state in which local authorities, primarily chiefs, headmen, and lineage heads, participate directly in state processes and decision-making. The advantage is that local leaders can better identify the needs and priorities of villagers, and be more accountable to their communities than can bureaucrats in a state apparatus. The 1992 constitution of Ghana put this insight to work, creating "District Assemblies" as the basic unit of national government, two thirds of which are elected and one third appointed, the latter being mostly traditional leaders or their representatives (Owusu 1992). Owusu observed that far from making chiefs and other non-state political leaders obsolete, these changes have put traditional leaders at the forefront of political change in the nation-state as a whole (Owusu 1996).

QUESTIONS FOR REFLECTION

1. How does Owusu's notion of participatory democracy, which relies upon decentralization of power toward local traditional leaders, differ from the way local governments at the city, town, or county level work in the United States?

2. Is it likely to be true that local traditional leaders are better able to identify local priorities than national leaders are?

Maxwell Owusu.

African countries where witchcraft beliefs are common, including Cameroon, campaigning politicians will often seek out and associate with sorcerers. While the Cameroonian government officially rejects witchcraft, some prominent politicians openly accept and perpetuate the idea that they draw on occult powers to defeat their political rivals, because it enhances their power among villagers for whom sorcery remains an important means of social control and authority (Rowlands and Warnier 1988).

Leaders of nation-states also often coopt local political actors and their power to serve their own or their nation-state's ends. In post-independence Ghana, for example, where chiefs, headmen, and extended family lineages control village-level resources and political processes, centralized governments have coopted traditional non-state leaders by rewarding some with high-level positions in the state bureaucracy. Such an appointment to a governmental position makes the leader responsible at the local level for enforcing national laws and mobilizing support for state-led development programs (Owusu 1996). For several decades, anthropologist Maxwell Owusu has researched how this kind of political power works in post-independence Ghana. He has advocated formally incorporating non-state political leaders into nation-state functions. In "Anthropologist as Problem Solver: Maxwell Owusu and Democracy in Ghana," we examine how his ideas have been put to work.

We have so far discussed the exercise of political power in terms of the cultivation of relationships, persuasion, the collection of information, or the strategic manipulation of others. But violence is also a strategic means of gaining and holding onto political power, and in some societies it seems more common and accepted than in others. In the next section, we explore this issue in more detail.

THINKING CRITICALLY ABOUT POLITICS

As this section shows, different anthropologists have approached political power in different ways. Do you think each of these approaches creates a fundamentally different picture of how political power works? Why or why not?

Why Do Some Societies Seem More Violent Than Others?

By the 1960s, a number of the societies anthropologists studied were experiencing intense post-independence violence, disruption, and conflict related to the end of European colonialism. This situation prompted an urgent concern to understand the relationship between political power and violence, and why political conflicts in some societies seemed to break out in violence more than conflicts did in other societies. What might be done to end and prevent future violence?

In pursuing answers to these questions, anthropologists have learned that violence is a form of power relations rooted in cultural processes and meanings, just as other strategies of political power, such as persuasion and manipulation, are.

What Is Violence?

Violence is typically defined as the use of force to harm someone or something. It is a highly visible and concrete assertion of power, and a very efficient way to transform a social environment and communicate an ideological message (Riches 1986).

Yet specifying what violence consists of is not always so straightforward, because violence is different things to different people (Eller 2006). The same person might acknowledge that shoving a person into a vat of boiling water is violent, yet may not view placing a lobster in that boiling water as violent. Another factor in assessing what is violent is intention: Did the perpetrator mean to do it (violent), or was it an accident (probably not violent)? And rationality: Did the perpetrator have control over his or her actions (violent), or was it a case of "losing one's mind" (probably not violent, or at least justified)? And legitimacy: Was it a legitimate act, such as a boxer beating on another boxer (sports, not violence), or deviant, such as a man beating his wife (violent)? Even the nature of force: Was the force personal, as in one person punching another (violent), or structural, as in economic conditions depriving a child of food (open to debate)? And depending on whether you are a victim, perpetrator, or witness, you are likely to have a different perspective on whether or not an act is violent.

Even though we might all agree that violence involves some element of harm and an assertion of power over others, people nevertheless have differing opinions on what constitutes violence. Some of these opinions are individually held, but some are related to differences in how we as members of a particular culture define violence and give meaning to it. Culture shapes not only how people think about violence but also how, why, and when they use it as a form of power over others.

Violence and Culture

Since Hobbes, Europeans and Americans have seen violence as a natural condition of humans. But anthropologists offer two major challenges to this view: (1) neither violence nor its opposite, nonviolence, is an inevitable condition of humanity; both are learned behaviors that express themselves in particular social and historical circumstances; and (2) violence is generally not chaotic and arbitrary, but tends to follow explicit cultural patterns, rules, and ethical codes.

NEITHER VIOLENCE NOR NONVIOLENCE IS INEVITABLE IN HUMAN SOCIETIES

In recent years, it has become fashionable to think of aggression and violence as genetically determined. But no animal or human carries genes for dominance, aggression, or passivity. These complex social and psychological conditions and states involve biological processes, such as the production of certain hormones, but they are not fixed properties or traits carried by genes.

So how should we deal with claims—some even made by anthropologists—that some societies are fierce and war-like and others peaceful? The answer, of course, is by demonstrating that neither violence nor nonviolence is universal (Fry 2006). Two famous examples—the Yanomami and the Semai—illustrate our point.

THE YANOMAMI AND THE SEMAI

Anthropologist Napoleon Chagnon (1968) described the Yanomami Indians of southern Venezuela, with whom he has worked since the early 1960s, as the "fierce people." According to Chagnon, the Yanomami have an aggressive style about nearly everything they do. They stage brutal raids against enemy settlements, and they routinely have violent responses to their fellow clansmen (Figure 8.5).

But other anthropologists, including Brian Ferguson (1995) and Jacques Lizot (1985), have seen the Yanomami in a different light, as warm and caring people who from time to time had to defend themselves against enemies. Ferguson's research suggests that Yanomami "fierceness" was not the traditional behavior of these Amazonian Indians, but the result of contact with foreigners: missionaries, prospectors, government officials, and anthropologists such as Chagnon, who has come under fire by Yanomami themselves for disrupting their society (Tierney 2002; see also the "Thinking Like an Anthropologist" box in Chapter 1).

A similar point can be made about a very different case, that of the Semai, egalitarian swidden farmers who live in the Malaysian rainforest. Anthropologist Robert Dentan (1968) characterized the Semai as peaceful and nonviolent because they committed little or no interpersonal violence during his field research. The Semai view themselves as peaceful and reject the idea that violence is a natural condition of human life. At the heart of Semai commitment to nonviolence is a valued concept of *persusah*, referring to the value of not causing trouble for others. But the Semai are not completely nonviolent: during the communist insurrection in Malaysia from 1948 to 1960, some Semai became soldiers and a few were renowned fighters. Although Dentan had consistently described the ethos of the Semai as nonviolent and peaceful, he did quote one former soldier who described himself and his comrades in the counterinsurgency as "drunk with blood" (1968:58–59). Robarchek

Figure 8.5   The "Fierce People."   In the ethnographic film *The Ax Fight*, from which this image is drawn, the filmmakers represent Yanomami lives as filled with aggression and near-constant violence. But is it really so?

and Dentan (1987) argue that the Semai are indeed socialized to be nonviolent, but when they were brought into the counterinsurgency they were socialized as soldiers and trained to kill.

The point of these examples is that violence and nonviolence are not absolute or static conditions. They are the result of cultural attitudes and particular social and historical conditions (Fry 2006).

Explaining the Rise of Violence in Our Contemporary World

Anthropologists have long observed that violence and the threat of violence, far from implying chaos, can actually encourage social order because they reflect culturally specific patterns, rules, and ethical codes. These patterns define when and why violence is acceptable, what forms of violence are appropriate, and who can engage in violent acts.

In news reports, pundits routinely explain the rise of violence around the globe as a chaotic outburst of meaningless "tribal" and "ethnic" tensions (Whitehead 2004). Such accounts appear to offer a tidy narrative that seems to explain so much of what is going on in our contemporary world, but they are based on a fundamental misunderstanding of the relationship between violence and culture.

IT IS NOT INEVITABLE THAT DIFFERENT ETHNIC GROUPS WILL FIGHT

The countries that made up the former Yugoslavia in southeastern Europe, in a region known as the Balkans, share the stereotype of ethnic and religious tribalism. We even have a word for it—*balkanization*—which refers to the fragmentation of society into hostile factions. During the Bosnian civil war in the 1990s, foreign journalists tended to describe acts of violence by Serbs, Croats, and Muslims as "ethnic violence" based on centuries-old hatred between these ethnic groups.

But this explanation ignores long histories of coexistence, cultural interchange, and peaceful relations that anthropologists had observed in the region (Lockwood 1975; Bringa 2005) (Figure 8.6). A more complex understanding of the conflict sees violence as a byproduct of a struggle over political power among nationalist leaders after the fall of communism. Seeking to consolidate their hold over political power and state institutions, nationalists on all sides used the media to broadcast daily doses of fear, hatred, and dehumanizing images of people from the other "ethnic" group (Bringa

Figure 8.6   A Peaceful Balkans.   At the time of the 1984 Olympic Games in the Bosnian capital city of Sarajevo, commentators celebrated longstanding peaceful relations between Serbs, Croats, and Muslims in this modern city, challenging any notion of "ancient seething hatreds" portrayed in later years.

2005). They used targeted violence on people of other ethnic backgrounds. All of these factors created fear and a sense of powerlessness among ordinary people. So when nationalist leaders eventually called on people to attack their neighbors of different backgrounds, some did just that, leading to now well-known incidents of incredible brutality and horror in places such as Srebrenica, the site of a mass killing of Bosnian Muslims by Bosnian Serbs (Oberschall 2000).

At the same time, many people found ways to protect their neighbors of different ethnic backgrounds from being attacked. In other words, even in a period of intense, artificially created ethnic conflict, not everybody participated in the violence, and many did not give in to the ethnic hatred that others promoted. Both points undermine any simplistic story of seething tribalism. Ethnic conflict is not an inevitable condition, and in this case it was manufactured to serve the political and ideological interests of certain leaders.

VIOLENCE IS A MEANINGFUL POLITICAL STRATEGY

In the United States, we sometimes hear in the media about events like suicide bombings in Iraqi markets and cafés; machete attacks on innocent people in Liberia, Rwanda, and Sierra Leone in Africa; or plane hijackings by some militant group. Commentators often call these shocking acts "meaningless" and "barbaric." But such acts are never meaningless: they are meaningful—to both victims and perpetrators—although the different sides interpret the violence very differently (Whitehead 2004). For one side the message is threat and hostility, and for the other it is a message of martyrdom and devotion to a cause.

When people refer to such acts as meaningless and barbaric, they interpret violence as emotional, beyond reason. In fact, violence and the threat of violence are often used as strategic tools for pursuing particular political ends. Consider, for example, the civil war in Sierra Leone (1991–2002), in which at least 50,000 people died. This conflict, waged between the government and a "people's army" called the Revolutionary United Front (RUF), gained widespread notoriety as a barbaric and brutal conflict.

According to British anthropologist Paul Richards (1996), the violence was anything but wanton and mindless. He explained that machete attacks, rape, throat slitting, and other acts of terror were "rational ways of achieving intended strategic outcomes" (Richards 1996:58). For example, during 1995 the RUF frequently cut off the hands of village women. This practice was strategically calculated to communicate a political message to the RUF's own soldiers and to prevent defections. RUF leaders reasoned that they could stop defections by stopping the harvest. To stop the harvest, they ordered the hand amputation of women who participated in harvesting grain. As news spread, the harvests stopped, and defections ended because soldiers did not want the same thing to happen to their own mothers and sisters. Richards does not justify these repulsive acts. Rather, his point is that violence is not "meaningless" but highly organized in a systematic, though brutal, fashion.

Not every conflict leads inevitably to violence. We explore this theme in more detail in our final section.

THINKING CRITICALLY ABOUT POLITICS

Since the early years of structural-functionalism, anthropologists have recognized that violence or the threat of violence, far from implying chaos, can encourage social integration and social order. How? Why?

✿ How Do People Avoid Aggression, Brutality, and War?

Although millions of people around the world rarely if ever have direct experiences of aggression, brutality, and war in their daily lives, this does not mean that disputes and conflicts do not arise, because they do everywhere, all the time. But, as we discussed, violence is not an inevitable human response to conflict. People always have creative and peaceful ways to manage or settle their disputes. Working out the problems that arise from those conflicting accounts inevitably touches on who has access to power and what allows them to hold it (Rasmussen 1991).

What Disputes Are "About"

Some disputes are explicitly about who can hold political power, but most disputes are also about other matters that are central to the political life of any community (Caplan 1995). Disputes are about property, who gets to make decisions, and rules of social interaction. They are also about dividing or joining people in new ways, because when arguments happen, people take sides.

Most North Americans assume that disputes are about winning and losing. We approach a lawsuit pretty much the same way we approach a sporting event, the point being to vanquish the other side. But for many peoples around the world, disputes are not "about" winning and losing but repairing a strained relationship.

When Trobriand Islanders play the game cricket, for example, the goal of the game is to end with a tie, not to win or lose (Kildea and Leach 1975). Sure, the players play hard and even get hurt in the process, but the game is really "about" reaffirming the social relationships that exist among the players and with their communities. When we look at how people manage disputes around the world, keep in mind that when presented with a dispute, most people prefer to restore harmony by settling the matter to the satisfaction of all parties.

How People Manage Disputes

Legal anthropology, the branch of political anthropology interested in such matters, has identified a number of ways people manage disputes (Nader and Todd 1978). Some strategies are informal, including avoidance, competition, ritual, and play. Others are formal, involving specialists or specialized institutions.

One of the easiest and most informal ways that people handle their disputes is to avoid the matter altogether, which allows tensions to subside. In small-scale communities, people have to get along, and avoiding certain subjects is often the best way of keeping the peace. People often turn to other informal strategies to handle tensions, such as telling jokes, laughter, gossip, song, duels, sporting

Figure 8.7   Rap Battles and Social Tension.   In urban hip-hop culture, "rap battles" involve two individuals engaging in competitive rapping in front of an audience. The individual with greater lyrical prowess—the ability to rhyme, to creatively "diss" (criticize) the opponent, and so on—is the winner. Rap battles are often born from social tensions between individuals or social factions, but they can also provide a creative means to reduce tensions as problems and status differences are publicly aired.

contests, ridicule, public humiliation, and even witchcraft accusations (Gulliver 1979; Watson-Gegeo and White 1990; Caplan 1995) (Figure 8.7).

When informal strategies do not work, people usually have more formal means of settling disputes. **Adjudication**, which is the legal process by which an individual or council with socially recognized authority intervenes in a dispute and unilaterally makes a decision, is one possibility. The image of a courtroom with a judge in a robe, a jury, and lawyers comes to mind. Not all societies do it this way, including the Kpelle [keh-**pay**-lay], rice cultivators of central Liberia. Anthropologist James Gibbs (1963) reported that while Kpelle could take their disputes to government courts, they avoided doing so because they viewed those courts as arbitrary and coercive (Gibbs 1963). Kpelle often turned to their own "moot courts," which are hearings presided over by respected kin, elders, and neighbors. Kpelle moot courts provided a thorough airing of grievances and a quick treatment of the problem before attitudes hardened. Instead of winner-take-all, their goal was to restore harmony.

In a **negotiation**, the parties themselves reach a decision jointly. British legal anthropologist Philip Gulliver (1979) observed that in a dispute between two close neighbors over land and water rights that took place in a small district in northern Tanzania in 1957, many factors influenced the ability and willingness of each side to negotiate a settlement. For example, one disputant was more popular and better connected in the community, and he thus had more allies to push his own agenda. But he was willing to negotiate because, like his rival, he was equally worried that the colonial court could intervene and impose a decision. He also worried that if the dispute was not settled, the other side might use witchcraft and further intensify the dispute.

Mediation entails a third party who intervenes in a dispute to aid the parties in reaching an agreement. Native Hawaiians commonly practice a kind of mediation called *ho'oponopono* (**hoh**-oh-poh-no-poh-no], or "setting to right" (Boggs and Chun 1990). This practice is intended to resolve interpersonal and family problems or to prevent them from worsening. It is based on the belief that disputes involve negative entanglements and setting things right spiritually will lead directly to physical and interpersonal healing (Boggs and Chun 1990). *Ho'oponopono* usually begins when a leader of high status—a family elder, a leader of a community church, or a professional family therapist—intervenes in a dispute, calling the adversaries and all immediate family members to engage in the process. After opening with prayers, the leader instructs participants in the process and guides a discussion in which all participants are expected to air their grievances and feelings openly and honestly. They direct them to the leader, not to one another, to avoid possible confrontation. At the end, the leader asks all sides to offer forgiveness and release themselves and each other from the negative entanglements.

Is Restoring Harmony Always the Best Way?

It is easy to romanticize dispute settlement traditions whose goal is to restore harmony. Legal anthropologist Laura Nader (1990) observed that harmony and reconciliation are cultural ideologies, and like other ideologies they uphold a particular social order and way of doing things, usually protecting the already powerful.

Nader observed that Zapotec Indians in the southern Mexican village of Talea [tah-**lay**-ah] whom she studied have a "harmony ideology." Taleans believe "a bad compromise is better than a good fight." They emphasize that people need to work hard to maintain balance and evenhandedness in their relationships with others. They go to local courts frequently, even for very minor disputes, to avoid escalation.

But peace and reconciliation have their price. Nader has seen how these ideologies can prevent a full airing of problems, delay justice, or be used as a form of social control. Harmony ideology sustains a particular power structure, serving the interests of some but not necessarily all.

Since the 1970s, restoring harmony has been a popular strategy in Western countries for conflict resolution studies and practice. Mediation and negotiated settlements deal with disputes from family and work-related problems to complex international clashes, including civil wars and wars between countries (Davidheiser 2007). These techniques are often called "alternative dispute management."

While some anthropologists welcome the rise of alternative dispute management (Avruch 1998), Nader (1995, 2001) questions its implicit harmony ideology.

She observes that many people involved in civil wars and other large-scale conflicts do not necessarily want harmony; they want justice, fairness, and the rule of law. This is a sentiment expressed by many Mozambicans, for example, whose civil war ended in a mediated settlement in 1992. Many Mozambicans believe the settlement, which brought with it the introduction of foreign aid institutions and International Monetary Fund stabilization policies, actually deepened their woes by generating more poverty and inequality than before the war (Hanlon 1996).

There is not necessarily a "best way" to solve a dispute. If there were, there would be no more disputes! In addition, dispute settlement is never a neutral act. In handling their disputes, people make ideological assumptions and enact social relationships that uphold particular power structures or, as Laura Nader suggests, even challenge those power structures.

THINKING CRITICALLY ABOUT POLITICS

Think about the last time you had a nonviolent dispute in your life. How did you handle it? Was one or more of the strategies we discussed—avoidance, adjudication, negotiation, or mediation—involved? How might the outcome have been different if you had pursued a different strategy than the one you did?

☙ Conclusion

If you pay much attention to political news on television or the Internet, you may have the impression that politics is mainly about politicians and their political parties, laws, and bureaucratic institutions. This impression offers only part of the story. Politics always involves some element of state power and bureaucratic processes. Every society has individuals who act a lot like North American politicians. From status leaders such as Big Men and councils of elders who settle disputes, to leaders of armed movements organizing violent acts, leaders everywhere use strategy, manipulation, persuasion, control over resources, and sometimes violence to obtain and maintain power over others.

Yet this view of politics is too narrow to appreciate the diverse forms that political power takes around the world. Not all societies train their young to deal with their problems through violence, and even those that accept violence place limits on its use, encouraging more peaceful ways of handling disputes. People not considered conventionally powerful have ways of challenging the power structure in their societies.

Politics is about relationships of cooperation, conflict, social control, and power that exist in any community and at all levels of social life, from the interpersonal and community levels to the national and transnational. The reason that people around the world have so many ways of managing and thinking about those relationships is the same reason cultural diversity persists in the world today: social processes like those involved in politics are always rooted in and emerge from people's everyday social interactions, belief systems, and cultural practices.

Key Terms

Acephalous society   p. 169

Action theory   p. 173

Adjudication   p. 186

Age-grades   p. 170

Band   p. 171

Centralized political system
    p. 171

Chiefdom   p. 171

Government   p. 169

Laws   p. 170

Mediation   p. 187

Nation-states   p. 177

Negotiation   p. 186

Non-centralized political
    system   p. 171

Political power   p. 173

Politics   p. 168

State   p. 171

Structural power   p. 174

Structural-functionalism
    p. 170

Tribe   p. 171

Violence   p. 181

Reviewing the Chapter

CHAPTER SECTION	WHAT WE KNOW	TO BE RESOLVED
Does every society have a government?	Not every society has a government as we know it, or even makes a distinction between those who govern and those who are governed. Some societies organize their political lives on the basis of principles such as egalitarian social relations, reciprocity, and kinship.	Although classical anthropological studies identified many political processes in non-state societies, anthropologists continue to study and debate how successful these processes have been in confronting the transnational forces that affect almost every society today.
What is political power?	Political power operates in multidimensional ways: it is action-oriented, it is structural, and it is gendered. It also tends to operate in particular ways in non-state contexts as well as in modern nation-states.	Anthropologists debate the relative importance of political power wielded by individuals and structural power in shaping fields of social action.
Why do some societies seem more violent than others?	Neither violence nor nonviolence is an inevitable condition. Both are learned behaviors expressed in particular social and historical circumstances.	Most peoples who have been characterized either as peaceful or as violent are not uniformly peaceful or violent, yet it is not always clear what conditions might have transformed an otherwise peaceful people into a violent one or vice versa.
How do people avoid aggression, brutality, and war?	Disputes arise in all societies, but they do not necessarily result in aggression, brutality, and war because people everywhere have many peaceful strategies for settling disputes.	Anthropologists continue to debate the effectiveness of the new field of alternative dispute management, especially in cross-cultural and international settings.

Race, Ethnicity, and Class

Understanding Identity and Social Inequality

During the late nineteenth century, Irish Americans became "white." Before then, other Americans considered them an inferior non-white racial group, even with their light-colored skin. The story of their transformation illustrates the fluidity with which racial identities, including whiteness, are culturally constructed.

Historically, the English, who had conquered and colonized Ireland in the sixteenth century, regarded Irish Catholics as beneath them—a separate and inferior **race** of people, race being a concept that organizes people into unequal groups based on specific physical traits that are thought to reflect fundamental and innate differences. The English institutionalized this concept by creating discriminatory laws known as the Penal Codes that denied Irish Catholics the right to vote, to live in incorporated towns, to attend university, and to buy,

Irish Lives in New York City. When the Irish first arrived in the United States, many of them moved into tenement buildings, often living side by side with freed slaves. Anglo Americans considered the Irish an inferior race and deserving of their poverty.

inherit, or receive gifts of land from Protestants (Ignatiev 1995). This discrimination was based on more than just religious, linguistic, or national differences: it was based on a racial worldview that emphasized Irish inferiority as part of the "natural order of things."

Beginning in the 1840s, large numbers of poor Irish emigrated to the United States, where the Anglo descendants of English settlers also regarded them as an inferior and separate race. They saw Irish and African Americans, or black people, as closely related, deriding the Irish as "Negroes turned inside out" and African Americans as "smoked Irish" (Ignatiev 1995). In the early years of mass emigration, Irish often lived side by side with freed slaves in segregated neighborhoods in Northeastern cities like New York and Boston. They worked the same low-prestige jobs and even intermarried.

Within a decade, however, this dynamic began to change. Irish workers began monopolizing certain trades and pushing black people out, sometimes violently. Seeing an opportunity to build its power base in Northern cities, the Democratic Party courted Irish voters. Some Irish leaders welcomed the political recognition, and in neighborhoods with no black voters, campaigners began to refer to "the white vote," symbolically redefining the Irish as white. By the end of the century, although many Irish Americans were still poor and considered of a lower class than their Anglo counterparts, they had achieved a level of social acceptance as white that would have been unimaginable several decades earlier.

The Irish are not alone in "becoming white" in North America. Jews, Italians, Finns, Greeks, Armenians, and certain Latin Americans—all of whom at one point were considered inferior non-white racial groups—have become white as well. In the process, they have also gone from lower-class status to gaining identification as "middle class."

American worldviews emphasize racial identities as the result of unchanging biological differences, yet no amount of research into the biological features of these groups will explain how and why those transformations in race and class took place. These changes emerged as a result of the dynamic ways racial and class identities are constructed, symbolized, and institutionalized in the socially stratified society that is the United States.

At the heart of understanding the relationship between identity and inequality is the question this chapter addresses: *If differences of identity are not rooted in biology, why do they feel so real, powerful, and unchangeable?* Embedded in this broader question are the following problems, around which this chapter is organized:

Is race biological?
How is race culturally constructed?
How are other social classifications naturalized?
Are prejudice and discrimination inevitable?

The order represented in the social hierarchy of any society is supported and justified by social institutions, political processes, and powerful symbolism. The categories may feel "natural" or inevitable, even morally necessary, but like all other cultural phenomena, they are constructed and dynamic. In order to show this, we have to begin by dispelling one of the most powerful ideas many Americans hold, that differences of race reflect biological differences between groups of people.

✥ Is Race Biological?

In 2005, the U.S. Food and Drug Administration (FDA) approved a new drug called BiDil for treatment of congestive heart failure among African Americans. It is the first drug ever intended and approved for a particular racial group, and studies have shown that it has benefits for African-American patients. For some scientists, medical researchers, and policy-makers, this situation confirms that racial groups have specific biological and genetic characteristics that can be treated with specific drugs.

But these claims do not hold up under critical scrutiny, and there is nothing about this situation that proves that African Americans are biologically different from other racial groups. How can this be? The answer lies in the political, economic, and social reasons this drug was developed in the first place, and the processes of its approval (Inda 2014). In recent years, the medical profession and the FDA have been under pressure from Congress and the public to reduce disparities in medical treatment among racial groups. Across the United States, racialized minorities— including African Americans, Latinos, and Native Americans—are more likely than white people to face serious obstacles to treatment, poor treatment, or no treatment at all.

Responding to this pressure and seeing an economic opportunity, the drug manufacturer targeted its efforts in developing BiDil exclusively for African Americans. After demonstrating the success of the drug, the company was able to gain a favorable patent from the FDA, giving it special commercial protection and enabling it to raise capital for the expensive trials among investors (Brody and Hunt 2006).

But here's the issue: the drug was tested only on African Americans. The drug's manufacturer and various experts have admitted that BiDil will probably work just as well on non–African Americans, but they have not tested it on other groups (Brody and Hunt 2006). At no point have any unique biological or genetic features of African Americans been identified that explain why BiDil works on them in particular. Indeed, all evidence suggests that congestive heart failure does not affect black people any differently than it does other social groups.

Most solutions to racial inequalities in health have focused on social and environmental problems—better access to healthcare, better living conditions, better diet, and so on—but in the wake of successful efforts to map the human genome, genetic thinking has come to exercise increasing influence over how such inequalities are imagined (Inda 2014). While the development of pharmaceuticals specifically for racial minorities may be new, attempts to "biologize" race as part of the natural order of things are not.

The Biological Meanings (and Meaninglessness) of "Human Races"

Since the eighteenth century, European and American scientists have played a key role in the **naturalization** of race—that is, the social processes that make race part of the natural order of things—by producing theories, schemes, and typologies about human differences. All of these typologies share the same basic flaw: there is no single biological trait or gene unique to any group of people, much less to any group that has been designated a "race." This point is such an important one for anthropologists that we need to examine it in greater detail.

THE PROBLEM OF CATEGORIZING HUMANS INTO "RACES"

For several centuries, European and American scientists have sought to naturalize race—that is, to categorize humans into racial groups and explain why nature organizes people into those groups. But many anthropologists have long argued that these efforts are scientifically futile. Why? For one, they recognize that racial markers, such as skin tone or facial features, are arbitrary and variable. In the human species, biological traits and genetic features never vary in neatly defined ways, much less in ways that correspond to the "racial" categories Americans are used to recognizing. Because of historical movement and genetic intermingling, human biological variations occur in a "clinal" fashion, which means that change is gradual across groups and that traits shade and blend into each other (Marks 1995). As a result, something like skin tone can be highly variable within any human population, and there are no clear lines between actual skin tones (Figure 9.1).

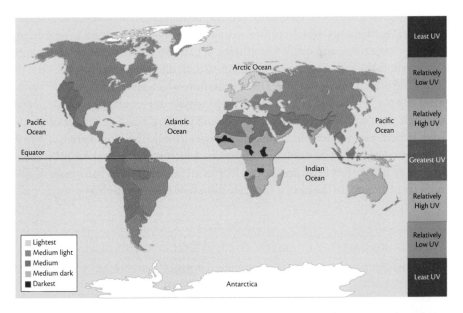

Figure 9.1   The Global Distribution of Skin Pigmentation.   This map shows a general correlation between ultraviolet light intensity and skin pigmentation, with people whose families have lived closer to the equator for many generations having darker skin than people whose ancestors have lived farther away from the equator.

Thanks to recent research in genetics, we also know that there is no single gene that codes race or is unique to any group of people conventionally thought of as a race (Long 2003). Moreover, genetically speaking, humans are a homogeneous species: there is far greater variation *within* human groups than there is *between* them (Long 2003). In other words, the aggregate sum of variations between the people whose origins lie in Africa is greater than the differences between that group as a whole and all Europeans, Asians, or any other commonly designated "racial" group. But these facts do not imply that race does *not* have biological consequences, because it does.

Race *Does* Have Biological Consequences

Even if the origins of racial groups are not genetically or biologically determined, race can *become* biology, by shaping people's biological outcomes due to disparities in access to certain kinds of healthcare and diets, exposure to certain kinds of diseases, and other factors that can make people either sick or healthy (Gravlee 2009). For example, epidemiological studies in the United States indicate well-defined differences between racial groups in terms of morbidity and mortality (incidence of disease and life expectancy, respectively). One illustration of this fact is that African Americans and other minority groups such as Latinos and Native Americans have shorter life expectancies and higher rates of many diseases, including hypertension, diabetes, certain cancers, stroke, renal failure, and cardiovascular disease (Gravlee 2009).

Race per se is not the *cause* of these health inequalities. Rather, these health inequalities are the *result* of race, or more specifically **racism**, which anthropologists define as the repressive practices, structures, beliefs, and representations that uphold racial categories and social inequality. One expression of racism is residential segregation by racial groups, which constrains opportunities such as access to education, certain occupations, and quality healthcare. It can also create social environments that promote the spread and distribution of disease, diet-related health problems, illegal drug use, and gang violence. **Discrimination**, which is negative or unfair treatment of a person because of his or her group membership or identity, has also been shown to have embodied consequences on individuals, producing a range of effects from hypertension to low birth weights (Gravlee 2009). The point here is not that different racial groups do not have differences in biology, but that these differences in biology, where they exist, are the result of social inequalities and processes of cultural construction. In the next section, we show how race is culturally constructed.

THINKING CRITICALLY ABOUT RACE, ETHNICITY, AND CLASS

The idea that racial differences are genetically and biologically determined is widely accepted by the U.S. public, and the contrary and more complicated view just presented has failed to gain widespread traction even as it offers a more empirically valid understanding of the relationship between race and biology. How do you think anthropologists could communicate these ideas and findings to the broader public?

❦ How Is Race Culturally Constructed?

Like all cultural "realities," the notions that Americans have about race are based on processes that naturalize certain meanings and actions as normal and even necessary. The development of a particular social order nearly always reflects and upholds this confounding of the culturally constructed and the natural. But these "races" are never self-evident; they are created (Gregory and Sanjek 1994). Scholars refer to the social, economic, and political processes of transforming populations into races and creating racial meanings as **racialization** (Omi and Winant 1996). Racialization always occurs under a particular set of cultural and historical circumstances, and different societies racialize groups differently, as the next two sections show.

The Construction of Blackness and Whiteness in Colonial Virginia and Beyond

After the English settled Jamestown in 1607, settlers began to raise tobacco as a cash crop. Labor shortages were a problem, so they began to bring indentured servants from England. They also began to rely on African labor. In 1619, for example, a group of African slaves held on a Portuguese ship were captured by an English ship and brought to Virginia colony as slaves to work. Some English-speaking Africans living in England also began to arrive in the colony as indentured servants (Parent 2003; Smedley 2007a, 2007b). These Africans were able to work off their debts and gain freedom from slavery. Some of the men even became prosperous traders and plantation owners and gained rights to vote and serve in the Virginia Assembly, just like any other man with property. Marriages between Africans and non-Africans were not uncommon. Unlike the Irish, whom the English considered racially inferior, Africans were respected because of their success at growing food in tropical conditions, their discipline and intelligence, and their ability to work cooperatively in groups (Morgan 1975; Smedley 2007a; Walsh 2013).

By the mid-1600s, the British began to rely more heavily on enslaved Africans to meet their labor needs and began to impose some restrictions on those slaves, among them restricted access to weapons and the practice of enslaving the children of slaves (Walsh 2013). At the same time, the Virginia colony was entering a period of crisis over land (Smedley 2007a). A few powerful men had taken most of the fertile land, and poor freedmen had difficulty finding any for themselves. Unhappy with their lot, in 1676, thousands of poor freedmen and indentured servants rebelled, in what is known as Bacon's Rebellion. Most were Europeans, but among them were several hundred of African origin. To prevent future unrest, the leaders began passing new laws aimed at gaining more control over laborers. A number of these laws separated out free Africans and their descendants, restricting their rights and mobility, including the ability to vote, own property, and marry Europeans (Parent 2003; Smedley 2007a). These laws took away basic rights that free African settlers had previously held. Within a few years, the colony's labor system was based completely on enslaved African labor, upheld by tight legal restrictions and physical controls over all Africans.

English colonial leaders also promoted a shift in thinking about Africans and their descendants. They began portraying Africans as uncivilized heathens, intellectually incapable of civilization. Such arguments justified African enslavement. They also began to homogenize all Europeans, regardless of ethnicity, class, or social status. In early public records, the word "Christian" commonly appeared next to the names of Europeans, but later it was replaced by "white." Poor white people received land as a way to encourage their identification with the colony's elites, preventing them from siding with Africans. By the end of the seventeenth century, the terms "black" and "white" came to symbolize the differences between the two groups, and the use of this racialized language helped to uphold the artificial lines of difference. Skin color became the chief way of marking status and difference.

The "biologizing" of race as a social category became extreme, particularly after the Civil War. In the South, people were defined as "black" if they were believed to have just "one drop" of African blood, meaning a single African ancestor. This notion, called "the one-drop rule," derives from a long-discredited belief that each race had its own blood type, which was believed to correlate with physical appearance and social behavior (Wright 1994:49). Widely promoted in the antebellum South, the rule was a way of enlarging the slave population with the mixed-race children of slaveholders (Figure 9.2).

As in the 1870s, today the vast majority of African Americans are of mixed ancestry. Over the years, the racialization of African Americans has been used, to a greater or lesser extent, to justify oppression and inequality as the "natural" order of things. The sharp "racial" lines drawn between "blacks" and "whites" upheld a particular social and political order and, more

Figure 9.2   The One-Drop Rule.   Mark Twain's classic 1894 novel *The Tragedy of Pudd'nhead Wilson* depicts the one-drop rule as a farcical tragedy. In it, Roxy (pictured here), a slave who is 1/16 black, switches her baby son, who is 1/32 black, with a white baby, knowing her son will grow up with privileges he would never enjoy if people knew he had even "one drop" of black blood.

importantly, served certain economic interests, especially of those who benefited from the cheap labor of racially marginalized people.

As this example suggests, American racial categories have never been static—far from it. In "Thinking Like an Anthropologist: Counting and Classifying Race in the American Census," we examine some of this dynamic history in more detail by considering how the U.S. government has classified people in the national census, held every ten years since 1790.

Racialization in Latin America

Another powerful demonstration of racialization comes from cross-cultural research in Latin America. In Latin America, the concept of "race" does not exist in many indigenous societies, but it is well established in societies shaped by European colonial expansion. Yet the distinct history of European conquest and state-building in Latin America has led to the results of racialization in this region being different from those in the United States.

Like the English in North America, the Spanish and Portuguese who colonized Latin America controlled African and Indian slaves by defining them as racially inferior and passing laws to control their rights and mobility (Wade 1997). But, unlike the English, they did not place such restrictions on sexual contact between Europeans and these other groups, leading to populations with many shades of skin color. As in the United States, "blackness" symbolizes an inferior and savage condition, while "whiteness" is considered civilized and superior. But these conditions are not firmly attached to skin color or other biological traits; they are linked to social behavior, attitude, and social class. "Blacks" may be people of many different shades of skin color, but they are poor and behave in "unrefined" ways, while "whites" act in a refined and courteous manner (Figure 9.3). "Black" people are still disadvantaged, but it is more obviously for "cultural" rather than "biological" reasons.

Figure 9.3 *Blanquismo* **in the Dominican Republic.** Between the 1920s and 1950s, the Dominican dictator Rafael Trujillo (1891–1961), pictured here in the center of the photo, promoted an official policy of *blanquismo* [blawn-**keys**-moh], or "whitening" of the population. This policy involved a massacre of black Haitians in 1935, invitations for white Europeans to immigrate to the island, and a celebration of European music, dance, and culture. Under *blanquismo*, dark-skinned individuals could be "white," but their whiteness depended on how closely they identified with European culture and attitudes.

Thinking Like an Anthropologist

Counting and Classifying Race in the American Census

Anthropologists begin their research by asking questions. In this box, we want you to learn how to ask questions as an anthropological researcher. Part One describes a situation and follows up with questions we would ask. Part Two asks you to formulate your own questions based on a different situation.

PART ONE: RACE AND THE 1850 CENSUS

Censuses interest anthropologists because they reveal the role of governments in classifying and categorizing groups of people. In addition, over time, census categories change, indicating broader shifts in social categories. The U.S. Census has noted the "color" of American residents from the very first census in 1790, but these categories have changed over time.

The U.S. Constitution requires a census every ten years to determine how many members each state should have in the House of Representatives. The Constitution mentions three kinds of people relevant to the population counted in the allocation of seats in Congress: free persons (each counted as one person), slaves (each counted as two thirds of a person), and Indians (who were not taxed and not counted until 1860).

The first American census (1790) recorded the head of each household and the number of individuals in each household in basic categories: Whites (by age group and gender), Other Free Persons, and Slaves. From 1800 to 1840, the census expanded the age groupings but used the same basic categories in each household.

In 1850, for the first time, the census recorded the name of every person in the United States and its territories (except American Indians). It also recorded the age, gender, color, occupation, and place of birth of every individual. Color is the most interesting classification because the census form mentions three possible categories: "White," "Black," or "Mulatto." The figure shows a form that was filled out in New Orleans's Fourth Ward.

Few Americans use the word "mulatto" anymore. It refers to mixed-race people, typically those who are part white and part black. Although the 1850 Census doesn't show them, in some parts of the South people informally used even finer-grained terms, such as "quadroon," referring to a person who is one-fourth black and three-fourths white, and "octoroon," a person who is one-eighth black.

All of these terms are obsolete and now considered offensive, but their use in that era suggests some important points. One is that Americans acknowledged the existence of people who are racially mixed and sought to classify them. Their use also reflects the same ideology that produced the "one-drop rule," in which mixed-race people are categorized as non-white.

After taking the census, the government produced an official summary of what it learned about the population to share with the public (something it still does). Interestingly, the summary never used the terms "Black" or "Mulatto." Instead, it distinguished people

SCHEDULE I.—Free Inhabitants in *the 4th Ward: 3d M* in the County of *Orleans* State of *Louisiana* enumerated by me, on the *7th* day of *September* 1850. *L. Findely* Ass't Marshal.

1850 U.S. Census Enumeration Sheet from New Orleans, Louisiana.   In Southern states like Louisiana, census takers were more sensitive to subtle differences in ethnicity than in most Northern states. While in Northern states people generally understood "color" to mean either black or white, the Southern states routinely recognized an intermediate category of mulatto. In this copy of the 1850 enumeration of New Orleans Ward 4, Precinct 3, whites are left blank, blacks are marked "B," and mulattos are indicated with "M." Note that although social status marked by these arbitrary racial categories was clear to everyone, these status differences did not keep whites, blacks, and mulattos from living in the same neighborhoods and even in the same households. (Although residential segregation existed at the time, it was organized not on the basis of race but on the basis of socioeconomic class and wealth.)

continues

Thinking Like an Anthropologist *continued*

in terms of whether they were "White," "Free Colored," or "Slave," despite the fact that the terms "Colored" or "Free Colored" never appeared on the enumeration forms, as we see in the image.

What questions does this situation raise for anthropological researchers?

1. What does the fact that the census forms used one set of categories but the public summary used a different set of categories tell us about American racial categories in the 1850s?
2. Why is it that it wasn't until the 1850s that the government wanted to record who was "mulatto" and "black"?
3. Although the terms "mulatto" and "black" might seem more precise than "colored," do these competing terminologies suggest an (aborted) effort to change public understandings of race?

PART TWO: THE 2000 AND 2010 CENSUSES

Following categorizations first established in the 2000 Census, the 2010 Census asked "What is this person's race?" and indicated that census takers could indicate one or more races. Its list of races includes "White," "Black, African Am., or Negro," and "American Indian or Alaska Native" as well as "Asian Indian," "Chinese," "Filipino," "Japanese," "Korean," "Vietnamese," "Other Asian," "Native Hawaiian," "Guamanian or Chamorro," "Samoan," "Other Pacific Islander," and "Some Other Race," followed by space to print a different option. In contemporary censuses, race is no longer an "either/or" category, and Americans can now check off any number of boxes to reflect the complicated interethnic blending now recognized by Americans. If you wanted to understand the dynamism of racial categories in the contemporary American census, what questions would you ask as an anthropological researcher?

Saying "Race Is Culturally Constructed" Is Not Enough

It is not enough to say that race is culturally constructed, because it might give the impression that race is not "real" (Hartigan 2006). Race is very real, of course, because racial groupings come with discrimination, exploitation, stigma, and negative biological and socioeconomic outcomes for some and privilege for others.

Put simply, racism is a potent force in making "race" real (Mullings 2005). Racism works through the prejudice that people express against people who are different from them, and through concrete social actions, such as violence or the denial of good wages and access to decent housing, education, and healthcare. Our point here is to emphasize that the concept of "race" is not a standalone concept: it goes hand in hand with prejudicial attitudes and a repressive social order that has real consequences for people's lives.

Of course, race is not the only means by which dominant groups establish and rationalize their social supremacy. In the next section, we consider how categories like ethnicity, class, and caste also operate through processes of naturalization.

THINKING CRITICALLY ABOUT RACE, ETHNICITY, AND CLASS

Racialization is not something that happened a long time ago; it is an ongoing process. Can you think of some examples of how it might still be taking place in the United States? Can you identify any conditions today that might shape dynamics of racialization differently from, say, during the period of the Virginia colony?

☙ How Are Other Social Classifications Naturalized?

All social hierarchies are rooted in and justified by the notion that social differences are part of the natural order of things rather than arbitrary cultural categories. Yet social hierarchies can be justified and upheld in different ways (Guimarães 1999). While racial ideologies tend to focus on aspects of physical appearance, other systems of classification divide people into groups based on economic status or occupation, behavioral characteristics, common descent, or symbolic purity. What they have in common with racial ideologies is that these divisions are perceived as inevitable and fixed even while in reality they might be quite dynamic.

Ethnicity: Common Descent

Along with race, ethnicity is a salient means of defining group identity and difference in the contemporary world. **Ethnicity** typically refers to membership in a group with a particular history, social status, or ancestry. Members of an ethnic group might be identifiable by any combination of distinctive social characteristics, such as language or dialect, clothing, foodways, etiquette, or bodily modifications such as tattoos or piercings.

The notion of shared "blood" and kinship is generally a central element of ethnicity. Members of ethnic groups often refer to each other as "brothers" and "sisters," might be expected to sacrifice themselves or their interests for the "fatherland" or "motherland," and often believe themselves to be descendants of a common ancestor or ancestral couple (van den Berghe 1999). For these reasons, the ethnicity concept often blends into other terms such as "nation," "nationality," and "tribe" (Barth 1969).

By invoking their common descent, ethnic groups establish a distinctive identity and, more important, establish their differences from other groups as part of the natural order of things. Despite an appearance of naturalness, however, ethnic groups do not form for genetic reasons. Some members of ethnic groups may eventually come to justify their identities in biological terms, but they are created for political, economic, and cultural reasons. This argument forms the basis of a theory of ethnicity called **instrumentalism**, which asserts that ethnic groups are not naturally occurring or stable but highly dynamic groups created to serve the interests of one powerful group or another (van den Berghe 1999).

THE RISE OF LATINO/A ETHNIC IDENTITY

A powerful illustration of how ethnic groups are established has been playing out in the United States in recent decades through the formation of "Hispanic" or "Latino/Latina" ethnic identity. With over 57 million people, Latinos/Latinas now constitute the largest ethnic minority in the United States. The "ethnic" label is applied because Latin Americans do not fit neatly into American racial categories based on skin color and other phenotypical characteristics.

But, as one astute journalist observed, "The theory is that there are no Latinos, only diverse people struggling to remain who they are while becoming something else" (Shorris 2001:9). Most "Latinos" actually think of themselves in terms of national origin—Mexican, Cuban, Puerto Rican, Colombian, Peruvian, and so forth (Fox 1997). There are many reasons for this situation. Different Latin American nations have different customs and identities, and well-developed notions of how they are superior (or inferior) to other Latin American nations. The proximity of Latin America to the United States means that individuals might migrate back and forth between the United States and their Latin American home countries frequently, undermining their sense of common identity with other Latin Americans in the United States. And in cities such as Chicago or New York City, where Mexicans, Dominicans, and Puerto Ricans might live in the same or adjacent neighborhoods, they may see the others as competitors for the same jobs and resources (Fox 1997).

Figure 9.4 Feeding "Latinos." The ethnic group "Latino," referring to a pan-Latin American identity in the United States, is only several decades old. Its emergence is aided by companies like Goya Foods, whose commercial success is based on downplaying national tastes and culinary traditions and emphasizing ingredients found across a wide spectrum of Latin American cuisines.

At the same time, however, powerful social forces are driving the construction of a homogeneous ethnic identity out of this diversity. One of these forces is the federal government, which beginning in 1980 included a category for "Hispanic" in the census ("Latino" was added in the 2000 Census), as a way of measuring the quantity of immigrants from Latin America. The federal government was also under pressure from Mexican-American and Puerto Rican civil rights groups, who were beginning to demand political recognition in U.S. society and inclusion in the census (Fox 1997). Government funding began flowing to people in the category, new legislation was developed to address them, and newly labeled politicians emerged with ambitions to gain power for themselves and their new constituencies. Market forces have also helped shape the category. For example, new media have emerged targeting that audience, including radio and television stations, such as Univision, that emphasize a common identity. In addition, new consumer products divorced from any single national origin have been created to appeal to a homogeneous group of Latinos (Dávila 2001) (Figure 9.4).

Class: Economic Hierarchy in Capitalist Societies

Most Americans think of themselves as "middle class," probably because, as the Declaration of Independence states, "all men are created equal." As a result, class remains largely hidden in American life. The social theorist Karl Marx saw class as the central organizing principle in capitalist societies, as the distinction between those who control the means of production (factory owners) and those whose labor produces the goods (workers). Here we understand **class** to be the hierarchical distinctions between social groups in society, usually based on wealth, occupation, and social standing.

The hiddenness of class in American cultural thought means that class tends to be the last factor introduced as an explanation of social success—as defined by wealth, privilege, and power—and failure, or poverty and social impotence (Ortner 2006:78). As much as they avoid talking about it directly, however, most Americans recognize that people are born into a particular social position due to the economic situations of their families. Indeed, this fact of birth has profound lifelong consequences, since one's class position typically shapes access to educational and occupational opportunities, possibilities for gaining wealth, even the towns and neighborhoods in which one lives (Figure 9.5).

Several generations ago, Americans regarded class

Figure 9.5. Class Divisions Represented in Popular Culture. The French term *parvenu* refers to a person of low origins who has obtained a great fortune. In popular culture, satirizing the "uncultured" ways of the parvenu is a common theme. A prototypical example is the 1960s television program The Beverly Hillbillies, in which the Clampett family from the Ozarks strikes oil and moves to the high-class California city of Beverly Hills. The show plays on stereotypes of poor, rural Southerners who misunderstand the ways of their more sophisticated neighbors.

differences as a biological phenomenon. To be wealthy was to be inherently superior, especially in terms of innate intelligence, and to be poor was to be born with inferior intelligence. These ideas have shifted with the growth of the middle class as an intermediate space between the richest and the poorest. Americans now naturalize class in other ways, primarily through the languages of race and ethnicity (Ortner 2006). For example, to be a WASP (white Anglo-Saxon Protestant) implies upper- or upper-middle-class status; to be Jewish implies middle-class status; and to be African-American or Latino implies lower- or lower-middle-class status. We all know that these distinctions are little more than crude stereotypes. Nevertheless, these intersections between class and race explain how Americans naturalize apparently neutral categories like middle, upper, or lower class (Ortner 2006).

In non-capitalist societies, native categories do not necessarily align with Western economic categories like class. But the spread of capitalism and consumption-oriented lifestyles around the world does create owner and worker classes, as well as middle classes with certain characteristic cultural tendencies that transcend national borders. For example, in his study of urban Kathmandu, Nepal, Mark Liechty (2002) found that the expansion of capitalist markets in recent decades had created a new middle class sandwiched between historically polarized Nepalese elites and commoners. Members of this new middle stratum explicitly distinguish themselves from those above and below them through their consumption of consumer goods and mass media, not unlike that of the American middle class. In one passage, Liechty describes a Hindu wedding in the suburbs to which he was invited. Expecting a traditional expression of Nepalese culture, he was surprised at how often a camera crew hired for the occasion interrupted and held up proceedings, even traditional dances.

The broader point here is that class is not shaped by biological imperatives. Rather, people create and re-create social classes in the context of broader historical and economic processes, often by defining themselves in contrast with other groups.

Caste: Moral Purity and Pollution

Caste primarily refers to the system of **social stratification** (the classification of people into unequal groupings) found in Indian society that divides people into categories of moral purity and pollution (Sharma 1999). The term derives from the Portuguese word for "pure breed" (*casta*), recognizing that one is born into a caste and should marry only someone of the same caste. Many millions of Indians consider the social divisions associated with their caste system as a "natural" and morally necessary aspect of the human condition.

Just as North Americans "see" race in the subtlest features of somebody's face, hair texture, or skin color, Indians "see" caste in people's occupations, the clothes they wear, how they talk, even their mannerisms. Caste has been described as India's "fundamental institution" (Béteille 1992) because the relationships of inequality upon which it is based are seen by Indians to be so self-evident and are so intertwined with how Indian society works.

Indians actually use two terms for what Westerners have named caste, *varna* [**vahr**-nah] and *jati* [**jah**-tee]. As outlined in classic Hindu religious texts, *varna* refers to the hierarchical division of society into four major groups: Brahmans (priests), Kshatriyas (warriors and rulers), Vaishyas (traders), and Shudras (artisans and servants). Another group outside these four is known as the "Untouchables" (*Dalit* or, formerly, *Harijan*). Related to these divisions is the perception that certain occupations and activities—such as metalworking, leatherworking, street sweeping, and trash collection—are inherently "polluting" in a ritual sense and thus should be left to the Untouchables. The small minority at the top of this system, the Brahmans (10% of the Indian population), are considered the most morally and ritually "pure" and enjoy the highest social status. Relative purity declines and pollution increases as one moves down the hierarchy.

In actual practice, Indians make many finer social distinctions beyond the four major categories of *varna*. They use the term *jati*, which translates in many Indian languages as "kind" or "species," to designate the actual manifestation of *varna* in practice. *Jati* are the actual social groupings, often based on occupation, that exist in a ranked hierarchy in relation to each other. A single village alone may have more than a dozen *jati*. Each has many internal divisions, so what appears like a single *jati* to outsiders may not actually seem that way to its members (Fuller 2004).

Jati and their many subdivisions are upheld by rigid rules that regulate social conduct, especially social and physical contact between groups and subdivisions. Within multi-caste villages, for example, people tend to live in residential clusters separated from other castes. Higher castes bar lower castes from using certain village wells and other public facilities, such as restaurants (Fuller 2004). Many other aspects of life—including whom an individual can marry, do business with, even have bodily contact with—are governed by the same set of strict rules.

Nevertheless, some Indians have begun to insist that caste's influence has diminished because of changing attitudes and the incorporation of ideals like democracy and the creation of formal government-supported affirmative-action programs (Sharma 1999) (Figure 9.6). This conviction is especially true among some Indians living in

Figure 9.6 Debating the Indian Census. In recent years, the inclusion of caste categories in the national census of India has sparked a national debate. Many fear that counting caste in the census grants legitimacy to caste-based politics, while others argue that the data obtained can help plan welfare measures.

urban settings, where everyday contact between members of different castes—sitting next to each other on a city bus, for instance—has weakened rigid rules governing contact between groups (Krishnamurthy 2004). However, while Untouchables now have legal rights, discrimination against them and others of low caste persists.

The social inequality upon which caste is constructed tends to be justified as a natural and inevitable aspect of individuals. However, just saying a particular form of social inequality is "natural" is never quite enough to fully explain its persistence. Social inequality is also upheld by prejudice and discrimination.

THINKING CRITICALLY ABOUT RACE, ETHNICITY, AND CLASS

The idea that class doesn't exist or is irrelevant in the United States is very powerful, yet social mobility (the ability to change classes) in the United States is restricted. In what ways do you think class mobility is restricted? How is the ideology that Americans have social mobility maintained?

❧ Are Prejudice and Discrimination Inevitable?

In the aftermath of the assassination of black civil rights leader the Reverend Dr. Martin Luther King, Jr, in 1968, Jane Elliott, a teacher in the all-white community of Riceville, Iowa, struggled with how to help her third-grade students understand prejudice and discrimination. She developed an exercise in which she divided the students into two groups, one made up of the blue-eyed kids and the other the brown-eyed kids. She told the blue-eyed kids that they were better and more intelligent than the brown-eyed kids, and treated them with special favors. She ridiculed the brown-eyed kids as less intelligent and unworthy, and shamed them mercilessly. She encouraged the blue-eyed kids to do the same, and they did (Peters 1970, 2005).

The impact of this experience on each group was remarkable. The blue-eyed kids began to feel superior and treated the brown-eyed kids, even those who were their close friends, with disdain. The brown-eyed kids felt humiliated, powerless, and downtrodden. Then, the next day, Elliott reversed the status of each group. Brown-eyed kids were now on top, and the effects on both groups were the same as before: feelings of pain and powerlessness for those in the lower-status group, and a sense of superiority for those in the higher-status group. Over the course of two days, Elliott and her class had constructed and role-played new social categories that closely resembled racial stereotypes in America, with powerful effects on everyone involved.

Elliott's classroom exercise has since become a common technique in antidiscrimination training in schools and organizations. It allows individuals who may never before have experienced **prejudice** (preformed, usually unfavorable opinions about people who are different) to experience it firsthand and in a deeply emotional way, to feel what it is like being treated as an inferior minority. It also demonstrates, with tremendous moral force, how the privileged benefit from, and even become complicit with, these attitudes, especially when people in authority (such as trainers, teachers, politicians, or CEOs) authorize and encourage discrimination (Figure 9.7).

There is nothing in human nature or biology that makes us treat people who are different from us as superior or inferior. Prejudice and discrimination are cultural processes, which is to say, they may feel natural and inevitable, but they are profoundly artificial constructions. Having said that, however, prejudice and discrimination are ubiquitous elements of socially stratified societies, a theme we explore in this next section.

Understanding Prejudice

Prejudice is based on taking arbitrary features and assigning qualities of social superiority and inferiority to them. Worldwide, there is a mind-boggling variety of markers upon which preju-

Figure 9.7   Politically Expedient Scapegoats. One of the ways some politicians advance their careers is to scapegoat certain groups, which means to unjustly blame them for society's problems. In Germany before the Second World War, Hitler and the Nazi Party built the Third Reich by blaming Jews, homosexuals, communists, and "Gypsies" (Roma) for their country's problems. In the contemporary United States, President Donald Trump has been heavily criticized for his tendency to scapegoat Mexican immigrants and Muslims, which has justified prejudice against and even encouraged mistreatment of people from these groups by Trump supporters.

dices are based. We are most familiar with skin color and hair texture, but other markers include gender behavior, sexual orientation, occupation, family lineage, and religious affiliation. Because people have multiple identities, the markers on which prejudices are based can be multiple and overlapping. Scholars call this phenomenon **intersectionality**, which refers to the circumstantial interplay of race, class, gender, sexuality, and other identity markers in the expression of prejudicial beliefs and discriminatory action. In the United States, for example, black men and women both experience racism, but black women also experience sexism. This intersection of race and gender prejudice can deepen their social marginality (Crenshaw 1989).

Where they exist, prejudices may feel deep, innate, and natural, but they are not static. As attitudes toward groups change, so do accompanying prejudices. There is no better illustration of this than the fact that between 2008 and 2017, the United States was led by a black president, Barack Obama, which would have been unimaginable only forty years before because of widespread prejudice against blacks. At the same time, the racist and sexist rhetoric surrounding the 2016 presidential elections demonstrated that millions of Americans still hold powerful prejudices against black people and other groups, among them Muslims, Latinos, and women.

Prejudices tend to express themselves through concrete processes of social rewards and unfair treatment, but they do not always lead to discrimination. In his classic study of prejudice from the 1950s, for example, Gordon Allport (1958) observed that prejudice expresses itself in a continuum from avoidance and non-contact to exclusion, physical aggression, and killing.

Most of us learn prejudices at a young age from people whom we regard as authorities, such as parents and other relatives, community leaders, and teachers. This point explains why our prejudices feel so natural. Yet where individuals have learned prejudices they can also *unlearn* them. Unfortunately, unlearning prejudice does not mean that discrimination automatically goes away. The reason is that discriminatory behaviors, where they exist, tend to be structured into people's social relations and institutions.

Discrimination, Explicit and Disguised

Discrimination may be a very visible feature of a society, upheld by its laws and openly accepted by social convention, as was true throughout the United States, Europe, and South Africa (among other places) for many decades. Or it may be hidden and subtle, operating in disguised but no less insidious ways. We examine both of these modes of discrimination in turn.

EXPLICIT DISCRIMINATION

Where discrimination is openly practiced, it is because discriminatory action has gained a certain level of social legitimacy and acceptance among members of the higher social strata, and sometimes by the victims themselves. Discriminatory action is often authorized through the creation of laws and bureaucratic processes that manage and enforce policies of institutionalized coercion and exploitation. It is legitimated because in some way it upholds a social order (blacks as servants to whites, for example, in the Jim Crow South) or promotes a new one (a racially homogeneous nation, as in the case of Nazi Germany and its discrimination against Jews, gay people, and others).

DISGUISED DISCRIMINATION

In contrast, many forms of discrimination are ambiguous, concealed, and difficult to prove. This fact is especially true where antidiscrimination laws now prohibit the most explicit forms of discrimination, such as in the United States, South Africa, Germany, and other countries once known for open discrimination against racial or ethnic minorities, the poor, or particular religious groups. Where civil rights struggles have succeeded, there may be a misleading sense that the playing field has become level (Mullings 2005).

Discrimination persists because bigotry does not necessarily disappear with changes in formal law. For example, throughout the United States, black people, poor people, and members of certain ethnic minority groups who enter shops and malls may be treated with suspicion and experience "racial profiling" or discrimination based on stereotypes. Shopkeepers and security personnel may keep a close eye on them because of stereotypes of these people as thieves. Real estate agents and landlords may steer potential customers away from areas where they do not "fit in," for racial or socioeconomic reasons, even though laws prevent housing segregation and discrimination. Media reports about crime often mention the accused's race or ethnicity, but only when the suspect is non-white, as if their race or ethnicity is the reason for the crime. Immigrants get tagged with labels like "illegal" and "criminal" and tied to the declining economic fortunes of other working people based on the perception that they take those people's jobs. To many people, especially members of higher-status groups, these situations may go unnoticed due to their subtlety or indirectness.

But in the contemporary United States, these disparities extend beyond matters of profiling in everyday life, and there are important differences in how the criminal justice system handles distinct racial groups that are more or less invisible to white middle-class Americans. For members of minority groups, for example, these problems include police violence and extrajudicial killings; higher conviction rates and harsher sentences; and higher incarceration rates (59% of the U.S. prison population is black or Latino, even though these groups make up only 29% of the overall U.S. population; Sakala 2014) (Figure 9.8).

Another proof of discrimination's existence is in the disadvantage that some groups experience that others do not (Rex 1999). For example, we know that in the United States, the educational outcomes of poor white and poor non-white students tend to be much weaker than those of white middle- and upper-middle-class students. There are numerous reasons for this situation, but a crucial one has to do with differences in funding levels for elementary and high schools in poor and middle-class areas. This factor directly affects the quality of teachers, the quality of facilities, and the kinds of programs a school can offer, each of which contributes to student success rates and has long-term consequences for a student's future educational, employment, and income possibilities (Kozol 1992). The underlying forces driving inequality in educational funding could be traced back to the size of the local tax base or employment levels in a community. Nevertheless, the result over the long term is uneven opportunities for different groups, and previously discriminated-against groups rarely end up on top.

What makes this example so loaded is that it is difficult to identify any single culprit for this situation, or even where the explicit racial or class bias lies. Inequality here is not a matter of personal ignorance, which is a common explanation for discrimination. On the contrary, it is clear that certain institutional routines and

Figure 9.8   Race Still Matters.   One of the most powerful effects of the Black Lives Matter movement is to challenge the post–Civil Rights era myth of America as a "color blind" society, showing that even with legislation protecting equal rights, systemic racial discrimination and inequality persist.

structural forces create and sustain unfair treatment independent of any particular individuals (Mullings 2005).

The Other Side of Discrimination: Unearned Privilege

The other side of discrimination is unearned privilege. It is easy for most Americans to recognize how skin color puts an individual at a disadvantage, but it is more difficult for many—especially white Americans—to identify the structural advantages and privileges that accrue to lighter skin.

As Peggy McIntosh (1997) observes, the privilege that comes with having white skin is "like an invisible weightless knapsack of special provisions, assurances, tools, maps, guides, codebooks, passports, visas, clothes, compass, emergency gear, and blank checks." A small sampling of these privileges includes being able to swear, dress in secondhand clothes, or talk with your mouth full and not have people attribute such things to your race; not being hassled by police or have people cross the street at night simply because of your skin color; and being sure that you can receive medical or legal help without your skin color working against you. These privileges exist regardless of whether a white individual holds bias against non-white people. The power of white privilege is that it posits whiteness as the norm and being non-white as different, even deviant (Hartigan 2005).

Of course, intersections of class, gender, sexuality, and so on complicate the picture of white privilege. In terms of class, for example, many poor white people would justifiably point to severe social disadvantages not experienced by higher-class white people (Hartigan 2005). But even these poor white individuals experience privileges not accessible to black people. For example, they are rarely pulled over by police because of their "race" in the way many African Americans are for "driving while black," and they rarely experience similar forms of racial profiling.

The broader point here is that social inequality—whether based on racial, class, ethnic, or religious categories—requires the consent of those who benefit from social inequality, who gain unearned privileges simply by being members of a privileged class (Mullings 2005:684). Thus, bringing about real social change requires those who benefit from the inequality to accept the immorality of the situation and support the change (McIntosh 1997).

THINKING CRITICALLY ABOUT RACE, ETHNICITY, AND CLASS

People rarely give up their privileges easily, but, as we have said throughout this chapter, social inequalities and prejudice are cultural processes and thus subject to change. Can you think of any social factors or changes in social relations that might produce a situation in which a group gives up its privileges?

🌱 Conclusion

Throughout this chapter, we have consistently argued one central point: in spite of the fact that the social categories most of us take for granted feel real, powerful, and unchangeable, there is nothing fixed or inevitable about them. All social hierarchies appeal to a natural order to justify the rankings and categories they assign to different groups. The markers by which these distinctions are made are arbitrary. If we really want to understand why some people are deemed inferior and others superior, we are better served to explore how belief systems and the dynamics of social power perpetuate prejudice, discrimination, and privilege, rather than searching for any preexisting biological or moral imperatives.

A final illustration of this point brings us back to where we opened this chapter, with the dynamics of whiteness. Irish Americans today are far less likely to experience discrimination on the basis of their identity than their ancestors did until a century ago. It is now common sense that they are "white." But whiteness has never been a straightforward category. Even today, the meanings and markers of whiteness are in flux. For example, Americans have been dropping ethnic identifications that were so common a generation ago—Irish-American, Italian-American, Polish-American, and so on—and adopting a generic "white" label (Gallagher 1997). This process has had the effect of replacing whatever national and ethnic identities groups sought to maintain during the first generations after immigrating to this country with a homogeneous racial identity that makes no such distinctions. Moreover, in becoming "white," these groups have come to be thought of as middle class and to share in the privileges of "whiteness," although the dynamics of intersectionality ensure that not all members of any social group are equally privileged or disadvantaged.

What is not in flux here—and this is the unfortunate power of social inequality in American history—is the fact that ideas of race, ethnicity, and class remain a powerful force, even if the individuals and groups assigned to these categories change over time. In hierarchical societies such as ours, inequality is often one of its most enduring features.

Key Terms

Caste   p. 204
Class   p. 203
Discrimination   p. 194
Ethnicity   p. 201

Instrumentalism   p. 201
Intersectionality   p. 207
Naturalization   p. 193
Prejudice   p. 206

Race   p. 190
Racialization   p. 195
Racism   p. 194
Social stratification   p. 204

Reviewing the Chapter

CHAPTER SECTION	WHAT WE KNOW	TO BE RESOLVED
Is race biological?	Races are socially, not biologically or genetically, determined. But due to racism and discrimination, race does have consequences for certain people's biological outcomes.	Anthropologists are still working to understand how social dynamics of race and racism express themselves through disparate biological outcomes.
How is race culturally constructed?	Races are never self-evident; they are culturally constructed through social and historical processes of racialization.	Saying "race is culturally constructed" is not enough, because race has real effects on people's lives, and anthropologists continue to explore the social outcomes and biological dimensions of race.
How are other social classifications naturalized?	All social hierarchies appeal to a "natural" order to justify themselves. This "natural" order may feel inevitable, even morally necessary, but like all other cultural phenomena, it is constructed and dynamic.	Race, ethnicity, class, and, in India, caste interact with each other in complex ways to produce identities, and anthropologists are continuing to work through these complexities.
Are prejudice and discrimination inevitable?	Prejudices are learned attitudes, and as a result they can also be unlearned. Even in the absence of privilege, discrimination may persist because it is structured into social relations in sometimes explicit, but more often than not disguised, ways.	Anthropologists continue to debate the main reasons social hierarchies are upheld. Some emphasize that discrimination and oppression against lower-stratum groups is the key factor, while others emphasize that it is based on the consent of those who gain unearned privileges simply by being members of a dominant group.

Gender, Sex, and Sexuality

The Fluidity of Maleness and Femaleness

During the 1990s, the West African country of Liberia was wracked by a civil war. Armed rebels sought to overthrow an oppressive dictatorship. During six years of conflict, at least 200,000 Liberians died and one million fled to neighboring countries as refugees. International news coverage of the conflict included jarring images of mutilated bodies, charred corpses, and child soldiers fighting for the rebels.

Interspersed with these images of brutality were images of male rebels dressed in women's clothing, wearing bras and wigs, sometimes striking effeminate poses for the foreign photojournalists. Such figure are hardly "soldiers" in the Western sense of the term. They contradict our basic assumptions about the masculinity of war (Moran 1997). Rather than try to explain the meaning of cross-dressing in this society, journalists dismissed it as a bizarre expression of an incomprehensible African mentality.

Cross-Dressing Warriors?   During the Liberian civil war, rebel cross-dressing represented a subtle expression of alternative masculinity and warriorhood.

According to rebels themselves, however, cross-dressing was deliberately taunting, a way to frighten their rivals. It made them feel invincible because they believed it would confuse enemy bullets. Whether cross-dressing actually warded off bullets is beside the point. Set against the backdrop of Liberian attitudes toward the government and its military, and against indigenous notions about the ideal qualities of warriorhood, cross-dressing made particular cultural and political sense.

First and foremost, cross-dressing helped rebels distinguish themselves from the government's uniformed "soldiers," who were despised because of corruption and their oppression of the populace. Government propaganda had promoted its soldiers as the country's masculine ideal, so cross-dressing was a protest against the soldiers and the state (Moran 1997). Cross-dressing also helped identify the rebels as "warriors," a social category of subtle complexity, an alternative masculinity commonly recognized in the villages where rebels operated. The male warriors' use of feminine symbols was meant to be playful. But it also communicated that true warriors are so powerful that they can overcome the biological and social constraints of maleness. In this society, men derive their special powers as warriors from a deliberate mixing of male and female symbols, thus drawing on the power of both.

Cross-dressing was not to last, however. Two years into the war, cross-dressing became less common as rebels adopted the hyper-masculinized image of Rambo, the macho commando, wearing cutoff sleeves and a headband. The new clothing and bearing continued to differentiate the rebels from government soldiers, this time by tapping into the power and romance of a Hollywood stereotype of strength, an image that brought with it new symbols of power and masculinity.

As wartime Liberia demonstrates, the characteristics that people associate with males and females are not set in stone. This point has two important dimensions. First, although all societies distinguish between male and female, the actual boundaries between these categories, and the specific qualities and roles assigned to each, can vary greatly from one society to another. Second, the qualities and roles associated with maleness and femaleness are not static; they can shift, especially in periods of social and political upheaval, and individuals relate to them in fluid ways.

Gender roles always have powerful meanings in any society, leading to the question at the heart of this chapter: *How do relations of gender and sex shape people's lives?* Embedded in this broader question are the following problems, around which this chapter is organized:

How and why do males and females differ?
Why is there inequality between men and women?
What does it mean to be neither male nor female?
Is human sexuality just a matter of being straight or queer?

Gender, sex, and sexuality are at the core of how we define ourselves in contemporary Western culture, shaping individual life conditions in important ways. But what any society associates with one or another gender, how individuals fluidly enact gender, and the circumstances under which gender is important are as constructed as any of the other elements of culture we have explored in this book. We begin by offering anthropological perspectives on male and female differences.

How and Why Do Males and Females Differ?

Walk into any kids' clothing store in a North American mall and the message is clear: boys and girls are fundamentally different. The boys' section is stocked with jeans, cargo pants, and blue or dark-colored T-shirts emblazoned with images of trucks, guns, or sports equipment. The girls' collection is full of frilly dresses and lace-lined shirts and pants in pastel colors like pink and purple, featuring images of butterflies, flowers, or baby animals. Judging by these articles, boys are adventuresome, active, and aggressive, while girls are nurturing, domestic, and sentimental (Figure 10.1).

These clothes convey powerful stereotypes about supposed differences in temperament and personality between males and females. In recent decades these stereotypes have become topics of intense debate in the United States, as we struggle over why women are excluded from certain kinds of jobs and positions of leadership, why men dominate certain professions and positions of power, and even which washrooms trans-gender individuals should be required to use. The issue is not whether our culture distinguishes males and females. The real issue is to explain why it views gender as a binary of two rigidly fixed options, and why it constructs the differences between males and females in the specific ways it does (Brettell and Sargent 2001).

Shifting Views on Male and Female Differences

The primary explanation our culture gives for differences between males and females is that they

Figure 10.1 Clothing and Sex/Gender Difference. North American ideas about sex/gender differences are powerfully expressed through the colors and characteristics of the clothing children are assigned from the earliest ages.

are "hardwired" differently. Differences in **sex**, usually understood in Western cultures as the reproductive forms and functions of the body, are even thought to produce differences in attitudes, temperaments, intelligences, aptitudes, and achievements between males and females. Some scientific support exists for these views: in all human societies boys tend to engage in more rough-and-tumble play, while girls tend to be more engaged in infant contact and care, suggesting that such behaviors are determined at a species level (Edwards 1993). Also, male and female brains appear to function differently: women's left-brained tendencies provide them with superior verbal skills, while men's right-brained tendencies give them superior visual and spatial skills (McIntyre and Edwards 2009).

But any conclusions about hardwired sex differences are muddied by evidence that culture and social relationships also shape the preferences and behaviors people associate with maleness and femaleness. For a long time, anthropologists referred to these cultural expectations of how males and females should behave as "gender." For example, the association of girls with pink and boys with blue feels natural and obvious to many Americans. But relatively few cultures associate a color with a particular gender, and a century ago in the United States, the colors were reversed, boys wearing pink and girls blue (Kidwell and Steele 1989). American attitudes toward boys and girls did not shift; what changed was the gender association of each color, which affects children's clothing preferences.

Since the 1930s, anthropologists have made a distinction between sex (biology) and gender (cultural expectations). But in recent years the distinction has been breaking down because it is difficult to tease apart just how much differences in male and female behavior are caused by "sex" (that is, shaped by biology) and how much they are caused by "gender" (cultural expectations) (Collier and Yanagisako 1987). Scientists believe that sex-specific biological influences on temperament are strongest during infancy and early childhood (McIntyre and Edwards 2009). But cultural influences on behavior are strong even early in a child's life, and these influences get much stronger as individuals age. Furthermore, "sex" is not simply a product of nature; it is also mediated and produced in the context of a specific culture. In light of this complexity, anthropologists increasingly reject an either-or perspective—that it's *either* biology *or* culture, *either* sex *or* gender—and accept that ideas and practices associated with male–female differences are shaped by a mix of biology, environmental conditions, individual choices, and sociocultural processes that construct the meanings of the categories of *male* and *female* (Worthman 1995).

Reflecting these intellectual shifts, anthropologists have changed their terminology and commonly refer to the ideas and social patterns a society uses to organize males, females, and those who exist between these categories as a **gender/sex system** (Morris 1995; Nanda 2000). Around the world, gender/sex systems are cross-culturally variable and historically dynamic. As the story of Liberian rebels that opens this chapter suggests, in any particular gender/sex system a spectrum of possibilities exists for defining and expressing masculinity and femininity, as does a shared understanding of when, how, and why it is important to do so.

Gender is still a meaningful concept for anthropologists. However, rather than being viewed as a matter simply of the cultural patterning of sexual differences over a biological substrate, it now refers to the complex and fluid intersections of biological sex, internal senses of self, outward expressions of identity, and cultural expectations about how to perform that identity in appropriate ways. Gender is not an essential entity, and so it cannot be used to explain behavioral differences between males and females. Rather, gender is fluid and dynamic, and people actively construct and enact gender within a range of culturally bound possibilities, norms, and constraints (McElhinny 2003). Clearly, this view diverges from the male–female binary that dominates Western cultural thought about gender.

Beyond the Male–Female Dichotomy

In the idealized world of science textbooks, human beings are a **sexually dimorphic** species, which means that males and females have a different sexual form. Men have X and Y chromosomes, testes, a penis, and various internal structures and hormones that support the delivery of semen. Secondary effects of these hormones include deep voices, facial hair, and, in some cases, pattern baldness. Women have two X chromosomes, ovaries, hormones, and internal structures that support the movement of ova, pregnancy, and fetal development, and the secondary effects of these hormones include breast development and a high voice.

You can probably name some minor exceptions to this rule—men with high voices, women with facial hair—but those variations are not enough to challenge anyone's certainties about male and female difference. On more systematic inspection, however, a sharp dichotomy between males and females breaks down. Chromosomes, gonads, internal reproductive structures, hormones, and external genitalia vary across our species more than you may realize (Fausto-Sterling 2000). Individuals who diverge from the male–female norm are called **intersex**, meaning they exhibit sexual organs and functions somewhere between male and female or including both male and female elements. Some individuals have both ovaries and testes; some have gonad development with separate but not fully developed male and female organs; and some have ovaries and testes that grow in the same organ. Many intersex individuals are infertile, but not infrequently at least one of the gonads functions well, producing either sperm or eggs.

One reputable estimate puts the frequency of intersex in the United States at 1.7% of all live births (Fausto-Sterling 2000). This figure of 1.7% is not universal; some populations have higher rates of intersex, and others lower rates. Yup'ik Eskimos in Alaska, for example, have a higher rate of intersex births: 3.5% of births have congenital adrenal hyperplasia, a condition resulting from a genetic mutation that can produce masculine genitalia in girls.

Different societies deal with intersex differently. Many cultures do not make anatomical features, such as genitalia, the dominant factors in constructing gender identities, and some cultures recognize biological sex as a continuum. But European and North American societies have considered intersexuality abnormal, sometimes immoral, most recently turning it into a medical problem. In the United States, most intersex children are treated shortly after birth with "sex-assignment surgery," in which a doctor eliminates any genital ambiguity through surgery, and doctors counsel the parents to raise the child to correspond with that sexual assignment.

The reasons behind parents' decisions to choose sex-assignment surgery for their intersex children are rarely medical; they derive from culturally accepted notions about how a boy's penis or a girl's vagina and clitoris should look. Surgeons work hard to construct culturally "appropriate" genitalia by removing body parts and using plastic surgery to construct "appropriate" genitalia. But there is no biological norm for penis or clitoris size or shape, and in fact, many boys are born with very small penises that get larger at puberty, and many girls are born with much larger than average clitorises that present no clinical problems (Fausto-Sterling 2000). The cultural issue surrounding these surgeries is ensuring that the genitals' size and shape will convince others—parents, caretakers, other children, and future sexual partners—that the person is a male or a female.

Sex-assignment surgery shows that "sex" is not simply a biological phenomenon, but is—*quite literally*—constructed upon cultural assumptions of a sexual binary in humans and about what an ideal male or female should look like. These cultural assumptions stand in contrast to the evidence of natural variations in the shape, size, and function of genitalia. Such surgeries seem well intentioned— to help intersex individuals avoid the emotional burdens of being different in a culture that does not accept sexual ambiguity. However, they have become highly controversial, especially among many intersex people themselves, some of whom have described it as mutilation (Figure 10.2).

Figure 10.2   "Human Rights for Hermaphrodites, Too!"   So says this man's T-shirt from a 2009 rally urging the International Olympic Committee (IOC) in Lausanne, Switzerland, to reject discrimination against athletes "suspected" of being intersex (the more common term these days for a hermaphrodite) who participate in international sporting competitions. The IOC has been criticized for supporting forced sexual identification tests and sexual reassignment surgery to "clarify" athletes' sex.

Do Hormones Really Cause Gendered Differences in Behavior?

The evidence of intersex destabilizes certainties about biologically rooted differences between males and females, but what about hormones? Don't they cause gendered behaviors? Hormones are chemicals that our bodies secrete into the bloodstream that regulate many of our bodily functions. Even miniscule amounts can have transformative effects on our bodies. Some athletes take anabolic steroids to build muscle mass and improve their performance, and some older men take testosterone injections to enhance their youthfulness and virility. Some women take hormones for birth control and during menopause to moderate hot flashes and mood swings.

These effects leave us with the impression that hormones play a major role in determining physical and even behavioral differences between males and females. But there are many popular misconceptions about hormones. One is that certain hormones are linked solely to a specific sex: testosterone to males, and estrogen and progesterone to females. These hormones do play a larger role in one sex than in the other; estrogen, for example, plays a larger role in women than in men in regulating reproductive cycles. But *both* males and females produce all of these so-called sex hormones because they are not connected solely to sexual functions. Hormones are versatile and are involved in the growth of several body systems. For example, in addition to producing testosterone, men's testes also produce estrogen, which is involved in bone growth and fertility (Fausto-Sterling 2000).

Popular beliefs in North America hold that sex-specific hormones cause particular behaviors, such as the notion that testosterone causes aggression and the drive to gain social dominance among males. This incorrect belief leads some U.S. states to perform chemical castrations on repeat male sex offenders. Yet hormones do not directly cause or trigger any particular behaviors, much less gender-specific behaviors. As a result, efforts to castrate male sex offenders have typically failed to reduce aggressive or violent behaviors (Fausto-Sterling 1992a:126; Worthman 1995).

Both males and females are capable of aggression and dominance, and societies differ in what they consider to be culturally appropriate levels of aggression expressed by men and women (Lee 1979; Brettell and Sargent 2001). For example, the egalitarian !Kung San (also known as Ju/'hoansi) expect both men and women to be aggressive, although in different ways. !Kung San women engage in verbal abuse, while homicides are usually committed by men. To understand when, why, and how !Kung San men and women express aggression, we have to consider not just biological factors influencing behavior, but also the immediate social causes of conflict, the availability of weapons, culturally approved expressions of hostility, and broader conditions, such as political-economic pressures that drive social conflict (Brettell and Sargent 2001:3).

Related to this whole issue of differences between men and women is yet another enduring question: Are women everywhere subordinate to men because of biological differences between them?

THINKING CRITICALLY ABOUT GENDER, SEX, AND SEXUALITY

In U.S. culture there is a widespread idea that female hormones enable mothers who have given birth to bond with their babies, providing the basis of effective mothering. While birth and the associated lactation do involve elevated production of certain hormones such as oxytocin, mothering is also a complex social relationship that must be understood in relation to cultural ideas about effective mothering. What cultural ideas do Americans have about effective mothering? Do you think that the production of childbirth-related hormones is necessary to be an effective mother?

Why Is There Inequality Between Men and Women?

Men hold most leadership roles in most societies around the globe. The few exceptions are generally small hunter-gatherer societies like the Batek of the Malay Peninsula in Southeast Asia. This small community lives in bands that anthropologists Kirk and Karen Endicott (2008) report are generally egalitarian in their gender roles, to the extent that the band they lived with during their fieldwork had a woman as its headman (Figure 10.3).

Figure 10.3 Batek Headwoman. This photo, taken in 1976, shows Batek headwoman Tanyogn in the Malaysian rainforest, plaiting a cord out of black fungus rhizomes to make a bracelet.

But such cases are unusual. In nearly all societies with any degree of social stratification, more men are in leadership roles than women, not only in political roles, but in economic and social roles involving trade, exchange, kinship relations, ritual participation, and dispute resolution (Ortner 1996:176). For example, in the United States today, only 19% of Congressional seats are held by women; in the workplace women earn on average 81% of what their male counterparts earn; and sex discrimination persists in social expectations, such as the notion that women should do housework. Very few of the privileges men have over women are predicated on physical strength. So why is inequality between the sexes such a common feature of many societies?

Debating "the Second Sex"

In 1949, French philosopher Simone de Beauvoir published an influential book titled *The Second Sex* in which she argued that throughout history women have been considered "the second sex," inferior in status and subordinate to men. Even before the publication of this book, during the Victorian era, a handful of women anthropologists, animated by the "first-wave feminism" that was beginning to challenge male domination and win the right to vote, wanted to understand if all societies treated women as unequally as Euro-American societies did. Nevertheless, it wasn't until the mid-1950s and early 1960s that anthropologists—inspired in great part by de Beauvoir's work and the emergence of "second-wave feminism"—began to pay greater attention to issue of gender/sex inequality.

Most feminist anthropologists rejected the idea that biological differences are the source of women's subordination. Instead, they argued that cultural ideologies and social relations impose lower status, prestige, and power on women than men. But here the agreement ends, and during the 1970s and 1980s a major debate took place over whether gender inequality is universal and what causes it.

On one side were those who argued that women's lower status is universal. Sherry Ortner, an influential participant in the debate, observed that the roots of female subordination lay in the distinction all societies make between "nature" and "culture" (Ortner 1974). Across many cultures, women are assigned symbolically to nature because of their role in childbearing, and thus they are viewed as uncultured and uncivilized. Men, on the other hand, are associated symbolically with culture and thus are viewed as civilized and superior.

On the other side were feminist anthropologists who argued that egalitarian male–female relations have existed throughout human history. Inequality exists, they observed, as the result of particular historical processes, especially the imposition of European capitalism and colonization on native peoples who were once egalitarian. For example, Eleanor Leacock (1981) argued that among the Montagnais-Naskapi [mohn-tan-**yay** nahs-kah-pee] of the Labrador Peninsula in Canada, women enjoyed equal status with men, held formal political power, exercised spiritual leadership, and controlled important economic activities before the arrival of Europeans. By the 1700s, however, dependence on the fur trade with Europeans undercut the traditional political system and economy, and Jesuit missionaries imposed compulsory Catholic schooling, which was hostile to women's independence and power. Eventually, the Montagnais-Naskapi developed a cultural view of women as inferior and subordinate.

Taking Stock of the Debate

On all sides of the feminist anthropology debate, participants recognized that inequality between men and women is, if not universal, at least pervasive. More important, the debate brought the study of what women say and do to the mainstream of the discipline. The emergence of this so-called anthropology of women successfully challenged the discipline's historical bias toward studying males and closed a gap in the ethnographic record by producing detailed studies of women's experiences and perspectives (Viswesaran 1997).

But the debate came to an impasse due to differences of interpretation over the evidence. Some participants also shifted their positions, including Ortner, who recognized that egalitarian relations between men and women can exist, although they are fragile and inconsistent (Ortner 1996). Critics of the debate, including some anthropologists, members of minority groups, and Third World academics, asserted that second-wave feminism made ethnocentric assumptions (Mohanty 1991). They pointed out that the mostly white, middle-class feminists involved in the movement had downplayed meaningful differences between women across cultures, assuming that all women viewed the fight for political equality as a single global priority. In many other countries, women's movements are more local and might be more oriented toward fighting militarism, challenging foreign ideals about beauty and ways of being a woman, or gaining access to local political processes or economic opportunities (Basu 2010).

Reproducing Male–Female Inequalities

The impasse in the debate also accompanied a shift in how anthropologists studied relations between men and women. A number of anthropologists insisted that it is necessary to focus on women *and* men, especially the dynamic relationships between them that take place in everyday life.

From this vantage point, inequality is not something static that people "possess"; it is something they "do." For example, patterns of inequality are reproduced in things as basic as everyday language. What American men and women say may include the same words but mean something different to each gender. As we explored in Chapter 4, such miscommunications happen because our culture has different expectations about how men and women should communicate.

BEING A MAN

Anthropologists also began to rethink "men." For decades anthropology involved men studying the lives of other men, but until recently very few anthropologists had examined men *as men*—that is, how men and women collectively view and shape what "being a man" means, and how men actually perform, or act out, manhood (Gutmann 1997). The anthropological study of **masculinity**, the ideas and practices of manhood, has not just opened new avenues of research for understanding how gender identities are constructed but has also generated new perspectives on male–female inequality, including the notion that ideals of masculinity are dynamic and do not in themselves necessarily assume male dominance (Figure 10.4).

For example, during the 1990s anthropologist Matthew Gutmann studied how men and women define what "being a man" means in a poor neighborhood of Mexico City (Gutmann 1996). Gutmann observed that certain ideals and practices of *machismo*—the Mexican stereotype of the dominant, assertive male—contribute to women's subordination. But Mexican masculinity has always been more subtle and dynamic than the stereotypes suggest. One reason is that broader social transformations—greater numbers of women are now working outside the home for money, boys and girls in schools are given equal status, and the feminist movement has influenced Mexican life—contribute to changing perceptions of manhood. Gutmann also observed that women argue, cajole, and issue ultimatums to men, forcing them to act contrary to *macho* stereotypes.

By focusing on the dynamic nature of male–female inequalities, anthropologists have come to understand that male domination and female subordination are reproduced and performed in complex ways in everyday life. But anthropologists have not studied only "men" and "women." They have also studied people who are neither men nor women, an issue we deal with in the next section.

Figure 10.4 Masculinity in Transition. In recent years, broad social transformations—such as greater numbers of women working outside the home for money, boys and girls in schools being given equal status, and the feminist movement—have contributed to changing perceptions of manhood across the United States, including the acceptance of men's greater involvement in parenting.

THINKING CRITICALLY ABOUT GENDER, SEX, AND SEXUALITY

Inequalities between men and women are reproduced and performed in many different ways in daily life. Can you identify examples in the following: Advertising? Sports? Language? Cooking? Shopping at a mall? At the same time, these inequalities are often challenged by both men and women. Can you find examples of such challenges in the same contexts?

✾ What Does It Mean to Be Neither Male Nor Female?

In many societies, some people live their lives as neither male nor female. They have a culturally accepted, and in some cases prestigious, symbolic niche and social pathway that is distinct from the cultural life plan of males and females (Herdt 1994). Anthropologists refer to this situation as **gender variance** (expressions of sex and gender that diverge from the male and female norms) or **third genders**, which recognizes the fact that many societies allow for more than two categories of gender/sex (in actuality ranging anywhere from three to five). Sometimes the terms are used interchangeably, as we do here.

Third gender has often been entangled in debates about **sexuality** (sexual preferences, desires, and practices), specifically as a form of homosexuality, since some third-gender individuals engage in what appear to be same-sex sexual activities (Herdt 1994). But sexual preferences intersect in complex ways with gender variance. People everywhere establish their gender/sex identities, including normative categories like "man" or "woman," not through sexual practices but through social performance: wearing certain clothes, speaking and moving in certain ways, and performing certain social roles and occupations. Here we consider three examples of gender variance in different contexts: the Navajo, India, and the contemporary urban United States.

Navajo *Nádleehé*

Gender variance has been historically documented in over 150 American Indian societies, although it is no longer an important institution except in a few of these societies. Today, where it exists, American Indian gender variance is often called "two-spirit," meaning that an individual has both male and female spirit. The phenomenon has been greatly misunderstood, largely because Western culture lacks the conceptual categories to translate the specific beliefs and customs related to gender variance in these societies (Roscoe 1994). For decades white Americans have used the term *berdache* [burr-**dash**], a derogatory Arabic term that refers to the younger partner in a male–male sexual relationship, to refer to gender variance among American Indians. This term assumes that gender-variant individuals are sexually attracted to individuals of their own sex, which is not always the case (Figure 10.5). Western moral thought also categorizes them as deviants when in fact, in a number of Indian societies, third-gender individuals held high social status.

The Navajo, who live in the Four Corners area of the Southwest, present an especially subtle and complex example of how one society has defined multiple genders. In Navajo society, *nádleehé* [nahk-**hlay**] are individuals held in high esteem who combine male and female roles and characteristics. They perform both male roles (such as hauling wood and participating in hunts and warfare) and female roles (such as weaving, cooking, sheepherding, and washing clothes). Some *nádleehé* dress in traditionally female clothing, while others dress in traditionally male clothing. Navajo families have traditionally treated *nádleehé* respectfully, even giving them control over family property. The *nádleehé* participate in

Figure 10.5   Two-Spirit Singers at a Gathering.   Unlike traditional gender variants in American Indian societies, many contemporary two-spirit individuals identify as gay. Due to anti-gay sentiment, they often experience hostility and discrimination in their home communities. They also feel alienated from white gay and lesbian communities and political activism, which does not acknowledge their unique cultural heritage and the issues of poverty and racism they face as Indians.

important religious ceremonies, serve as spiritual healers, and act as go-betweens in arranging marriages and mediating conflicts.

The Navajo recognize five genders, two of them being male and female (W. Thomas 1997). The term *nádleehé* (in English, "one who changes continuously") refers to intersex individuals whom they consider a third gender. The fourth and fifth genders are also called *nádleehé*, but they are distinct from intersex individuals. The fourth gender is the masculine-female, female-bodied individuals who do not get involved in reproduction and who work in traditional male occupations (hunting and raiding). Today they often serve as firefighters or auto mechanics. The fifth gender is the feminine-male, male-bodied individuals who participate in women's activities of cooking, tending to children, and weaving. Feminine-males may engage in sexual relations with males, although Navajo do not consider these to be same-sex relationships.

Beginning in the 1800s, Christian missionaries tried to eliminate the *nádleehé*. Prominent *nádleehé* began to be more discreet about exposing their identities to the outside world, a situation that continues today (W. Thomas 1997). Although *nádleehé* continue to exist, many young Navajos, especially those raised off reservation, might not identify themselves as *nádleehé* but as "gay" or "lesbian," adopting Western forms of identification that really have nothing to do with traditional Navajo gender notions.

Indian *Hijras*

In India, *hijras* [**hee**-drahs] are members of a third gender who have special social status by virtue of their devotion to Bahuchara Mata, one of many versions of the Mother Goddess worshiped throughout India (Nanda 1994) (Figure 10.6). *Hijras* are males who are sexually impotent, either because they were born intersex with ambiguous genitalia or because they underwent castration. They are viewed as "male plus female" because they dress and talk like women, take on women's occupations, and act like women, though in exaggerated, comic, and burlesque fashion.

Individuals from many religious backgrounds—Hindu, Christian, and Muslim—become *hijras*, but their special status emerges from the positive meanings Hinduism attributes to individuals who embody both male and female characteristics and to individuals who renounce normal social conventions. In Hindu thought, males and females exist in complementary opposition. The female principle is active, both life-giving and destructive, while the male principle is inert and latent. When they become *hijras* by undergoing castration (or if they are intersex they can join a *hijra* community), men can become powerful enough to tap into the beneficent and destructive powers of the female principle, as vehicles for the Mother Goddess. *Hijras* are thus viewed both as carrying the ability to bless and as inauspicious and stigmatized, and many Indians fear the ability *hijras* have to issue curses.

Figure 10.6   *Hijras* in India.   The *hijras* pictured here are protesting against Indian Penal Code Section 377, which criminalizes same-sex relationships. Protestors have sought to overturn the law, alleging that the law, which was created during the British colonial era, is outdated and justifies daily abuse and harassment of members of the gay, lesbian, bisexual, and transgender communities, including *hijras*, by police.

Hijras live in communes of up to twenty people, led by a *guru* (teacher). They live outside the normal bounds of social convention, having renounced their caste position and kinship obligations. The primary social role of *hijras* is to provide blessings when a boy is born (a major cause of celebration in India) or to bless a couple's fertility at a wedding. *Hijras* are typically a raucous presence at these events, making crude and inappropriate jokes, performing burlesque dances, and demanding payment for their services. Although it is stigmatized within *hijra* communities, some *hijras* also engage in sex acts with men for pay. These *hijras* are not necessarily considered "gay"; Indian society does not consider human sexuality as a dichotomy between gay and straight as ours does, and *hijras* are not considered males anyway.

Although British colonialism tried to outlaw *hijras*, they continued to exist largely by conducting their initiation rites in secret. In recent decades they have had to adapt to a changing Indian society. Government family-planning programs have reduced birth rates, and urban families increasingly live in apartment buildings with security guards who prevent the entrance of *hijras* when they arrive to bless a baby. In response, *hijras* have exploited new economic opportunities, asking for alms from shop owners and expanding their involvement in the sex industry (Nanda 1994:415).

Trans in the United States

Even in the United States, where the culture emphasizes the male–female binary, gender variance exists. Our culture has long recognized the existence of individuals who dress, act, or otherwise present themselves in a manner inconsistent with what the majority of Americans would expect based on their biological sex. Many in the mainstream have stigmatized these people as deviant, immoral, even mentally ill, and some have targeted them for violence and hate crimes.

Beginning in the early 1990s, political activists began challenging the stigma and pushing for formal rights for gender variants. The term these activists use, *trans*, is shorthand for **transgender**, which refers to someone to whom society assigns one gender who does not perform as that gender but has taken either permanent or temporary steps to identify as another gender (Valentine 2003). *Trans* has become a catchall term to describe a wide variety of people who had once been seen as separate: transsexuals (people who have had sexual reassignment surgery or strongly desire it), transvestites (people who cross-dress), drag queens (men who wear exaggerated women's clothing, usually for performances), drag kings (women who dress in exaggerated men's clothing), intersex individuals, and people who consider themselves to be neither exclusively male nor exclusively female. It rapidly became a common term in academia, psychiatry, and politics, where trans activists have been effective in promoting legislation on the issue of hate crimes (Figure 10.7). Increasing acceptance of trans terminology has been accompanied by use of another term, **cisgender**, which refers to people whose gender

Figure 10.7   Transgender Activism in New York City.

identity aligns with their biological sex at birth as male or female. Although some intersexual individuals and others criticize the use of this term as implementing a new binary (trans vs. cis), its use is increasingly widespread in academia and medical fields.

Many of the people who occupy the category of "trans" do not necessarily identify themselves as such, suggesting that there is no single community or accepted form of "being trans" in America. American anthropologist David Valentine has explored this issue in ethnographic research among mostly male-to-female trans-identified people at drag balls, support groups, cross-dresser organizations, clinics, bars, and clubs in New York City. Valentine observed that many individuals resist the label "transgender" because they see it as including them with so many different groups, thus diluting their own issues (Valentine 2007:101).

For some people, uncertainty about the trans label is related to the ongoing hostility in the United States against people who diverge from male and female norms. We explore this issue in more detail in "Thinking Like an Anthropologist: Anthropological Perspectives on American (Non)Acceptance of Trans People."

The meanings of *trans* are still in formation, though our culture still does not provide trans individuals a legitimate symbolic niche and social pathway. One reason is perhaps that many Americans view trans identities through a moralistic lens, as an expression of a perverse sexuality, a notion anthropologists reject. As we show in the next section, sexuality is also a distinctive issue with its own complexities and cultural variability.

THINKING CRITICALLY ABOUT GENDER, SEX, AND SEXUALITY

Societies in which gender variance is common tend to also be societies that are tolerant toward ambiguity and complexity in other areas of life, such as religious beliefs. How and why might a society develop an acceptance of ambiguity and complexity? Beyond gender and religious beliefs, in what other aspects of social life might one expect to see a tolerance for ambiguity?

Thinking Like an Anthropologist
Anthropological Perspectives on American (Non) Acceptance of Trans People

Anthropologists begin their research by asking questions. In this box, we want you to learn how to ask questions as an anthropological researcher. Part One describes a situation and follows up with questions we would ask. Part Two asks you to formulate your own questions based on a different situation.

PART ONE: TRANS PEOPLE AND PUBLIC BATHROOMS IN PERSPECTIVE

In the past several years, a number of American universities, corporations, and communities have been creating gender-neutral (or "all gender") bathrooms to accommodate people who do not identify as either male or female. The establishment of these bathrooms is rooted in a number of concerns, among them accessibility, personal privacy, inclusion, and preventing discrimination. Because federal law does not extend nondiscrimination protections to LGBTQ (lesbian, gay, bisexual, trans, and queer) people, each state, county, and city government can enact its own legislation protecting the rights of LGBTQ individuals, including access to gender-neutral bathrooms.

It is in this context that city councilors in Charlotte, North Carolina, in February 2016, passed an ordinance prohibiting discrimination in the city on the basis of sexual orientation or gender identity in public accommodations, including public bathrooms. Conservative politicians and religious leaders around the state denounced Charlotte's law as a moral failing and worried

openly that trans people, who they inaccurately stereotyped as sexual predators, would assault innocent bathroom users. State legislature quickly passed a bill called HB 2 (or House Bill 2), which prevented Charlotte and other cities from implementing nondiscrimination provisions for LGBTQ people, and required individuals to use the bathrooms that correspond to the sex identified on their birth certificate.

HB 2 provoked outrage around the country, and many prominent corporations and organizations boycotted North Carolina at the cost of millions of dollars to the state economy. Trans celebrity Caitlyn Jenner even publicly declared that if she found herself in North Carolina she would use a women's bathroom.

Commenting on this situation, anthropologist Elijah Adiv Edelman (2016) observed that characterizations of trans people as sexual predators are inaccurate and often obscure the fact that trans people are at much greater risk of being

Caitlyn Jenner, Trans Celebrity.

continues

Thinking Like an Anthropologist *continued*

victims of sexual assault and violence. He also noted that the anxieties around trans people's access to bathrooms are not about bathrooms themselves, but anxieties many Americans feel about the "unnaturalness" of sex and gender ambiguity. It is this sense of unnaturalness that leads many to justify violence against trans people, explaining why trans people are among the most vulnerable to sexual violence in our society. What worries Edelman is that bills like HB 2 formalize state support for that violence.

This situation raises a number of questions for anthropologists, including the following:

1. What kinds of symbolic representations of trans people exist in debates over their rights and their use of public facilities?
2. What forms of vulnerability and violence do trans people experience in contemporary American society?
3. How and why have a number of American individuals, corporations, institutions, and state offices come to accept that

LGBTQ individuals should receive state protection from discrimination?
4. What beliefs, political interest groups, and social factors contributed to the creation of HB 2?
5. What role should anthropological researchers take in public debates over trans rights?

PART TWO: THE CULTURAL AND SOCIOPOLITICAL MEANINGS OF CAITLYN JENNER'S FAME

In 2015, television personality and former Olympic athlete Bruce Jenner announced a name and gender change, becoming Caitlyn Jenner. Americans had long been fascinated with Jenner—especially as an accomplished Olympian and a participant in the reality show *Keeping Up with the Kardashians*—but since this announcement, interest in Jenner's life has exploded. What questions might you ask as an anthropological researcher about the cultural meanings and sociopolitical effects of Caitlyn Jenner's fame as a trans woman in American society?

❂ Is Human Sexuality Just a Matter of Being Straight or Queer?

Most of us assume that sexuality (sexual preferences, desires, and practices) is an either/or issue, that people are *either* straight *or* queer. We also assume that most humans are heterosexual. The term we use to indicate heterosexuality—"straight"—implies that it is normal and morally correct, while anything else is deviant, bent, or "queer," a term that once had derogatory connotations but in recent years has been appropriated by LGBTQ communities and given a more positive connotation.

But human sexuality is far more complex and subtle, something that social scientists began to realize after Indiana University biologist Dr. Alfred Kinsey conducted a series of sexuality studies during the 1940s (Figure 10.8). Kinsey and his colleagues surveyed the sexual lives and desires of American men and women, discovering that sexuality exists along a continuum. They found, for example, that 37% of the male population surveyed had had some sexual experience with other men, most of which occurred during adolescence, and at least 25% of adult males had had more than incidental same-sex sexual experiences for at least three years of their lives (Kinsey 1948; Fausto-Sterling 1992b). Many of these men did not think of themselves or lead their lives as gay; this suggests quite clearly that in practice, people's sexuality does not fall into absolute categories. More important, Kinsey's research challenged views of same-sex sexuality that consider it a pathological and deviant condition, indicating that psychologically "normal" people may express their sexuality in many ways.

Figure 10.8 Controversial Knowledge. Kinsey's work was highly controversial during a period in American history when same-sex sexual encounters and sexual promiscuity were widely considered to be unacceptable.

As a flexible phenomenon, human sexuality has numerous possible expressions. Some of these expressions include lesbian sexuality (sexual attraction between women), gay sexuality (sexual attraction between men), straight sexuality (sexual attraction between men and women), asexuality (non-sexuality or lack of sexual attraction), bisexuality (sexual attraction to both men and women), demisexuality (sexual attraction only to individuals with whom one has an emotional bond), and pansexuality (sexual attraction to individuals of any gender, including individuals outside the gender binary). Sexuality is not an essence buried deep in a person's psychological self or genetic makeup (Lancaster 2004), or just a matter of personal preference or individual orientation. Like other forms of social conduct, sexuality is learned, patterned, and shaped by culture and the political-economic system in which one lives (Weston 1993).

Cultural Perspectives on Same-Sex Sexuality

Anthropological attention to same-sex sexuality goes back to the discipline's early years when in the 1920s a handful of anthropologists wrote about sexual desires and practices in certain non-industrialized societies (Lyons and Lyons 2004). But it was not until the 1960s and 1970s—when the emergence of a gay movement in the United States spurred even greater scholarly attention to issues of sexuality—that anthropologists began paying more consistent attention to issues of sexuality more generally, and the cultural dynamics of same-sex sexuality more specifically (Weston 1993). More recently the global HIV/AIDS pandemic, the visibility of openly gay celebrities in media and television, and the push for legal rights for gay people have focused even more anthropological attention on issues of same-sex sexuality (Lewin and Leap 2009; Parker 2009).

One of the difficulties anthropologists studying same-sex sexuality in other societies have faced is the problem of adequately naming what they are studying (Weston 1993). Most North Americans hold the view that people are born straight or gay, implying a fixed and stable condition and identity. This notion originated in the late nineteenth century, when medical science and psychology turned what people had previously considered "perverse" *behaviors* into biopsychological *conditions* requiring medical intervention. In many other cultures, this idea of same-sex sexuality as a fixed and either/or condition does not exist.

One example comes from the work of anthropologist Gilbert Herdt, who studied male initiation rituals of the Sambia people of Papua New Guinea. Boys undergo six elaborate stages of initiation that involve behavior he calls "insemination." To be a strong, powerful warrior requires *jerungdu* (the essence of masculine strength), a substance a boy can acquire only from ingesting the semen of a man. Before insemination the boys must purge harmful feminine essences with a rite that mimics female menstruation: sharp grasses are shoved up the noses of the boys to make them bleed off the lingering essences of their mother's milk. Finally, they receive *jerungdu* in the form of semen directly from young married men on whom they perform fellatio. During the early stages of the initiation the boys are inseminated orally by young married men at the height of their sexual and physical powers. When the initiates reach later stages of initiation—after marriage but before they become fathers—younger initiates will fellate them. The final stage of initiation occurs after the birth of their first child. Now in their twenties or thirties, the men have sex only with women.

Herdt (1981) described these initiation activities as "ritualized homosexuality." The problem with this terminology is that Western notions of "homosexuality" imply an inborn condition or identity, yet after marriage Sambia men shift their erotic focus to women. Furthermore, for the Sambia these ritual acts are not erotic per se, but intended to develop masculine strength. Herdt and others who study similar rites now refer to them as "semen transactions" or "boy-inseminating rites."

Anthropologists have also learned that concepts of same-sex sexuality differ across cultures. In Latin American countries like Mexico (Carrier 1976), Nicaragua (Lancaster 1992, 1997), and Brazil (Parker 1989), a man who engages in same-sex sexual practices is not necessarily identified as (nor would he consider himself) "gay." For example, Brazilian sexual culture distinguishes between active and passive participants in sexual intercourse, typically considering the active agent masculine and the passive agent feminine. The metaphorical language people use to describe sex acts reflects these distinctions: *dar* [darr; "to give"] is the passive role of being penetrated during intercourse, while *comer* [koh-**mehr**; "to eat"] is the action of penetration (Parker 1989). "Women" and *viados* (a colloquial term meaning "fags" or gay men) are those who "give" (receive penetration), while "men" are the active ones who "eat" (penetrate). The result is that a man who penetrates another man would not consider himself—nor would he be considered by others—to be gay, yet the man being penetrated would be considered gay.

As Richard Parker (2009), an anthropologist who has studied Brazilian sexual culture, points out, these implicit sexual meanings can have major consequences for designing public health programs. Parker observes that in the early years of the HIV/AIDS crisis, Brazilians uncritically accepted the notion derived from the United States and Europe that HIV/AIDS was a "gay disease" transmitted through sex between men and affecting only the gay population. To create effective public health interventions, Parker advised, it was necessary to build programs around the specific Brazilian cultural meanings of sexuality, and not ignore the risky behaviors of men who did not consider themselves susceptible to HIV because they were "not gay."

Controlling Sexuality

Long ago, anthropologists observed that every society places limits on people's sexuality by constructing rules about who can sleep with whom. Modern governments routinely exert great control over sexuality, implementing and enforcing laws that limit the kinds of sexual relations their citizens can have. For example, in dozens of countries, and even in twenty-one U.S. states, adultery is considered by the law to be "injurious to public morals and a mistreatment of the marriage relationship" (Adultery 2009) and is treated by authorities as a civil offense (subject to fines) or even a crime (subject to jail time). Until the U.S. Supreme Court overturned such laws in 2003, fifteen states still outlawed "sodomy," or sex acts considered "unnatural" or "immoral" such as anal sex, oral sex, or same-sex sex acts. In our country, the most contentious public issues—including debates about abortion, gay people in the military, and the right to same-sex marriage—involve questions over whether and how the government should control the sexuality of its citizens.

Family-planning programs can also be viewed as another manifestation of government control over sexuality, especially women's sexuality (Dwyer 2000). China's well-known "One Child Policy," which limited most families to one child, has reduced fertility rates and unemployment significantly, but it also involved unprecedented government control over sexuality, including (until 2002, when it was outlawed) forced abortions and sterilizations of women who exceeded their quota or were deemed unfit to reproduce.

THINKING CRITICALLY ABOUT GENDER, SEX, AND SEXUALITY

Many queer activists in the United States and Europe have accepted and promote the idea that they were "born" with their sexual identity and that they have no choice in the matter. How do you think anthropologists, who view sexuality as culturally patterned, socially conditioned, and not inborn, should respond to this idea?

❦ Conclusion

The concept of sexuality connects back to concepts we considered earlier in this chapter, namely gender and sex. Although they traditionally have distinct definitions, each of these concepts touches on an issue of central importance to human existence, which is our capacity for sexual reproduction. Yet, these concepts are intertwined in complex ways, shaping the ideas and social patterns a society uses to organize males, females, and others who do not fit these neat categories, such as intersexuals and gender variants.

It is important to remember that however natural our ideas about these matters may feel to us, they are not universal. Returning to the Liberian example of cross-dressing warriors that opened this chapter, it would be quite easy—but deeply mistaken—to explain warrior cross-dressing as some kind of erotic fantasy, just because that is how many of us think of cross-dressing in our own culture. Crossdressing Liberian warriors were self-consciously engaging with their own traditional notions of sex and gender, specifically mixing male and female symbols to draw on the mystical power of both.

It is also good to remember that matters of sex, gender, and sexuality are not necessarily as stable as they feel to us. Just as Liberian rebels were rather quick to drop cross-dressing in favor of Rambo-style clothing, our own notions of sex, gender, and sexuality are dynamic and fluid as well. Not only does our own society have more diversity and flexibility in sexual practices than our cultural categories tend to acknowledge, the very notion of sexuality as an inborn condition is a relatively new one in Western history. The reason these things feel so stable to us in our everyday experience is that they are powerful cultural constructions reproduced and upheld in our everyday lives and most important social institutions.

Key Terms

Cisgender   p. 227

Gender   p. 217

Gender variance   p. 224

Gender/sex systems   p. 216

Intersex   p. 217

Masculinity   p. 222

Sex   p. 216

Sexuality   p. 224

Sexually dimorphic   p. 217

Third genders   p. 224

Transgender   p. 227

Reviewing the Chapter

CHAPTER SECTION	WHAT WE KNOW	TO BE RESOLVED
How and why do males and females differ?	Every society makes a distinction between "male" and "female." But not all societies have the firm binary between males and females we find in Western cultures. Gender/sex systems are cross-culturally variable dynamic, and not all attach the same meanings to biological differences, or even think differences in biology are important for explaining differences between males and females.	Anthropologists continue to work out the relative influences of biological, environmental, and cultural factors on shaping gender/sex.
Why is there inequality between men and women?	Biological differences are not the source of women's subordination. Rather, cultural ideologies and social relations impose on women lower status, prestige, and power than men.	The debate over the universality of women's subordinate status was never resolved, and in recent years new debates have emerged about the extent to which gender inequalities are performed by women and men.
What does it mean to be neither male nor female?	Many gender/sex systems around the world allow for gender variance and third genders. Gender variants generally establish their unique identities through social performance: wearing certain clothes, speaking and moving in certain ways, and performing certain social roles and occupations.	Western terminology and concepts are not always able to capture the complexity of how other cultures conceive of matters of sex, gender, and sexuality, which raises questions about how to best represent such phenomena.
Is human sexuality just a matter of being straight or queer?	Human sexuality is variable and patterned by cultural ideologies and social relations. It is also not a fixed or exclusive condition.	Anthropologists continue to work through the complex and subtle ways in which sexuality interacts with gender and sex, as well as other identities like class, race, and ethnicity.

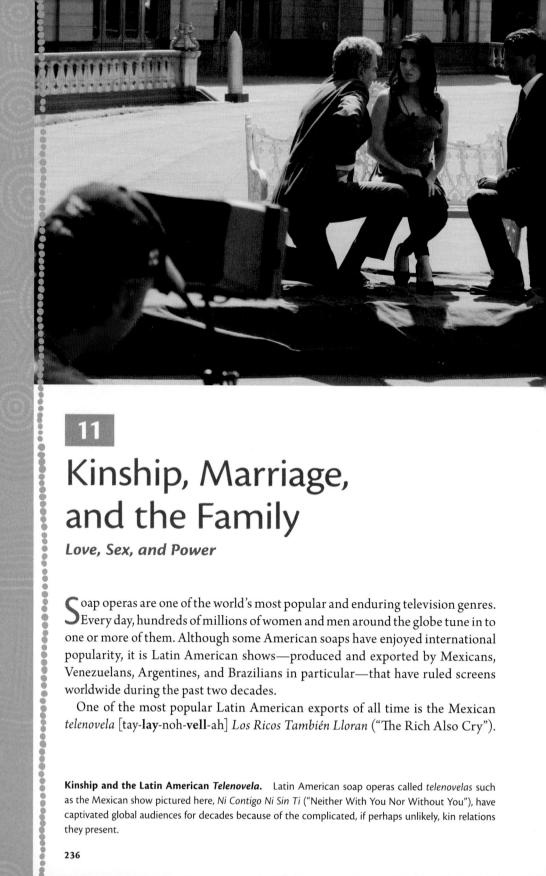

11

Kinship, Marriage, and the Family

Love, Sex, and Power

Soap operas are one of the world's most popular and enduring television genres. Every day, hundreds of millions of women and men around the globe tune in to one or more of them. Although some American soaps have enjoyed international popularity, it is Latin American shows—produced and exported by Mexicans, Venezuelans, Argentines, and Brazilians in particular—that have ruled screens worldwide during the past two decades.

One of the most popular Latin American exports of all time is the Mexican *telenovela* [tay-**lay**-noh-**vell**-ah] *Los Ricos También Lloran* ("The Rich Also Cry").

Kinship and the Latin American *Telenovela*. Latin American soap operas called *telenovelas* such as the Mexican show pictured here, *Ni Contigo Ni Sin Ti* ("Neither With You Nor Without You"), have captivated global audiences for decades because of the complicated, if perhaps unlikely, kin relations they present.

Produced in 1979, it has enjoyed tremendous popularity and been rebroadcast in dozens of countries throughout the Americas, Europe, Asia, and Africa to the present day. *Telenovelas* (as such shows are called in Spanish) usually run for only a few months and have a clear ending, unlike U.S. soaps, which are long-running and open-ended.

The basic plot of *Los Ricos También Lloran*, which many subsequent *telenovelas* have imitated, is as follows. A beautiful and poor young woman named Mariana becomes a maid for a rich and powerful family. She and the youngest son in the family, Luis Alberto, have a scandalous love affair and eventually get married. She has a baby son, Beto, but in a fit of temporary madness she gives him away to an old woman on the street.

During the next eighteen years, Mariana searches desperately for Beto and miraculously finds him when he begins dating Marisabel, who is Mariana and Luis Alberto's adopted daughter (though she doesn't know she's adopted). Mariana tells Marisabel who Beto really is. Marisabel becomes hysterical at the thought of incest with her brother. Mariana does not, however, tell Luis Alberto, fearing he will get angry with her. He gets angry anyway because she spends so much time with Beto that Luis Alberto suspects the two are having an affair. In the final episode Luis Alberto confronts Beto and Mariana with a gun. In the program's final moments, Mariana screams "Son!" Luis Alberto goes ballistic. Beto screams, "Father, let me embrace you!" and the family is, against all odds, reunited at long last.

Dark family secrets, suspicious spouses, unruly children, irresponsible parents, and possible incest make for gripping television, to say the least! But to an anthropologist—if not also for many viewers around the world—the fascination this show holds is not due simply to its unlikely storyline but to its presentation of the complexities of love, sex, and power that are part and parcel of being in any family, anywhere in the world.

Also noteworthy is the show's assumption that blood relations are the central defining relationships in people's lives—after all, Luis Alberto's anger disappears when he realizes Beto is his son, and Marisabel would probably not be so hysterical if she knew Beto wasn't her biological brother. For anthropologists, it is a noteworthy assumption mainly because it reflects one particular culture's way of defining family relationships. Around the world not all cultures give the same weight to biological relatedness for defining a family.

The biological facts of procreation are only one aspect of what it means to have a family. What is more important is how these biological facts are interpreted and the special rights and obligations that these facts confer on individuals. At the heart of anthropology's interest in families is the question: *How are families more than just groups of biologically related people?* Embedded within this larger question are the following questions, around which this chapter is organized:

What are families, and how are they structured in different societies?
How do families control power and wealth?
Why do people get married?
How are social and technological changes reshaping how people think about family?

The kinds of influence and control people can exert on their relatives vary widely from one society to another. Yet, anthropologists have long recognized that we cannot understand a society until we understand the core relationships of kinship, marriage, and family around which people's social lives are lived. So let us begin by considering what makes a group of relatives a family.

❦ What Are Families, and How Are They Structured in Different Societies?

Families are important in nearly every society. They give members a sense of comfort and belonging and provide them part of their identity, values, and ideals. They control wealth and the material necessities of life. And, importantly, they assign individuals with basic roles, rights, and responsibilities in relation to other relatives.

It probably feels natural to you that your own family does all (or most) of these things. What is *not* natural is how and why your family is organized and achieves these things in the ways it does. Like other aspects of culture we've explored throughout this book, **kinship**—the social system that organizes people in families based on descent and marriage—is patterned in culturally specific and dynamic ways. We begin by exploring its dynamism, and then we examine the different ways families can be organized cross-culturally.

Families, Ideal and Real

In every society a gap exists between that society's ideal family and the real families that exist, the reason being that all families are dynamic. For example, as individuals grow older they move out of their **natal family**—the family into which they were born and in which they are usually raised—to marry and start their own families. In addition, broader social and economic conditions change the composition, size, and character of the ties between family members, as the example of the American family illustrates.

"TRADITIONAL" AMERICAN FAMILIES

American politicians and religious leaders frequently extol the virtues of the "traditional" family. But just what family do these people have in mind as their model? Most likely, it is some version of the family in the television show *The Adventures of Ozzie and Harriet* (which aired from 1952 to 1966), with a working husband/father who is the head of the household, a loving stay-at-home wife/mother, and two or three children living in a spic-and-span suburban home.

The problem is that the Ozzie and Harriet ideal is not a "traditional" family, but a new pattern—the independent American suburban family—that emerged in the 1950s and lasted for less than twenty years. Only twenty years before then, during the Great Depression of the 1930s, American birth rates had fallen sharply; with limited income, most families refrained from having children. The birth rate remained low from 1942 to 1946 because so many men were serving in the military during World War II. But once these millions of men returned, they began to marry and start families. The 1950s were a time of unprecedented economic growth, and the baby boom—77 million babies in fifteen years—encouraged expansion of new subdivisions filled with these young families. By the late 1950s around 60% of all Americans lived in such families.

During the late 1960s and 1970s these young postwar families had grown up, children moved out, and some couples divorced. These changes paralleled changes in the economy as women began to join the workforce in larger numbers, lowering wages for entry-level jobs. By the 1980s it was hard for young American families to get by on one salary. Two-income households brought in more wages but put stress on couples, who still needed someone to cook their meals, clean their houses or apartments, and look after their children. Nowadays, families tend to have one or two children rather than three or four. Divorce has become much more common than ever before in American life, and today only half of American households are headed by a married couple. When divorced couples with kids get remarried, the composition of a family (with multiple sets of stepparents and stepsiblings)—and especially the obligations individuals in the family have to each other—can get quite complicated.

Nuclear and Extended Families

Still, the **nuclear family**—the family formed by a married couple and their children—is the most important family structure in the United States. Ours is not the only society with nuclear families—nuclear family units occur in and are important to nearly every society around the world. Indeed, for many decades anthropologists wrote of the nuclear family as the most basic unit of kinship (Radcliffe-Brown 1941:2).

Using a basic **kinship chart** (a visual representation of family relationships), we can graph a man's nuclear family easily enough, and we can add another nuclear family for his wife's natal family, and add children (Figure 11.1). Such charts describe biological connections, such as mother–daughter or father–daughter, without expressing the content of these different relationships. For example, when a child is young the relationship between parent and child may involve teaching and training. But when a widowed mother moves in with her child's family, the content of the relationship is entirely different, even though the biological relationship has not changed.

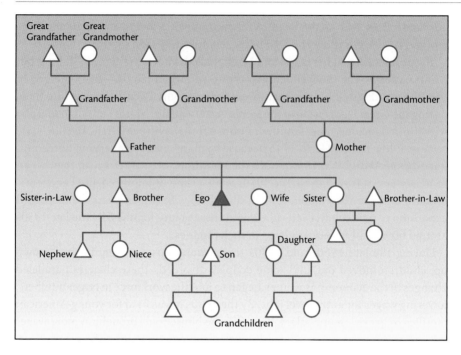

Figure 11.1   A Kinship Chart Plots out All Sorts of Kin Relations.   Here the chart shows members of the extended family from a husband/father's perspective (identified as "Ego" in the chart). Of course, the chart could be drawn from the wife/mother's perspective as well.

One important feature of nuclear and natal families is that they usually function as **corporate groups,** which are groups of people who work together toward common ends, much as a corporation does. The family's goals are not just the goals of one family member, but of the group as a whole. In every society around the world, families are supposed to look after the needs of all members of the family—parents, children, and any other family members who happen to be in residence.

Family groups may also consist of larger groups of relatives beyond the nuclear family, which anthropologists call **extended families**. Extended families may live together and function as a corporate group, or they may merely acknowledge ties with one another. In nineteenth-century America, for example, it was common for households to include a nuclear family at its core, as well as some mix of elderly parents, a single brother or sister, the orphaned children of the wife's sister, and perhaps another niece or nephew. Nowadays, for many Americans only special events like funerals, weddings, and family reunions bring large extended families together (Figure 11.2).

Clans and Lineages

Anthropologists use the term **clan** to refer to a special group of relatives who are all descended (or claim to descend) from a single ancestor. In many societies, links to these ancestors can be quite vague, and in a number of societies these ancestors are animals or humans with distinctive non-human characteristics. Clans are often as important as nuclear families in the small-scale societies anthropologists have studied in Oceania, Africa, and the Americas—so much so that in the 1940s French anthropologist Claude Lévi-Strauss (1949/1969) challenged the importance of the nuclear family as the basic unit of kinship, arguing instead for the importance of clans as basic units of kinship. Clans typically control land and other resources, as well as any individual member's access to those resources. They are also usually **exogamous**, which means that

Figure 11.2   Extended Families in North America.   (Top) An Indian family from the Kainai tribe in the Canadian plains about 1900. (Bottom) An American extended family gathers for a reunion in Mt. Carmel, Illinois, in 1904. Everyone in the photo is descended from one deceased couple, parents of seven of the senior women pictured.

members of the clan must marry someone from another clan, which has the effect of building political, economic, and social ties with other clans. Clans come in three types: patrilineal, matrilineal, and cognatic. **Lineages** are very similar to clans, but lineages tend to be composed of people who are directly descended from known ancestors, while clan membership is often more vague and assumed rather than empirically known.

PATRILINEAL CLANS AND LINEAGES

The most common clans and lineages in non-industrial societies are **patrilineal**, such as those found among the Omaha Indians, the Nuer of South Sudan, and most groups in the Central Highlands of Papua New Guinea. In these societies, clan members claim to be descended through males from the same ancestor (Figure 11.3). These clans are **unilineal** (based on descent through a single descent line, in this case males). Most Americans will easily understand patrilineal descent because in the United States we have traditionally inherited our surnames patrilineally—that is, taking on the family name from the father.

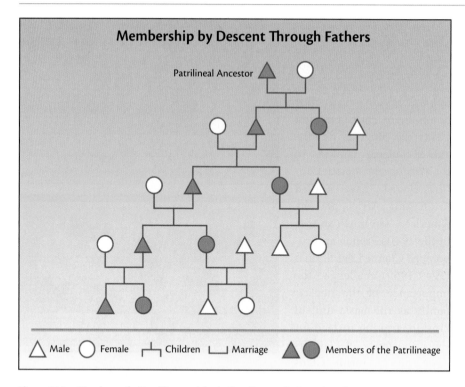

Figure 11.3   Members of a Patrilineage (shaded).   Descent is through males.

MATRILINEAL CLANS AND LINEAGES

Anthropologists have also observed **matrilineal** clans and lineages that reckon descent through women, and are descended from an ancestral woman (Figure 11.4). In these societies, such as the Trobriand Islanders discussed in other chapters, every man and woman is a member of his or her mother's clan, which is also the clan of their mother's mother. Other members of this clan include the mother's brother and the mother's mother's brother. A person's strongest identity is with his or her relatives in a mother's clan and lineage.

Matrilineality is not the same as matriarchy, in which women hold political power. Matrilineality is only about identity and group membership. In matrilineal societies, land is usually owned by the clan or by a lineage within a larger clan. While women may have some say in who uses clan land for gardens or for gathering material for building houses, it is usually the men in the clan who have control over these resources. As such, a young man will look to his mother's brother for guidance and assistance, just as this uncle had looked to his mother's brother for direction when he was young.

COGNATIC CLANS

A third kind of clan is the **cognatic** clan (or bilateral clan), such as is found among the Samoans of Central Polynesia. Samoans reckon descent through both the

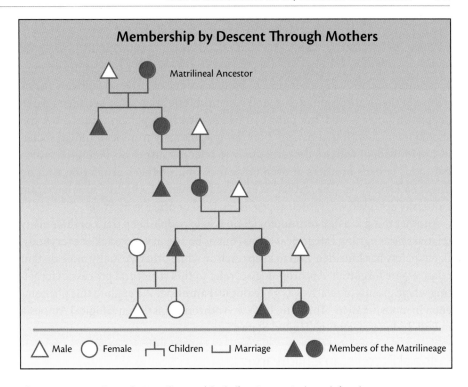

Membership by Descent Through Mothers

Matrilineal Ancestor

Male   Female   Children   Marriage   Members of the Matrilineage

Figure 11.4   Members of a Matrilineage (shaded).   Descent is through females.

mother and the father, allowing people to be members of both their mother's and their father's clan. The main difference between a cognatic clan and a unilineal clan is that in cognatic clans one can be a member of any of several clans, and in some societies multiple membership is possible or even typical. Matrilineal and patrilineal clans, in contrast, are naturally bounded by who a person's mother or father is, respectively.

Kinship Terminologies

Another way to think about the structure of families is to explore terms that people in different societies use to refer to their relatives. Since the 1860s, when American anthropologist Lewis Henry Morgan (1871) collected kinship terminologies from many different languages around the world, anthropologists have collected thousands of different kinship terminologies, but it happens that all of them can be grouped into six basic patterns Morgan had identified. Morgan and several other anthropologists from the cultural evolution school tried to identify some kinship terminologies as more evolved and sophisticated than others. Anthropologist A. L. Kroeber (1909) identified and summarized the basic principles of kinship terminologies by arguing that kinship terminologies are shaped by the kind of clan organization found in a society, not by a group's position on some evolutionary scale.

This early research on kinship terminologies was important because it demonstrated the existence of a few basic systems of organizing people. Anthropologists also realized that kinship terminologies do not just provide descriptive names that indicate relationships between individuals, but can also indicate the specific nature of the relationship, rights, and responsibilities that exist between related people. In other words, the term you use to identify a person shapes how you should interact with that person. For example, in many American Indian societies, an individual will use the term *father* to refer not just to his biological father, but to his father's brothers or even other men of his father's generation with no direct biological ties. The "father" is expected to interact with his "son" in certain culturally accepted ways, such as providing food or other assistance.

Another thing kinship terminologies do is help people keep track of their many relatives by assigning categorical terms. But nobody can keep track of everybody. Each society has kinsmen vital to keep track of, while others, usually more distant relatives, are forgotten. Anthropologists refer to this structural process of forgetting whole groups of relatives as **genealogical amnesia**. We explore this phenomenon in more detail in "Thinking Like an Anthropologist: Genealogical Amnesia in Bali, Indonesia, and the United States."

Cultural Patterns in Childrearing

Nearly a century ago, the anthropologist Margaret Mead began studying how families raised children in different cultures. Between the 1930s and the 1950s, Mead was associated with a loosely connected group of scholars known as the **culture and personality movement**, whose focus was on how patterns of childrearing, social institutions, and cultural ideologies shaped individual experience, personality characteristics, and thought patterns (Hsu 1972). They asserted that how a child is bathed, fed, and attended to in the first years of life shapes that child's approach to the world into adulthood.

In her first fieldwork project on kinship and social organization in American Samoa (Mead 1930a, 1930b), Mead observed how Samoan families were caring for their children. She wrote about these things in her popular book *Coming of Age in Samoa* (1928), where she explained that Samoan adolescent sexuality lacked a lot of the psychological distress and anxiety typical of American adolescent sexuality. The reason for this, she believed, is that Samoan approaches to childrearing involve children in work early in their lives and don't judge maturity by a child's age but according to outward physical changes, such as those associated with puberty.

Today, it is clear from a variety of more recent studies by anthropologists and sociologists that parental investment of time and nurturing makes a difference in what children aspire to achieve as adolescents and adults. Anthropologists in particular have focused on how middle-class and upper-middle-class families have an ideology and the resources to emphasize education and concerted self-improvement, while poor families with fewer resources have less time for nurturing children because they are struggling to keep their families fed and clothed (see, e.g., Stack 1997; Lareau 2003).

Thinking Like an Anthropologist

Genealogical Amnesia in Bali, Indonesia, and the United States

Anthropologists begin their research by asking questions. In this box, we want you to learn how to ask questions as an anthropological researcher. Part One describes a situation and follows up with questions we would ask. Part Two asks you to formulate your own questions based on a different situation.

PART ONE: GENEALOGICAL AMNESIA AND NAMING PATTERNS ON THE ISLAND OF BALI

In the late 1950s, American anthropologists Hildred and Clifford Geertz (1964, 1975) studied Balinese kinship patterns on the lush, tropical island of Bali in Indonesia. The Balinese have a bilateral kinship system, which means that an individual is related equally to relatives in his or her mother's and father's family (much as Americans are). People are more or less "closely" related, at least in theory, to everyone who is descended from any one of their sixteen great-great-grandparents. That is a lot of relatives!

How do the Balinese keep track of them all? The Geertzes found that people don't. While Balinese lived in large extended family groups, the number of relatives they actually interacted with was limited to a few dozen members. Most informants were aware of only a couple hundred kinsmen rather than the thousands that were theoretically possible. The Geertzes referred to this forgetting of relatives as "genealogical amnesia."

Genealogical amnesia was not about how particular individuals literally forgot some of their relatives, but about how features of normal social life encourage people to focus on some relatives so that other relatives gradually drift off their radar screen.

The Geertzes learned that genealogical amnesia was not random, but quite systematic. It is the result of a particular naming system. All Balinese have personal names, and as in the United States and other countries, parents often name their children after grandparents, aunts and uncles, and great-grandparents. But after Balinese men and women marry they are no longer called by their personal names; they are referred to as "father of so-and-so" or "mother of so-and-so." As their children get older and marry, these parents will begin to be referred to as "grandfather of so-and-so" or "grandmother of so-and-so." (Anthropologists call this naming

A Modern Balinese Family Attending a Ceremony. Most members of this extended family live together in several households inside the same house yard.

continues

Thinking Like an Anthropologist *continued*

practice **teknonymy**, a system of naming parents by the names of their children.)

In Bali the teknonyms assigned to individuals kept changing over time as people got older. The effect of this was that none of the younger people had ever heard the personal names of their grandparents and great-grandparents. The effect of this rather simple naming system was that everyone knew they were related to everyone who was a descendant of a great-grandparent—who would be known as "great-grandfather of so-and-so" or "great-grandmother of so-and-so." But it also obscured relatives, since all the personal names several generations back were no longer used in conversation. Members of earlier generations were known only by the names of their first-born grandchildren or great-grandchildren, and even these identifications became difficult to pick out of daily conversation after people in those generations had died.

What questions does this situation raise for anthropological researchers?

1. How does being a grandchild of someone with a particular teknonym help you identify other close relatives?
2. What happens to people's knowledge of their common kin ties once their great-grandparents die?
3. How might people be able to identify kin relations more easily if everyone used personal names rather than teknonyms?

PART TWO: GENEALOGICAL AMNESIA IN AMERICAN FAMILIES

In the United States, naming practices also produce a systematic pattern of genealogical amnesia. One of the most obvious effects of genealogical amnesia comes from the practice of women dropping their maiden names when they marry. This practice was typical until the 1970s, and it remains fairly common today. What questions would you ask about genealogical amnesia in the United States as an anthropological researcher?

Whether societies place emphasis on small nuclear family groups or extended kin groups organized as lineages or clans, families organize corporate activities within the group and relationships with people in other groups. Let us turn now to how families control wealth and power.

THINKING CRITICALLY ABOUT KINSHIP, MARRIAGE, AND THE FAMILY

Lewis Henry Morgan thought of American kinship as the most rational way of reckoning kin relationships, and he referred to our system as a descriptive rather than classificatory system because relatives on the mother's side were called the same thing as relatives on the father's side. But, in fact, terms like *aunt*, *uncle*, and *cousin* group together very different kinds of relatives under the same label, which makes our system a "classificatory" system. Using your own family as an example, discuss how these terms are classificatory, even if *mother, father, son,* and *daughter* are not.

✽ How Do Families Control Power and Wealth?

Whatever form of family we might find in a society, one of its key functions is controlling and managing its members' wealth. The most obvious way for a family, lineage, or clan group to control its wealth is by defining rights over the productive and reproductive abilities of its women and children, as well as defining the inheritance rights of family members when someone dies. We explore each of these issues in turn next.

Claiming a Bride

In the non-industrial societies that anthropologists studied in the early and mid-twentieth century in Africa, South America, and the Pacific, it was clear that women provided much of the labor needed to plant, weed, and harvest food from their fields and gardens. When a couple marries, the groom's family gives valuables to the bride's family in what has been called bridewealth, bride price payments, or simply **bride price.** Bride price compensates the woman's natal family for the loss of her productive and reproductive activities (Figure 11.5).

The patrilineal Zulu tribes of southern Africa, for example, traditionally used cattle for their bride price payments. When a young man had identified a young woman that he was interested in as a wife, his male relatives began negotiations about her bride price, which Zulu call *lobola.* These negotiations marked the beginning of the couple's engagement. Typically the man sought the assistance of male relatives in his patrilineage. The bride price was paid through a series of gifts from the groom to his father-in-law, the first gift of several head of cattle occurring at the time of the marriage. Later the man would give additional gifts of cattle until the entire bride price had been given. Anthropologist Max Gluckman (1940) reported that the South African government viewed these multiple *lobola* payments as a practice that disrupted the flow of young men to the mines as laborers. It seems that these men wanted to stay in their villages working to assemble the cattle they needed and were not eager to set off as mine workers. The government plan was to limit *lobola* to eleven

Figure 11.5 Bride Price. Cash has replaced traditional shell valuables in many bride price payments in Papua New Guinea.

head of cattle, all of which should be paid at the time of marriage. This plan, together with a tax levied on each Zulu hut, forced young men to work in the mines but disrupted the normal pattern of marriage, since most wives stayed back in their husband's village and there was no opportunity for the man to build bonds with his father-in-law.

In some tribal societies, other kinds of valuables can be given as bridewealth, including wild game in some Amazon communities or pigs and shell valuables in many New Guinea societies. In other societies, a young man has to work for his wife's family for a year or more, performing what can be called bride service.

Recruiting the Kids

As with bride price payments aimed at paying for rights in women, child price payments are another kind of payment to a woman's family, intended to buy rights in the woman's children. Such payments compensate the woman's family for a child who belongs to a different clan and allow the father to recruit the child to his clan. This sort of transaction over children is most typical in societies with patrilineal clans, rather than in those with matrilineal clans, where the children belong to their mother's clan and typically live with her. In some societies, child price payments can be paid all at once, but the power of these transactions can best be understood in societies like the Daribi of the Highlands of Papua New Guinea, where payments may take place over many years. Anthropologist Roy Wagner (1967, 1969) described these gifts as countering the rights and claims of the child's uncle (mother's brother) over these children. This uncle could claim the child to his clan if the payments were not made. Because so many transactions between clans are about creating alliances, the ongoing series of payments preserve and perpetuate the relationship between the child's father and the uncle. In this case, the payments in the form of gifts define and bind the two clans, just as they link the two men in an ongoing alliance. Both men get something from the relationship, including assistance from the other when needed.

Dowry in India

Another traditional form of marriage payment occurs in the highly stratified communities of India. Here, high-caste families traditionally gave a **dowry** consisting of a large sum of money—or in-kind gifts of livestock, furniture, or even electronics—to a daughter to ensure her well-being in her husband's family. Sometimes the dowry was given, at least in part, to the husband as a way of attracting a prosperous and hardworking husband. The Indian government outlawed the practice of dowry in 1961, but in many parts of the country the practice continues as before.

In recent years abuses of dowry have become common, reaching more than 3,000 incidents a year, attracting the attention of the Indian government, state governments, and international human rights groups. In these cases, members of the husband's family threaten the bride if more dowry is not forthcoming. In the most severe cases, the men's families have even killed the bride because her family would not contribute more dowry.

Controlling Family Wealth Through Inheritance

Families also control wealth, property, and power through rules of inheritance. The death of an individual can create a crisis in a family, because members have to decide how to redistribute land and whatever kinds of wealth that person may have held, which can create conflict. Rules of inheritance typically ensure an orderly process and, more important, ensure that wealth and property stay in the family.

In Western countries, such rules have been codified in law for a long time. For example, centuries ago Great Britain acknowledged the right of primogeniture, in which the eldest son inherited a man's entire estate, including all lands and other wealth. Elder brothers might give some allowance to their younger brothers, but these younger sons had no claim to the estate and often went into the Church or the military, or migrated to distant lands. The goal of primogeniture was to preserve large landed estates together with the money and other wealth needed to maintain them.

Inheritance Rules in Non-Industrial Societies

Inheritance rules also exist in small-scale non-industrial societies, in spite of the fact that many lack a formal legal code. In many of these societies the most valuable property is land, but it might also include livestock, locally recognized valuables, vegetables, and rights in people. Not surprisingly, when people die in these societies land and some forms of durable personal property are the most important things to be inherited. In tribal and chiefly societies land is typically controlled by clans or some other form of extended family group.

In any society, inheritance usually goes to legitimate heirs—typically the children of a socially recognized married couple. But marriage is such a complicated social institution that we should consider what motivates people to get married in the first place, as well as the less obvious benefits that come to married people.

THINKING CRITICALLY ABOUT KINSHIP, MARRIAGE, AND THE FAMILY

Although most Americans who get engaged think that the upcoming marriage is about them as a couple, in fact marriage brings together two sets of families and friends. Consider the most recent wedding you attended, or ask a friend or relative about a wedding they attended as a guest. Who paid for different parts of the celebration (reception, officiant, wedding license, flowers, bridesmaids' dresses, groomsmen's tuxes, etc.)? Who was expected to give gifts, and to whom were those gifts expected to be given? How do the dollars and cents of a wedding outline the structure of American families and kin groups?

❧ Why Do People Get Married?

For at least two centuries, American pastors, priests, and rabbis have preached that sex is reserved for marriage, as it is primarily for procreation. Yet the reality of American life is that sexual behavior is not limited to married couples, and marriage is about a lot more than sex. In this section we explain some of the reasons people have for getting married, as well as some of the diverse forms that marriage can take.

Why People Get Married

For most Americans, marriage is about love and sex, and we take for granted our individual right to choose a marriage partner. But in most societies around the world, marriage is about cultivating political and economic relations between families. In such contexts, a common belief is that marriage is too important to be left to the whims of an individual, and so accepted practice is for family members to choose an individual's marriage partner.

Marriage also provides social recognition of the ties between the couple, if not also their families, as well as social legitimacy to the children. The importance of public recognition partially helps explain why same-sex marriage has become a key political issue in the past decade in many societies, including the United States, Canada, Mexico, and Argentina. Whoever is getting married, weddings proclaim to the world that the couple is united and brings the two families together to acknowledge the couple as a unit.

Forms of Marriage

Just as we have seen the definition of marriage widening in some states and countries to include same-sex marriages, the tendency around the world has increasingly been to limit the number of partners to a couple. In many traditional societies in Africa, Asia, the Americas, and the Pacific, **polygamy** (or plural marriage) was far more common previously than it is today. The most common form of plural marriage is **polygyny**, in which one man is married simultaneously to two or more women. In parts of Africa and Melanesia, for example, having more than one wife indicates an important man with greater wealth, higher social status, or more importance in the community. From a woman's point of view, being in a polygynous marriage can mean that other wives provide support in conducting household duties, such as raising children and cooking. But as these indigenous economies have been drawn into the global system, the number of men with two or more wives has declined, as it is increasingly considered too costly and too old-fashioned (Figure 11.6).

The other form of plural marriage is **polyandry**, in which one woman has two or more husbands at one time. Few societies around the world are known to have allowed polyandry, and the best-known are the Toda, one of the hill tribes in India (Rivers 1906; Dakowski 1990), and the Sherpas of Nepal, who formerly used polyandry to keep large estates from being divided into tiny estates (Ortner 1989). Among both the Todas and the Sherpas, a group of brothers marries the same woman, a practice known as fraternal polyandry, which limits the tensions among co-husbands.

Some anthropologists suggest that polyandry is uncommon because of the dominance of men's roles over women's in most societies. Let's consider some of the power that families have over their members.

Sex, Love, and the Power of Families Over Young Couples

All societies around the world have rules about who can have sex with or get married to whom. Parents and other family members may object to certain possible partners, such as if a woman chooses a partner from the wrong socioeconomic, religious, educational, or ethnic background. And nearly every society has prohibitions against sex and marriage with people who are too closely related.

THE INCEST TABOO

Many things can happen within a family, but two things that should not happen are sex and mar-

Figure 11.6 Polygamy Is Largely in Decline Around the World. (Top) A polygamous family in the Palestinian city of Ramallah in the early twentieth century; today, most Palestinian men have only one wife. (Bottom) Fundamentalist Mormons, who have broken away from the Mormon Church based in Salt Lake City, are the main group that still practices polygyny in the United States.

riage. The prohibition on sexual relations between close family members is generally called the **incest taboo**, and this taboo is as close to a universal feature of human societies as anything.

There are two well-known exceptions to the incest taboo, both of which ironically prove this taboo's generality: in ancient Egypt, during the reigns of the pharaohs, and in Hawaii, before Europeans encountered the islands for the first time in 1778. In both societies, ruling monarchs could engage in incest because they were considered living gods who could preserve the divine essence of their being only by marrying a sibling.

For relationships beyond the nuclear family—such as marriage of cousins—societies vary in what they allow. In Africa, Southeast Asia, South America, Australia, and New Guinea, the incest taboo includes prohibitions on marriage with some kinds of cousins, particularly in societies with a unilineal clan system. And in most clan-based societies, the prohibition on marriage within the clan suggests that this extension of the incest taboo defines the boundaries of the clan, just as the boundaries of incest define the boundaries of the nuclear family.

WHY IS THERE AN INCEST TABOO?

Social scientists have suggested two general explanations for the incest taboo. The most common is that it prevents birth defects. The main problem with this explanation is that in small-scale societies only incest within the nuclear family, such as brother–sister pairings, leads to higher rates of birth defects. Even then, higher rates of defects do not mean every child suffers defects. Within a small community of 300 or 500 individuals, the risk of birth defects from marriages between first cousins is not much different from random mating. Everyone in a small community is already interrelated, and the odds of deleterious (harmful) gene combinations are effectively the same for marriage with a first cousin and for random pairings.

A second explanation, called the "Westermarck Effect," explains the incest taboo as a natural psychological revulsion toward marriage (or having sex) with close relatives. First-cousin marriage was common in many places and even in the United States, where it is allowed in more than half of the states and was historically considered an appropriate match. Recently, evolutionary psychologists like Steven Pinker (1997) have adopted this explanation, arguing that natural selection has selected genes that cause us to feel little sexual attraction for people we have grown up with. There are three critiques of this evolutionary model as an explanation for the incest taboo: (1) no gene (or combination of genes) has been identified as linked to the proposed revulsion; (2) the range of relatives prohibited by the incest taboo varies too widely from society to society to be explained by selection; and (3) it is probable that the incest taboo itself is what generates psychological revulsion. That is to say, people are repulsed by sibling marriage because it violates the cultural rules of incest.

Both of these explanations assume that the incest taboo emerges from biology. But anthropologists have suggested that the incest taboo emerges from the context of ordinary life rather than from our biology. They point to the research of Melford Spiro (1958), an anthropologist who studied life in an Israeli kibbutz in the 1950s. Spiro found that the adolescents who lived together in large communal settings avoided marrying or even dating members of their communal group. There was no rule against marriage or sex within the group, but there simply was no sexual attraction because they thought of other members as siblings. Something like this occurs in U.S. college dormitories where individuals are warned against the "hallway hookup" and "floorcest" (Sivo 2005).

In the next section, we consider how changing social and technological situations produce new situations for families to make sense of and create new kinds of kin relations.

THINKING CRITICALLY ABOUT KINSHIP, MARRIAGE, AND THE FAMILY

Americans often think that marriage is about "love," but marriage is also about economics: being married and having a family cost money. Recent studies have determined that the average age at marriage in the United States has been rising for several decades as middle-class incomes have declined. Discuss how the economics of modern American life help shape the decision to get married.

How Are Social and Technological Changes Reshaping How People Think About Family?

In the 1960s, the birth control pill allowed women in Western countries like the United States, France, and Great Britain an unprecedented level of direct control over their sexuality. This technological development contributed to a so-called sexual revolution centered around the desire for "casual sex." For all the entanglements of kinship discussed previously, the prospect of having a child does not facilitate casual sex!

By the 1980s, the technological cutting edge shifted away from efforts to prevent pregnancy to efforts to improve fertility and overcome infertility. Some couples also sought to create families through adoption, only to find that there are few babies available to be adopted. In recent decades, anthropologists interested in matters of kinship have become attuned to the fact that these new social and technological developments have begun to complicate people's understandings of kinship relations.

International Adoptions and the Problem of Cultural Identity

Adoption has been a human phenomenon for as long as there have been humans. The mid-twentieth century saw the rise of adoption agencies that could arrange adoptions across U.S. states. More recently intercultural adoptions became common, and in the 1990s a new phenomenon emerged—international adoption, in which a child is adopted across international borders.

Since the 1980s, international adoptions from China, Russia, and Eastern Europe have posed a number of new issues for both the host countries and the families in the receiving countries. Not surprisingly, international adoption has political implications for relationships between donor countries and receiving countries. It also has raised important questions about the cultural identities of the adoptees, who find themselves in an intercultural position from which they must navigate complex politics of race, class, and culture in the United States.

In Vitro Fertilization

People often talk about in vitro fertilization (IVF) as a way to produce "test-tube babies." The technique takes eggs from the mother or a female donor and sperm from the father or a male donor. Fertilization can occur by incubating an egg and sperm in a Petri dish or by injecting one sperm cell into the egg. After the embryos have reached the six- to eight-cell stage they are implanted in the womb of the mother, where some of the embryos can implant in the uterus and lead to a successful pregnancy. Although only 25% to 45% of all IVF attempts produce a successful pregnancy, IVF has become an important procedure, accounting for nearly 1% of all American births annually (Elder and Dale 2000).

IVF has created a variety of new kinship relationships that people never had to cope with before. For most couples, the preferred situation was the mother's egg and father's sperm implanted into the mother, based on the belief that blood relations are the most important. But in situations where a man or woman cannot provide either sperm or an egg, other possibilities present themselves: a mother's egg, a donor's sperm; a donor's egg, a father's sperm; a donor's egg and sperm; and any of these in a surrogate uterus. The social relationships between the individuals involved in any of these scenarios do not transfer easily to categories like "mother" and "father," since who provides the biological material may differ from who raises the child or provides the womb to nurture it during pregnancy.

Surrogate Mothers and Sperm Donors

For British anthropologist Marilyn Strathern (1996) the new reproductive technologies offer insights into the ways that ordinary people understand kinship, as these new situations can lead to litigation in the courts where families are being defined, constructed, and dismantled in innovative ways because suddenly there are new parties in the family: surrogate mothers, sperm donors, multiple men claiming to be fathers, and the like. Strathern suggests that traditionally biology and social ties should work together to create kinship bonds between parents and children, but these new technologies disrupt those bonds.

To be sure, conception always presented some possible ambiguity about biological paternity, since any number of men besides the husband may have had intercourse with a woman. Paternity tests are also never fully reliable. Even when DNA tests indicate the husband as the biological father, his closest kin cannot always be excluded.

The new reproductive technologies—where sperm donors, egg donors, and IVF are involved—introduce even more ambiguities about who was the biological mother or even the biological father. Even eggs and semen from a married couple that are intended to be used for IVF can be inadvertently mixed up with specimens from other individuals before fertilization. And, some gay men wanting a child may request that their semen samples be mixed together intentionally so that one of the men is the biological father, but neither knows whether it is him or his partner.

Surrogacy introduces still more complexities. A surrogate mother agrees to have an embryo implanted in her womb, carries the baby to term, and after the baby is born the child belongs to the couple who provided the embryo. Surrogate mothers are rarely related genetically to the children they carry to term, but their body has nurtured the child for nine months, which constitutes some ambiguous link between the surrogate mother and the child. Studies by anthropologists of surrogate mothers suggest that very few surrogates have any desire to keep the newborns (Ragoné 1996). Most see their role as quite separate from that of the child's mother; their job is to help unfortunate couples by carrying their babies to term, sometimes (but not always) for a fee.

After several decades of viewing these new reproductive technologies as simple technological advances, it is becoming clear that parental rights are not about biology but about how people in different cultures choose to interpret and emphasize some biological claims over others.

THINKING CRITICALLY ABOUT KINSHIP, MARRIAGE, AND THE FAMILY

Americans have strong feelings that parents have rights over their children. Consider how these parental rights become less clear-cut under the following conditions: (a) the parents have adopted a child, but the birth parents are in the same community; (b) the parents have given up their child for adoption, and they know the family the child lives with; (c) the couple's newborn is the result of the mother's egg and an anonymous sperm donor, who has learned he is the biological father; and (d) the egg was from an anonymous donor, the sperm from the father, and the child was carried to term by a surrogate mother.

❧ Conclusion

Although the tendency in our own culture—if not also in the Mexican *telenovela* discussed in the opening of this chapter—is to emphasize that kinship and family are primarily matters of blood relationships, anthropologists view the matter rather differently, having seen the great variety of ways in which different societies construct families and kinship relations. Not only are families imbued with social and cultural expectations, but the very biological acts of sexual intercourse to conceive children are currently being revised with the rise of new reproductive technologies.

Families are at the heart of most systems of social relationship, although the Israeli kibbutzim suggest that communal living situations can in some ways overwhelm this most basic social unit. In non-industrial societies, families are vitally important to most aspects of social life. But industrialization has put pressure on large families and has encouraged individual nuclear families rather than large, unwieldy extended families and clans. And families are important to individuals even when, as in our society, the active family units are pared down to parents and a small number of children.

But no matter how dazzling the diverse kinds of families we might find in different societies, whether matrilineal lineages, patrilineal clans, nuclear families, or some other social form, these ways of understanding and working with relatives seem inherently natural. In nearly every society, individuals look at their families as one of the most natural and biologically based institutions. Just as we saw in the previous chapter, where ideas of sex and gender seem inherently natural, so too do the families around which we structure our lives.

Key Terms

Bride price p. 247	Extended families p. 240	Nuclear family p. 239
Clan p. 240	Genealogical amnesia p. 244	Patrilineal p. 241
Cognatic p. 242	Incest taboo p. 251	Polyandry p. 250
Corporate groups p. 240	Kinship p. 238	Polygamy p. 250
Culture and personality	Kinship chart p. 239	Polygyny p. 250
movement p. 244	Lineage p. 241	Teknonymy p. 246
Dowry p. 248	Matrilineal p. 242	Unilineal p. 241
Exogamous p. 241	Natal family p. 238	

Reviewing the Chapter

CHAPTER SECTION	WHAT WE KNOW	TO BE RESOLVED
What are families, and how are they structured in different societies?	All societies change their understandings of family, kinship, and social relationship as their societies adapt to new external factors.	It is impossible to predict how any society's system of kinship will change without understanding the other social, economic, environmental, and political changes in that society.
How do families control power and wealth?	Kin relationships are about social ties between individuals as much as they are about biological ties. All societies have developed ways of ensuring that the family group has some control over the collective resources or the labor of its members.	Many anthropologists consider social and cultural factors, such as the desire to control wealth or to exercise power over individuals, to be more decisive in explaining how and why people have kinship relations. Yet some still insist that there is a biological basis to kin relations.
Why do people get married?	Our own cultural model of basing marriage on love and sex is not important to all societies, especially those in which marriage is about creating social, economic, and political ties with other groups.	Although we know that economics has an impact on who gets married and who does not, it is not clear what the long-term impact of delayed marriage or the growing number of unmarried couples with children will be.
How are social and technological changes reshaping how people think about family?	Although international adoptions and new reproductive technologies are changing the biological relationships in families, they are not having much impact on the social roles within families.	It is unclear how new reproductive technologies and international adoptions will change how people think of the expectations, relationships, and meanings of kinship over time.

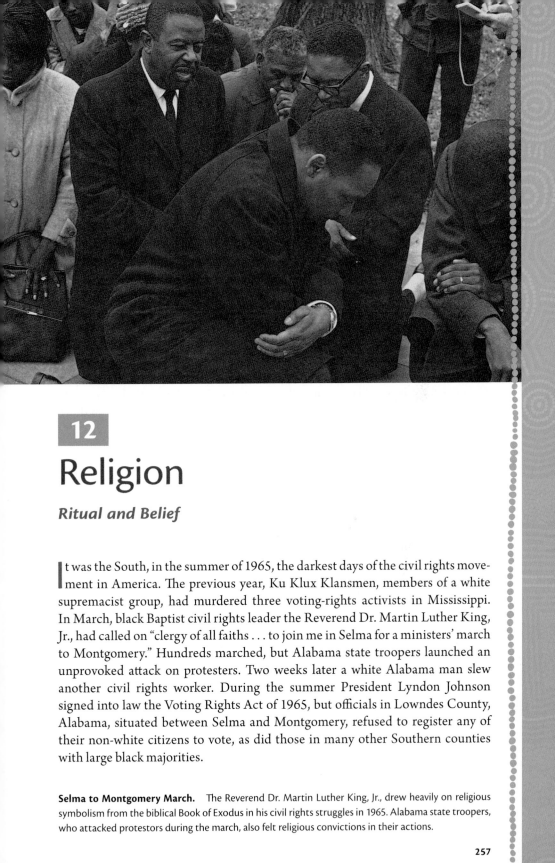

12

Religion

Ritual and Belief

It was the South, in the summer of 1965, the darkest days of the civil rights movement in America. The previous year, Ku Klux Klansmen, members of a white supremacist group, had murdered three voting-rights activists in Mississippi. In March, black Baptist civil rights leader the Reverend Dr. Martin Luther King, Jr., had called on "clergy of all faiths . . . to join me in Selma for a ministers' march to Montgomery." Hundreds marched, but Alabama state troopers launched an unprovoked attack on protesters. Two weeks later a white Alabama man slew another civil rights worker. During the summer President Lyndon Johnson signed into law the Voting Rights Act of 1965, but officials in Lowndes County, Alabama, situated between Selma and Montgomery, refused to register any of their non-white citizens to vote, as did those in many other Southern counties with large black majorities.

Selma to Montgomery March.   The Reverend Dr. Martin Luther King, Jr., drew heavily on religious symbolism from the biblical Book of Exodus in his civil rights struggles in 1965. Alabama state troopers, who attacked protestors during the march, also felt religious convictions in their actions.

Into this cauldron of politics, fear, and religion came twenty-six-year-old white seminary student Jonathan Daniels of Keene, New Hampshire. Daniels had marched through Lowndes County with Dr. King in March 1965, and he spent the summer in Lowndes County protesting racial discrimination and trying to register black voters. In August he participated in a demonstration with Father Richard Morrisroe, a young, white Catholic priest from Chicago, and twenty-seven other activists. All of them were arrested and held for a week in the Lowndes County Jail in the quiet little town of Hayneville. After six days, the entire group was released on their own recognizance.

Outside, it was hot and dusty, so Daniels and Father Morrisroe set off down the street with two young black female activists, Ruby Sales and Joyce Bailey, to buy soft drinks at the only store in town that regularly served black customers. As Daniels opened the screen door, Special Deputy Sheriff Tom Coleman confronted him, holding a 12-gauge shotgun. Coleman shouted, "This store is closed. Get off this goddam property before I blow your goddam brains out, you black bastards." With that he aimed his gun at Ruby Sales. Seeing what was happening, Daniels pushed Sales to the ground and moved between her and the gun. Coleman fired at pointblank range. The blast threw Daniels out the door and into the street, killing him instantly. Morrisroe grabbed Bailey's hand and ran down the street with her, as Coleman shot him in the back, wounding him critically. The two women ran for cover, and Coleman stopped shooting.

This incident arose because of a set of conflicting beliefs—those that motivated Tom Coleman versus those that motivated Jonathan Daniels. Today, we may find Coleman's prejudicial belief in the so-called racial inferiority of blacks even more difficult to understand than Daniels's religiously inspired altruism. Nevertheless, the bigger issue here is how we make sense of the existence of such different beliefs. It leads us to focus on the phenomenon of beliefs and behaviors, which can vary so radically.

At the heart of anthropology's approach to belief and religion is the question: *Why do people believe things that others consider wrong?* Embedded in this broader question are the following problems, around which this chapter is organized:

How should we understand religion and religious beliefs?
What forms does religion take?
How do rituals work?
How is religion linked to political and social action?

Over the past century anthropologists have come to realize that religious beliefs offer people a roadmap for their behavior: how they should live and how they should understand other people's behaviors, actions, and ideas. At their very heart, religious beliefs create meaning for people through the use of powerful rituals and religious symbols, all of which we discuss in greater depth in this chapter.

How Should We Understand Religion and Religious Beliefs?

Western intellectuals and social scientists have historically found the subject of religion problematic. When scholars in the nineteenth century confronted peoples around the world who held mystical views, most considered these ideas to be nonscientific mumbo-jumbo, and their adherents to be people of limited intellectual capacity. But by the 1870s, when anthropology was emerging as an academic discipline, scholars began to look systematically for theories that would help them understand religious beliefs. Anthropologists came to recognize the cultural importance of religious beliefs early, although theories differed on how to make sense of them. In this section we consider four different definitions of religion that anthropologists have suggested, several of which are still commonly used today. Among these is our own approach to religion that builds on the others. In our view, the most effective way to think of **religion** is as a symbolic system that is socially enacted through rituals and other aspects of social life that relate to ultimate issues of humankind's existence.

Understanding Religion, Version 1.0: Edward B. Tylor and Belief in Spirits

To make sense of the exotic religious beliefs of non-Western cultures, the British anthropologist Sir Edward B. Tylor (1871) suggested that religion had to do with belief in spiritual beings. For him, primitive religions were based on a fundamental error in thinking. He reasoned that people in all societies had dreams, but the so-called primitive peoples had misinterpreted their dreams as reality, transforming the characters in their dreams into souls or spirits. Tylor called such beliefs in spirits **animism**, which refers to the belief that inanimate objects such as trees, rocks, cliffs, hills, and rivers are animated by spiritual forces or beings. For him the ideas that trees and rocks might have souls and that carved images might contain spirits were just other examples of this same "primitive" misunderstanding. Tylor also reasoned that as societies evolved and became more complex, the supernatural beings they believed in gave way first to demigods and mythical heroes, then to gods and goddesses, then to a single, all-powerful God, and finally to science. Although many anthropologists later came to reject Tylor's evolutionary theories, his basic approach remained influential in anthropology for many decades.

Understanding Religion, Version 2.0: Anthony F. C. Wallace on Supernatural Beings, Powers, and Forces

By the 1950s, anthropologists in the United States had long abandoned the idea that American Indians and other non-Western peoples were "primitive." They had also come to accept, as Paul Radin argued in his influential book *Primitive Man as Philosopher* (1927), that there was nothing simple-minded in the myths, legends, and religious practices of tribal peoples. When American anthropologists began to look at how American Indian religions had changed—and continued to change—in the context of white expansion and domination, they saw systematic shifts in Indian thinking to make sense of changing times (Figure 12.1).

One of the major figures of this period was Anthony F. C. Wallace, who had studied religious change among the Seneca, one of the Iroquois tribes in upstate New York (1956, 1970). For Wallace, religious change could be observed most easily in the changing religious ceremonies and **rituals** (stylized performances involving symbols that are associated with social, political, and religious activities). He recognized that these rituals made sense only in terms of religious beliefs. His definition of religion became standard in anthropology because it linked beliefs with rituals: "beliefs and rituals concerned with supernatural beings, powers, and forces" (Wallace 1966:5).

This approach to religious beliefs and behavior bounded the field of religion in ways that fit comfortably with traditional European and American views, which also emphasized the supernatural. But Wallace's definition is static, offering little or no direction for understanding how or why religious ideas and practices change. If a society practiced some tribal religion but then converted to Christianity, Islam, or Buddhism, Wallace's definition could help us document what had changed, but little else. It could not tell us what difference these changes in belief make for real people's lives. Moreover, this sense of religion tends to depict

Figure 12.1 The Ghost Dance. The Ghost Dance, which originated among the Sioux around 1890, was an innovative religious movement among various tribes in the Great Plains. It was the Sioux's attempt to recover self-respect and control over traditional resources through ritual, but it led to disastrous consequences at Wounded Knee in 1890, when U.S. Army soldiers misinterpreted the ritual and killed at least 150 Lakota Sioux.

deeply religious people as intellectually limited, and it does not explain why people hold on to their religious beliefs and practices with such passion.

Understanding Religion, Version 3.0:
Religion as a System of Symbols

Unsatisfied with Wallace's notion of religion as simply belief in the supernatural, the American cultural anthropologist Clifford Geertz (1966) proposed another kind of definition of religion that could help explain why beliefs are deeply held and motivational, even to the point of risking harm to oneself, as we saw with the example of Jonathan Daniels. Geertz argued that religion was a cultural system, or as he put it, a "system of symbols." It consisted of five elements:

> Religion is (1) a system of symbols which act to (2) establish powerful, pervasive, and long-lasting moods and motivations in men by (3) formulating conceptions of a general order of existence and (4) clothing these conceptions with such an aura of factuality that (5) the moods and motivations seem uniquely realistic. (1966:4)

The most important feature of this definition is that it centers on symbols that seem intensely real and factual. For example, one of the central symbols in Christianity generally is the most improbable, the notion that after his execution Christ rose from the dead. Likely or not, hundreds of millions of people around the world accept Christ's resurrection as a historical fact.

Furthermore, the systems of meaning that these symbols generate can create a sense of moral purpose or meaning in people's lives and move them to action. These conceptualizations of the world offer a set of unquestioned assumptions about the world and how it works, called a **worldview**. The notion of culture adopted in this textbook ultimately derives from this understanding of religion as a cultural system. So when we suggest that culture is about how people naturalize certain meanings and actions as normal, we are arguing that culture consists of symbols that are created and given meaning by social life, not just in religious contexts. People's understandings of the world provided by these symbols, like Geertz's religion, seem uniquely realistic and cloaked in an aura of factuality; the world seems uniquely natural. The symbols describe a *model of* how the world is, as they simultaneously depict a *model for* how the world (morally) should be.

Most anthropologists continue to find Geertz's approach to religion useful. Following Geertz, they have tried to understand the worldview and ethos of a religion, adopting what is often called an **interpretive approach**, a style of analysis that looks at the underlying symbolic and cultural interconnections within a society.

One problem with Geertz's approach is that his definition of religion reads as if he is describing a lone believer, sitting quietly surrounded only by his own moods and thoughts as company. But a key feature of religious beliefs and behavior is that they are rooted in social behavior and social action. By acting together, the community of believers begins to accept the group's symbolic interpretations of the world as if they were tangible, authentic, and real rather than merely interpretation.

Understanding Religion, Version 4.0: Religion as a System of Social Action

In July 2013, three million Brazilians turned out in Rio de Janeiro to celebrate mass with Pope Francis, the first Roman Catholic pope from Latin America. In this massive public ritual we can see that religion is important for these millions of believers, and that it is an intensely exciting and social experience. It is a very different experience from a single nun on retreat praying quietly by herself for days at a time. Yet both experiences are "religious" in that they deal with worshipers' understandings of the world and how important the supernatural power of God is in people's lives. Both also get their power from their social context—whether it involves being among millions of others or by oneself—and from being so different from ordinary daily life. Indeed, the social experience of religious practice is what makes the beliefs, the organization of religion in daily life, and the religious symbols have meaning for every person present (Figure 12.2).

Thus, when we speak of religion in this book, we define it as a symbolic system that is socially enacted through rituals and other aspects of social life that relate to ultimate issues of humankind's existence. This definition implies several elements that earlier scholars have emphasized:

1. The existence of things more powerful than human beings. Although in many societies it takes the form of some supernatural force, we prefer to think of it as a worldview or cosmology that situates the place of human beings in the universe.

2. Beliefs and behaviors surround, support, and promote the acceptance of the underlying idea that things more powerful than humans actually exist.

3. Symbols that make these beliefs and behaviors seem both intense and genuine.

4. Social settings, usually involving important rituals, that people share while experiencing the power of these symbols of belief.

Armed with this sense of religion, let us apply this understanding of religion to one of the great problems of meaning of our time: making sense of why some people willingly put themselves at great risk to promote some greater cause.

Making Sense of the 2015 Terrorist Attacks in France: *Charlie Hebdo*

France has seen various kinds of terrorist attacks for the past two centuries. For the most part, the motivations behind these attacks have been clearly political. In the 1960s, for example, during the Algerian struggle for independence, France experienced a series of attacks conducted by right-wing French nationalist groups opposed to Algerian independence. In

Figure 12.2 Expressing Religiosity. Religious rituals are social activities, and many around the world are energetic and boisterous rather than somber, sedate, and pensive as some Americans may assume. On the top is a West African ritual performance that brings the gods into contact with the community, and on the bottom is a modern mega-church in America in which participants take on a vibrant role in the service.

recent years, France and other European countries have experienced a series of jihadist attacks, much as the United States has. What differentiates these contemporary attacks is that the motivations behind them are largely tied to religious views, and that the attackers seem so willing to put aside their personal safety—and even die—for their cause.

The first high-profile jihadist attack in France came in 2015 at the offices of the satirical magazine *Charlie Hebdo* in Paris, killing twelve and wounding eleven people. It was apparently motivated by the fact that the magazine had published a satirical cartoon on its cover featuring a depiction of the Prophet Muhammad.

Nowhere in the **Quran**, the holy scripture of Islam, is there any overt prohibition on artistic images of the Prophet. However, prohibitions against figural art, especially images of the Prophet, do appear in certain *hadiths*—sayings attributed to the Prophet that were recorded by his followers after his death and have been used as legal precedent where the Quran is silent. Nevertheless, some jihadist groups see these images as mocking the Prophet and making fun of Islam.

Such notions run counter to the liberal Western European and American ideas of free speech. In spite of Muslim criticisms, the *Charlie Hebdo* staff periodically published satirical cartoons of the Prophet, much as it did of the Pope, Jesus, and political leaders across the globe. The jihadist group Al-Qaeda in the Arabian Peninsula (AQAP) responded by publishing in its propagandist magazine *Inspire* a hit list of suitable targets that included a number of the staff of *Charlie Hebdo* (Kapferer 2015; Zagato 2015).

On the morning of January 7, 2015, two brothers of Arab descent born in Paris to Algerian immigrant parents broke into the *Charlie Hebdo* offices, killing most of the magazine's staff and shouting "God is great" in Arabic. Both were killed in a shootout with police. The brothers had been radicalized by AQAP jihadists in Yemen, where one of the brothers had visited, and by other radical Islamists they had encountered while serving short prison sentences for robbery. They had framed their justification for the attacks as inspired by Islam, although the political aspects of their actions were obvious.

For their part, European leaders and the public were galvanized into action, holding solidarity marches and rallies in Paris and other cities. The tag phrase *Je suis Charlie* ("I am Charlie") appeared on buttons, T-shirts, and banners as a symbol of the counterterrorist position. Standing with *Charlie Hebdo* was intended to mean standing for Western democratic ideals in which individual freedom of speech is guaranteed, with the same reverence as that given by the jihadists to the defense of the Prophet and their ban on cartoons.

Anthropologist Angelique Haugerud (2016) suggests that the response to the Charlie Hebdo shootings symbolically supported the notion, already common in the West since the September 11 destruction of the World Trade Center in New York City, that liberal democracies were engaged in a "clash of civilizations" between Western Europe, America, and Canada on the one hand and the Islamic world on the other.

Anthropologists have strongly rejected the view that there is any "clash of civilizations," arguing that the idea that foreign enemies exist and must be overcome allows leaders to take advantage of their own people, their resources, and their free speech (Gusterson 2005; Haugerud 2016). From an anthropological perspective, the "clash of civilizations" explanation for jihadist attacks such as the one against *Charlie Hebdo*'s offices misses the point; these situations can be traced to tensions that have arisen over discrimination, poverty, limited access to education, and other inequities among Muslims, in contrast to the better financial, social, and political conditions of non-Muslims in many countries around the world. The terrorists' ideas are simultaneously religious and political acts using religious symbols.

When European leaders joined solidarity marches, they inadvertently reinforced the view that Islam was at war with Western values, despite the fact that each had previously denied there was any ideological difficulty integrating Muslim citizens into their societies. Both the jihadists in their antisocial actions and these world leaders in their walks arm in arm down city streets created meaning through social action. Both communities offered a *model of* the world as they had perceived it as well as a *model for* how the world should be. They then rooted those beliefs in social action by attacking their enemies or standing together in solidarity.

Before taking a closer look at how religious beliefs and behaviors are linked to political and social action in the world, it is necessary to turn to another major preoccupation of the anthropology of religion, the different forms that religion takes around the world.

THINKING CRITICALLY ABOUT RELIGION

Consider how each of the four definitions or understandings of religion would explain why a religious cult like the Jim Jones cult in Guyana or the early Mormons in Nauvoo, Illinois—where they were attacked by non-Mormons—emerged. Alternatively, use these four explanations or definitions to interpret local reaction in your own community toward people with widely different religions.

✿ What Forms Does Religion Take?

Early anthropologists like Edward B. Tylor largely saw all "primitive" societies as having a "primitive" religion. While anthropologists today reject the notion that some peoples are more "primitive" and others more "civilized," it is clear that societies with simple technologies and small populations traditionally had very different religions from those that have formed in states with centralized governments and more sophisticated technologies. But there is no evidence that one form inevitably evolves into another, as the early anthropologists believed.

The variety of human religions that exists seems to correspond to the kinds of social orders that exist in different scales of society. Societies with small populations, for example, developed few governmental institutions larger than the family, clan, or village, and their religious institutions were typically focused on these same primary institutions.

Clan Spirits and Clan Identities in New Guinea

Nearly all New Guinea societies are organized around families and groups of families that belong to the same clan, and these clans are typically associated with particular kinds of spirits. The Ningerum of Papua New Guinea, for example, who have a very low population density of seven to fifteen people per square mile, are concerned with various clan spirits that inhabit their traditional clan lands.

These clan spirits have a full range of human emotions, but they become dangerous when they get jealous or angry, whereupon they can cause sickness or even
death to people from other clans or even among the children and elders of their
own clans. When they are happy and well attended to by the living with gifts of
food, especially pork, they bring good harvest in the gardens, success in hunting,
and healthy, prosperous families. All Ningerum rituals, aside from a few specific
healing rites, emphasize dealing with all of these clan-based spirits, and at major
feasts pigs are sacrificed to these spirits to honor them with a bit of pork and other
gifts made to them.

Totemism in North America

Early anthropologists studying American Indian societies observed that
people were identified with particular animals, often claiming to be descended
from these animals. These people indicated their clans, lineages, tribes, or other
social groups with certain revered emblems, usually animals, plants, places,
and geographic or meteorological features. Anthropologists usually refer to
these emblems as totems, and **totemism** as the system of thought that associates particular social groups with specific animal or plant species. Totems
help create social cohesiveness by stressing group identity, focusing group and
private rituals on totems. Some Native American societies simultaneously em-
ployed color symbolism, directional symbols, and species as totems.

We see a version of to-
temism in American cul-
ture as well, especially with
sports teams or military
units named after animals or
a particular social group, cultivating among fans and soldiers a sense of belonging to a
social order larger than oneself (Linton 1924). But these
totems are largely secular in
orientation, while traditional
tribal societies, such as those
along the Northwest Coast
of North America, usually
understood themselves to be
related to the totemic animal
in some supernatural way
(Figure 12.3).

Figure 12.3 Chiefly Totems. Totemic images identified with the clan and social position of a Kwakiutl chief on
Vancouver Island, British Columbia. The main images on the
two pole are eagles; other elements associated with the eagle
moiety are grizzly bears. The figure at the bottom of the left
pole holds a ceremonial copper plaque, suggesting the importance of the chief. These poles capture the social identity, the
social position, and the accomplishments of the chief, all expressed through the carved memorial pole.

Shamanism and Ecstatic Religious Experiences

As early as the sixteenth century, European travelers from Russia and central Europe encountered tribes in Siberia whose religious rituals involved spiritual leaders called **shamans**, religious leaders who communicate the needs of the living with the spirit world, usually through some form of ritual **trance**—a semiconscious state typically brought on by hypnosis, ritual drumming and singing, or hallucinogenic drugs like mescaline or peyote. These specialists were not political leaders but were focused on healing and ensuring the health and prosperity of the community, using drum rituals to connect with the spirits.

These practices are found in one form or another on all continents, but especially North and South America, Africa, and Asia. The details of these shamanic traditions vary widely, but they are often associated with small-scale societies with more or less egalitarian political structures. Anthropologist Napoleon Chagnon and Timothy Asch's 1973 film *Magical Death* shows one of the best-known examples of shamanic healing. In this film, a Yanomami shaman heals his family by ingesting hallucinogenic snuff made from a local plant. As in many shamanic traditions, this shaman is assisted by his **spirit familiar** (a spirit that has developed a close bond with the shaman), who helps him see other spirits and heal his children. In societies more familiar to Americans, such as some Pentecostal and charismatic Christian traditions, the ecstatic religious experience that has long been associated with shamans is encouraged by members of the congregation through witnessing, singing, and **speaking in tongues** (the phenomenon of speaking in an apparently unknown language, often in an energetic and fast-paced way).

Whether it is religions like those of the Ningerum, totemism among Native American groups, or shamanism, each stresses group identities and links these identities to various religious symbols.

Ritual Symbols That Reinforce a Hierarchical Social Order

Ritual symbols can be used to reinforce the social hierarchy and the political order at the same time that they interact with divine beings and powers. In the former kingdom of Benin in what is now Nigeria in West Africa, for example, the Oba (king) was believed to be divine (Figure 12.4). The fiercest animal in the region, the leopard, became a symbol of royal power, projecting an image of the Oba's power over his people. The Oba's palace was a model for the structure of the cosmos and the social order. People with the higher political and ritual statuses occupied the more central areas, while commoners were only allowed to enter marginal parts of the palace. Among the Benin, rituals, royal palaces, and the royal art together provided a model of the divine nature of the ruler, supporting a social order in which the ruler dominated over all others (Bradbury 1957; Dark 1962, 1982; Eboreime 2003).

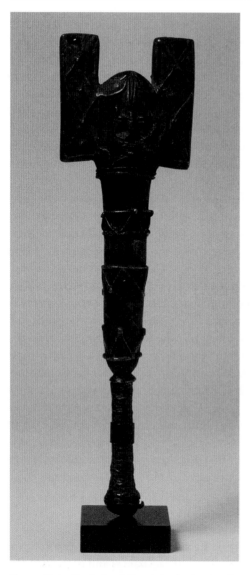

Figure 12.4 Symbols of Royal Authority in the Benin Kingdom. For the people of the kingdom of Benin, bronze figures and reliefs represented royal connections to the gods. (Hood Museum of Art, Dartmouth College, Hanover, New Hampshire)

Polytheism and Monotheism in Ancient Societies

The kingdoms and dynasties of ancient Egypt provided a similar model of the social order replicated in many of its most important rituals. The pharaoh was a king ruling over a vast empire of people along the Nile and Mediterranean coast and extending into what is now Israel and the Arabian Peninsula. Everything about Egyptian ritual—as well as the construction of great pyramids and structures like the Sphinx—celebrated a complex hierarchy of officials and priests, with the pharaoh as a divine figure at the head of the state and its religious organizations. But the pharaoh was not the only divine figure; Egyptians held that there were a host of other, more powerful deities, making their religion one of **polytheism** (belief in many gods). All of these gods demanded the attention of humans or, it was thought, they might harm the human world with droughts, plagues, locusts, and floods of the Nile River.

Nearly all of the ancient societies in the Middle East and the Mediterranean were polytheistic with complex state rituals, all of which promoted and supported an image of the state and its human leaders as superior to ordinary men. The main exception to polytheism in the ancient world was the ancient Hebrews, whose religion focused on a single god called Yahweh. In all likelihood, Yahweh began as a local deity that was worshiped and venerated by one of the tribes of Israel that became the ancient Hebrews (Armstrong 1994). When the Hebrews established

Yahweh as the God of Israel, they began a long-term shift to **monotheism** (belief in a single god). The key feature of monotheism was that it symbolized a single universal faith because the single God was presented as the deity of all, whereas polytheism encouraged different groups to identify with different local gods, in much the same way that totemism works.

World Religions and Universal Understandings of the World

Most of us are more familiar with the universal monotheistic **world religions**— or religions that claim to be universally significant to all people—of Judaism, Christianity, and Islam than the small-scale religions discussed previously. All three of these monotheistic world religions provided a general message that was applicable to all people, not just the members of a small clan or social group. For the most part, all three provided a positive, uplifting message for adherents, and all three also became state religions, whose religious message and ritual supported the government of the state.

Islam illustrates the ways a local monotheistic religion can become universalized through a set of beliefs and social order. Islam emerged during the seventh century in the Arabian Peninsula when the Prophet Muhammad received holy scripture in the form of poetry from a single, universal God—called Allah in classical Arabic. Most non-Muslims are startled to learn that the Prophet had one Christian wife and lived peaceably among a mix of Muslims, Jews, and Christians in Medina, until members of one of the Jewish tribes attempted to assassinate him. Jesus, Mary, John the Baptist, Moses, Abraham, and Adam, among others, are discussed at some length in the Quran, and all are considered prophets. From a Muslim point of view, Muslims, Christians, and Jews are all "people of the book," meaning that each has scripture received through prophets from God. But followers of Islam, which is the newest of these three religions, feel that God's message was most accurately received by the Prophet Muhammad and that Christians and Jews didn't get the entire message from God.

Asia has also produced important world religions that reflect particular histories of social stratification and universalistic belief. Hinduism was a polytheistic religion that emerged in India thousands of years ago. Like the polytheistic religions of the Middle East, Hinduism supported the authority of local princes and kings, and it focused on achieving good relations between people and various gods. Sometime in the fourth to sixth centuries BCE, a man named Siddhartha Gautama emerged as the founder of a new faith called Buddhism in reaction to Hinduism. According to Buddhist traditions, after selfishly pursuing his own pleasure through licentious living, he was mysteriously awakened to his misdeeds and promoted a life of reflection and active commitment to the Buddhist path, accepting the Buddha, the *Dharma* (the Buddha's teachings), and the *Sangha* (the Buddhist community). Unlike most other religions, Buddhism encourages its members to strive toward greater enlightenment. In this sense Buddhism is neither monotheistic nor polytheistic, but is more like a moral code of conduct.

The rituals often involve meditation and devotional acts aimed at turning people from worldly desires (wealth, sex, power, etc.) to concern for other people and all other creatures, and a state of enlightenment called *Nirvana*.

How Does Atheism Fit in the Discussion?

Finally, we must ask if atheists, agnostics, and nonbelievers have a religion. If all humans have some sort of worldview, then *everyone* has some sort of perspective on life analogous to religion. Secular people must also have symbolic systems that give meaning and purpose to their lives. For some, secular rituals that celebrate the state or nation, particular occupations, or other identities may achieve many of the same ends as religious rituals. For others, practicing scientific research may construct a worldview similar to that of people with more traditional religious beliefs. Geertz's definition of religion was specifically designed to be as useful for secular worldviews with a rich array of secular symbols as it is for more traditional religions.

THINKING CRITICALLY ABOUT RELIGION

Consider any three different societies we have discussed in this book. Discuss the extent to which the scale of the society—measured in terms of population or number of people within the same administrative or governing body—is reflected in the complexity of technology and the complexity of religious concepts. How do these three measures of complexity—population size, technological complexity, and sophistication of religious ideas—match up? What does this kind of comparison tell us about evolutionary models of society?

❦ How Do Rituals Work?

All rituals have certain key features, including that they are repetitive (happening at set times or before or after certain events) and stylized (following a set order of words or actions). What distinguishes religious ritual from daily habits such as brushing one's teeth is that none of us invests such special significance in tooth brushing. Moreover, at the heart of all ritual action exists a particular mode of thought that we call "magical." What do we mean?

Magical Thought in Non-Western Cultures

For anthropologists, **magic** is an explanatory system of causation that does not follow naturalistic explanations—such as being struck by a weapon or infected by some virus—often working at a distance without direct physical contact. Informants who live in communities where magic is practiced nearly always accept magical explanations as real, and they often believe deeply that they are frightening or dangerous. Magic can have many goals, usually goals that are out of reach through an individual taking direct action. The practitioner may want his or her gardens to flourish or his hunt to be successful. She may want the food at her feast to go further than it normally would, or to attract the affections of a handsome young man in a neighboring hamlet. Techniques may involve incantations, spells, unusual behaviors, and the manipulation of any number of special objects, all in an effort to cause some desired event to occur. Rarely do anthropologists worry about proving whether magical practices actually bring about their desired ends or not. It is usually enough to understand that members of a community accept that these processes occur. But why do these puzzling practices make any sense to the people who practice magic?

Sympathetic Magic: The Law of Similarity and the Law of Contagion

The English anthropologist Sir James G. Frazer coined the term **sympathetic magic** to refer to any magical rite that relies on supernatural powers to produce its outcome without working through a specific supernatural being such as a spirit, demon, or deity. Drawing on dozens of examples from around the world, Frazer showed that sympathetic magic works on two principles that he called the law of similarity and the law of contagion. Both involved sympathetic magic because the person or object acted upon did so in sympathy with the magical actions (Figure 12.5).

Frazer identified the law of similarity as some point of similarity between an aspect of the magical rite and the desired goal. A good illustration is a so-called voodoo doll, in which people make a doll or image of their enemy. By poking or stabbing the image, they hope to produce pain in the same part of the victim's body. Alternatively, a magical rite could follow the law of contagion, in which things that had once been in physical contact with one another could have an effect even when they were no longer in contact. According to the law of contact, mundane objects we've touched or produced as individuals, such as a cigarette butt, a scrap of partly eaten food, hair, nail clippings, sweat, urine, and feces, carry part of our essence, and harmful things done to them by an ill-intentioned magician can by extension hurt us.

Although Frazer depicted imitative and contagious magic as occurring in separate situations, it is clear that these two principles often occur together, drawing simultaneously on the similarities and previous

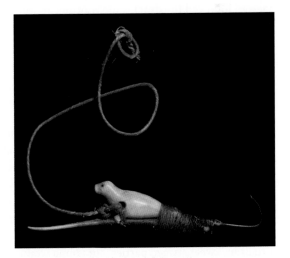

Figure 12.5 Sympathetic Magic Among the Inuit. Attached to this fishhook is a charm carved of ivory in the shape of a seal. The charm is meant to ensure that the hook will be successful in catching fish like a seal is successful in catching fish. (Hood Museum of Art, Dartmouth College, Hanover, New Hampshire)

contacts. A good example is the Christian ritual of communion, in which followers consume bread and wine (Figure 12.6).

Figure 12.6   The Christian Eucharist or Communion. The similarity of red wine to blood and wafers to flesh establishes the similarities between the ritual objects and their meaning. Consuming them during the ritual invokes the law of contagion to spread the blessings of God among all the people.

Magic in Western Societies

Americans tend to believe that modernization has eliminated magical thought in our culture. Yet many of the elements observed in non-Western societies also occur in contemporary America. In his study of baseball players, for example, anthropologist George Gmelch (1978) noted that players often have lucky jerseys, good-luck fetishes, or other objects that become charms. For these players, ordinary objects acquire power by being connected to exceptionally hot batting or pitching streaks. These charms follow the law of similarity. For three months during a winning season, one pitcher Gmelch interviewed followed the exact same routine: at lunch he went to the same restaurant and had two glasses of iced tea and a tuna-fish sandwich, and for an hour before the game he wore the same sweatshirt and jockstrap he had worn the first day of the streak. He was afraid that changing anything he had done before the first winning game might produce a bad result.

Rites of Passage and the Ritual Process

The most important type of ritual is the **rite of passage**, a life-cycle ritual that marks a person's (or a group's) transition from one social state to another. In 1909 the French sociologist Arnold van Gennep (1960) outlined the structure of rituals that marked that passage of individuals from one status to another. Rites of passage include marriage rituals, in which individuals change status from being single to being married, and rituals that mark the transition from childhood to adulthood. Initiations are common around the world, even in industrial societies such as ours that carry out such rituals in "sweet sixteen parties" for young women, when we graduate from school, and the like. Funerals represent another rite of passage; they focus on the deceased but are largely about the transition survivors will experience. In "Thinking Like an Anthropologist: Examining Rites of Passage," we explore the link between symbols and the construction of meaning in two American rituals: funerals and graduations.

Thinking Like an Anthropologist
Examining Rites of Passage

Anthropologists begin their research by asking questions. In this box, we want you to learn how to ask questions as an anthropological researcher. Part One describes a situation and follows up with questions we would ask. Part Two asks you to formulate your own questions based a different situation.

PART ONE: STATE FUNERAL FOR PRESIDENT RONALD REAGAN

When former president Ronald Reagan died on June 5, 2004, America began a week of national mourning and state ritual that dominated television and radio. State funerals, like inaugurations, are rites of passage that create a model of the state and become a model for how the state should be. Such secular rituals support and help create a sense of nationalism, American pride, a feeling of belonging to the nation, and a way of linking all Americans to state institutions. All funerals, of course, also have an important personal function: disposing of a dead body, and helping the deceased's friends and relatives adjust to the loss. It was no different when Reagan passed away. Distant relatives and close friends paid their respects to his widow and children. But because of his former role as president of the United States, his death became a rite of passage and transition for all Americans.

The former president died in southern California, and the family decided that he would be buried at the Ronald Reagan Presidential

A Public Funerary Ritual.   Mourners file in to view former president Ronald Reagan's flag-draped casket as he lies in state in the rotunda of the U.S. Capitol building in Washington, D.C., on June 10, 2004.

continues

Thinking Like an Anthropologist *continued*

Library in Simi Valley, California. The most efficient way to conduct a funeral would be to hold it in California. But most of the ritual occurred in Washington, D.C., the center of the government that he had led.

Flown to Andrews Air Force Base, the flag-draped coffin was brought to the Washington Monument, where it was transferred to a horse-drawn caisson, on which it would proceed slowly up Constitution Avenue to the Capitol. The procession was led by a riderless horse, carrying boots pointed backward in the stirrups, symbolic of the dead (former) commander in chief. Three pairs of horses pulled the caisson, with riders only on the three left horses. When the procession reached 4th Street, twenty-one F15 planes made a flyover, and the coffin was carried the rest of the way up to the Capitol by eight-man teams representing each branch of the military. At this point, there was a twenty-one-gun salute, and the band played "Hail to the Chief" and "The Battle Hymn of the Republic." Mrs. Reagan was waiting inside the Capitol to meet the coffin.

After a short ceremony the former president's body was to lie in state in the Rotunda, at the center of the Capitol building. The flag-draped casket rested on the simple pine frame covered with black cloth that had first held the coffin of Abraham Lincoln in 1865. Present were important politicians who had served in the Reagan administration or in the Bush administration. Only the Reagan family was given seats for the ceremony. After the ceremony, Mrs. Reagan and the dignitaries left, but the public was allowed to file in and around the casket throughout the night. Thousands filed past the casket to pay their respects in solemnity and silence until 7 the next morning.

The next morning a motorcade took the body to the National Cathedral for the national funeral service, with eulogies from President George W. Bush, former president George H. W. Bush, former British prime minister Margaret Thatcher, and former Canadian prime minister Brian Mulroney. After the funeral, a motorcade brought the body back to Andrews, whereupon it was flown to California for a private interment ceremony attended only by the Reagan family and close family friends.

What questions does this situation raise for anthropological researchers?

1. How do the ritual symbols, such as the use of a caisson, riderless horse, twenty-one-plane flyover, twenty-one-gun salute, and so on, add meaning to the ritual?
2. What added meaning was given to the event by holding it in Washington, D.C., that could not have been accomplished at the Reagan Library in California?
3. What meaning was created by the particular dignitaries who attended the Rotunda ceremony?
4. What model of social order was conveyed by the particular order in which people viewed the flag-draped casket? What was accomplished by prolonging the viewing for thirty-six hours?

PART TWO: YOUR HIGH SCHOOL GRADUATION

Reflect on your own high school graduation, which was likely marked by special costumes, processions, music, speeches, and actions (such as shifting the tassel to one side of the hat) that acknowledged your shift from one status to another. Viewing this graduation as a rite of passage, what questions would you ask about this situation as an anthropological researcher?

For anthropologist Victor Turner (1967, 1969), all rituals invoke symbols that can convey the underlying meanings of the ritual. Ritual symbols can consist of objects, colors, actions, events, or words. Often symbols point to, suggest, or take meaning from myths or sacred texts known to participants, such as the cross or the wine and wafers in Christian church services. When American brides wear white, they are symbolically expressing their purity, whereas when Chinese wear white at a funeral they are expressing their grief. What is common throughout these examples is that rituals create solidarity and meaning for participants and represent tradition for a group of people.

THINKING CRITICALLY ABOUT RELIGION

Compare the ritual symbols used in a televised Sunday morning service conducted by a Protestant televangelist with those used in a televised Sunday morning Roman Catholic mass. Although both services are religious rituals for Christian sects, they look very different. How do the different structures in the two services suggest different meanings derived from the same scripture?

How Is Religion Linked to Political and Social Action?

Time magazine's cover for April 8, 1966, asked the provocative question, "Is God Dead?" Playing off the nineteenth-century German philosopher Friedrich Nietzsche's famous claim that "God is dead"—suggesting that the **secular worldview**, or a worldview that does not accept the supernatural as influencing current people's lives, had finally overtaken the religious one in Europe—*Time* was suggesting that the same secularizing trend was at work in America. But *Time* was so wrong. More than fifty years later, we can see the persistent power of religion in the United States, in politics, in social discourse, in civil rights, and on TV. American church membership has risen gradually since the late 1940s to almost 75% of American adults today. So, why was *Time* magazine so wrong?

One reason is that American churches responded to social change not by ignoring it but by challenging it. Churches and other religious organizations became increasingly political, often supporting one political party or the other. In nearly every society, political and religious institutions are not only engaged with one another, they are frequently the same institutions. The broader point here is that religious values, symbols, and beliefs typically either challenge or uphold a particular social order. We illustrate this point by considering the forceful rise of religious fundamentalisms around the world.

The Rise of Fundamentalism

Since the 1960s, the most significant change in U.S. religion has been how much more active religious organizations have become in public life, particularly among the conservative churches that call themselves **fundamentalist**, people belonging to conservative religious movements that advocate a return to fundamental or traditional principles. Fundamentalist TV preachers have expanded their broadcasting since the early 1980s, and conservative religious groups and religious organizations have been as deeply involved in elections and politics as ever. This is not unique to the United States; across the world, conservative groups have turned to fundamentalism to make sense of and to confront changes that were happening all around them.

Understanding Fundamentalism

Scholars have had difficulty agreeing on a definition of *fundamentalism*. Traditionally, **fundamentalism** in America has been associated with extremely literal interpretation of scripture, particularly prophetic books in the Bible. Recently the American media has often associated fundamentalism with Islam, violence, extremism, and terrorism, but both views are far too narrow and biased, because most of the world's religions have their own conservative, "back to fundamentals" branches, and most are not so outwardly violent.

To correct these biases, in the 1990s a team of researchers working on the Fundamentalism Project at the University of Chicago studied conservative religious movements within Christianity, Islam, Zionist Judaism, Buddhism, Hinduism, Confucianism, and Sikhism (Marty and Appleby 1991; Almond, Appleby, and Sivan 2003). Not all of these diverse movements rely on literal readings of scripture, and for some groups sacred writings are of little consequence. Nor do fundamentalist groups necessarily reject everything modern. Most have embraced television, computers, the Internet, and other digital technologies to get the word out.

The Fundamentalism Project (Marty and Appleby 1991:viii–x) found several key themes common to all of these conservative religious movements. These include the following:

- They see themselves as fighting back against the corrosive effects of secular life on what they envision as a purer way of life. They fight for a worldview that prescribes "proper" gender roles, sexualities, and educational patterns. Their interpretation of the purer past becomes the model for building a purer, godlier future.
- They are willing to engage in political, even military, battles to defend their ideas about life and death, including issues that emerge in hospitals and clinics dealing with pregnancy, abortion, and the terminally ill.
- They work against others, whether infidels, modernizers, or moderate insiders, in the process reinforcing their identity and building solidarity within their community.
- They have passion, and the most passionate are those who "are convinced that they are called to carry out God's or Allah's purposes against challengers" (Marty and Appleby 1991:x).

The broader point here is that fundamentalists are not isolated from the world of politics; rather, they are actively engaged in it. What is so striking about fundamentalism for anthropologists is that unlike religion in most small-scale societies, fundamentalism does not typically support the existing political order but fights against it. What we do see in fundamentalism is that membership and a sense of belonging to a congregation or denomination is an important feature of religious organizations in industrial societies, where it is easy for individuals to feel anonymous. Indeed, part of the power of any religious organizations (churches, synagogues, mosques, and other religious centers) is that they bring people together, provide them with social support, and give them an identity within a broader secular world.

THINKING CRITICALLY ABOUT RELIGION

Consider the Fourth of July ritual that takes place in your home town. How do the parades and the speeches and fireworks build symbolic support for the state and federal governments and for the U.S. military? How do the symbols support the existing government?

❦ Conclusion

A month after Tom Coleman shot Jonathan Daniels in Hayneville, Alabama, an all-white jury found Coleman not guilty of manslaughter. This was a cause of disbelief for many who sympathized with Daniel's worldview. For example, Daniels's home-town newspaper, the *Keene Sentinel*, editorialized that "White Southerners and Northerners who hold [similar] views . . . do not, and apparently cannot, understand why a white man would risk his life to help a Negro register to vote or teach Negro children to read. They simply do not understand that, to men like Jonathan Daniels, all men are brothers, and skin color means nothing. . . . In dying, not only was Jonathan Daniels minding his own business, but he was attending to His business."

When Daniels first went to Alabama, he did so with a moral and religious commitment to what he understood as social justice. His actions were driven by a worldview that called him to help create a world suggested by his reading of scripture and his understanding of God. But at the same time, Tom Coleman acted out of his own worldview, one clearly shared by the jury. At that time in America, many people were proud of their prejudices and found many justifications for them, even in their religions. As much as people today may disapprove of Coleman's actions and of those on the jury, these actions were motivated by a shared set of assumptions about what the world should be like. Coleman acted in defense of that worldview. Just as Daniels's actions made sense in terms of his belief system, Coleman's beliefs and understandings about the world made sense to a large part of his community.

Whether or not we agree with such a perspective, we can never understand the actions of others without understanding a community's worldview and the powerful moods and motivations it creates. These are the benefits of approaching conflicting beliefs from "the native's point of view."

Key Terms

Animism   p. 259

Fundamentalism   p. 276

Fundamentalist   p. 275

Interpretive approach   p. 261

Magic   p. 270

Monotheism   p. 269

Polytheism   p. 268

Quran   p. 263

Religion   p. 259

Rite of passage   p. 272

Rituals   p. 260

Secular worldview   p. 275

Shaman   p. 267

Speaking in tongues   p. 267

Spirit familiar   p. 267

Sympathetic magic   p. 271

Totemism   p. 266

Trance   p. 267

World religions   p. 269

Worldview   p. 261

Reviewing the Chapter

CHAPTER SECTION	WHAT WE KNOW	TO BE RESOLVED
How should we understand religion and religious beliefs?	Anthropologists long emphasized that religion is about the supernatural. But more recent approaches emphasize the symbolic and action-oriented character of religious beliefs.	Many anthropologists accept that we can learn a great deal about the worldviews of the peoples we study, but not all anthropologists believe that we can fully understand how any individual sees and feels about his or her world.
What forms does religion take?	Traditional societies with limited social stratification tend to have simpler religions than the religions of complex societies, but this correlation is not inevitable.	We don't really know what environmental, political, or social conditions produce more complex forms of religious ideas.
How do rituals work?	Rituals use symbols that convey deep meanings about the world and how it should be. All rituals rely on some version of magical thinking. Ritual symbols themselves rely heavily on metaphor and other kinds of resemblances for conveying meaning.	It is not entirely clear why humans in all societies so readily accept ideas and beliefs that can be so easily shown to be incomplete, if not wrong.
How is religion linked to political and social action?	Religions have always been linked to political organizations and the social order. Anthropologists reject the idea that as the world modernized it would become more secular, drawing on the widespread rise of fundamentalism to demonstrate the continuing social and political importance of religion.	There is no real consensus among anthropologists as to how much political institutions can shape religious symbols, rituals, and worldviews, even though it is obvious that groups in power often try to.

The Body

Biocultural Perspectives on Health and Illness

During the fall of 2014, television screens, newspaper headlines, radio news broadcasts, and social media proclaimed the same terrifying message: an American outbreak of Ebola. The Ebola virus produces fearsome effects in humans, including the hemorrhaging of blood and other bodily fluids, with an average mortality rate of 50%. For several months the contagious virus had spread across Liberia, Sierra Leone, and Guinea in West Africa, a region that had until then never seen a single case of Ebola. Thousands had already died in that region, where the virus had reportedly killed as many as eight out of ten infected patients.

The first person to be diagnosed with Ebola in America was a Liberian named Thomas Eric Duncan, who was visiting family in Dallas. Duncan had contracted

Quarantine. When a Liberian man who had contracted Ebola in West Africa died of the disease in Dallas and an American doctor who had been helping Ebola patients in West Africa became sick with the disease soon after returning to New York City in 2014, the tabloids went wild. Media reports, along with the overreactions of public officials such as New Jersey governor Chris Christie and New York governor Andrew Cuomo, intensified public panic around the possibility of an Ebola outbreak in America.

Ebola before his trip when he helped carry a dying neighbor to a local clinic, where his uncovered hands came in contact with blood seeping through her skin. After noticing a fever, Duncan went to a Dallas hospital, but he was sent home. His fever worsened and he returned to the hospital two days later, when doctors began to suspect that he might have Ebola. Two nurses soon came down with fevers, and they were later confirmed as having become infected through contact with Duncan. One of these nurses had flown to Ohio and back before being diagnosed, and she had developed a fever before boarding her return flight. News of her travel sent the nation into a panic as the media coverage raised the specter of domestic airplane flights spreading the disease around the country.

Meanwhile, several American volunteer health workers who had been in West Africa got wrapped up in high-profile situations as public panic around Ebola grew. One was Dr. Craig Spencer, who had gone to Guinea to help with the crisis and returned to his home in New York City without symptoms. He eventually developed a fever and checked into a local hospital, where it was confirmed he had contracted Ebola despite wearing heavy protective gear when he was working with Ebola patients. Under growing pressure driven by 24-hour news coverage, the three governors in the tristate area around New York implemented mandatory quarantine orders for anyone who arrived from West Africa with a fever.

In the midst of this situation, a volunteer nurse named Kaci Hickox who had worked with Ebola patients in West Africa arrived at the Newark airport. The new mandatory screening order meant that everyone on the plane was screened with a routinely unreliable forehead thermometer that uses a beam of light on the forehead. Hickox's temperature was found to be slightly higher than normal, and she was immediately quarantined in a makeshift facility, a tent in the parking lot of the Newark airport. Initially, New Jersey governor Chris Christie insisted that Hickox would need to be quarantined for three weeks, a period Hickox and other medical professionals objected to as unnecessarily long. However, a few days later, after showing no further signs of fever or any other symptom of Ebola, Hickox was released and transported to her home in rural Maine.

The 2014 Ebola outbreak was devastating in West Africa, where it killed more than 10,000 people. Extreme poverty, years of armed conflict, broken public healthcare systems, burial practices involving the handling of infected bodies, and inadequate understanding of how the virus could be spread all contributed to this situation. But in spite of the public reaction, Ebola was never a serious risk in America, where the population is healthier and biomedical institutions are stronger than in West Africa. Nevertheless, understanding the reaction of the American media, politicians, and public is not a biomedical problem; it is a cultural one. Cultural beliefs and relationships always shape how people think of the body and its impairment, leading to the question central to this chapter: *How does culture influence our experience of health and illness?* We can answer this question by considering a number of more focused questions around which this chapter is organized:

How do biological and cultural factors shape our bodily experiences?
What do we mean by health and illness?
How and why do doctors and other health practitioners gain social authority?
How does healing happen?
How can anthropology help us address global health problems?

The Ebola epidemic shows how anthropology has a great deal to say about health and illness. Anthropologists have developed useful tools for understanding the links between culture, reactions to disease, and how our bodies respond to disease. This chapter explores how anthropologists put that knowledge to work in addressing real-world health crises. Let us first consider how biology and culture jointly shape the experience of our bodies.

How Do Biological and Cultural Factors Shape Our Bodily Experiences?

Since at least the 1920s, anthropologists have struggled with questions about the relative importance of our human biology as compared with the profound effects that culture has on individuals in any community around the world. In the nineteenth century anthropologists like Edward B. Tylor (1871) and Lewis Henry Morgan (1877) thought that biology could explain why indigenous peoples in Africa, Australia, or the Americas had such modest technologies and tools to work with when compared with Europeans and white Americans. Their answer: the bodies and minds of "primitive" people were not as developed as people from European stock. For a number of decades after 1920, it looked as if culture could shape who and what people were (e.g., Mead 1928). But in recent years, especially since the emergence of genetics and DNA research as a prominent subfield of biology, it has appeared to many Americans as if it is "all in our genes" or our biological "hardwiring." From this perspective, biology, genes, or hormones can explain sexual orientation, criminality, IQ, wealth, education, and who becomes CEO of a Fortune 500 company.

Today anthropologists are deeply skeptical of grandiose claims about biological destiny. This sort of "it's all in your genes and hormones" thinking is a cultural idiom our society uses to understand human nature, just as other societies use other idioms and metaphors to understand their own individual and collective selves. This is not to deny that biology plays a role in who we are as individuals, but our biology works together with our culture to make us who we are and to determine what we can accomplish and which maladies we will experience. A full appreciation of the human condition requires that we avoid thinking of ourselves as *either* cultural *or* biological (natural) beings, but through a new and emerging paradigm that emphasizes humans as **biocultural** beings in which biological, psychological, and cultural processes interact in complex ways.

The idea of human nature and bodily experience as something fixed in our biology has been central to Western European and American ideas about humanity for more than a century. The fundamental problem with this sort of understanding is that it simply cannot account for who gets sick, who succeeds in school or business, or how other aspects of our lives and identities develop. We examine why in the next two sections.

Uniting Mind and Matter: A Biocultural Perspective

One place to mend the divide between biology and culture is in the human **mind**, the emergent qualities of consciousness and intellect that manifest themselves through thought, emotion, perception, will, and imagination. There is increasing biocultural evidence indicating that even our most basic cognition does not happen separately from our bodies. The human nervous system is a complex neurological network that reads and regulates chemical and biological conditions throughout the entire body, not just our thinking brains. Human biology sets certain broad outer limits that all humans share, but the actual character of cognitive processes differs from one individual to the next and across cultures because of the influence of external factors.

These external factors include social context and culture, with which the nervous system interacts through individual cognition. For example, culture shapes some basic aspects of perception. People growing up in societies with little two-dimensional art must learn how to understand photographs after first seeing them (Shore 1996). Cultural differences in perception suggest that mental development varies with cultural practices. Research has also demonstrated that the mental stresses people experience because of rapid social and political-economic change have physical and bodily consequences, including raising blood pressure, affecting immunity to disease, and creating symptoms of fatigue or feelings of inadequacy (Dressler 2005). These mental stresses may accompany other biological impacts, including changes in diet, nutrition, and general health (Daltabuit and Leatherman 1998). The mind manifests itself through the whole person, throughout an individual's lifetime (Toren 1996).

Culture and Mental Illness

Studies of people with psychological problems across the globe have brought into question whether the psychological dynamics observed in Western countries are universal—that is, based purely in human biology. Numerous conditions, among them schizophrenia, anxiety, depression, attention-deficit disorders, and narcissistic personality disorders, vary greatly in their incidence in different cultures, suggesting that culture has a profound effect on the ways humans think about their psychology and display mental disorders. Cross-cultural differences in how people from different backgrounds express even the most basic psychological and emotional processes and conditions has an important consequence: we have to approach mental illness in a culturally relative way.

Psychological abnormality is always defined culturally because what is considered abnormal is based on socially accepted norms. Not all societies define the same conditions as psychologically abnormal, nor do they necessarily share the same mental illnesses. A well-known example of a so-called **culture-bound syndrome** (a mental illness unique to a culture) is *koro*, the condition unique to Chinese and Southeast Asian cultures in which an individual believes his external genitalia—or, in a female, nipples—are shrinking and even disappearing.

Societies can even change what they consider a disorder, homosexuality being one such example. Although today few people view same-sex sexual attraction as an illness, until 1974 American psychiatrists classified homosexuality as a mental disorder, and until 1990 the U.S. Immigration and Naturalization Service used the classification of homosexuality as "abnormal" as a reason for excluding gay and lesbian immigrants.

Because different societies define mental illnesses differently based on different cultural understandings of individual psychology, treatments differ accordingly. For example, on the Indonesian island of Bali, persons are not conceived of as isolated or indivisible, as we conceive of them in the West. Spirits and deceased ancestors commonly reside in individuals. Madness (*buduh*) can be caused by inherited factors, congenital influences, an ancestral or divine curse, or the blessings of gods (Connor 1982). The task of the village-level healer, called the *balian*, is to identify the specific causes of madness, which are usually related to some kind of social disruption or family conflict. The *balian* then resolves the conflict or disharmony in the family or neighborhood (Connor 1982) (Figure 13.1). Western psychiatry's approach, which often involves isolating the individual through institutionalization or providing pharmaceuticals, would clearly be inappropriate, if not socially disruptive, in these circumstances.

Figure 13.1 Balinese *Balians*. *Balians* are ritual specialists and healers who use a mix of traditional herbs, prayers, massage, and other rituals.

Nevertheless, as documented in Ethan Watters's book *Crazy Like Us: The Globalization of the American Psyche* (Watters 2011), Western psychological terms, notions, and illnesses have been globalizing rapidly in recent years. For example, mental illnesses such as depression, anorexia, and post-traumatic stress disorder seem to now exist in places that have never had them before, such as Hong Kong, Sri Lanka, and Tanzania. Watters suggests that much of this is taking place because of the increasingly global flows of Western media and psychiatric practices, as well as the expansion of pharmaceutical companies into new markets throughout the globe. Watters argues that such practices, which are usually based on an assumption of "hyper-individualism," destabilize indigenous notions and ways of treating mental illness in social context.

We can bring these insights about psychological processes and mental illness beliefs even further with a biocultural approach that combines cultural and biological insights. Rebecca Seligman has conducted research on Candomblé, a spirit-possession religion in Brazil (Figure 13.2). Seligman asked a simple question: Why do certain people become spirit mediums and others do not? Biomedicine explains mediumship as a psychological disturbance with a biological basis, but it fails to explain how and why such a disturbance might express itself specifically through mediumship. The cultural approach argues that oppressed and marginalized individuals gravitate toward mediumship, but it fails to explain why not all dispossessed people become mediums (Seligman 2005).

Seligman found that there is no single pathway to mediumship, but the interaction of biological, psychological, and cultural factors plays a crucial role. Among these are a physiological ability to achieve dissociation (trance states); conditions of poverty and oppression that cause emotional distress, which is often experienced through bodily pain; and a cultural outlet and social role that reward people who exhibit the qualities of mediumship. Seligman concludes that without this holistic perspective on a medium's experience, we cannot appreciate the complexity of how people become mediums.

Now that we have explained how even the most basic matters of human cognition and psychology are not simply the

Figure 13.2 Candomblé Mediumship. In Brazil, where some two million people practice Candomblé, temples where rituals are carried out are managed by women priests, known as "mothers-of-saint," often with support from men priests ("fathers-of-saint").

function of our biological hardwiring, we can productively understand more broadly how *all* matters of disease, health, and illness are powerfully shaped by culture.

THINKING CRITICALLY ABOUT THE BODY

If individual psychology differs from one culture to another, what might this suggest about the academic and clinical disciplines of psychology in which most psychologists treat patients who are Americans? What might these psychologists consider when dealing with recent immigrants from Africa or Asia?

❧ What Do We Mean by Health and Illness?

At first thought, health and illness seem to be straightforward concepts. Dictionaries often define the word *health* as the "soundness of body and mind" or as "freedom from disease" and *illness* as being "unhealthy," or having a "disease," "malady," or "sickness." The problem is that ideas like "soundness of body" and "malady" do not suggest any objective measure of when we have health and when it has left us. For example, most people feel sore after a hard workout at the gym, and many people have mild seasonal allergies and sinus conditions that rarely impair their daily lives but can be annoying. Are these people healthy?

The borderland between health and illness is more ambiguous than we might have originally assumed. This ambiguity results from two interlaced dynamics: the "subjectivity of illness," which is how people perceive and experience their condition on a personal level, and the "**sick role**," the culturally defined agreement between patients and family members to acknowledge that a patient is legitimately sick. We consider each in turn.

These issues are at the heart of medical anthropology, which is the subfield of anthropology that tries to understand how social, cultural, biological, and linguistic factors shape the health of human beings (Society for Medical Anthropology 2014). Doctors tend to focus on treating sickness and disease, while public health officials have traditionally focused on preventing outbreaks of disease. Medical anthropologists look at the diverse aspects of illness, its prevention, and its treatment. At its core, medical anthropology begins with the fact that, as much as we might like health and illness to be objective categories, health and illness are always subjective states.

The Individual Subjectivity of Illness

Illness is a subjective experience, but it is also shaped by cultural and social expectations. This insight is credited to sociologist Earl L. Koos, who in the 1940s conducted a classic study of attitudes toward health and illness in a mainstream

American community he called Regionville. In his study, he interviewed many hundreds of ordinary Americans about being sick. For example, he asked one working-class woman about being sick, to which she replied:

> I wish I really knew what you mean about being sick. Sometimes I've felt so bad I could curl up and die, but had to go on because the kids had to be taken care of, and besides, we didn't have the money to spend for the doctor—how could I be sick? . . . How do you know when you're sick, anyway? Some people can go to bed most any time with anything, but most of us can't be sick—even when we need to be. (Koos 1954:30)

This statement demonstrates both the subjectivity of illness and how health and illness are inherently linked to social behavior and expectations, not to mention social status or social position. When our symptoms impair us so much that we cannot effectively perform the normal social and economic duties expected of us—jobs, school, and, in this case, caring for her family—we can see that our social position within our families and communities affects how we understand and define health.

To understand when a particular symptom is considered significant enough to provoke someone to seek medical care, we have to understand the ordinary expectations of the people involved. In the United States, these expectations are linked to issues like social class, gender, age, the kind of work the person ordinarily performs, and the person's routine lifestyle. The poor and working class routinely work more physically, eat less healthy food, and pay less attention to their health concerns than do wealthier people. It is not that lower-class people do not care about health, of course. They simply have less time for doctors' visits, work in jobs they could lose if they miss a day, and eat the least expensive foods, which as we discussed in Chapter 6 ("Sustainability"), are the processed foods made available by the industrial food system. And they often have less adequate health insurance, or no health insurance at all.

A number of cross-cultural anthropological studies confirm that cultural background also shapes the subjectivity of illness. For example, anthropologist Katherine Dettwyler (2013) conducted research in Mali, a West African nation at the southern edge of the Sahara. There she observed high infection rates of schistosomiasis, a liver and bladder infection caused by a parasitic worm that lives in water. This worm enters the human body through the feet and legs, causing sores on the skin and releasing blood into the urine. Dettwyler found this condition so common in Mali that by puberty nearly all rural men have blood in their urine. Instead of viewing red urine as a shocking symptom, as Americans would, Malians understood it as a normal condition typical of the transition to adulthood. For these adolescents it meant they were becoming men, not that they had an infection (Figure 13.3).

Figure 13.3   Undernourished Adolescent in Mali.   In Mali, undernourishment is caused by a heavy disease load as much as by poor nutrition in the diet.

The "Sick Role": The Social Expectations of Illness

In all societies around the world, when a person is ill there are expectations of how that person, as well as friends and family, should behave. For Americans, this typically means the sick person should not go to school or work, should stay in bed and rest, should be given chicken soup, and so on. But these patterns vary cross-culturally. One of this book's authors, Robert Welsch, experienced this kind of cultural difference while conducting field research in Papua New Guinea among the Ningerum people.

One day, Welsch noticed that his body ached all over and his forehead burned with a high fever. It was malaria. At first he retired to his bed to rest, but the fever turned into chills, followed by sweats and an even worse body ache. He took antimalarial pills and aspirin, but the headache became so bad it was unbearable to lay his head on a pillow. Like most Americans he wanted to be by himself and endure this agony alone.

But Ningerum villagers did not sit idly by. As Welsch's condition worsened, more and more of his friends in the village came by the house to sit and chat and smoke. He later realized that most people in the village attributed his sudden symptoms to sorcery: someone in the area had used magic to hurt him, and people expected him to die. If it was sorcery there was nothing anyone in the village could really do for him, but nobody wanted to be accused of having caused his death. The only sure way to avoid suspicion of being a sorcerer was to demonstrate concern. Fortunately for everybody, by the eighth day, the fever broke, and the headache and body ache subsided. The villagers who had been keeping vigil for several days went back to their normal activities.

In this instance, the anthropologist and the villagers had very different ideas of how they expect patients and caregivers to behave. Anthropologists refer to these unwritten rules as the sick role, or the responsibilities and expected behaviors of sick people by their caregivers (Parsons 1951). To be considered legitimately sick—rather than as malingering, or faking sickness—one must accept specific responsibilities and a new social role, which exempts one from one's ordinary daily roles and responsibilities such as school or work. Two key aspects of the sick role are to want to get well, and to cooperate with medical experts.

A great example of this phenomenon comes from our own childhoods. During cold and flu season in the winter, many schoolchildren feel under the weather and want to stay home. When parents agree to let their children stay home, many kids may decide later in the day that it would be fun to go out and play in the snow. But "Dr. Mom" steps in with her authoritative zeal to explain that if you are sick enough to stay home, you are too sick to go outside to play. Playing outside does not demonstrate that you want to get well—which is a key aspect of American ideas of the sick role—and slipping out of the house in defiance of Dr. Mom's explicit orders to stay in bed is not compliance with her medical expertise (Figure 13.4).

Both of these responsibilities, wanting to get well and cooperating to do so, may simultaneously come into play in your own college classes. For example, when absent from a class or especially an exam, the legitimately sick student may need a note from a doctor or a clinic, demonstrating that the student wants to get better and has sought medical care.

Welsch found that Ningerum people had a different sick role model, believing that if patients still enjoy a minimum of physical strength, they should themselves deal with the illness. For the Ningerum patient to get help with his or her care and treatment, the patient is obliged to display to family and friends precisely how sick and disabled he or she is. Patients convey this information through their actions or visible physical signs of illness rather than through their words. Startling symptoms such as fainting, bleeding, vomiting, shrieking, and sudden weight loss call family members to action. Patients can also display the severity

Figure 13.4   Dr. Mom.   "Dr. Mom" expects her patient to remain in bed when staying home from school.

of their condition by using props like a walking stick to limp cautiously across the village plaza, shedding clothing, refusing to eat, or smearing their chests and legs with mud and dirt. All these actions communicate to family and friends that the patient is sick, and (silently) demand that family members show their sincere concern for the patient. Not to do so would suggest that one was not sensitive to a relative's needs—indifference that, to the Ningerum, whose culture prescribes very close kinship ties, would suggest not being fully human.

While culture shapes a community's expectations of the sick role, our medical schools and hospitals have created a culture of medicine that often leads to tensions between the views of professionals and those of laypeople. These tensions often have to do with the social authority given to doctors that makes the relationship asymmetrical, a topic we consider next.

THINKING CRITICALLY ABOUT THE BODY

The "sick role" concept works well for acute diseases like measles, bad colds, and chickenpox, when patients are expected to want to get better and to help in their own care by following medical advice. To meet these expectations, patients are often considered exempt from participating in ordinary social activities, and they generally are not blamed for causing their own sickness. Compare the sick role for an acute infection with that for a chronic condition like diabetes, chronic shortness of breath, or severe arthritis.

❧ How and Why Do Doctors and Other Health Practitioners Gain Social Authority?

Medical doctors in the United States have one of the most prestigious, respected, and well-paid occupations. The prestige and social authority doctors enjoy, however, is relatively new. Throughout most of the eighteenth and nineteenth centuries, American doctors had low social status. Medicine was not sophisticated, and doctors often doubled as barbers. During the Civil War, surgeons were little more than butchers who amputated with large, dirty saws, using no antibiotics, few painkillers, and no antiseptics (Starr 1982).

Many people assume that doctors gained prestige and authority because new medical discoveries and technologies improved their ability to heal people. Antibiotics like penicillin, for example, have made a huge difference in treating disease. But the major advances in health we take for granted today were mostly improvements in preventing diseases rather than curing them. Clean water, sanitation, and other public hygiene programs saved more lives than doctors' treatments have. So how do we explain the social authority of doctors? Medical anthropologists have studied the social authority of healers in many societies. They identify several processes at work, the most important being the social processes that privilege the healers' perspectives over those of their patients and the designation of otherwise normal conditions as health problems.

The sociologist Eliot Freidson (1970) was among the first to identify the professionalization of the field of medicine as responsible for giving the doctor's perspective privilege over the understandings of ordinary people. It is not that doctors necessarily knew more about what the patient experiences during an illness, but doctors had been trained to treat a wide variety of diseases. Subsequently, the medical sociologist Paul Starr (1982) argued that during the twentieth century medical doctors in the United States had used their professional status to increase their incomes, the level of respect they received from the public, and the exclusive right to determine the course of treatment for particular patients. American physicians formed professional associations like the American Medical Association, which allowed them to control how many new doctors were being trained. But while American physicians had achieved professional privileges, great respect, and high salaries, few of these perks were enjoyed by doctors in most other countries.

The Disease–Illness Distinction: Professional and Popular Views of Sickness

Around the world, patients often view their illnesses differently from the doctors or healers who treat them. In the Western world, patients often feel that their doctors do not understand the intensity of their pain and other symptoms. What frequently emerges is a clash of professional and popular (or layperson's) understandings that we call the disease–illness distinction, in which doctors focus on **disease**, the purely physiological condition, and patients focus on **illness**, their actual experience of the disease (Eisenberg 1977); see Figure 13.5.

In our culture the doctor, not the patient, has the greater authority in identifying and defining health and illness. Sociologist Eliot Freidson (1970:205) explained this authority as

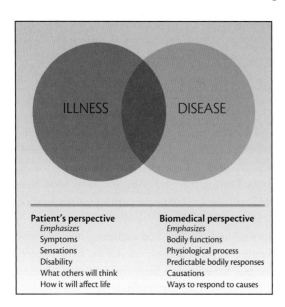

Patient's perspective	Biomedical perspective
Emphasizes	*Emphasizes*
Symptoms	Bodily functions
Sensations	Physiological process
Disability	Predictable bodily responses
What others will think	Causations
How it will affect life	Ways to respond to causes

Figure 13.5   The Disease–Illness Distinction.   Patients are concerned with the illness: symptoms, how they feel, and how their activities are affected by these symptoms. Doctors tend to focus on the underlying causes of the symptoms that they speak of as disease.

the result of a social process: "In the sense that medicine has the authority to label one person's complaint an illness and another's complaint not, medicine may be said to be engaged in the creation of illness as a social state which a human being may assume." American social structure also upholds the doctor's view as the officially sanctioned one. Because of the doctor's professional training, the hospital, governments, insurance providers, and, in extreme cases, even the courts recognize the diagnosis of the physician as legitimate. At the same time, the patient who has to live with the symptoms generally lacks any ability to authorize a prescription or treatment, or even offer an official diagnosis.

Understanding the distinction between doctors' and patients' perspectives is a key approach in contemporary medical anthropology. In the 1950s and 1960s anthropologists typically accepted Western medicine as superior and authoritative in much the same ways that Freidson suggests. Anthropologists generally assumed that health problems in developing countries were due to ignorance of medical knowledge and technology. A breakthrough came when Arthur Kleinman, a medical anthropologist who conducted research in Taiwan, argued that the key to understanding such differences in perspective is that healers and patients often have different **explanatory models of illness**, which are explanations of what is happening to the patient's body. Kleinman asserted that the goal of medical anthropology research was not to decide who was right in their explanation, but to accept that different people would come to the illness with different concerns and different kinds of knowledge.

Kleinman's approach also helped medical anthropologists realize the limitations of scientific knowledge, and they began to challenge whether the doctors always had such special and privileged knowledge. Perhaps the patient understood some aspects of his or her body that the physician did not, and perhaps could not, understand. We have already discussed the subjectivity of pain and other symptoms. But in addition, medical knowledge is constantly changing, so how could doctors always have all the answers for how to treat their patients?

For example, consider what the medical profession has advised about breastfeeding for infants. Breastfeeding was universal until the 1950s, when baby formula was developed, and most American pediatricians promoted formula as a technologically superior way to ensure the health of the baby. By the 1970s, new scientific analyses of the contents of breast milk indicated that breast milk contained antibodies that helped the child ward off infections. Rather than viewing breast milk as unsophisticated, the medical world began to see it as nature's way of protecting the child (Figure 13.6). About the same time in many developing countries, international aid workers were promoting baby formula as a way of producing strong, healthy babies. But by the 1990s, it became clear that this practice was not ideal: babies became malnourished because their poor mothers could not afford enough formula, and where clean drinking water was scarce, mothers often

Figure 13.6   Changing Views on Infant Formula and Breastfeeding. Since the 1970s, breastfeeding has had a resurgence in the United States after it became known that a mother's breast milk gives antibodies and partial immunity to infections to her baby.

had no choice but to use unsanitary water for their baby formula, resulting in much higher rates of fatal diarrhea.

With the spread of AIDS in the developing world, we now know that mothers infected with HIV can give the infection to their infants through breast milk. So, as a result, aid workers are once again, at least in communities where incidences of HIV infection are high, recommending baby formula. Who knows where the science of breast milk will settle in another generation? But as with nearly every other aspect of medicine, few scientific facts have remained, or will remain, static.

Since medical knowledge is constantly changing, it is no wonder that new diseases and drugs to treat them are constantly emerging. One way this knowledge changes is when the professional medical system casts its net of authority out farther, to cover conditions that were not previously understood as medical problems.

The Medicalization of the Non-Medical

Over the past fifty years, the healthcare industry has expanded dramatically, taking over more and more of our individual personal concerns. It has done so by redefining certain social, psychological, and moral problems as medical concerns. This process of viewing or treating as a medical concern conditions that were not previously understood as medical problems is called **medicalization**.

Alcoholism is a good example of this phenomenon. Excessive use of alcohol has been a problem throughout the history of the United States, producing opposition to it in the form of the temperance movement in the nineteenth and early twentieth centuries, and Prohibition in the 1920s. For a long time, alcoholism was seen as a moral failing that caused (usually) men to abandon their jobs and families. By the 1980s, psychiatrists, HMOs, and health insurance companies began to view alcoholism as a disease defined as "recurrent substance use resulting in failure to fulfill major role obligations at work, school, home" (American Psychiatric Association 1994). Defining alcohol abuse as a disease, rather than as a crime, socially inappropriate behavior, sinful behavior, or moral failing, reclassifies it as a medical concern.

Three major reasons have been suggested for medicalizing the non-medical. The first is financial: pharmaceutical companies, hospitals, and insurance companies stand to make larger profits when they can define a new disease for which they can provide treatment, care, and coverage. A second explanation is that the medicalization enhances the social authority of physicians. A third explanation concerns Americans' current preference for viewing social problems in scientific rather than moral or social terms.

THINKING CRITICALLY ABOUT THE BODY

Fifty years ago, alcoholism was considered a moral failing, a behavioral problem found when people have no strong moral code to live by and do bad things to their families and others. Compare this earlier understanding of alcoholism with the now common view that alcoholism is a disease. How do you think this shift happened?

❧ How Does Healing Happen?

When Robert Welsch was studying healing practices among the Ningerum, one of his informants came down with malaria. Welsch offered him some anti-malarial tablets, but his informant could not swallow them because they tasted bad. After several days of lying in bed, the man's nephew performed a traditional ritual, smearing clay on his uncle's painful chest, reciting magic words, and apparently removing a packet consisting of some small object wrapped in a banana leaf from the sick man's chest. Within two hours, the man was up and about with his walking stick heading for the spring where he showered, a visible sign to everyone in the village, including the anthropologist, that he was feeling better (see Welsch 1983).

To the Western mind, such examples of traditional healing strain credibility. But anthropologists around the world have observed similar responses to a wide variety of non-medical treatments. We do know that the human body is remarkably resilient. If we cut ourselves superficially while chopping vegetables, the wound will bleed and scab over, and gradually new skin will cover the cut. We do not fully understand how healing works, but we know that healing is more complex than most Americans recognize. Healing is a complex biocultural process: it is not just about pills and surgeries, but about the meaning that the sick person and the healers give to treatments in a specific cultural context. Healing is a complex biocultural process. Medical anthropologists generally accept that treatments help our bodies heal in four distinct therapeutic processes: (1) clinical processes, (2) symbolic processes, (3) social support, and (4) persuasion (Csordas and Kleinman 1996). We consider each of these processes next.

Clinical Therapeutic Processes

Most professionals working with Western medicine assume that effective treatment comes from **clinical therapeutic processes**, which involve a doctor observing a patient's symptoms and prescribing a specific treatment, such as a pill. The medicines involved in this treatment have some active ingredient that is assumed to address either the cause or the symptom of a disorder. One example is an antibiotic, which is thought to kill a type of bacterium. Another is a vaccination, which inserts a small amount of the virus or bacterium—usually already dead—into the blood, triggering the body's immune system to react by creating antibodies so the body can fight off the infection in the future.

Sometimes doctors understand how these physiological processes work; at other times they may not understand the healing process but assume that it works by some plausible but unproven process. Whatever the case, for medical anthropologists and medical researchers there is still more to understand because these clinical processes do not account for healing such as in the Ningerum case presented earlier.

Symbolic Therapeutic Processes

In most tribal societies that medical anthropologists studied in the twentieth century, there were some treatments that used herbs, teas, and potions. The explanatory models used in these societies sometimes drew on clinical models, but often the herbs and potions were important not so much for their chemical properties but for their symbolic ones. Although the chemical composition of the herb or potion might help the patient heal, people were largely unaware of these properties and used them in rituals for other reasons.

In such cases, healing rituals act as a **symbolic therapeutic process** by virtue of their role in structuring the meanings of the symbols used. The symbolism of healing rituals comes from a number of sources, invoking our olfactory senses and our senses of taste and touch. It can also involve chanting, drumming, singing, and other sounds that set particular moods. Typically, the rituals provide a symbolic temporal progression, as in the form of a mythological story, that the affliction is supposed to follow for the patient to recover and heal.

For example, the French anthropologist Claude Lévi-Strauss (1961) documented a healing ritual among the Kuna [**koo**-nah] Indians of Panama in which, over a period of many hours, the shaman sings, produces smells, and touches a woman in the midst of a difficult birth. The ritual chanting recounts a mythological story in which a child overcomes diverse obstacles to reach its goal. These things relax the mother and her baby so the child can emerge from the womb, just as the hero of the story reaches his final goal. Medical anthropologists Thomas Csordas and Arthur Kleinman (1996) suggest that this kind of ritual is very common around the world because so many societies have found it efficacious.

Social Support

The **social support therapeutic process** involves a patient's social networks, who typically surround the patient, much like Welsch's experience among the Ningerum. Although relatives and friends may perform some (usually) minor treatments on the patient, the major thrust of this therapeutic process comes from the presence of family members who provide comfort and aid to the sick person. Feeling aided and supported by his or her relatives may affect the patient's bodily functions. For example, diabetics often have better control of their blood sugars when they are with supportive family members, but poorer control when feeling isolated.

Persuasion: The Placebo Effect

Persuasion is another powerful therapeutic process. Consider the **placebo effect**, in which a patient is given a non-medicine as if it were a medicine. The classic example of a placebo is a sugar pill given instead of some prescription drug with an active pharmaceutical ingredient. What makes it a placebo is that the sugar pill has a beneficial effect, even though it has no pharmacological or clinically active component. Usually, patients are told that they will receive a powerful medication or procedure, even though they will actually receive the placebo. This strategy, however, worries many people, including doctors, because it amounts to lying to a patient; dispensing placebos challenges professional ethical codes of behavior and even some federal laws in the United States.

Up to now it has been hard to explain the placebo's effect clinically, since the placebo seems to work through persuading the patient that the drug is effective. Something must be happening within the patient's body, but it seems to lie outside the bounds of ordinary medicine.

A dramatic illustration of the power of the placebo effect comes from a French study conducted in the 1990s. In this study, researchers divided a group of hospitalized cancer patients with mild to moderate cancer pain into four groups to test the effectiveness of naproxen, at the time a new painkiller that many people now know by the brand name Aleve. None of the patients experienced so much pain that they required opiates, and the study put none of the patients in significant distress. First the patients were randomly assigned to one of two groups as they came out of cancer surgery. One group was told they would be in a random trial of a powerful new pain reliever and would receive either the test drug or an inert placebo. The second group was told nothing. Members of this second group were unaware they were in a test and would assume that they were receiving standard hospital care. Half of the patients in each group were randomly given either an inert placebo or naproxen, thus creating four groups in all. Nurses, who were unaware of the details of the study, asked patients to evaluate their pain reduction hourly using a pain scale from 1 to 100 that represents the pain experienced (Bergmann et al. 1994; Kaptchuk 2001).

All the patients given naproxen showed a reduction in pain, confirming that naproxen is an effective painkiller. But patients who were given the placebo and told they were in the study had greater pain relief than those who were given naproxen but were told nothing about their pain treatment regimen. Figure 13.7 illustrates this study's findings. Even more remarkable, this study suggests something that most researchers were not anticipating and had not appreciated. Figure 13.7 shows the large gap in experiences of pain relief between the two groups who were given naproxen. Theoretically, if we assume that naproxen works physiologically, both groups should have experienced similar levels of pain relief. But they did not: the placebo effect enhanced the pain relief in the test group who received naproxen and were told they were in the trial. In other words, those patients in the test group knew they were in the study and expected to get good results from their painkiller. What this tells us is that the placebo effect probably enhances all clinical interventions whether they are pharmaceuticals, surgeries, or other procedures. When patients *believe* that a pharmaceutical or medical procedure is effective, they regularly see improvements.

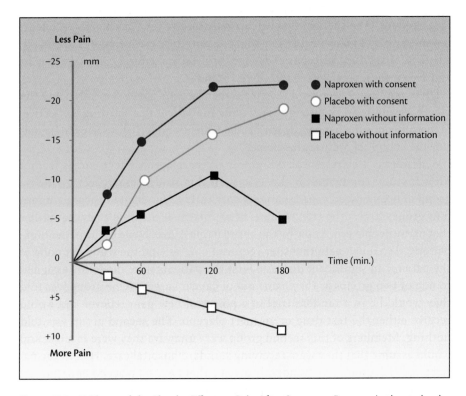

Figure 13.7   Evidence of the Placebo Effect on Pain After Surgery.   Everyone in the study who received naproxen experienced pain reduction, but people told about the study who received only the placebo experienced more relief from pain than did patients who received naproxen but were not told about the study. (After Bergmann et al. 1994.)

The insight that culture and social processes influence the healing process is a powerful insight of medical anthropology. So how do anthropologists put such insights to work? We consider this question in our last section.

THINKING CRITICALLY ABOUT THE BODY

The naproxen study demonstrates the power of the placebo effect. Discuss what this study might mean for a doctor prescribing a "powerful" antibiotic or some brand-new treatment for a condition in a patient he or she sees in his or her clinic.

🌱 How Can Anthropology Help Us Address Global Health Problems?

Anthropologists have long recognized that they can contribute to alleviating global health problems by understanding the healthcare systems available to different peoples around the world, how diseases are transmitted within and between communities, and how people use the resources available to them. In recent years, anthropologists have also become more engaged and proactive in trying to improve health conditions in the communities, countries, and regions in which they work. We explore both of these themes—understanding and actively addressing global problems—below.

Understanding Global Health Problems

One of the first attempts at addressing global health problems came in the 1950s when medical anthropologists, working through the Institute of Inter-American Affairs, helped design public health programs and rural clinics to promote better health in rural Latin America (Erasmus 1952; Foster 1952; Simmons 1955). Their goal, which they reached with only moderate success, was to find ways for encouraging rural peasants to make better use of newly introduced clinics and improved vaccinations as a way of lowering infant mortality.

By the 1970s, it seemed that Western medicine would fix the world's health problems, and anthropology's role in explaining different cultural systems of healthcare was largely irrelevant. After the eradication of smallpox in 1979, the World Health Organization (WHO) believed that eradication of polio and other infectious diseases was simply a matter of time. But as AIDS and other public health crises spread worldwide, and even polio proved more intractable than researchers had expected, medical anthropologists increasingly saw the need to increase their involvement in understanding what were rapidly becoming global health problems. We explore two issues here: medical pluralism and patterns of disease transmission.

UNDERSTANDING MEDICAL PLURALISM: COMPARING
DIFFERENT HEALTHCARE SYSTEMS

Medical anthropologists have long recognized that there are many sophisticated non-Western systems of medicine—in places like India, China, and the Arab world—that had been effective for centuries before the medical systems of the United States and Western Europe developed antiseptics, antibiotics, and vaccines. As India, China, and the Arab world began to establish modern industrial societies, their healthcare facilities were integrating Western medicine with traditional practices. Medicine was not replacing these ancient traditions but supplementing them. Nearly all other societies draw on more than one medical tradition simultaneously, a concept called **medical pluralism**, which refers to the coexistence and interpenetration of distinct medical traditions with different cultural roots.

An example of medical pluralism comes from anthropologist Carolyn Nordstrom (1988), who studied Ayurveda, a traditional medical system developed in India and Sri Lanka. Ayurvedic practitioners diagnose health problems using the classical Ayurvedic practice of reading the pulse, and they mix herbs in specified ways. But practitioners also draw upon traditional Sinhalese (referring to the people of Sri Lanka) medical ideas and practices. Nordstrom learned that practitioners often mix traditional Sinhalese herbal preparations along with those they have learned at an Ayurvedic college, and that many Ayurvedic healers frequently use stethoscopes and thermometers and dispense standard Western medicines along with their herbal preparations. She also observed that some Sinhalese Buddhist monks incorporated Ayurvedic and Buddhist principles in their therapeutic work, sometimes adding Sinhalese preparations as well (Figure 13.8).

The broader point here is that in an increasingly globalized world, medical anthropologists are learning that all medical systems are now plural systems. Successfully addressing global health problems must take this fact into account.

In "Anthropologist as Problem Solver: Nancy Scheper-Hughes on an Engaged Anthropology of Health," we consider another way that anthropologists are becoming increasingly proactive in addressing health problems around the world.

Figure 13.8   Medical Pluralism.   Modern Ayurveda often adopts elements from biomedicine.

Anthropologist as Problem Solver
Nancy Scheper-Hughes on an Engaged Anthropology of Health

Medical anthropologist Nancy Scheper-Hughes has conducted research in a variety of contexts around the world: in the parched lands and shantytowns of northeast Brazil, in the squatter camps of South Africa, and in the AIDS sanatoria of Cuba. In each of these contexts, she saw structural poverty and blatant examples of what she called "useless suffering." For years anthropologists have adopted a position of cultural relativism that she feels often puts us in a position of trying to be morally neutral when confronting issues of institutional or state violence against "vulnerable bodies and fragile lives." In her view, to be ethical, anthropologists need to focus critically on the institutions and embedded power relations that shape the health of poor, underserved, and disadvantaged people.

Scheper-Hughes has also studied the illegal sale of body parts (Scheper-Hughes and Wacquant 2003; Scheper-Hughes 2004). As part of this work, she has interviewed a Brazilian organ trafficker in his prison cell, people whose kidneys had been sold, and other people involved in this trafficking. In July 2009, Scheper-Hughes assisted authorities in arresting a Brooklyn man accused of selling black-market kidneys. The *New York Daily News* heralded her as having an anthropological "'Dick Tracy' moment" when she turned over information to the FBI that allowed them to bring this suspected organ-trafficker to justice (Daly 2009). This led to the exposure of an extensive network that involved people in several countries. She told NPR's Brian Lehrer (National Public Radio 2009), "I had begun to unravel a huge network—a criminal network that really looks like, smells like, a kind of a mafia. The head office of the pyramid scheme originated in Israel; with brokers placed in Turkey; in New York City; in Philadelphia; in Durban; in Johannesburg; in Recife, Brazil; Moldova—all over the place." She went on to say, "And I used my ethnographic investigative skills to just go country-hopping and try to connect the dots. Eventually, it brought me to Isaac Rosenbaum being the head broker for Ilan Peri in Israel, who is the don, basically, of the operation, and who is a slippery guy."

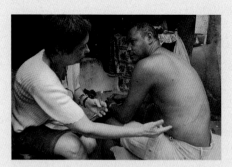

Nancy Scheper-Hughes. Here the anthropologist interviews a man who was trafficked from his home in Recife, Brazil, to Durban, South Africa, so his kidney could be illegally sold. For his kidney he received $6,000, a large sum of money in the slums of Brazil.

QUESTIONS FOR REFLECTION

1. To what extent is understanding the perspective of people without a voice a contribution to addressing and resolving health issues?

2. Anthropology has become a much more "hands-on" discipline in the past two decades. But does such involvement in shaping policy get in the way of our being able to understand all perspectives holistically?

UNDERSTANDING PATTERNS OF DISEASE TRANSMISSION

Medical anthropologists have also played a key role in making sense of how infectious diseases spread within a population, which is as much an anthropological or sociological task as it is a medical one. For example, anthropologists have played a key role in helping researchers understand the transmission of HIV, the virus that causes AIDS. In the United States and Europe, public health officials have promoted the use of condoms to interrupt the spread of HIV. But promoting condoms has not proved so effective in several African countries, Haiti, and certain Southeast Asian countries, each of which had patterns of transmission that differ significantly from those in the United States. By studying these patterns of transmission, anthropologists played a central role in helping medical researchers understand how culture was shaping HIV transmission.

In East Africa, for example, HIV was first noticed along major highway routes where male long-haul truckers became infected through sexual contacts with infected female sex workers, taking the infection to women in the next truck stop town (Nyamwaya 1993). Truck stops produced ideal conditions for transmission of HIV because they provided a meeting place for truckers and sex workers who had connections to wide-ranging and international social networks. Anthropologist and geographer Ezekiel Kalipeni (2004) suggests that epidemiologists and medical researchers had completely missed seeing these patterns. He argues that medical researchers explained the observed distribution of cases in terms of traditional patterns of African sexuality. Traditional culture was demonized, and the appearance of modern lifestyles, population growth, social inequality, and mounting poverty that was sending villagers in many African countries to urban centers and new forms of employment all went ignored. Anthropologists provided detailed observations of people's ideas about the disease and their explanatory models, as well as specific information about the sexual practices and behaviors of women and men, helping illuminate the patterns of HIV transmission (McGrath et al. 1992; Nyamwaya 1993).

Anthropological Contributions to Tackling the International HIV/AIDS Crisis

As their understanding of global health problems has become more sophisticated, anthropologists have become more assertive in putting their ideas to work. One way they do this is by working with communities to design aspects of the public health system to meet the needs, understandings, and cultural expectations of people in the community. To continue with the example of the HIV/AIDS crisis, we examine the work of Paul Farmer.

Using anthropology's holistic perspective to understand communities and their social problems, anthropologist and physician Paul Farmer (1992) began research for his dissertation in Haiti. As an undergraduate, Farmer had majored in anthropology at Duke University. In 1983, before beginning medical school at

Harvard, he spent some time in Cange, a community in the mountainous central plateau of Haiti. In this extremely poor area, he could see firsthand that the social, economic, political, and health problems were interconnected. Farmer saw these connections before HIV/AIDS had been identified and before large numbers of HIV/AIDS cases had been diagnosed in Haiti. When the HIV/AIDS epidemic broke out, the connections between the health of Haitians and socioeconomic and political conditions became even more obvious.

Working with another M.D.-Ph.D. student, Jim Yong Kim, who went on to head the World Bank (see Chapter 7), Farmer helped found an organization in the highland district of Cange in 1987. They called this organization Partners in Health (2010) and developed a small health center. The international health community was initially focused on treating HIV/AIDS patients and on dealing with other public health concerns to slow the spread of HIV/AIDS. But Farmer and Kim had larger goals that they saw as related to health in the Haitian community. They began encouraging local people to plant trees in the once-lush forested region that had been devastated from poverty and rapid population growth. Farmer and Kim put together an integrated program that attacked the causes of poverty and environmental degradation as a way of improving health. Just over a decade after establishing this program, Farmer and Kim saw the district returned to something like its lush original environment, along with solid improvements in local health (Kidder 2003).

THINKING CRITICALLY ABOUT THE BODY

Medical anthropologists have traditionally been involved in public health efforts to vaccinate children, to provide clean drinking water, and more recently to assist with combating HIV/AIDS. Why would such public health efforts be a natural role for anthropologists, rather than involvement in clinical settings that include physicians and their patients in modern urban settings?

❦ Conclusion

This chapter's focus on issues of our bodies reflects what most of us feel, implicitly, is the most natural part of our beings. But how we understand our bodies and minds and how we make sense of impairments to them are inevitably shaped by the culture we have grown up in and by the concerns and preoccupations people around us have. Whether we are considering chronic pain, psychological issues like post-traumatic stress disorder (PTSD), or infectious diseases like Ebola or HIV, the cultural expectations of the community always shape people's response to any illness condition.

As we saw with the 2014 outbreak of Ebola, discussed in the chapter opener, people living in different cultures, with varying views and cultural expectations, react differently to essentially the same set of facts. In an effort to protect their citizens, each country's leaders approach problems of health and epidemics somewhat differently, because in each case it is not the virus or the epidemiology but the local cultural assumptions that shape these leaders' actions. When individuals become ill in different cultures, they and their families also respond in locally appropriate ways, interpreting the signs, symptoms, and implications in locally meaningful ways.

Recent research even suggests that our bodies respond according to our expectations about the effectiveness of a treatment. Western physicians have dismissed such responses as merely the "placebo effect," but for millennia societies have looked after their sick with herbs and local rituals that seem to bring relief to the sick.

The research medical anthropologists are conducting today comprises some of the most important applied projects in the discipline. But these research projects have demonstrated that global health concerns and modern epidemics are much more than medical problems. Like everything else in life, health and illness are linked to the kinds of society we live in, our biology, the historic traditions that have motivated and shaped our communities, and the meaning and significance we give to these biological and social facts. These biocultural linkages taken together are what make us human.

Key Terms

Biocultural   p. 281
Clinical therapeutic
    process   p. 294
Culture-bound
    syndrome.   p. 283
Disease   p. 290

Explanatory model of
    illness   p. 291
Illness   p. 290
Medical pluralism   p. 298
Medicalization   p. 292
Mind   p. 282

Placebo effect   p. 295
Sick role   p. 285
Social support therapeutic
    process   p. 295
Symbolic therapeutic
    process   p. 294

Reviewing the Chapter

CHAPTER SECTION	WHAT WE KNOW	TO BE RESOLVED
How do biological and cultural factors shape our bodily experiences?	Biocultural perspectives and evidence are breathing new life into classic anthropological interests in cognition, psychologies, and our bodily experiences, suggesting that "human nature" is not a singular condition.	Anthropologists continue to debate how the cultural variability around psychology, emotions, and mental states relates to biological and other psychological processes.

CHAPTER SECTION	WHAT WE KNOW	TO BE RESOLVED
What do we mean by health and illness?	A person's culture shapes his or her interpretation of symptoms and understanding of the illness condition.	How people in any particular society will interpret the symptoms of illness can be determined only by detailed evidence from illness episodes in a particular society.
How and why do doctors and other health practitioners gain social authority?	By dealing with human concerns as medical or biomedical problems, our society implicitly gives power to health practitioners who can prescribe drugs and other therapies.	It is not entirely clear why some peoples around the world are so ready and willing to give authority to healers, while people in other societies are not so willing.
How does healing happen?	Not all healing can be explained by the clinical processes familiar to physicians and medical students. Healing has important social and cultural dimensions.	While the power of the placebo effect is demonstrated, we still don't understand why it can work on our bodies.
How can anthropology help us address global health problems?	Clinical solutions to global health problems cannot work effectively without understanding the local culture of the people whose health-related behavior we want to improve, as well as the fact that due to medical pluralism most societies combine distinct healing systems.	Until now there has been no single solution to a health problem that will work in all societies; it is not clear if there are general strategies applicable to most societies.

14
Materiality

Constructing Social Relationships and Meanings With Things

In November 1989, the Royal Ontario Museum (ROM) in Toronto, Canada, opened a blockbuster exhibition on the art of Africa called *Into the Heart of Africa*. This was the ROM's first major exhibition of its African collection, and it promised to expose the Canadian public to the delights of African art.

The curator, cultural anthropologist Jeanne Cannizzo, wanted to do more than just show off the ROM's collection. She wanted to look at how the museum had obtained pieces in this collection in the first place. She worked with the families of Canadian servicemen who had served in Africa in the nineteenth century and World War I. She also contacted families of missionaries who had served in Africa between 1875 and 1925. Much of the ROM's African collection had been donated by these missionaries and servicemen, who had acquired African

Exhibiting African Art.   This object appeared as part of the *Into the Heart of Africa* exhibit, which opened on November 16, 1989, and closed on August 6, 1990, at the Royal Ontario Museum in Toronto, Ontario, Canada. It is a gold necklace made by an unidentified Asante artist, c. 1874.

objects as souvenirs. Cannizzo also assembled photographs taken by the missionaries and servicemen during their time in Africa along with statements from their writings, hoping to explore the attitudes of the men and women who had collected the objects in the first place (Cannizzo 1989; Butler 2008). Her idea was to let the photographs and statements speak for themselves, which was a consequential decision.

The catalog released with the show's opening explains that the goal of this approach was to show that the majority of the Canadians serving in Africa in the early twentieth century would have assumed—like most anthropologists of the day—that Europeans and Canadians were culturally superior to Africans (Cannizzo 1989). Cannizzo hoped to use irony to let the public explore and challenge the mindsets and prejudices of the wrong, but well-meaning, Canadians of the early 1900s.

Museum staff quickly realized that visitors took away quite different meanings from the exhibition, and almost no one in the public saw the perspective of the anthropologist as Cannizzo had intended it. Worse, Cannizzo's use of irony backfired. Some visitors thought the collectors' own words and images seemed to indicate that Cannizzo and the museum supported the racist attitudes that had predominated in the period between 1875 and 1925, when both Cannizzo and the museum wanted to critique these views.

Nobody was happy with the exhibition. Black community leaders wrote critical letters to the Toronto-based newspaper *The Globe and Mail* arguing that the exhibition "infantilize[d] the African peoples depicted" and celebrated a racist view of Africans (quoted in Tator, Henry, and Mattis 1998:40). They staged daily protests outside the ROM condemning the museum and its staff as racist. At the same time, the families of the Canadian servicemen and missionaries who had loaned their photographs to the museum felt that the good intentions of their relatives in the early twentieth century were being ignored. Although the museum's director stood by the exhibition and its curator, Cannizzo resigned several months before the exhibition closed. The four other museums in Canada and the United States scheduled to receive the exhibition canceled, wanting none of the tension and controversy that the exhibition had produced.

As anthropologist Simon Ottenberg (1991:81) suggests, "curating an exhibition is a political act." In this case, his words seem like an understatement. But there is something else going on here, and it is about the objects themselves. The objects and photographs in the exhibition were real objects. We call this concrete, physical presence their **materiality** (having the quality of being physical or material), the theme we will explore in this final chapter. Although the tensions surrounding the ROM's *Into the Heart of Africa* exhibition were not about the material characteristics of the photographs and objects in the show, different people gave these tangible objects different meanings, a fact that raises the question central to this chapter: *What is the role of objects and material culture in constructing social relationships and cultural meanings?* Embedded within this larger question are several more focused questions around which this chapter is organized:

Why is the ownership of artifacts from other cultures a contentious issue?
How can anthropology help us understand objects?
How do the meanings of things change over time?
How do objects come to represent our goals and aspirations?

This chapter examines **material culture**, the objects made and used in any society. Traditionally, the term referred to technologically simple objects made in preindustrial societies, but *material culture* may refer to all of the objects or commodities of modern life as well, including the latest electronic gadgets we use. When we take objects seriously and consider all the ways people use objects to communicate with others, define themselves through objects, and control others using objects, we can see that anthropology is not "simply" about people but about the intertwining of people and material things.

❧ Why Is the Ownership of Artifacts From Other Cultures a Contentious Issue?

In the United States, the discipline of anthropology began in museums, arising amidst the scramble to put together collections of cultural, archaeological, linguistic, and biological data to document the human story. At first, most of the material culture displayed in these museums was from Native Americans in Western states. From 1850, many of these objects were held in the Smithsonian Institution in Washington, D.C.

By the time of the Chicago World's Fair of 1893, the Smithsonian's curators had assembled impressive anthropological exhibits. But rather than rely exclusively on the national collection, the organizers of the World's Fair hired anthropologist Frederic Ward Putnam of Harvard's Peabody Museum of Archaeology and Ethnology (established in 1866) to organize its own anthropological exhibits. Putnam competed with the Smithsonian researchers to present the cultures and prehistory of the New World, sending out teams of researchers to acquire new collections from dozens of Indian tribes and to excavate Indian mounds in Ohio, pueblos like Mesa Verde in the Southwest, and ancient sites in Peru. At the end of the Fair, most of the collections were purchased for the newly formed Field Museum (Hinsley and Wilcox 2016).

What followed during the early twentieth century was an international scramble for collections from societies that Western scholars thought of as "primitive" (Cole 1985; Schildkrout and Keim 1998; O'Hanlon and Welsch 2000). Major American museums were actively competing with one another for objects, in the process employing a lot of anthropologists. At first, nobody was concerned about who owned all of these objects, since in a legal sense they belonged to the individual museums. But in recent decades, questions of ownership and control over these objects have become a contentious issue. Shouldn't the people whose direct ancestors made or used these objects have some rights over these collections? Who has the moral right to display and interpret them? Do the museums who own these objects have the right to say whatever they want about another culture's objects, or should the people from whom the objects were collected have a say? These questions were, of course, at the heart of the ROM's *Into the Heart of Africa* controversy.

Questions of Ownership, Rights, and Protection

Until recently, in the United States there have been no special laws protecting the rights of American Indian peoples or their material culture. It has always been assumed that Indian tribes and their members have the right to sell off their possessions to a visiting traveler or anthropologist, or at trading posts developed as places for Indians to sell their handicrafts beginning in the late nineteenth century (Wade 1985). In many tribes today it is forbidden or controversial to sell off commonly held ritual objects, but historically the assumption was if a museum or a private collector purchased some American Indian object, it belonged to that institution or individual. What changed?

AMERICAN INDIANS' RIGHTS AND CALLS FOR REPATRIATION

In the nineteenth century, rights to Indian lands were governed by treaties and later by legislation. As a result of the Dawes Act of 1887, the majority of land on most reservations was sold off to non-Indian owners by 1950. By the mid-1960s, when civil rights legislation began to protect African Americans, American Indians began pressing their claims against drilling, mining, pipelines, and agri-business farming on their reservations, issues that persist today. They also protested the ways their peoples and cultures were depicted in movies, books, and museums. But the claims that seemed to reach the American public's consciousness most directly were those against archaeological excavations of sacred Indian sites and cemeteries.

During the 1970s, activists associated with the **American Indian Movement (AIM)**, a prominent American Indian rights group founded in 1968, began to protest the disrespectful ways national, state, and local officials treated Indian remains (Banks 2004). They also pointed to histories of forced settlement on reservations; punishment for speaking their native languages in government schools; and pressures on reservations to sell their lands to white Americans.

Calls for **repatriation**, or the return of human remains and artifacts to the communities of descendants of the people to whom they originally belonged, came to stand for respect for Indian identity. But at the time, the United States had only a few basic laws to protect archaeological sites, and only on government lands.

THE TRAGEDY OF SLACK FARM AND THE PASSAGE OF NAGPRA

An incident in Kentucky in 1987 led to new state and federal laws that make it a felony to disturb archaeological sites on both government-owned and private lands everywhere. Anthropologists and archaeologists had been aware of an important late prehistoric site on the property known as Slack Farm near Uniontown, Kentucky, that included an intact cemetery containing more than 1,000 Indian graves, plus grave goods (pots, beads, pipes, arrowheads, and ritual artifacts). The owners of the land sold rights to dig on this site for $10,000 to a group of pot hunters, who dug up the site with abandon, leaving skeletal material and broken pots all over. The state police arrested and fined the looters on the misdemeanor charge of desecrating a venerated object (Fagan 1988; Arden 1989). This incident was so offensive to American Indian groups, anthropologists, and archaeologists that it led the Congress to pass the **Native American Graves Protection and Repatriation Act** of 1990 (NAGPRA).

NAGPRA requires the repatriation of human remains and artifacts found with those remains to the families of the dead individuals. The law also requires all museums or other institutions that hold human remains or cultural objects from any native group included in the act to inform tribal representatives of their holdings. If the group feels that an object is of special cultural, religious, or historic significance, it may petition the institution to return or repatriate the object. Although many museums own objects from other countries, NAGPRA covers only material from American cultural groups, including American Indians, Hawaiian Islanders, Native Alaskans, and the indigenous peoples of American Samoa and Guam.

Some archaeologists and anthropologists worried that information about the prehistory of Native Americans would be lost if reburial of bones and grave goods became commonplace (Buikstra 1983). Others rejected the Indian position altogether; as one prominent archaeologist was once heard to say, the Indians would "get my bones over my dead body."

Despite such concerns, many sets of human remains have been returned to various tribes, along with objects of very special significance to the tribal groups involved. Most important cultural institutions have taken advantage of NAGPRA to establish or reestablish relationships with Native American groups over repatriation concerns. These efforts have involved the creation of close relationships between museums and the tribes whose objects they display. For their part, tribal groups have used repatriation to celebrate the significance of their traditional culture and to push for greater respect for indigenous peoples from mainstream America (Figure 14.1).

Although NAGPRA applies only to native groups within the United States, building relationships with native groups in other countries is just as important, as we explore in "Anthropologist as Problem Solver: John Terrell, Repatriation, and the Maori House at The Field Museum."

PROTECTION OF HISTORIC SITES AROUND THE WORLD

Many countries have implemented legislation and programs of their own to recognize and protect historic sites, and most governments support UNESCO's **World Heritage Sites program**, which provides financial support to maintain sites of importance to humanity. The majority of the 814 cultural heritage sites currently recognized by UNESCO's program have played a key role in human history. Five of them are sites where early fossil hominids have been found in Africa, China, and Australia. Others are key archaeological sites such as

Figure 14.1 Repatriating a Chilkat Blanket to the Tlingit at a Memorial Potlatch in Sitka, Alaska, Fall 2002. (*Top*) Tlingit elders who organized the memorial potlatch wearing Chilkat blankets or button blankets: Edwell John, from Dakl'aweidi (Killer Whale) clan; Joe Murray, representing Dakl'aweidi clan; Joe Murray, representing Dakl'aweidi clan; a man from Kaagwaantaan (Wolf) clan; Dan Brown, of Teikweidee (Brown Bear) clan; and Randy Gamble, of Kaagwaantaan clan. They wear headdresses from their respective clans. (*Bottom*) Kellen Haak, registrar of the Hood Museum of Art at Dartmouth College, presents the Museum's Chilkat blanket being returned to the Deisheetaan (Beaver) clan in the Raven moiety. To his left are Nell Murphy (from the American Museum of Natural History in New York), anthropologist Sergei Kan (from Dartmouth College, speaking for the group), and Terri Snowball (from the National Museum of the American Indian in Washington, D.C.). Tlingit leaders in this photo include Alan Zuboff, of L'eeneidi (Dog Salmon) clan, and Garfield George, of Deisheetaan clan.

the pyramids of Giza and the temples and palaces of Ancient Thebes in Egypt, Angkor Wat in Cambodia, Chichén Itzá in Mexico, Mesa Verde in Colorado, and the moai statues on Rapa Nui (Easter Island), all of which are typical of what we

Anthropologist as Problem Solver
John Terrell, Repatriation, and the Maori Meeting House at The Field Museum

At the heart of any Maori community in New Zealand is a meeting house where rituals, business, and other important community processes take place. Meeting houses have elaborately carved images in their posts and ridge poles, which not only symbolize a Maori family's ancestry, but embody the spirits of these ancestors as well.

In 1905, The Field Museum in Chicago purchased a nearly complete meeting house named Ruatepupuke [roo-ah-tay-pah-**poo**-kay] that originally came from Tokomaru Bay, New Zealand. The museum bought it from a European curio dealer who had convinced one member of the family to sell this house. The structure had been quietly and quickly dismantled and shipped overseas. For the Maori family, this was a shameful act that amounted to selling off their ancestors.

When archaeologist John Terrell became The Field Museum's curator of oceanic archaeology and ethnology in 1971, he began researching

John Terrell Speaking at a Workshop Held in the Meeting House at The Field Museum in Chicago.   A112618c by Diane Alexander White and Linda Dorman. Courtesy of The Field Museum

this Maori meeting house. He brought specialists to the museum to examine the carvings, including Hirini (Sidney) Moko Mead, one of the leading Maori anthropologists. Terrell also visited Tokomaru Bay to confirm what he and other specialists had suspected—that this was indeed their meeting house that had been sold and packed off around 1900.

Terrell then began working with elders at Tokomaru Bay, discussing the future of the structure. Some of the young people wanted their house and their ancestors to come back to the community. But after talking over the matter with Terrell, the elders agreed to keep the house in Chicago, so long as The Field Museum would work with the community to restore the structure. Terrell, in collaboration with Tokomaru elders, chose Maori curators, conservators, and artists to help with the restoration (Hakiwai and Terrell 1994).

The house went on display for the public in 1986 as part of an exhibition called *Te Maori*, and Maori elders were invited to help with the opening. Later, more than twenty elders, both men and women, came to Chicago to perform the rituals that would bring their ancestral spirits from the museum's lower level, where the house had been for many decades, to the second floor, where the house would be reassembled. Elders have been involved with planning and executing all important decisions about Ruatepupuke ever since. They selected their own Maori curator and conservator, as well as a Maori artist who was tasked with carving new pieces missing from the front of the structure. Maori curator Arapata Hakiwai discovered several boards from this meeting house in Te Papa, the national museum of New Zealand, and Tokomaru elders requested that these carved boards join the house in Chicago where they belonged; the museum complied with this request. The people of Tokomaru Bay are now well known by Maori across New Zealand because their meeting house is so prominently displayed overseas. By working with Terrell and The Field Museum, the people of Tokomaru Bay transformed an embarrassing situation into an object of national pride.

By April 2007, a number of the elders who had been involved with The Field Museum passed away. The younger generation had not been as involved with the museum, and some were talking about bringing Ruatepupuke back to Tokomaru Bay. The Field Museum invited some fifty Maori from Tokomaru Bay, both elders and younger members of the community, to celebrate the meeting house and Maori culture for a week. After this experience, many of those young people recognized that if they want a place for their

cultural traditions on the world stage, they can be more successful by working with The Field Museum than they ever could be on their own. As in the 1980s, John Terrell continues to work hard to engage with indigenous communities who made and formerly owned the artifacts his museum now holds. Together, the curator and the Maori community have found alternative solutions to the question of repatriation of cultural objects that for Maori are the embodiment of their ancestors.

QUESTIONS FOR REFLECTION

1. What does this example illustrate about the role archaeologists and anthropologists can play in explaining and promoting a community's culture around the world?

2. Many archaeologists have assumed there is a natural tension between them and indigenous peoples. To what extent do you feel this tension is inevitable?

3. Archaeologists and anthropologists have always been the outsiders who most understand the native cultures they study. Why have indigenous peoples so often wanted to challenge their ownership of artifacts?

often think of as ancient historic and prehistoric sites. Many others are historic cities like Fez in Morocco.

Cultural Resource Management: Not Just for Archaeologists Any More

In response to the legislation introduced in the past few decades, the need for specialists who can study the architecture and cultural significance of historic sites has grown. All of these efforts are often referred to as **cultural resource management** (CRM), which is a form of applied anthropology. CRM's goal is to protect and manage the cultural resources of every community, especially important historic and prehistoric sites and structures. Much of what CRM does is document and interpret historic and prehistoric sites and structures for living communities. The vast majority of archaeological work in the Americas and around the world is done by contract archaeologists, and CRM has become a major focus for those seeking careers in archaeology. But a growing number of applied cultural anthropologists are working in the CRM field with historic and cultural sites and materials. And most communities have an historical society, historic district, or heritage commission that regularly hires consultants to interpret historical and cultural resources in their towns and cities.

An increasing number of American Indians have also earned postgraduate degrees in archaeology and anthropology and use the techniques of CRM to preserve their tribe's cultural heritage. Nearly all tribes that use CRM view heritage management differently than most federal government agencies do (Anyon, Ferguson, and Welch 2000:132). One key difference is that non-Indian agencies nearly always see heritage resources as tangible places and things, and scientific study as a way of finding a middle ground between the heritage resource and some other use. Emphasizing their spiritual connections to the past, tribes tend to prefer avoiding the disturbance of the heritage resource altogether, including scientific investigation (Dongoske et al. 1995).

The social conflicts around objects are complex, suggesting that the meanings and uses of objects are not straightforward matters. In the next section we deepen this point by pulling back and reviewing what we can learn about societies by looking at objects anthropologically.

THINKING CRITICALLY ABOUT MATERIALITY

How do the meanings of museum collections of American Indian material culture change depending on who is thinking about them? How would these meanings be different if the objects were historical artifacts from a white pioneer community in the National Museum of American History?

How Can Anthropology Help Us Understand Objects?

Until the 1980s, anthropologists tended to look at the study of objects principally as evidence of cultural distinctiveness. They approached cultural and artistic objects as expressions of a society's environmental adaptation or aesthetic sensibilities, or as markers of ethnic identity. Viewed in this way, arts and crafts were considered an expression of a particular tradition, time, or place, but even more so, an expression of the individual creativity of the artist or craftsperson. This way of looking at objects may seem reasonable, but in the mid-1980s anthropologists began to look at objects in a new way. In particular, they started to recognize that objects were capable of conveying meaning in many different ways simultaneously, many of these ways symbolic.

The Many Dimensions of Objects

The late historian of anthropology George W. Stocking Jr. edited an influential book called *Objects and Others: Essays on Museums and Material Culture* (1985). Stocking's introduction to this book explained that anthropology's history began with the study of objects in museums decades before anthropologists even began conducting their own field research. Using these collections, they developed crude analyses of how civilized, barbaric, or primitive a society was from the kinds of objects they had or did not have. Later, when anthropologists started conducting fieldwork, they noticed firsthand the importance of objects in rituals, social exchanges, and political activities. They used objects to understand the meaning of rituals, the interconnections between people who exchanged particular objects, and the social stratification within a society that could be seen in the presence or absence of objects in a particular household or community. In its most basic sense, this approach has endured until the present.

But the importance of Stocking's work was his argument that objects are multidimensional, and if we really want to understand them, we have to recognize and try to understand not just their three basic physical dimensions—height, width, depth—but at least four other dimensions as well, among them time (history), power, wealth, and aesthetics, making a total of seven dimensions.

The dimension of *time* or *history* refers to the fact that objects in museums came from somewhere and each had an individual history. In part this asks the following: When, by whom, and how were they produced? How did they get to the museum or their current location? How have interpretations of them changed over time? The dimension of *power* reveals the relations of inequality reflected in objects, especially why the objects of non-Western people sit in ethnographic museums, while very few non-Western peoples have museums or repositories where local people can view Western objects. During the heyday of colonialism, European and American anthropologists collected thousands of objects from the peoples they studied. Rarely could a community know enough about how these objects might be displayed or studied to be able to give informed consent. *Wealth* reflects the fact that people use objects to establish and demonstrate who has wealth and social status. We have seen how American museum directors saw showy and impressive objects as being quite valuable for their museums and their museums' reputations. Similarly, only the wealthy can typically own original examples of important early artworks. The dimension of *aesthetics* is reflected in the fact that each culture brings with it its own system or patterns of recognizing what is pleasing or attractive, which configurations of colors and textures are appealing, and which are not. All of these patterns, of course, change over time in the style of artworks, but also in the designs of commonplace objects like pottery (Kubler 1962).

What intrigued Stocking most about objects, especially those now found in museums, was that these things were a historical archive in multiple dimensions that can tell us a great deal about the cultures that made and used these objects as well as the relationships between the collectors' societies and the communities who originally made them. Furthermore, objects could offer a window for understanding local symbolic systems of meaning. This point was more expansive than just being focused on the objects found in art and ethnographic museums. His insights can actually be applied to any everyday object. Consider, for example, a shiny new bicycle.

A Shiny New Bicycle, in Multiple Dimensions

Picture a shiny new bicycle chained to a bicycle rack on your campus (Figure 14.2). Like all objects, this bicycle has the physical properties of height, length, and width, dimensions that are quite important for any individual mounting one: think of how difficult it is to ride a bicycle that is too big or small.

Objects are defined by more than their physical traits, however. Objects also embody a temporal dimension of having a past, present, and future. The shape and form of this particular object has emerged from improvements on the functions of generations of bicycles, used by generations of cyclists as a childhood toy, as an inexpensive mode of transport, for racing, or for casual weekend riding. If we think of a bicycle in the abstract, we can choose from among all of these meanings and uses of a bicycle. The particular owner of this bicycle has certain associations that come to mind when he or she thinks of a bicycle, and these associations may be quite different from cyclists who race, from mothers who pedal around the neighborhood with their children, or from bike messengers who spend their days cycling through busy urban traffic. The owner's view of his or her bicycle may be shaped by previous bicycles he or she has owned; it may be influenced by feelings that the owner is being ecologically "green" and choosing an environmentally friendly mode of transportation. And such images shape how the owner views himself or herself today or how he or she imagines the future (Vivanco 2013).

This bicycle—like practically every other object North American consumers purchase—is also a commodity that as parts

Figure 14.2   The Bicycle, Like All Objects, Is Multidimensional.

and as a finished product has circulated through a

complex economic system, supported by an equally complex set of regulatory rules. As deeply personal as the selection and purchase of an object like a bicycle may be for us as individuals, it was made on an assembly line overseas by dozens of workers, each contributing a small part to the finished effort. So the bicycle has traveled through a worldwide network of economic linkages, warehouses, and shippers to get to its current owner.

In that process, the manufacturer and the mainstream culture generally have carefully cultivated the current owner's desire to own and use this object. The owner has purchased this particular bicycle and not a more expensive one, and not a beaten-up secondhand one. The owner may even have replaced an older bike with this newer and more efficient one, imagining himself as more of a racer than he really is, or thinking of herself as more environmentally conscious than she might actually be. And our impressions of particular bicycles may be shaped by the images we have seen of them in films, TV programs, ads, and shiny brochures advertising a particular brand of bicycle (Vivanco 2013).

Finally, this bicycle, like most other objects we own, is a useful object, not only for where or how far it can take us, not just in how much it can help keep us healthy from the exercise it provides, not simply from the fuel it saves us, but from the impressions of us that it creates in others as they see us ride.

The point of our bicycle example is that *any* mundane object can help us imagine ourselves, our past, and where we are headed. Although Stocking's seven dimensions do not cover all the aspects or dimensions suggested about our shiny new bicycle, they do offer a simple first glance at how we feel we should look at objects anthropologically.

The Power of Symbols

Now that we have you thinking about objects in multiple dimensions, we can turn to the aesthetic. By studying the art traditions and objects of non-Western peoples, anthropologists have encountered diverse ideas about aesthetics. The African carving in Figure 14.3 is a good case in point. The African carver of that sculpture was not trying to depict the human form, but was displaying the distinctive characteristics of supernatural beings by symbolically representing them as anatomical features.

There is every reason to believe that the carvers of such figures, and perhaps others living in their communities when the figures were created, imagined that their spirits and demons looked like the carvings they produced. But when others grow up and the only depiction of a particular spirit is the carving that represents that spirit, they will likely understand the spirit to look just like the carvings.

The Symbols of Power

Just as the aesthetic dimensions of objects shape an object's meaning, powerful people use aesthetics in ways to demonstrate and legitimate their social, political, or religious power. Wealthy North Americans and Europeans, for example,

Figure 14.3 Rethinking African Art. When Western audiences were first introduced to objects like this *Nkisi* figure from the Democratic Republic of Congo pictured here, they often responded dismissively and ethnocentrically. They misunderstood African notions of aesthetics. In this *Nkisi* figure, displayed at the Hood Museum of Art at Dartmouth College, each additional element adds meaning and power to the object. The most important here are the nails. Each nail pounded into the carving requested some favor from the spirit in this figure, and it also strengthened the spirit. (Courtesy of Hood Museum of Art, Dartmouth College, Hanover, New Hampshire)

may own and display paintings or sculptures by well-known artists to demonstrate their high social position. In many traditional African kingdoms, the kings and chiefs who ruled these communities distinguished themselves from ordinary people with symbols of rank and authority—staffs, chairs, thrones, clothing, and so forth—artfully carved or woven in a particular local style or aesthetic. Similarly, in many religions authorities employ aesthetics to indicate that the holder of an item possesses divine power as well as power here on earth.

What sets these objects of power apart is in part their aesthetic style that establishes the objects, and by extension their owners, as important and special. But the aesthetic settings and ways in which such objects are used and displayed can also symbolically communicate the power of their owners. An interesting illustration comes from the island of Walis along the north coast of Papua New Guinea, as witnessed by Rob Welsch, one of the authors of this textbook, in 1993. A century earlier, a religious cult leader name Barjani had foretold the coming of Europeans and was believed to be a prophet. After his death, his family's clansmen had erected a shrine for him, where people in need of supernatural assistance could leave a small amount of money or tobacco to ensure Barjani's assistance. When Welsch and his colleague, John Terrell, went to see the shrine, they were mostly interested in the building's historically important architectural style.

The real surprise came when they climbed the small ladder to peer into Barjani's shrine. The interior of the small shrine held a single object in a place of honor on a simple but small platform of palm leaves: an old and well-worn bowler hat. This was Barjani's hat, an object that possessed its power from Barjani's having worn it, but also from being the only object in the shrine. The meaning of this hat, standing out starkly in such an unexpected place, came partly from its association with Barjani and partly from his association with the foreigners he had predicted would come. In addition, the fact that it was a foreign object that few if any other Walis Islanders could have owned must have made it both exotic and valuable as a relic of this local prophet (Figure 14.4).

Figure 14.4   Barjani's Shrine on Walis Island in Papua New Guinea.   Inside, the room was empty except for Barjani's bowler hat and offerings or gifts that had been left in exchange for Barjani's help.

Although Barjani's hat is for Walis Islanders a statement about relations between themselves and powerful outsiders, it is also a window into the historical context of both their society and the changing meaning that this bowler hat has had over its century of existence. To pursue this issue further, let us consider the next question around which this chapter is organized, which is how objects change meaning over time.

THINKING CRITICALLY ABOUT MATERIALITY

Most people take the objects around them at face value, but anthropologists think about things in more multidimensional ways. Consider some object, statue, artwork, building, or other physical feature on your campus and outline its different dimensions as an anthropologist might. What new insights about your campus, your school's history, or the school's distinctive local culture do you get from this analysis?

🌱 How Do the Meanings of Things Change Over Time?

Anthropologists today study some of the very same museum collections that anthropologists studied over a century ago, but they interpret them differently. This is a key aspect of what Stocking was getting at when he indicated that objects have a temporal dimension: all objects change over time, *if not in their physical characteristics, then in the significance we give to them.*

Around the same time that Stocking was laying out his framework for understanding objects in seven dimensions, another group of anthropologists was developing a set of complementary theories and techniques for analyzing in depth the issue of how objects change over time. Declaring that "things have social lives," they published a book called *The Social Life of Things: Commodities in*

Cultural Perspective (Appadurai 1986) in which they laid out some useful concepts and approaches for thinking anthropologically about objects. So how can an *inanimate* object have a *social* life?

The Social Life of Things

The idea that inanimate things have social lives is based on the assumption that things have forms, uses, and trajectories that are intertwined in complex ways with people's lives. Just as people pass through different socially recognized phases of life, objects have "careers" (in the sense of having a course or progression) with recognizable phases, from their creation, exchange, and uses, to their eventual discard. Along the way, it is possible to identify social relationships and cultural ideologies that influence each period in this career. Across cultures, these relationships and ideologies can vary drastically.

Consider a pair of running sneakers sold at a mall. This pair of sneakers may start as cotton fabric and rubber in a Chinese factory. But the shoes mean something quite different there from what they will mean to the mall salesperson, or from what they will mean to you when you first wear them to some social event. The shoes may have aged only a few weeks from the time they were made until you wear them; the change in significance comes not from aging, but from moving from one person to another. That pair of shoes has a complicated life, taking on meanings from the contexts it passes through and, to the sensitive observer, revealing a whole range of complex social relations in the process. And throughout it all, the same pair of shoes has changed.

Three Ways Objects Change Over Time

All objects change over time, but they can do so in different ways. Most objects age and weather with time, of course, usually becoming less significant because they get old and worn out. But for the purposes of understanding the social life of things, there are three major ways that objects change over time:

1. The form, shape, color, material, and use changes from generation to generation.
2. An object changes significance and meaning as its social and physical contexts change.
3. A single object changes significance and meaning as it changes hands.

Let us consider a few examples of each of these kinds of changes to illustrate how the social meanings of an object can change over time.

CHANGING FORM FROM GENERATION TO GENERATION

Nearly every manufactured product has changed over time as styles and social preferences have changed. While we usually understand these changes as gradual improvements in form or technology, they are just as often due to introducing innovations or differences in style, simply to be different. One of the best examples comes from an anthropological study of ladies' fashion.

Just before World War II, anthropologists Jane Richardson and Alfred Kroeber (1940) published an analysis of skirt length in women's dresses over the previous 300 years. Studying all sorts of pattern books, sketches, and photographs of women's dresses, they documented how styles of dresses had changed over this period. They found that skirt length had risen and fallen in ways that most women were unaware of. In a more or less predictable way, hem length fluctuated from extremes of long to short over a fifty-year period or cycle (Figure 14.5). Subsequent studies since 1940 have suggested that this cycle has now shortened to about twenty or twenty-five years (Bernard 2011:355).

What is the cause of these cyclical changes? One is that fashionable women want to wear the latest fashion, and this desire encourages many others to follow their lead. Second, the factories and seamstresses that make women's dresses have a vested interest in these objects changing. They want to sell new dresses, and the best way to sell new dresses is if the styles change so much that everyone's closet is filled with "old-fashioned" dresses. But there is more to it than simply encouraging new sales, because the symbolism of being fashionable relies on constantly changing preferences. All of this activity involves many thousands of people in the fashion industry, from the high-end designers to the most inexpensive stores and even the consignment shops, who all rely on—and help produce—those changing preferences.

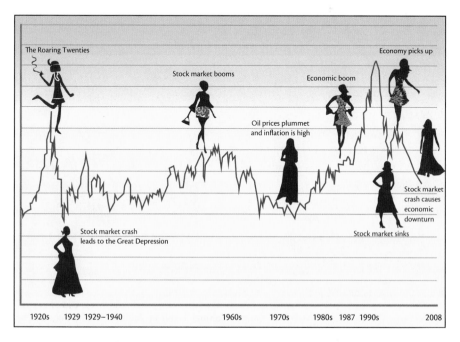

Figure 14.5   Shifting Dress Styles.   Although dress styles in Europe and America have changed in many ways from period to period, they reflect cyclical trends in stylistic and aesthetic innovation (after Richardson and Kroeber 1940 and Bernard 2011).

CHANGING MEANING WITH CHANGING CONTEXTS

Contexts often change as environments and technologies change as well. Tahitians, like other Polynesians, had no knowledge of iron until Europeans first visited their islands (Figure 14.6). On June 18, 1767, the British captain Samuel Wallis was the first Westerner to reach Tahiti, and that day Tahitians learned about the powerful abilities of iron tools for cutting, chopping, and carving. After learning about iron tools, Tahitian men started plotting ways they could get access to Wallis's steel. The traditionally sexually restrained Tahitian society became transformed almost overnight as men sent their wives, daughters, and sisters out to Wallis's ship, the HMS *Dolphin*, to engage in sex in exchange for any sort of iron tools: knives, axes, or even nails that could be fashioned into cutting tools. The following year, the French captain Louis-Antoine de Bougainville arrived at Tahiti, and a year later British captain James Cook first reached Tahitian shores; they both found Tahitian women to be so sexually promiscuous that the crew nearly dismantled their small lifeboats in a quest for much desired nails. On his second voyage, Cook brought along quantities of nails and hoop iron to satisfy the local desire for iron. Of course, these interactions with Tahitian women created the stereotype that Polynesians were traditionally very promiscuous, when in fact it was the horny sailors combined with the Tahitian desire for iron that

Figure 14.6   Queen Oberea Welcomes Captain Samuel Wallis at Tahiti.   When Wallis and his crew reached Tahiti in 1767, the queen and captain exchanged gifts that included some small iron cutting tools. Tahitians found the iron tools to be far superior to the stone and shell cutting tools they had been using, and they quickly developed a strong desire for iron that transformed their society.

had transformed Tahitian society and introduced sexual license to these islands (Howe 1984). As this example shows, new technologies can have profound impacts on local communities.

CHANGING MEANING FROM CHANGING HANDS

The most powerful examples of objects that change meaning when they pass into different hands come from the situations where an anthropologist or collector buys an object from exotic villagers for a museum. Often, a collector will buy an object such as a stone axe that people in the village feel is useful. But for the collector, the object is not going to be used, except as an example of a traditional society's technology and way of life. Once the object reaches a museum, its meaning changes profoundly; it no longer has a useful function but becomes a rare example of something from an exotic culture far away in time and space.

Geographic movements of objects mean that objects also move across differences in both cultural and individual perspectives. Commodities, as we have suggested previously, provide examples of the changing significance of objects as these objects change hands. But rather than focus too directly on how commodities create meaning, let us consider how objects represent and even help us create who we are.

THINKING CRITICALLY ABOUT MATERIALITY

The meaning of an object clearly depends on the context from which its owner views it. Consider some possession that excited you some years ago when you bought it or were given it as a gift. How do you think about this object today? What has changed to make it more or less valuable to you? Is it valuable to you in a different way today, or has it lost its value altogether?

❧ How Do Objects Come to Represent Our Goals and Aspirations?

When we ask how objects can represent our goals and aspirations, we are really addressing three interconnected issues: (1) objects express our personal and collective pasts, (2) objects help us express and even formulate our goals and aspirations, and (3) objects can be used in ways that manipulate what our goals and aspirations should be. We consider each of these issues in this final section of the chapter.

The Cultural Biography of Things

To understand how objects help us express our individual pasts, it is helpful to consider an idea first proposed by the anthropologist Igor Kopytoff (1986) in an essay included in the book we mentioned before, *The Social Life of Things*. Kopytoff explains that in some societies, including pre–Civil War America, some people have been seen as property. This observation forced him to recognize that *all* tangible property has a biography that is profoundly shaped by culture. Paying attention to the biography of a thing—its life course from its origins through its distribution, uses, and eventual discard—can uncover important social relationships and cultural dynamics.

As an illustration of this concept, think about this: the objects we choose to keep and display in our rooms, houses, and offices remind us of important things in our lives. But they also communicate important things about us to others. Consider, for example, the posters and other objects you or one of your friends has hung up in a dorm room. College students are especially sensitive to what these things communicate about them, so they carefully choose the objects they put on display, and they are usually ready to tell stories of how these objects fit into their lives. Friends may have different perceptions of the same symbolic objects, because their perceptions are rooted in differing cultural biographies of the same symbolic object. These different perceptions, of course, were at the center of the controversy over the ROM's *Into the Heart of Africa* exhibition.

The Culture of Mass Consumption

People do not simply imprint themselves and their pasts *onto* objects. They also formulate who they are and express themselves *through* objects, especially their goals and aspirations about their lives. A useful vantage point from which to observe this dynamic is in the contemporary **culture of mass consumption**—a term that refers to the cultural perspectives and social processes that shape and are shaped by how goods and services are bought, sold, and used in contemporary capitalism—because this culture is so ubiquitous in so many people's lives (Figure 14.7).

Understanding the culture of mass consumption is important because it explains the changes in human relations that came with the rise of commodity production.

Rather than looking at consumption as an *antisocial* act, anthropologists have concluded that it is a deeply *social* act. Possessing consumer goods is a key means through which people define and express who they are: their social status, economic means, gender identities, aesthetic sensibilities, individual qualities of taste and discernment, and identification with a certain social class or interest group (Bourdieu 1984; Miller 1987, 1998).

Figure 14.7 Keeping in Touch. Modern devices such as smartphones allow us to keep in touch with friends, but they are also examples of what Marx called our "commodity fetish"—they control our attention and have become objects of obsessive desire and worship.

How Advertisers Manipulate Our Goals and Aspirations

If large corporations want to survive and expand, they have to convince consumers to buy their products and not those of one of their competitors. To convince you to buy their product, they bombard you with advertising that will encourage you to think that their product is necessary for a fulfilling life and that their brand is more likely to help you reach your goals than any other brand. Advertisers proudly announce that they are simply passing on useful information to consumers, but we know that they are really trying to convince us that we need *their* product. We think of this ad-making as part of the process of manipulating our world through a symbolic framing or reframing of their products.

Many TV commercials speak to needs that people already have, from basics like food and clothing to less essential things such as being attractive to other people. The challenge for an advertiser is to get individuals to think that its product is the better one for them. So makers of consumer goods segment their audiences, targeting their products toward particular individuals based on audience demographics, such as gender, socioeconomic class, sexual orientation, and so on.

Most of these ads are fairly obvious about who they are for and what the product does, but they often have other goals that many—perhaps most—Americans do not consciously understand. Consider the ads produced to sell Budweiser beer. How do these ads try to convince consumers that Budweiser beer is better than other beer, since they provide no comparisons with other brands and never speak about price? The ads are not really about the beer, but about young men's aspirations to be liked by other guys and to have a good time. What they actually present is a lot of guys, and usually a bunch of attractive young women, at some sort of party having a good time. If we step back from the ads, we know that nearly any beer in the same setting would create the same party atmosphere, but here Budweiser products are framed as being the consumer's link to a great party. The ads construct what their makers feel twenty-something men desire, and they symbolically associate Budweiser products with this desired goal in order to sell these products. Most ads work by tapping into preexisting goals and aspirations—for example, the desire for approval from others or to have a good time. The beer company presents its product as able to fulfill these desires, whether the beer tastes good or is unpalatable.

THINKING CRITICALLY ABOUT MATERIALITY

Consider a store near your campus. What are the characteristics of the consumers this store hopes to sell to? How does this store market specifically to this demographic group? How does the store position certain products to catch the attention of this target demographic? What aspirations is this store emphasizing to get its target audience's attention? Why might some other marketing imagery, or array of commodities in the store or in advertising, be less effective in selling these products?

❦ Conclusion

Understanding how material objects are given meaning by their social context is central to appreciating how societies and cultures make sense of their world. Meaning is not intentionally constructed or interpreted; rather, it flows naturally from social patterns that make certain interpretations seem obvious and logical, and others seem foolish, implausible, or simply wrong. In the nineteenth century, most white North Americans and Europeans interpreted native Africans wearing loincloths as less refined and less cultured than themselves because this was the meaning of such clothing in Western culture. At the same time, African villagers likely saw white men—who were trying to demonstrate their cultural refinement and superiority by wearing elaborate suits, ties, vests, and high collars even in tropical Africa—as resembling some of the tribal chiefs who were constantly covered in elaborate robes and ornaments. In each case, people were behaving in their ordinary cultural ways, and they could not interpret the meaning of the other group's costumes any differently. But these meanings were not inherent in the clothes themselves—they had been constructed from years of observing ordinary people in normal social settings.

The issues raised by the materiality of simple objects—whether a piece of clothing, an art object, a photograph, an historical building, or a commonplace object we use in daily life—highlight a broader dynamic that affects the social and cultural construction of meaning in every culture across the globe. The meanings of objects change over time, and the meaning of the past itself changes as social contexts change. Control over the past is a highly contentious issue, but control of the meaning of today's objects, even the significance of a smartphone, is equally contentious. This dynamic has two dimensions. One lies in who has control over access to the resources, both historical and cultural, from which we can document and uncover the story of how things came to be. The other is that interpretations of the material world, whether from the past or the present, differ according to social interests. So the interpretation of objects, artifacts, archaeological sites, and human remains always has a wide variety of legal, moral, and political implications. These implications are constructed by many different people, each with a different set of personal and social agendas. We call this the cultural construction of meaning, whether applied to objects, bodies, practices, or human experiences, and it is this that shows us what cultural anthropology is all about.

Key Terms

American Indian Movement
(AIM)   p. 307
Cultural resource management
(CRM)   p. 311
Culture of mass
consumption   p. 322

Material culture   p. 306
Materiality   p. 306
Native American Graves
Protection and Repatriation
Act (NAGPRA)   p. 308
Repatriation   p. 308

World Heritage Sites
program   p. 309

Reviewing the Chapter

CHAPTER SECTION	WHAT WE KNOW	TO BE RESOLVED
Why is the ownership of artifacts from other cultures a contentious issue?	Ownership of artifacts raises difficult moral, social, and political questions about who has the right to control and display objects. NAGPRA legislation has clarified some of these issues.	NAGPRA does not completely resolve conflicts over who should control archaeological objects, because some museum skeletal collections are themselves poorly documented. Archaeologists, museums, and American Indians still need to negotiate what happens to the objects.
How can anthropology help us understand objects?	All objects, old and new, from the most special to the most mundane, have multiple dimensions.	Stocking's original notion of seven dimensions to objects is a useful starting point for analyzing objects. But there is debate over whether these are always the most useful dimensions for analyzing all objects, as well as which dimensions he may have missed.
How do the meanings of things change over time?	All objects change over time, if not in their physical characteristics then in the significance people give to them. Meanings change because of generational change, changes in social and technological context, and as objects change hands.	Anthropologists have not yet systematically explored whether the importance of objects changes and has always changed in the same ways, or if different kinds of societies (literate vs. preliterate; stratified vs. egalitarian, etc.) change the meanings of things in precisely the same ways.
How do objects come to represent our goals and aspirations?	Three interrelated issues need to be considered: objects express people's personal and collective pasts; objects help people express and even formulate their goals and aspirations; and objects can be used in ways that manipulate what people's goals and aspirations should be.	Although many anthropologists assume that mass-producing commodities has transformed societies' approach to objects and thus their goals and aspirations, it seems likely that the process of commodification is more complex than recent studies have suggested.

Epilogue

Cultural Anthropology and the Future of Human Diversity

Beginning around the year 2000, people from many countries began traveling to and buying property in a village called Bugarach (population 189), which is near the Pyrenees mountains in the far south of France. Calling themselves "esoterics," these individuals had identified a nearby mountain peak as a good place to survive what they predicted was going to be a cataclysmic transformation of the world that would take place on December 21, 2012. They had come to this conclusion based on a reading of the Mesoamerican Long Count calendar, one of several calendars used by the ancient Maya that traces back to mythical creation times. They believed that the calendar marked that particular day in 2012 as a special moment of cosmic transformation, provoking the destruction of the world as we know it but also ushering in a great spiritual awakening for humankind. Esoterics believed the mountain was occupied by an alien spaceship that would transport the faithful to safety.

Uncertain Futures.   Based on predictions that the world would come to an end on December 21, 2012, "esoterics" began traveling to Bugarach, France, where they hoped an alien spaceship in the mountain pictured here might transport them to safety and a new spiritual awakening. Even though their predictions did not come true, many esoterics still believe that big changes are going to come. Like people everywhere, they want to know what the uncertain future will bring so they can prepare themselves for it.

Over the next decade, thousands of people poured into the area, many of them to climb the peak and some of them to settle there. As 2012 approached, many locals were growing exasperated with the chaos caused by all the activity, and the village's mayor threatened to call the army. Not long before that fateful day arrived, police showed up and began limiting access to the mountain. Finally, the day came . . . and there was no cosmic cataclysm. This fact didn't cause most of the esoterics to ditch their predictions of big changes to come, just to reassess when these things will occur, and many of them remain in the Bugarach area.

For many of you, these beliefs and motivations may seem strange, exotic, and difficult to understand. And yet there is something deeply human that drove the esoterics to put so much stock in the Maya calendar in their quest to create meaningful lives, and that is the desire to know what the future holds. Wanting to predict the future is a common human urge. Sometimes it is driven by simple curiosity about how things taken for granted today might differ in the future. But there is also a pragmatic concern of knowing what to do now to prepare for what is to come. Across the world, people have developed many esoteric bodies of knowledge to explore and satisfy this urge, and those with access to that special wisdom often carry great social authority. The list includes diviners, oracles, seers, soothsayers, prophets, healers, and fortune tellers. It also includes scientists in disciplines like climatology, physics, and medicine, and a few in social scientific fields like economics, behavioral psychology, and political science. Although we tend to separate the first group from the second because of the latter's use of the scientific method, in their specific cultural contexts, all of these actors can make useful and sometimes highly reliable predictions about what is to come. People regularly take action as a result of their pronouncements.

But as Yoda, that iconic source of wisdom in popular culture, once observed, "Difficult to see. Always in motion is the future." Although few anthropologists are likely to consider the *Star Wars* movies to be a source of authoritative and rigorous cultural insight, his observation does align strongly with what we know about human social complexity. It also relates to one of the reasons anthropologists are deeply hesitant to offer predictions about the future. The human future *is* always in motion. People are not robots, programmed to carry out codes instilled in them by their enculturation. Every anthropological fieldworker knows that people will *tell* you one thing, only to *do* something different. Usually they are not doing this because they are lying or because they are irrational and cannot think straight. They do it because human action is fluid, situational, and context-dependent. Anthropology has developed many strategies—among them the holistic and cross-cultural perspectives (Chapter 2) and a diverse and effective toolkit of fieldwork methods (Chapter 3)—for understanding the fluidity of human thought and action.

Moreover, cultures—those collective processes through which we construct and naturalize certain meanings and actions as normal and even necessary—are themselves dynamic, emergent, and changing. As we have explored in this book, no group of people has ever been totally static and homogeneous, not least be-cause different people have different life experiences due to particularities of age, gender, social identity, and other factors, as well as distinct social expectations for how to communicate with others (Chapter 4). Creativity, uncertainty, and social conflict are key aspects of everyday social relations everywhere. Thanks to the widening scale of social relationships associated with globalization and transna-tional interconnection (Chapter 5), the processes of cultural dynamism seem to have intensified and manifest themselves in almost all aspects of people's lives in the contemporary world.

This dynamism is present in what we may think of as the material aspects of life: in foodways and environmental relationships (Chapter 6), and in economic activity and political relationships (Chapters 7 and 8). Even though some aspects of human life seem stable and fixed, no society is entirely static in matters of social identity and gender (Chapters 9 and 10), or even in the most traditional topic that anthropologists have studied, kinship relations (Chapter 11), which have been undergoing change in recent years, driven largely by changing attitudes toward gender, race, ethnicity, and family. Finally, we can see dynamic processes in our religious beliefs and activities (Chapter 12), our interpretations of health and ill-ness (Chapter 13), and our interactions with material objects (Chapter 14).

Nevertheless, there is one thing anthropologists are reasonably certain about as we look to the future, and that is the persistence of human diversity. Diver-sity, understood by anthropologists as variety and multiplicity, is a basic pattern of nature and the basis upon which natural systems—oceans, forests, mountain ecosystems, and so on—and the species within them thrive.

We can appreciate these patterns among people simply by recognizing the sheer variety of ways of being human in the world. While processes of global-ization do appear to contribute to some kinds of cultural convergences around the world—we see it especially in the alignment of certain kinds of economic activity and consumption patterns—the anthropological record is also full of fas-cinating details about how, through the processes of culture, people everywhere turn alien cultural imports into something more familiar. Although there is still debate about how and why these processes play out as they do, most anthropolo-gists have come to accept that human diversity persists because of, not in spite of, interconnections across cultures.

Anthropology also offers a useful reminder that knowing what to do in the present does not require being able to predict the future. Anthropologists are ex-perts at identifying the causes of many different kinds of social problems, and whether it is helping craft a new constitution in Ghana or figuring out ways to address farmworker food insecurity in Vermont (Chapters 8 and 6, respectively), anthropologists have offered effective problem-solving strategies. The variety of practical issues anthropologists have taken on is as diverse as the human con-dition and reflects engagement with the big issues most of us are worried about in the contemporary world: improving human health and well-being; addressing difficulties of cross-cultural communication; adapting to the challenges of environmental sustainability; handling tensions around international relations, terrorism, and violence; understanding the effects of religious fundamentalism; and moving toward the construction of social justice; among others.

What unites all of these anthropologists are certain shared intellectual commitments, including the holistic perspective, critical relativism, and a rejection of ethnocentrism. Another is the ability to "think like an anthropologist." To a large extent this has to do with how we pose questions, rooted in recognizing that 99% of a good answer is a good question. Doing anthropology means being habitually curious about how and why people do the things they do in their everyday lives, and gaining the skills and confidence to ask useful questions—to ourselves as thought experiments, and to others in empirical research—that help focus attention not just on what is happening but on how to interpret it.

Anthropologists have been asking rigorous questions about human diversity for over a century. A number of those classic questions and the answers to them have constituted anthropology's contributions to knowledge. At the same time, many debates remain unresolved, new questions emerge all the time, and anthropology's relationships and intersections with many other disciplines in the humanities and natural and social sciences make for a lot of cross-fertilization that brings new issues into consideration. Anthropology is a dynamic and engaged discipline.

But it is not necessary to be a professional anthropologist to appreciate all these things. With some effort and an open mind, anybody can realize that there is great value and life-long relevance in learning how to be curious, observe and listen to others, ask meaningful questions, record accurate information, recognize several truths at once, and establish and maintain ethical and collaborative relationships with diverse kinds of people. We feel that there is much to be gained—for a successful career, a meaningful life, or both—for those of you who make the effort to incorporate these activities and approaches into your daily encounters with those around you. While the future of human diversity as a whole does not necessarily depend on *you* doing these things, it will make your understanding of the diverse world in which you live much, much richer.

Glossary

Note: The number at the end of each definition denotes the chapter in which the term is defined.

Accent. A regional or social variation in the way a language is pronounced (e.g., an Alabama accent). (4)

Acephalous society. A society without a governing head, generally with no hierarchical leadership. (8)

Action anthropology. An approach to anthropological research that seeks to study and, at the same time, improve community welfare. (3)

Action theory. An approach in the anthropological study of politics that closely follows the daily activities and decision-making processes of individual political leaders, emphasizing that politics is a dynamic and competitive field of social relations in which people are constantly managing their ability to exercise power over others. (8)

Adjudication. The legal process by which an individual or council with socially recognized authority intervenes in a dispute and unilaterally makes a decision. (8)

Age-grades. Groupings of age-mates, who are initiated into adulthood together. (8)

American Indian Movement (AIM). The most prominent and one of the earliest American Indian activist groups, founded in 1968. (14)

Animal husbandry. The breeding, care, and use of domesticated herding animals such as cattle, camels, goats, horses, llamas, reindeer, and yaks. (6)

Animism. The belief that inanimate objects such as trees, rocks, cliffs, hills, and rivers are animated by spiritual forces or beings. (12)

Anthropogenic landscapes. Landscapes modified by human action in the past or present. (6)

Anthropological linguistics. The study of language from an anthropological point of view. (4)

Anthropology. The study of human beings, their biology, their prehistory and histories, and their changing languages, cultures, and social institutions. (1)

Anthropology of development. The field of study within anthropology concerned with understanding the cultural conditions for proper development, or, alternatively, the negative impacts of development projects. (5)

Applied anthropology. Anthropological research commissioned to serve an organization's needs. (1)

Appropriation. The process of taking possession of an object, idea, or relationship and making it one's own. (7)

Archaeology. The study of past cultures by excavating sites where people lived, worked, farmed, or conducted some other activity. (1)

Balanced reciprocity. A form of reciprocity in which the giver expects a fair return at some later time. (7)

Band. A small, nomadic, and self-sufficient group of anywhere from 25 to 150 individuals with face-to-face social relationships, usually egalitarian. (8)

Biocultural. The complex intersections of biological, psychological, and cultural processes. (13)

Biological anthropology. The study of the biological aspects of the human species, past and present, along with those of our closest relatives, the nonhuman primates. (1)

Bride price (or bridewealth). Gifts or money given by the groom's clan or family to compensate the bride's clan or family for the loss of one of its women along with her productive and reproductive abilities. (11)

Call system. Patterned sounds, utterances, and movements of the body that express meaning. (4)

Capitalism. An economic system based on private ownership of the means of production, in which prices are set and goods distributed through a market. (7)

Carrying capacity. The population an area can support. (6)

Caste. The system of social stratification found in Indian society that divides people into categories according to moral purity and pollution. (9)

Centralized political system. A political system, such as a chiefdom or a state, in which certain individuals and institutions hold power and control over resources. (8)

Chiefdom. A political system with a hereditary leader who holds central authority, typically supported by a class of high-ranking elites, informal laws, and a simple judicial system, often numbering in the tens of thousands with the beginnings of intensive agriculture and some specialization. (8)

Cisgender. Someone whose gender identity aligns with their biological sex at birth as male or female. (10)

Clan. A group of relatives who claim to be descended from a single ancestor. (11)

Class. The hierarchical distinctions between social groups in society, usually based on wealth, occupation, and social standing. (9)

Clinical therapeutic process. A healing process that involves the use of medicines that have some active ingredient that is assumed to address either the cause or the symptom of a disorder. (13)

Cognate words. Words in two languages that show the same systematic sound shifts as other words in the two languages, usually interpreted by linguists as evidence for a common linguistic ancestry. (4)

Cognatic. Reckoning descent through either men or women from some ancestor. (11)

Colonialism. The historical practice of more powerful countries claiming possession of less powerful ones. (1)

Commodities. Mass-produced and impersonal goods with no meaning or history apart from themselves. (7)

Commodity money. Money with another value beyond itself, such as gold or other precious metals, which can be used as jewelry or ornament. (7)

Comparative method. A research method that derives insights from a systematic comparison of aspects of two or more cultures or societies. (1)

Consumers. People who rely on goods and services not produced by their own labor. (7)

Consumption. The act of using and assigning meaning to a good, service, or relationship. (7)

Corporate groups. Groups of people who work together toward common ends, much as a corporation does. (11)

Creole language. A language of mixed origin that has developed from a complex blending of two parent languages and exists as a mother tongue for some part of the population. (4)

Cross-cultural perspective. Analyzing a human social phenomenon by comparing that phenomenon in different cultures. (2)

Cultural anthropology. The study of the social lives of living communities. (1)

Cultural appropriation. The unilateral decision of one social group to take control over the symbols, practices, or objects of another. (2)

Cultural construction. The meanings, concepts, and practices that people build out of their shared and collective experiences. (2)

Cultural determinism. The idea that all human actions are the product of culture, which denies the influence of other factors like physical environment and human biology on human action. (2)

Cultural economics. An anthropological approach to economics that focuses on how symbols and morals help shape a community's economy. (7)

Cultural imperialism. The promotion of one culture over others through formal policy or less formal means, like the spread of technology and material culture. (5)

Cultural landscape. The culturally specific images, knowledge, and concepts of the physical landscape that help shape human relations with that landscape. (6)

Cultural relativism. The moral and intellectual principle that one should seek to understand cultures on their own terms and withhold judgment about seemingly strange or exotic beliefs and practices. (1)

Cultural resource management (CRM). Research and planning aimed at identifying, interpreting, and protecting sites and artifacts of historic or prehistoric significance. (14)

Culture. The taken-for-granted notions, rules, moralities, and behaviors within a social group. (1)

Culture and personality movement. A school of thought in early and mid-twentieth-century American anthropology that studied how patterns of childrearing, social institutions, and cultural ideologies shaped individual experience, personality characteristics, and thought patterns. (11)

Culture-bound syndrome. A mental illness thought to be unique to a particular culture or ethnic group. (13)

Culture of mass consumption. The cultural perspectives and social processes that shape and are shaped by how goods and services are bought, sold, and used in contemporary capitalism. (14)

Culture of migration. The cultural attitudes, perceptions, and symbolic values that shape decision-making processes around, and experiences of, migration. (5)

Customs. Long-established norms that have a codified and lawlike aspect. (2)

Delayed reciprocity. A form of reciprocity that features a long lag time between receiving a gift and paying it back. (7)

Descriptive linguistics. The systematic analysis and description of a language's sound system and grammar. (4)

Development anthropology. The application of anthropological knowledge and research methods to the practical aspects of shaping and implementing development projects. (5)

Dialect. A regional or social variety of a language in which the vocabulary, grammar, and pronunciation differ from those of the standard version of the language (e.g., African American Vernacular English). (4)

Diffusionists. Early twentieth-century Boasian anthropologists who held that cultural characteristics result from either internal historical dynamism or a spread (diffusion) of cultural attributes from other societies. (5)

Discrimination. The negative or unfair treatment of an individual because of his or her membership in a particular social group or category. (9)

Disease. The purely physiological condition of being sick, usually determined by a physician. (13)

Diversity. The sheer variety of ways of being human around the world. (1)

Division of labor. The cooperative organization of work into specialized tasks and roles. (7)

Dowry. A large sum of money or in-kind gifts given to a daughter to ensure her well-being in her husband's family. (11)

Ecological footprint. A quantitative tool that measures what people consume and the waste they produce. It also calculates the area of biologically productive land and water needed to support those people. (6)

Economic anthropology. The subfield of cultural anthropology concerned with how people make, share, and buy things and services. (7)

Economic system. The structured patterns and relationships through which people exchange goods and services. (7)

Emic perspective. A cultural insider's perspective on his or her culture. (3)

Empirical. Verifiable through observation rather than through logic or theory. (1)

Enculturation. The process of learning the cultural rules and logic of a society. (2)

Environmental anthropology. The field that studies how different societies understand, interact with, and make changes to the natural world. (6)

Environmental justice. A social movement addressing the linkages between racial discrimination and injustice, social equity, and environmental quality. (6)

Ethics. Moral questions about right and wrong and standards of appropriate behavior. (1)

Ethnicity. A concept that organizes people into groups based on their membership in a group with a particular history, social status, or ancestry. (9)

Ethnobiology. The subfield of ethnoscience that studies how people in non-Western societies name and codify living things. (6)

Ethnocentrism. The assumption that one's own way of doing things is correct, and that other people's practices or views are wrong or ignorant. (1)

Ethnographic method. A research method that involves prolonged and intensive observation of and participation in the life of a community. (1)

Ethnohistory. The study of cultural change in societies and periods for which the community had no written histories or historical documents, usually relying heavily on oral history for data. Ethnohistory may also refer to a view of history from the cultural insider's point of view, which often differs from an outsider's view. (3)

Ethnoscience. The study of how people classify things in the world, usually by considering some range or set of meanings. (4, 6)

Etic perspective. An outside observer's perspective on a culture. (3)

Evolution. The adaptive changes organisms make across generations. (1)

Exchange. The transfer of objects and services between social actors. (7)

Exiles. People who are expelled by the authorities of their home countries. (5)

Exogamous. A social pattern in which members of a clan must marry someone from another clan, which has the effect of building political, economic, and social ties with other clans. (11)

Explanatory model of illness. An explanation of what is happening to a patient's body, by the patient, by the patient's family, or by a healthcare practitioner, each of whom may have a different model of what is happening. (13)

Extended families. Larger groups of relatives beyond the nuclear family, often living in the same household. (11)

Fiat money. Money created and guaranteed by a government. (7)

Fieldnotes. Information the anthropologist collects or transcribes during fieldwork. (3)

Fieldwork. Long-term immersion in a community, normally involving firsthand research in a specific study community or research setting where the researcher can observe people's behavior and have conversations or interviews with members of the community. (3)

Food security. Access to sufficient nutritious food to sustain an active and healthy life. (6)

Foodways. Structured beliefs and behaviors surrounding the production, distribution, and consumption of food. (6)

Foraging. Obtaining food by searching for it, as opposed to growing or raising it. (6)

Formal economics. The branch of economics that studies the underlying logic of economic thought and action. (7)

Functionalism. A perspective that assumes that cultural practices and beliefs serve social purposes in any society. (2)

Fundamentalism. Conservative religious movements that advocate a return to fundamental or traditional principles. (12)

Fundamentalist. A person belonging to a religious movement that advocates a return to fundamental or traditional principles. (12)

Gender. The complex and fluid intersections of biological sex, internal senses of self, outward expressions of identity, and cultural expectations about how to perform that identity in appropriate ways. (10)

Gender variance. Expressions of sex and gender that diverge from the male and female norms that dominate in most societies. (10)

Gender/sex system. The ideas and social patterns a society uses to organize males, females, and those who exist between these categories. (10)

Genealogical amnesia. The structural process of forgetting whole groups of relatives, usually because they are not currently significant in social life. (11)

Genealogical method. A systematic methodology for recording kinship relations and how kin terms are used in different societies. (3)

General purpose money. Money that is used to buy nearly any good or service. (7)

Generalized reciprocity. A form of reciprocity in which gifts are given freely without the expectation of return. (7)

Globalization. The widening scale of cross-cultural interactions caused by the rapid movement of money, people, goods, images, and ideas within nations and across national boundaries. (5)

Government. A separate legal and constitutional domain that is the source of law, order, and legitimate force. (8)

Green Revolution. The transformation of agriculture in the Third World, beginning in the 1940s, through agricultural research, technology transfer, and infrastructure development. (6)

Headnotes. The mental notes an anthropologist makes while in the field, which may or may not end up in formal fieldnotes or journals. (3)

Holism. Efforts to synthesize distinct approaches and findings into a single comprehensive interpretation. (1)

Holistic perspective. A perspective that aims to identify and understand the whole—that is, the systematic connections between individual cultural beliefs, practices, and social institutions—rather than the individual parts. (2)

Horticulture. The cultivation of gardens or small fields to meet the basic needs of a household. (6)

Human Relations Area Files (HRAF). A comparative anthropological database that allows easy reference to coded information about several hundred cultural traits for more than 350 societies. The HRAF facilitates statistical analysis of the relationship between the presence of one trait and the occurrence of other traits. (3)

Hybridization. Persistent cultural mixing that has no predetermined direction or endpoint. (5)

Illness. The psychological and social experience a patient has of a disease. (13)

Immigrants. People who enter a foreign country with no expectation of ever returning to their home country. (5)

Incest taboo. The prohibition on sexual relations between close family members. (11)

Industrial agriculture. The application of industrial principles to farming. (6)

Industrialization. The economic process of shifting from an agricultural economy to a factory-based economy. (1)

Informant. Any person an anthropologist gets data from in the study community, especially a person who is interviewed or who provides information about what the anthropologist has observed or heard. (3)

Instrumentalism. A social theory that ethnic groups are not naturally occurring or stable but instead are highly dynamic groups created to serve the interests of one powerful group or another. (9)

Intensification. Processes that increase agricultural yields. (6)

Interpretive approach. A kind of analysis that interprets the underlying symbolic and cultural interconnections within a society. (12)

Interpretive theory of culture. A theory that culture is embodied and transmitted through symbols. (2)

Intersectionality. The circumstantial interplay of race, class, gender, sexuality, and other identity markers in the expression of prejudicial beliefs and discriminatory actions. (9)

Intersex. Individuals who exhibit sexual organs and functions somewhere between male and female elements, often including elements of both. (10)

Intersubjectivity. The realization that knowledge about other people emerges out of relationships and perceptions individuals have with each other. (3)

Interview. Any systematic conversation with an informant to collect field research data, ranging from a highly structured set of questions to the most open-ended ones. (3)

Kinship. The social system that organizes people in families based on descent and marriage. (11)

Kinship chart. A visual representation of family relationships. (11)

Language. A system of communication consisting of sounds, words, and grammar. (4)

Language ideology. Widespread assumptions that people make about the relative sophistication and status of particular dialects and languages. (4)

Laws. Sets of rules established by some formal authority. (8)

Life history. Any survey of an informant's life, including such topics as residence, occupation, marriage, family, and difficulties, usually collected to reveal patterns that cannot be observed today. (3)

Limited purpose money. Objects that can be exchanged only for certain things. (7)

Lineage. A group composed of relatives who are directly descended from known ancestors. (11)

Linguistic anthropology. The study of how people communicate with one another through language and how language use shapes group membership and identity. (1)

Linguistic relativity. The idea that people speaking different languages perceive or interpret the world differently because of differences in their languages. (4)

Localization. The creation and assertion of highly particular, place-based identities and communities. (5)

Magic. An explanatory system of causation that does not follow naturalistic explanations, often working at a distance without direct physical contact. (12)

Market. A social institution in which people come together to exchange goods and services. (7)

Masculinity. The ideas and practices of manhood. (10)

Material culture. The objects made and used in any society. Traditionally, the term referred to technologically simple objects made in preindustrial societies, but *material culture* may refer to all of the objects or commodities of modern life as well. (14)

Materiality. Having the quality of being physical or material. (14)

Matrilineal. Reckoning descent through women, who are descended from an ancestral woman. (11)

Means of production. The machines and infrastructure required to produce goods. (7)

Mediation. The use of a third party who intervenes in a dispute to help the parties reach an agreement and restore harmony. (8)

Medical pluralism. The coexistence and interpenetration of distinct medical traditions with different cultural roots in the same cultural community. (13)

Medicalization. The process of viewing or treating as a medical concern conditions that were not previously understood as medical problems. (13)

Migrants. People who leave their homes to live or work for a time in other regions or countries. (5)

Mind. Emergent qualities of consciousness and intellect that manifest themselves through thought, emotion, perception, will, and imagination. (13)

Modes of subsistence. The social relationships and practices necessary for procuring, producing, and distributing food. (6)

Money. An object or substance that serves as a medium of exchange, a store of value, or a unit of account. (7)

Monotheism. Belief in a single god. (12)

Morphology. The structure of words and word formation in a language. (4)

Multi-sited ethnography. An ethnographic research strategy of following connections, associations, and putative relationships from place to place. (5)

Natal family. The family into which a person is born and in which she or he is (usually) raised. (11)

Nation-states. Independent states recognized by other states, composed of people who share a single national identity. (8)

Native American Graves Protection and Repatriation Act (NAGPRA). The 1990 law that established the ownership of human remains, grave goods, and important cultural objects as belonging to the Native Americans whose ancestors once owned them. (14)

Naturalization. The social processes through which something becomes part of the natural order of things. (9)

Negative reciprocity. A form of reciprocity in which the giver attempts to get something for nothing, to haggle his or her way into a favorable personal outcome. (7)

Negotiation. A form of dispute management in which the parties themselves reach a decision jointly. (8)

Neoclassical economics. An approach to economics that studies how people make decisions to allocate resources like time, labor, and money in order to maximize their personal benefit. (7)

Non-centralized political system. A political system, such as a band or a tribe, in which power and control over resources are dispersed between members of the society. (8)

Norms. Typical patterns of actual behavior as well as the rules about how things should be done. (2)

Nuclear family. The family formed by a married couple and their children. (11)

Nutrition transition. The combination of changes in diet toward energy-dense foods (high in calories, fat, and sugar) and declines in physical activity. (6)

Obesity. Having excess body fat to the point of impairing bodily health and function. (6)

Open-ended interview. Any conversation with an informant in which the researcher allows the informant to take the conversation to related topics that the informant rather than the researcher feels are important. (3)

Othering. Defining colonized peoples as different from, and subordinate to, Europeans in terms of their social, moral, and physical norms. (1)

Overweight. Having an abnormally high accumulation of body fat. (6)

Participant observation. The standard research method used by cultural anthropologists that requires the researcher to live in the community he or she is studying to observe and participate in day-to-day activities. (3)

Participatory action research. A research method in which the research questions, data collection, and data analysis are defined through collaboration between the researcher and the subjects of research. A major goal is for the research subjects to develop the capacity to investigate and take action on their primary political, economic, or social problems. (3)

Pastoralism. The practice of animal husbandry. (6)

Patrilineal. Reckoning descent through males from the same ancestors. (11)

Philology. Comparative study of ancient texts and documents. (4)

Phonology. The systematic pattern of sounds in a language, also known as the language's sound system. (4)

Pidgin language. A mixed language with a simplified grammar, typically borrowing its vocabulary from one language but its grammar from another. (4)

Placebo effect. A healing process that works on persuading a patient that he or she has been given a powerful medicine, even though the "medicine" has no active medicinal ingredient. (13)

Political ecology. The field of study that focuses on the linkages between political-economic power, social inequality, and ecological destruction. (6)

Political power. The processes by which people create, compete, and use power to attain goals that are presumed to be for the good of a community. (8)

Politics. Those relationships and processes of cooperation, conflict, social control, and power that are fundamental aspects of human life. (8)

Polyandry. When a woman has two or more husbands at one time. (11)

Polygamy. Any form of plural marriage. (11)

Polygyny. When a man is simultaneously married to more than one woman. (11)

Polytheism. Belief in many gods. (12)

Postcolonialism. The field that studies the cultural legacies of colonialism and imperialism. (5)

Practicing anthropology. Anthropological work involving research as well as involvement in the design, implementation, and management of some organization, process, or product. (1)

Prejudice. Preformed, usually unfavorable opinions that people hold about people from groups who are different from their own. (9)

Prestige economies. Economies in which people seek high social rank, prestige, and power instead of money and material wealth. (7)

Primary materials. Original sources such as field-notes that are prepared by someone who is directly involved in the research project and has direct personal knowledge of the research subjects. (3)

Proto-language. A hypothetical common ancestral language of two or more living languages. (4)

Push-pull factors. The social, economic, and political factors that "push" people to migrate from their homes and that "pull" them to host countries. (5)

Qualitative method. A research strategy that produces an in-depth and detailed description of social behaviors and beliefs. (1)

Quantitative method. A methodology that classifies features of a phenomenon, counting or measuring them, and constructing mathematical and statistical models to explain what is observed. (1)

Quran. The main body of scripture in Islam, consisting of verses of classical Arabic poetry understood to be revealed to the Prophet Muhammad by Allah, often in dreams or in the midst of other activities.

These verses were memorized by the Prophet's followers and written down after his death. (12)

Race. A concept that organizes people into groups based on specific physical traits that are thought to reflect fundamental and innate differences. (9)

Racialization. The social, economic, and political processes of transforming populations into races and creating racial meanings. (9)

Racism. The repressive practices, structures, beliefs, and representations that uphold racial categories and social inequality. (9)

Rapid appraisal. Short-term, focused ethnographic research, typically lasting no more than a few weeks, about narrow research questions or problems. (3)

Reciprocity. The give-and-take that builds and confirms relationships. (7)

Redistribution. The collection of goods in a community and then the further dispersal of those goods among members. (7)

Refugees. People who migrate because of political oppression or war, usually with legal permission to stay in a different country. (5)

Religion. A symbolic system that is socially enacted through rituals and other aspects of social life that relate to ultimate issues of humankind's existence. (12)

Repatriation. The return of human remains or cultural artifacts to the communities of descendants of the people to whom they originally belonged. (14)

Rite of passage. Any life cycle rite that marks a person's or group's transition from one social state to another. (12)

Rituals. Stylized performances involving symbols that are associated with social, political, and religious activities. (12)

Salvage paradigm. The paradigm that held that it was important to observe indigenous ways of life, interview elders, and assemble collections of objects made and used by indigenous peoples. (1)

Scientific method. The standard methodology of science that begins from observable facts, generates hypotheses from these facts, and then tests these hypotheses. (1)

Secondary materials. Sources such as censuses, regional surveys, or historical reports that are compiled from data collected by someone other than the field researcher. (3)

Secular worldview. A worldview that does not accept the supernatural as influencing current people's lives. (12)

Sex. Understood in Western cultures as the reproductive forms and functions of the body. (10)

Sexuality. Sexual preferences, desires, and practices. (10)

Sexually dimorphic. A characteristic of a species in which males and females have different sexual forms. (10)

Shaman. A religious leader who communicates the needs of the living with the spirit world, usually through some form of ritual trance or other altered state of consciousness. (12)

Sick role. The culturally defined agreement between patients and family members to acknowledge that a patient is legitimately sick, which involves certain responsibilities and behaviors that caregivers expect of the sick. (13)

Social institutions. Organized sets of social relationships that link individuals to each other in a structured way in a particular society. (2)

Social sanction. A reaction or measure intended to enforce norms and punish their violation. (2)

Social stratification. The classification of people into unequal groupings. (9)

Social support therapeutic process. A healing process that involves a patient's social networks, especially close family members and friends, who typically surround the patient during an illness. (13)

Sociolinguistics. The study of how sociocultural context and norms shape language use and the effects of language use on society. (4)

Speaking in tongues. The phenomenon of speaking in an apparently unknown language, often in an energetic and fast-paced way. (12)

Spheres of exchange. Bounded orders of value in which certain goods can be exchanged only for others. (7)

Spirit familiar. A spirit that has developed a close bond with a shaman. (12)

State. The most complex form of political organization, associated with societies that have intensive agriculture, high levels of social stratification, and centralized authority. (8)

Structural power. Power that not only operates within settings, but also organizes and orchestrates the settings in which social and individual actions take place. (8)

Structural-functionalism. An anthropological theory that the different structures or institutions of a society (religion, politics, kinship, etc.) function to maintain social order and equilibrium. (8)

Substantive economics. A branch of economics, inspired by the work of Karl Polanyi, that studies the daily transactions people engage in to get what they need or desire. (7)

Surplus value. The difference between what people produce and what they need to survive. (7)

Swidden agriculture. A farming method in tropical regions in which the farmer slashes and burns a small area of forest to release plant nutrients into the soil. As soil fertility declines, the farmer allows the plot to regenerate to forest. (6)

Symbol. Something—an object, idea, image, figure, or character—that represents something else. (2)

Symbolic therapeutic process. A healing process that restructures the meanings of the symbols surrounding the illness, particularly during a ritual. (13)

Sympathetic magic. Any magical rite that relies on the supernatural to produce its outcome without working through a specific supernatural being such as a spirit, demon, or deity. (12)

Syntax. The pattern of word order used to form sentences and longer utterances in a language. (4)

Taste. A concept that refers to the sense that gives humans the ability to detect flavors, as well as the social distinction associated with certain foodstuffs. (6)

Teknonymy. A system of naming parents by the names of their children. (11)

Theory. A tested and repeatedly supported hypothesis. (1)

Third genders. A category found in many societies that acknowledge three or more gender categories. (10)

Totemism. A system of thought that associates particular social groups with specific animal or plant species called "totems" as an emblem. (12)

Tradition. Practices and customs that have become most ritualized and enduring. (2)

Traditional ecological knowledge. Indigenous ecological knowledge and its relationship with resource management strategies. (6)

Trance. A semiconscious state typically brought on by hypnosis, ritual drumming and singing, or hallucinogenic drugs like mescaline or peyote. (12)

Transactional orders. Realms of transactions a community uses, each with its own set of symbolic meanings and moral assumptions. (7)

Transgender. Someone to whom society assigns one gender who does not perform as that gender but has taken either permanent or temporary steps to identify as another gender. (10)

Transnational. Relationships that extend beyond nation-state boundaries but do not necessarily cover the whole world. (5)

Tribe. A type of pastoralist or horticulturist society with populations usually numbering in the hundreds or thousands in which leadership is more stable than that of a band, but usually egalitarian, with social relations based on reciprocal exchange. (8)

Unilineal. Based on descent through a single descent line, either males or females. (11)

Value. The relative worth of an object or service that makes it desirable. (7)

Values. Symbolic expressions of intrinsically desirable principles or qualities. (2)

Violence. The use of force to harm someone or something. (8)

World culture. Norms and values that extend across national boundaries. (5)

World Heritage Sites program. A UNESCO-run program that provides financial support to maintain sites of importance to humanity. (14)

World religions. Religions that claim to be universally significant to all people. (12)

World systems theory. The theory that capitalism has expanded on the basis of unequal exchange throughout the world, creating a global market and global division of labor, dividing the world between a dominant "core" and a dependent "periphery." (5)

Worldview. A general approach to or set of shared, unquestioned assumptions about the world and how it works. (12)

References

Adultery. 2009. "Adultery: Criminal Laws, Enforcement of Statutes, as a Defense, Divorce, Cross-Reference." Accessed on 8/18/2009: http://law.jrank.org/pages/4112/Adultery.html.

Allport, Gordon. 1958. *The Nature of Prejudice.* Abridged edition. New York: Doubleday Anchor Books.

Almond, Gabriel A., R. Scott Appleby, and Emmanuel Sivan. 2003. *Strong Religion: The Rise of Fundamentalisms Around the World.* Chicago: University of Chicago Press.

Alonso Camal, Bartolomé. 1997. "Indios, antropologia y descolonization." In Patricio Guerrero, comp., *Antropologia Aplicada* 1997:315–322.

American Psychiatric Association. 1994. *Diagnostic and Statistical Manual of Mental Disorders: DSM-IV.* Washington, D.C.: American Psychiatric Association.

Ames, Michael. 1999. "How to Decorate a House: The Re-negotiation of Cultural Representations at the University of British Columbia Museum of Anthropology." *Museum Anthropology* 22:41–51.

Amuyunzu-Nyamongo, Mary. 2006. "Challenges and Prospects for Applied Anthropology in Kenya." In Mwenda Ntarangwi, David Mills, and Mustafa Babiker, eds., *African Anthropologies: History, Critique and Practice,* pp. 237–49. Dakar: CODESRIA.

Anderson, Eugene N. 2005. *Everyone Eats: Understanding Food and Culture.* New York: New York University Press.

Anyon, Roger, T. J. Ferguson, and John R. Welch. 2000. "Heritage Management by American Indian Tribes in the Southwestern United States." In F. O. McManamon and A. Hatton, eds., *Cultural Resource Management in Contemporary Society: Perspectives on Managing and Presenting the Past,* pp. 142–159. London: Routledge.

Appadurai, Arjun, ed. 1986. *The Social Life of Things: Commodities in Cultural Perspective.* Cambridge: Cambridge University Press.

Appadurai, Arjun. 1996. *Modernity at Large: Cultural Dimensions of Globalization.* Minneapolis: University of Minnesota Press.

Arden, Harvey. 1989. "An Indian Cemetery Desecrated: Who Owns Our Past." *National Geographic* 175:376–92.

Armstrong, Karen. 1994. *A History of God: The 4,000-Year Quest of Judaism, Christianity and Islam.* New York: Ballantine Books.

Asch, Timothy, and Napoleon Chagnon. 1997. *The Feast.* Videocassette. Watertown, MA: Documentary Educational Resources. [Released as 16 mm film, 1970.]

Atran, Scott. 2001. "The Vanishing Landscape of the Petén Maya Lowlands: People, Plants, Animals, Places, Words, and Spirits." In Lisa Maffi, ed., *On Biocultural Diversity: Linking Language, Knowledge, and the Environment,* pp. 157–76. Washington, D.C.: Smithsonian Institution Press.

Avruch, Kevin. 1998. *Culture and Conflict Resolution.* Washington, D.C.: United States Institute of Peace.

Bailey, F. G. 1969. *Stratagems and Spoils: A Social Anthropology of Politics.* London: Basil Blackwell.

Banks, Dennis. 2004. *Ojibwa Warrior: Dennis Banks and the Rise of the American Indian Movement,* by Dennis Banks with Richard Erdoes. Norman: University of Oklahoma Press.

Barnes, Jessica, and Michael Dove. 2015. *Climate Cultures: Anthropological Perspectives on Climate Change.* New Haven, CT: Yale University Press.

Barth, Frederick. 1969. *Ethnic Groups and Boundaries: The Social Organization of Culture Difference.* New York: Little Brown & Co.

Bartlett, Robert. 1982. *Gerald of Wales, 1146–1223.* Oxford: Oxford University Press.

Basch, Linda, Nina Glick Schiller, and Cristina Szanton Blanc. 1993. *Nations Unbound: Transnational Projects, Postcolonial Predicaments, and Deterritorialized Nation-States.* Basel: Gordon and Breach.

Basu, Amitra, ed. 2010. *Women's Movements in the Global Era: The Power of Local Feminisms.* Boulder, CO: Westview Press.

Bates, Daniel G. 1998. *Human Adaptive Strategies: Ecology, Culture, and Politics.* Boston: Allyn and Bacon.

Benedict, Ruth. 1946. *The Chrysanthemum and the Sword: Patterns of Japanese Culture.* Boston: Houghton Mifflin.

Bennett, John W. 1996. "Applied and Action Anthropology: Ideological and Conceptual Aspects." *Current Anthropology* 37:S23–S53.

Bergmann, J. F., O. Chassany, J. Gandiol, P. Deblois, J. A. Kanis, J. M. Segresta, C. Caulin, and R. Dahan. 1994. "A Randomized Clinical Trial of the Effect of Informed Consent on the Analgesic Activity of Placebo and Naproxen in Cancer Pain." *Clinical Trials Meta-Analysis* 29:41–47.

Berlin, Brent. 1973. "Folk Systematics in Relation to Biological Classification and Nomenclature." *Annual Review of Systematics and Ecology* 4:259–71.

Berlin, Brent, and Paul Kay. 1969. *Basic ColorTerms: Their Universality and Evolution.* Berkeley: University of California Press.

Bernard, Russell H. 2011. *Research Methods in Anthropology: Qualitative and Quantitative Approaches.* Lanham, MD: AltaMira Press.

Béteille, André. 1992. "Caste and Family in Representations of Indian Society." *Anthropology Today* 8:13–18.

Bird-David, Nurit. 1993. "Tribal Metaphorization of Human-Nature Relatedness: A Comparative Analysis." In K. Milton, ed., *Environmentalism: The View from Anthropology,* pp. 112–25. London: Routledge.

Blim, Michael. 2000. "Capitalisms in Late Modernity." *Annual Reviews of Anthropology* 29:25–38.

Boas, Franz, ed. 1911. *Handbook of North American Indian Languages.* Bulletin of the Bureau of American Ethnology, No. 40. Washington, D.C.: Government Printing Office for the Smithsonian Institution.

Boas, Franz. 1940. *Race, Language, and Culture.* New York: Macmillan.

Bodley, John. 1999. *Victims of Progress.* 4th ed. New York: McGraw-Hill.

Boggs, Stephen T., and Malcolm Naea Chun. 1990. "Ho'oponopono: A Hawaiian Method of Solving Interpersonal Problems." In Karen Ann Watson-Gegeo and Geoffrey White, eds., *Disentangling: Conflict Discourse in Pacific Societies,* pp. 123–53. Stanford, CA: Stanford University Press.

Bohannon, Paul, and Laura Bohannon. 1968. *Tiv Economy.* Evanston, IL: Northwestern University Press.

Boseley, Sarah. 2012. World Bank's Jim Yong Kim: "I Want to Eradicate Poverty." *The Guardian.* 25 July 2012. Accessed on February 17, 2017: https://www.theguardian.com/global-development/2012/jul/25/world-bank-jim-yong-kim-eradicate-poverty.

Bourdieu, Pierre. 1977. *Outline of a Theory of Practice.* Cambridge, UK: Cambridge University Press.

Bourdieu, Pierre. 1984. *Distinction: A Social Critique of the Judgement of Taste.* Cambridge, MA: Harvard University Press.

Bourgois, Philippe. 1995. *In Search of Respect: Selling Crack in El Barrio.* New York: Cambridge University Press.

Bradbury, R. E. 1957. *The Benin Kingdom and the Edo-speaking Peoples of South-Western Nigeria.* London: International African Institute.

Brettell, Caroline. 2003. *Anthropology and Migration: Essays on Transnationalism, Ethnicity, and Identity.* Lanham, MD: Rowman and Littlefield.

Brettell, Caroline B., and Carolyn F. Sargent, eds. 2001. *Gender in Cross-Cultural Perspective.* 3rd ed. Upper Saddle River, NJ: Prentice Hall.

Bridges, K., and W. McClatchey. 2009. "Living on the Margin: Ethnoecological Insights from Marshall Islanders at Rongelap Atoll." *Global Environmental Change* 19:140–46.

Bringa, Tone. 2005. "Haunted by Imaginations of the Past: Robert Kaplan's Balkan Ghosts." In Katherine Besteman and Hugh Gusterson, eds., *Why America's Top Pundits Are Wrong: Anthropologists Talk Back,* pp. 60–82. Berkeley: University of California Press.

Brockington, Dan. 2002. *Fortress Conservation: The Preservation of the Mkomazi Game Reserve.* Bloomington: Indiana University Press.

Brody, Howard, and Linda Hunt. 2006. "BiDil: Assessing a Race-Based Pharmaceutical." *Annals of Family Medicine* 4:556–560.

Brown, Michael. 2003. *Who Owns Native Culture?* Cambridge, MA: Harvard University Press.

Brownell, K. D. 2002. "The Environment and Obesity." In C. G. Fairburn and K. D. Brownell, eds., *Eating Disorders and Obesity: A Comprehensive Handbook.* 2nd ed., pp. 433–38. New York: Guilford Press.

Buikstra, Jane. 1983. "Reburial: How We All Lose—An Archaeologist's Opinion." *Council for Museum Anthropology Newsletter* 7:2–5.

Butler, Shelly Ruth. 2008. *Contested Representations: Revisiting Into the Heart of Africa.* Peterborough, ON: Broadview Press.

Cannizzo, Jeanne. 1989. *Into the Heart of Africa.* Toronto: Royal Ontario Museum.

Caplan, Pat, ed. 1995. *Understanding Disputes: The Politics of Argument.* Oxford: Berg Publishers.

Carrier, James. 1995. *Gifts and Commodities: Exchange and Western Capitalism Since 1700.* London: Routledge.

Carrier, James. 1996a. "Exchange." In Alan Barnard and Jonathan Spencer, eds., *Encyclopedia of Social and Cultural Anthropology,* pp. 218–21. London: Routledge.

Carrier, James. 1996b. "Consumption." In Alan Barnard and Jonathan Spencer, eds., *Encyclopedia of Social and Cultural Anthropology,* pp. 128–29. London: Routledge.

Carrier, Joseph M. 1976. "Family Attitudes and Mexican Male Homosexuality." *Urban Life* 5: 359–75.

Carroll, John B., ed. 1956. *Language, Thought, and Reality: Selected Writings of Benjamin Lee Whorf.*

Cambridge, MA: Technology Press of Massachusetts Institute of Technology.

Chagnon, Napoleon. 1968. *Yanomamö: The Fierce People*. New York: Holt, Rinehart and Winston.

Chambers, Robert. 1997. *Whose Reality Counts? Putting the Last First*. 2nd ed. London: Intermediate Technology Publications.

Chapin, Mac. 2004 . "A Challenge to Conservationists." *World Watch Magazine* November/December 2004: 17–31.

Chossudovsky, Michel. 1997. *The Globalization of Poverty: Impacts of IMF and World Bank Reforms*. Atlantic Highlands, NJ: Zed Books.

Clifford, James, and George Marcus, eds. 1986. *Writing Culture: The Poetics and Politics of Ethnography*. School of American Research Advanced Seminar. Berkeley: University of California Press.

Cohen, Jeffrey. 2004. *The Culture of Migration in Southern Mexico*. Austin: University of Texas Press.

Colchester, Marcus. 2003. "The Vth World Parks Congress: Parks for People or Parks for Business?" *World Rainforest Movement Bulletin No. 75*, October 2003. Accessed on February 15, 2005: http://www.wrm.org.uy/bulletin/75/parks.html.

Cole, Douglas. 1985. *Captured Heritage: The Scramble for Northwest Coast Artifacts*. Seattle: University of Washington Press.

Collier, Jane, and Sylvia Yanagisako, eds. 1987. *Gender and Kinship: Essays Toward a Unified Analysis*. Stanford, CA: Stanford University Press.

Connor, Linda. 1982. "Ships of Fools and Vessels of the Divine: Mental Hospitals and Madness, A Case Study." *Social Science and Medicine* 16:783–94.

Counihan, Carole. 1999. *The Anthropology of Food and Body: Gender, Meaning, and Power*. New York: Routledge.

Counts, Dorothy A. 1980. "Fighting Back Is Not the Way: Suicide and the Women of Kaliai." *American Ethnologist* 7:332–51.

Crate, Susan. 2008. "Gone the Bull of Winter? Grappling with the Cultural Implications of and Anthropology's Role(s) in Global Climate Change." *Current Anthropology* 49:569–95.

Crenshaw, Kimberle. 1989. "Demarginalizing the Intersection of Race and Sex: A Black Feminist Critique of Antidiscrimination Doctrine, Feminist Theory, and Antiracist Politics." *University of Chicago Legal Forum* 140:139–67.

Csordas, Thomas, and Arthur Kleinman 1996. "The Therapeutic Process." In Carolyn F. Sargent and Thomas M. Johnson, eds., *Medical Anthropology: Contemporary Theory and Method*. Revised ed., pp. 3–20. Westport, CT: Praeger.

Dakowski, Bruce. 1990. "Everything Is Relatives: W. H. R. Rivers." In *Pioneers of Social Anthropology: Strangers Abroad* (Documentary Film Series).

Videorecording. Princeton, NJ: Films for the Humanities and Sciences.

Daltabuit, Magalí, and Thomas Leatherman. 1998. "The Biocultural Impact of Tourism on Mayan Communities." In Alan Goodman and Thomas Leatherman, eds., *Building a New Biocultural Synthesis: Political-Economic Perspectives on Human Biology*, pp. 317–38. Ann Arbor: University of Michigan Press.

Daly, Michael. 2009. Anthropologist's "Dick Tracy Moment" Plays Role in Arrest of Suspected Kidney Trafficker. *New York Daily News*, July 24, 2009. Accessed August 18, 2009: http://www.nydailynews.com/news/ny_crime/2009/07/24/2009-07-24_seven_year_quest_to_end_rosenbaum_evil_work_pays_off.html.

D'Andrade, Roy. 1995. *The Development of Cognitive Anthropology*. Cambridge, UK: Cambridge University Press.

Dark, Philip J. C. 1962. *The Art of Benin: A Catalogue of an Exhibition of the A. W. F. Fuller and Chicago Natural History Museum Collections of Antiquities from Benin, Nigeria*. Chicago: Chicago Natural History Museum.

Dark, Philip J. C. 1982. *An Illustrated Catalogue of Benin Art*. Boston: G. K. Hall.

Davidheiser, Mark. 2007. "Overview of Peace and Conflict Resolution Study and Practice." *Anthropology News* October: 11–12.

Dávila, Arlene. 2001. *Latinos, Inc.: The Marketing and Making of a People*. Berkeley: University of California Press.

Delaney, Carol. 1988. "Participant Observation: The Razor's Edge." *Dialectical Anthropology* 13:291–300.

Dentan, Robert Knox. 1968. *The Semai: A Non-Violent People of Malaya*. New York: Holt, Rinehart, and Winston.

de Saussure, F. 1916. *Cours de linguistique générale*. Paris: Payot.

de Saussure, F. 1986. *Course in General Linguistics*. LaSalle, IL: Open Court.

Dettwyler, Katherine A. 2013. *Dancing Skeletons: Life and Death in West Africa*. 2nd ed. Prospect Heights, IL: Waveland.

Dobrin, Lise M. 2008. "From Linguistic Elicitation to Eliciting the Linguistic Lessons in Community Empowerment from Melanesia." *Language* 84:300–24.

Dongoske, K., M. Yeatts, T. Ferguson, and L. Jenkins. 1995. "Historic Preservation and Native American Sites." *SAA Bulletin* 13:13, 39.

Douglas, Mary. 1966. *Purity and Danger: An Analysis of the Concepts of Pollution and Taboo*. New York: Praeger.

Douglas, Mary, and Baron Isherwood. 1978. *The World of Goods*. Harmondsworth, UK: Penguin.

Dressler, William. 2005. "What's Cultural About Biocultural Research?" *Ethos* 31:20–45.

Dreyer, Edward L. 2007. *Zheng He: China and the Oceans in the Early Ming Dynasty, 1405–1433.* New York: Pearson Longman.

Dwyer, Leslie. 2000. "Spectacular Sexualities: Nationalism, Development, and the Politics of Family Planning in Indonesia." In Tamar Mayer, ed., *Gender Ironies of Nationalism: Sexing the Nation*, pp. 25–62. New York: Routledge.

Eboreime, Joseph. 2003. *The Installation of a Benin Monarch: Rite de Passage in the Expression of Ethnic Identity in Nigeria.* Paper from the ICOMOS 14th General Assembly. Accessed on March 3, 2005: http://www.international.icomos.org/victoriafalls 2003/papers/B3–1%20-%20Eboreime.pdf.

Edelman, Elijah Adiv. 2016. "Why We Need to Stop Talking About Trans People in the Bathroom." *Anthropology News.* Accessed on February 17, 2017: http://www.anthropology-news.org/index .php/2016/06/22/why-we-need-to-stop-talking-about-trans-people-in-the-bathroom/.

Edwards, Carolyn P. 1993. "Behavioral Sex Differences in Children of Diverse Cultures: The Case of Nurturance to Infants." In Michael E. Pereira and Lynn A. Fairbanks, eds., *Juvenile Primates: Life History, Development, and Behavior*, pp. 327–38. New York: Oxford University Press.

Eisenberg, Leon. 1977. "Disease and Illness: Distinctions Between Professional and Popular Ideas of Sickness." *Culture, Medicine and Psychiatry* 1:9–23.

Elder, Kay, and Brian Dale. 2000. *In Vitro Fertilization.* 2nd ed. Cambridge, UK: Cambridge University Press.

Eller, Jack David. 2006. *Violence and Culture: A Cross-Cultural and Interdisciplinary Approach.* Belmont, CA: Thomson Wadsworth.

Endicott, Kirk, and Karen Endicott. 2008. *The Headman Was a Woman: The Gender Egalitarian Batek of Malaysia.* Long Grove, IL: Waveland Press.

Erasmus, Charles John. 1952. "Changing Folk Beliefs and the Relativity of Empirical Knowledge." *Southwestern Journal of Anthropology* 8:411–28.

Escobar, Arturo. 1991. "Anthropology and the Development Encounter: The Making and Marketing of Development Anthropology." *American Ethnologist* 18:658–82.

Escobar, Arturo. 1995. *Encountering Development: The Making and Unmaking of the Third World.* Princeton, NJ: Princeton University Press.

Esteva, Gustavo. 1992. "Development." In Wolfgang Sachs, ed., *The Development Dictionary*, pp. 6–25. London: Zed Books.

Fabian, Johannes. 1971. "On Professional Ethics and Epistemological Foundations." *Current Anthropology* 12:230–2.

Fabian, Johannes. 2001. *Anthropology With an Attitude: Critical Essays.* Palo Alto, CA: Stanford University Press.

Fagan, Brian M. 1988. "Black Day at Slack Farm." *Archaeology* 41:15–73.

Farmer, Paul. 1992. *AIDS and Accusation: Haiti and the Geography of Blame.* Berkeley: University of California Press.

Fausto-Sterling, Anne. 1992a. *Myths of Gender: Biological Theories About Women and Men.* 2nd ed. New York: Basic Books.

Fausto-Sterling, Anne. 1992b. "Why Do We Know So Little About Human Sex?" *Discover Magazine.* June 1992. Accessed on August 19, 2009: http://discovermagazine.com/1992/jun/ whydoweknowsolit64.

Fausto-Sterling, Anne. 2000. *Sexing the Body: Gender Politics and the Construction of Sexuality.* New York: Basic Books.

Fazioli, K. Patrick. 2014. "The Erasure of the Middle Ages from Anthropology's Intellectual Genealogy." *History and Anthropology* 25:336–55.

Ferguson, James. 1994. *The Anti-Politics Machine: "Development," Depoliticization, and Bureaucratic Power in Lesotho.* Minneapolis: University of Minnesota Press.

Ferguson, R. Brian. 1995. *Yanomami Warfare: A Political History.* Santa Fe, NM: School of American Research Press.

Finney, Ben R. 1973. *Big Men and Business: Entrepreneurship and Economic Growth in the New Guinea Highlands.* Honolulu: University of Hawaii Press.

Fluehr-Lobban, Carolyn. 2003. *Ethics and the Profession of Anthropology: Dialogue for Ethically Conscious Practice.* Walnut Creek, CA: AltaMira Press.

Food and Agriculture Organization of the United Nations (FAO). 2012. *Undernourishment Around the World.* Accessed on September 11, 2013: www .fao.org/docrep/016/i3027e/i3027e02.pdf.

Foster, George M. 1952. "Relationships Between Theoretical and Applied Anthropology: A Public Health Program Analysis." *Human Organization* 11:5–16.

Foster, Robert. 2008. *Coca-Globalization: Following Soft Drinks from New York to New Guinea.* New York: Palgrave/Macmillan.

Foucault, Michel. 1978. *The History of Sexuality, Vol. 1: An Introduction.* Trans. Robert Hurley. New York: Vintage Books.

Fox, Geoffrey. 1997. *Hispanic Nation: Culture, Politics, and the Constructing of Identity.* Tucson: University of Arizona Press.

Freidson, Eliot. 1970. *Profession of Medicine: A Study of the Sociology of Applied Knowledge.* New York: Dodd, Mead.

Friedman, Jonathan. 1994. *Cultural Identity and Global Process*. London: Sage Publications.

Friedman, Jonathan. 1999. "The Hybridization of Roots and the Abhorrence of the Bush." In Michael Featherstone and Scott Lash, eds., *Spaces of Culture: City-Nation-World*, pp. 230–55. London: Sage.

Fry, Douglas. 2006. *The Human Potential for Peace: An Anthropological Challenge to Assumptions About War and Violence*. New York: Oxford University Press.

Fuentes, Agustín. 2007. "Monkey and Human Interactions: The Wild, the Captive, and the In-between." In R. Cassidy and M. H. Mullin, eds., *Where the Wild Things Are Now: Domestication Reconsidered*, pp. 123–45. Oxford: Berg.

Fuller, C. J. 2004. *The Camphor Flame: Popular Hinduism and Society in India*. Princeton, NJ: Princeton University Press.

Gallagher, Charles. 1997. "White Racial Formation: Into the Twenty-First Century." In Richard Delgado and Jean Stefancic, eds., *Critical White Studies: Looking Behind the Mirror*, pp. 6–11. Philadelphia: Temple University Press.

García Canclini, Nestor. 1995. *Hybrid Cultures: Strategies for Entering and Leaving Modernity*. Minneapolis: University of Minnesota Press.

Gardner, R. Allen, Beatrix T. Gardner, and Thomas E. van Cantfort, eds. 1989. *Teaching Sign Language to Chimpanzees*. Albany: State University of New York Press.

Geertz, Clifford. 1963. *Agricultural Involution: The Processes of Ecological Change in Indonesia*. Berkeley: University of California Press.

Geertz, Clifford. 1966. "Religion as a Cultural System." In Michael Banton, ed., *Anthropological Approaches to the Study of Religion*, pp. 1–46. ASA Monograph 3. London: Tavistock.

Geertz, Clifford. 1973. *The Interpretation of Cultures: Selected Essays*. New York: Basic Books.

Geertz, Clifford. 1988. *Works and Lives: The Anthropologist as Author*. Stanford, CA: Stanford University Press.

Geertz, Hildred, and Clifford Geertz. 1964. "Teknonymy in Bali: Parenthood, Age-Grading, and Genealogical Amnesia." *Journal of the Royal Anthropological Institute of Great Britain and Ireland* 94:94–108.

Geertz, Hildred, and Clifford Geertz. 1975. *Kinship in Bali*. Chicago: University of Chicago Press.

Gellner, Ernest. 1983. *Nations and Nationalism*. Ithaca, NY: Cornell University Press.

Genz, Joseph. 2011. "Navigating the Revival of Voyaging in the Marshall Islands: Predicaments of Preservation and Possibilities of Collaboration." *The Contemporary Pacific* 23:1–34.

Gibbs, James L., Jr. 1963. "The Kpelle Moot." *Africa* 33:1–11.

Gledhill, John. 2000. *Power and Its Disguises: Anthropological Perspectives on Politics*. London: Pluto Press.

Global Justice Now. 2016. "10 Biggest Corporations Make More Money than Most Countries in the World Combined." Accessed on February 17, 2017: http://www.globaljustice.org.uk/news/2016/sep/12/10-biggest-corporations-make-more-money-most-countries-world-combined.

Gluckman, Max. 1940. "Analysis of a Social System in Modern Zululand." *Bantu Studies* 14:1–30, 147–74.

Gmelch, George. 1978. "Baseball Magic." *Human Nature* 1:32–39.

Godelier, Maurice. 1999. *The Enigma of the Gift*. Chicago: University of Chicago Press.

Gonzalez, Roberto. 2001. *Zapotec Science: Farming and Food in the Northern Sierra of Oaxaca*. Austin: University of Texas Press.

Goodenough, Ward. 1965. Yankee Kinship Terminology: A Problem in Componential Analysis. *American Anthropologist* New Series, Vol. 67, No. 5, Part 2: Formal Semantic Analysis (Oct., 1965), pp. 259–87.

Gow, David. 1993. "Doubly Damned: Dealing with Power and Praxis in Development Anthropology." *Human Organization* 52:380–97.

Graeber, David. 2011. *Debt: The First 5,000 Years*. New York: Melville House Publishing.

Gravlee, Clarence. 2009. "How Race Becomes Biology: Embodiment of Social Inequality." *American Journal of Physical Anthropology* 139:47–57.

Gregory, Steven, and Roger Sanjek, eds. 1994. *Race*. New Brunswick, NJ: Rutgers University Press.

Grimm, Jacob. 1822. *Deutsche Grammatik*. Göttingen: Dieterichsche Buchhandlung.

Grove, Richard. 1995. *Green Imperialism: Colonial Expansion, Tropical Island Edens and the Origins of Environmentalism, 1600–1860*. Cambridge, UK: Cambridge University Press.

Gudeman, Stephen. 1986. *Economics as Culture: Models and Metaphors of Livelihood*. London: Routledge and Kegan Paul.

Gudeman, Stephen. 2001. *The Anthropology of Economy: Community, Market, and Culture*. Oxford: Blackwell.

Guha, Ramachandra. 2000. *Environmentalism: A Global History*. New York: Longman.

Guimarães, Antonio Sérgio Alfredo. 1999. "Racism and Anti-Racism in Brazil." In Roger S. Gottlieb (series ed.) and Leonard Harris (volume ed.), *Key Concepts in Critical Theory: Racism*, pp. 314–30. Amherst, NY: Humanity Books.

Gulliver, Phillip H. 1979. *Disputes and Negotiations: A Cross-Cultural Perspective*. New York: Academic Press.

Gusterson, Hugh. 2005. "The Seven Deadly Sins of Samuel Huntington." In Catherine Besteman and Hugh Gusterson, eds., *Why America's Top Pundits Are Wrong: Anthropologists Talk Back*, pp. 24–42. Berkeley: University of California Press.

Gutmann, Matthew C. 1996. *The Meanings of Macho: Being a Man in Mexico City*. Berkeley: University of California Press.

Gutmann, Matthew C. 1997. "Trafficking in Men: The Anthropology of Masculinity." *Annual Review of Anthropology* 26:385–409.

Hakiwai, Arapata, and John Terrell. 1994. *Ruatepupuke: A Maori Meeting House*. The Field Museum Centennial Collection. Chicago: The Field Museum.

Hale, Kenneth L. 1992. "On Endangered Languages and the Safeguarding of Diversity." *Language* 68:1–3.

Hanlon, Joseph. 1996. "Strangling Mozambique: International Monetary Fund 'Stabilization' in the World's Poorest Country." *Multinational Monitor* 17(7–8) July/August: 17–21.

Hannerz, Ulf. 1992. "The Global Ecumene." In *Cultural Complexity: Studies in the Social Organization of Meaning*, pp. 217–67. New York: Columbia University Press.

Hansen, Karen Tranberg. 2000. *Salaula: The World of Secondhand Clothing and Zambia*. Chicago: University of Chicago Press.

Harris, Marvin. 1979. *Cultural Materialism*. New York: Random House.

Hartigan, John, Jr. 2005. *Odd Tribes: Towards a Cultural Analysis of White People*. Durham, NC: Duke University Press.

Hartigan, John, Jr. 2006 . "Saying 'Socially Constructed' Is Not Enough." *Anthropology News*, February 2006, p. 8.

Harvey, L. P. 2007. *Ibn Batuta*. London: I. B. Tauris & Oxford Centre for Islamic Studies.

Haugerud, Angelique. 2016. "Public Anthropology in 2015: Charlie Hebdo, Black Lives Matter, Migrants, and More." *American Anthropologist* 118:585–601.

Herdt, Gilbert H. 1981. *Guardians of the Flutes: Idioms of Masculinity*. New York: McGraw-Hill.

Herdt, Gilbert H. 1994. "Introduction: Third Sexes and Third Genders." In Gilbert Herdt, ed., *Third Sex, Third Gender: Beyond Sexual Dimorphism in Culture and History*, pp. 21–81. New York: Zone Books.

Hinsley, Curtis M., and David R. Wilcox, eds. 2016. *Coming of Age in Chicago: The 1893 World's Fair and the Coalescence of American Anthropology*. Lincoln: University of Nebraska Press.

Ho, Karen. 2009. *Liquidated: An Ethnography of Wall Street*. Durham, NC: Duke University Press.

Hobbes, Thomas. 1909. *Leviathan*. Oxford: Clarendon Press.

Hoben, Alan. 1995. "Paradigms and Politics: The Cultural Construction of Environmental Policy in Ethiopia." *World Development* 23:1007–21.

Hobsbawn, Eric, and Ranger, Terence, eds. 1983. *The Invention of Tradition*. Cambridge, UK: Cambridge University Press.

Horn, David. 1994. *Social Bodies: Science, Reproduction, and Italian Modernity*. Princeton, NJ: Princeton University Press.

Howe, K. R. 1984. *Where the Waves Fall: A New South Sea Islands History From Its First Settlement to Colonial Rule*. Honolulu: University of Hawaii Press.

Hsu, F. L. K. 1972. "Psychological Anthropology in the Behavioral Sciences." In F. L. K. Hsu, ed., *Psychological Anthropology*, pp. 1–19. Cambridge, MA: Schenkman Publishing Co.

Humphrey, Caroline. 2002. *The Unmaking of Soviet Life: Everyday Economies After Socialism*. Ithaca, NY: Cornell University Press.

Ignatiev, Noel. 1995. *How the Irish Became White*. New York: Routledge.

Igoe, James. 2004. *Conservation and Globalization: A Study of National Parks and Indigenous Communities from East Africa to South Dakota*. Belmont, CA: Wadsworth.

Inda, Jonathan Xavier. 2014. *Racial Prescriptions: Pharmaceuticals, Difference, and the Politics of Life*. Burlington, VT: Ashgate.

Inda, Jonathan, and Renato Rosaldo, eds. 2002. *The Anthropology of Globalization: A Reader*. Malden, MA: Blackwell.

International Obesity Task Force (IOTF). 2013. "The Global Epidemic." World Health Organization Fact Sheet. Accessed on September 10, 2013: http://www.iaso.org/iotf/obesity/obesitytheglobalepidemic/.

International Telecommunication Union (ITU). 2016. "ICT Facts and Figures 2016." Accessed on February 17, 2017: http://www.itu.int/en/ITU-D/Statistics/Pages/facts/default.aspx

Kalipeni, Ezekiel. 2004. *HIV and AIDS in Africa: Beyond Epidemiology*. Malden, MA: Blackwell.

Kambas, Michele, and Antonio Bronic. 2016. Out of Sight, Out of Mind? Europe's Migrant Crisis Still Simmers. Reuters, August 10, 2016. Accessed on February 17, 2017: http://www.reuters.com/article/us-europe-migrants-idUSKCN10L13T?il=0.

Kapferer, Bruce. 2015. Afterword. In Alessandro Zagato, ed., *The Event of Charlie Hebdo: Imaginaries of Freedom and Control*, pp. 93–114. Critical Interventions, Vol. 15. Oxford: Berghahn.

Kaplan, David, and Robert A. Manners. 1972. *Culture Theory.* Prospect Heights, IL: Waveland Press.

Kaptchuk, Ted J. 2001. "The Double-blind, Randomized, Placebo-controlled Trial: Gold Standard or Golden Calf?" *Journal of Clinical Epidemiology* 54:541–49.

Kearney, Michael. 1995. "The Local and the Global: The Anthropology of Globalization and Transnationalism." *Annual Review of Anthropology* 24:547–65.

Kearney, Michael. 1996. *Reconceptualizing the Peasantry: Anthropology in Global Perspective.* Boulder, CO: Westview Press.

Khanmohamadi, S. 2008. "The Look of Medieval Ethnography: William of Rubruck's Mission to Mongolia." *New Medieval Literatures* 10:87–114.

Kidder, Tracy. 2003. *Mountains Beyond Mountains.* New York: Random House.

Kidwell, Claudia Brush, and Valerie Steele, eds. 1989. *Men and Women: Dressing the Part.* Washington, D.C.: Smithsonian Institution Press.

Kildea, Gary, and Jerry Leach. 1975. *Trobriand Cricket: An Ingenious Response to Colonialism.* DVD. Berkeley, CA: Berkeley Media.

Kingsolver, Ann. 1996. "Power." In Alan Barnard and Jonathan Spencer, eds., *Encyclopedia of Social and Cultural Anthropology,* pp. 445–48. London: Routledge.

Kinsey, Alfred. 1948. *Sexual Behavior in the Human Male.* Philadelphia: W. B. Saunders.

Koos, Earl Lomon. 1954. *The Health of Regionville.* New York: Columbia University Press.

Kopytoff, Igor. 1986. "The Cultural Biography of Things: Commoditization as Process." In Arjun Appadurai, ed., *The Social Life of Things: Commodities in Cultural Perspective,* pp. 64–91. New York: Cambridge University Press.

Korten, David. 1995. *When Corporations Rule the World.* West Hartford, CT: Kumarian Press.

Kozol, Jonathan. 1992. *Savage Inequalities: Children in America's Schools.* New York: Harper Perennial.

Krech, Shepard. 1999. *The Ecological Indian: Myth and History.* New York: W. W. Norton.

Krishnamurthy, Mathangi. 2004. "Resources and Rebels: A Study of Identity Management in Indian Call Centers." *Anthropology of Work Review* 25(3–4): 9–18.

Kroeber, Alfred L. 1909. "Classificatory Systems of Relationship." *Journal of the Royal Anthropological Institute of Great Britain and Ireland* 39:77–84.

Kroeber, Alfred L. 1923. "American Culture and the Northwest Coast." *American Anthropologist* 25(1): 1–20.

Kubler, George. 1962. *The Shape of Time: Remarks on the History of Things.* New Haven, CT: Yale University Press.

Kurtz, Donald V. 2001. *Political Anthropology: Paradigms and Power.* Boulder, CO: Westview Press.

Labov, William. 1990. "Intersection of Sex and Social Class in the Course of Linguistic Change." *Language Variation and Change* 2:205–54.

Labov, William, Sharon Ash, and Charles Boberg. 2006. *The Atlas of North American English: Phonetics, Phonology, and Sound Change: A Multimedia Reference Tool.* Berlin: Mouton de Gruyter.

Lahsen, Myanna. 2015. "Digging Deeper into the Why: Cultural Dimensions of Climate Change Skepticism Among Scientists." In Jessica Barnes and Michael Dove, eds. *Climate Cultures: Anthropological Perspectives on Climate Change,* pp. 221–48. New Haven, CT: Yale University Press.

Lakoff, Robin. 1975. *Language and Woman's Place.* New York: Harper and Row.

Lancaster, Roger. 1992. *Life Is Hard: Machismo, Danger, and the Intimacy of Power in Nicaragua.* Berkeley: University of California Press.

Lancaster, Roger. 1997. "On Homosexualities in Latin America (and Other Places)." *American Ethnologist* 24:193–202.

Lancaster, Roger. 2004. "The Place of Anthropology in a Public Culture Shaped by Bioreductivism." *Anthropology News* 45:4–5.

Lareau, Annette. 2003. *Unequal Childhoods: Class, Race, and Family Life.* Berkeley: University of California Press.

Larner, John. 1999. *Marco Polo and the Discovery of the World.* New Haven, CT: Yale University Press.

Leacock, Eleanor. 1981. *Myths of Male Dominance.* New York: Monthly Review.

Lechner, Frank, and Boli, John. 2005. *World Culture: Origins and Consequences.* Malden, MA: Blackwell.

Lee, Richard. 1969. "!Kung Bushmen Subsistence: An Input-Output Analysis." In Andrew P. Vayda, ed., *Environment and Cultural Behavior,* pp. 47–79. Garden City, NY: Natural History Press.

Lee, Richard. 1979. *The !Kung San: Men, Women, and Work in a Foraging Society.* Cambridge, UK: Cambridge University Press.

Lentz, Carola. 1999. "Changing Food Habits: An Introduction." In Carola Lentz, ed., *Changing Food Habits: Case Studies From Africa, South America, and Europe,* pp. 1–25. Newark, NJ: Harwood Academic Publishers.

Lévi-Strauss, Claude. 1949/1969. *The Elementary Structures of Kinship.* Boston: Beacon Press.

Lévi-Strauss, Claude. 1961. "The Effectiveness of Symbols." In *Structural Anthropology,* pp. 186–205. New York: Basic Books.

Lewellen, Ted C. 1983. *Political Anthropology: An Introduction.* South Hadley, MA: Bergin & Garvey Publishers.

Lewellen, Ted C. 2003. *Political Anthropology: An Introduction.* 3rd ed. Westport, CT: Praeger.

Lewin, Ellen, and William L. Leap, eds. 2009. *Out in Public: Reinventing Lesbian/Gay Anthropology in a Globalizing World.* Malden, MA: Wiley-Blackwell.

Liechty, Mark. 2002. *Suitably Modern: Making Middle Class Culture in Kathmandu.* Princeton, NJ: Princeton University Press.

Linton, Ralph. 1924. "Totemism and the A. E. F." *American Anthropologist* 26:296–300.

Little, Peter, and Michael Painter. 1995. "Discourse, Politics, and the Development Process: Reflections on Escobar's 'Anthropology and the Development Encounter.'" *American Ethnologist* 22:602–9.

Lizot, Jacques. 1985. *Tales of the Yanomami: Daily Life in the Venezuelan Forest.* Trans. by Ernest Simon. Cambridge, UK: Cambridge University Press.

Locke, John. 2003. *Two Treatises on Government: And a Letter Concerning Toleration.* New Haven, CT: Yale University Press.

Lockwood, William G. 1975. *European Moslems: Economy and Ethnicity in Western Bosnia.* New York: Academic Publishers.

Long, Jeffrey. 2003. *Human Genetic Variation: The Mechanisms and Results of Microevolution.* Paper presented at the American Anthropological Association 2003 annual meeting on November 21, 2003, Chicago, Illinois. Accessed on May 24, 2007: http://www.understandingrace.com/resources/papers_author.html.

Lonely Planet. 2014. "Why Are Hearts the Symbol for a Rustic Toilet in Swedish Countryside?" Thorn Tree Forum. Country Forums: Scandinavia & the Nordics: Sweden. Accessed August 2014: https://www.lonelyplanet.com/thornt ree/forums/europe-scandinavia-the-nordics/topics/why-are-hearts-the-symbol-for-a-rustic-toilet-in-swedish-countryside.

Lovgren, Sven. 2003. "Map Links Healthier Ecosystems, Indigenous Peoples." *National Geographic News,* February 27, 2003. Accessed on February 15, 2005: http://news.nationalgeographic.com/news/2003/02/0227_030227_indigenousmap.html.

Lyons, Andrew P., and Harriet D. Lyons. 2004. *Irregular Connections: A History of Anthropology and Sexuality.* Lincoln: University of Nebraska Press.

MacBeth, Helen. 1997. *Food Preferences and Taste: Continuity and Change.* New York: Berghahn Books.

Mair, Lucy. 1969. *Anthropology and Social Change.* New York: Humanities Press.

Malinowski, Bronislaw. 1922. *Argonauts of the Western Pacific: An Account of Native Enterprise and Adventure in the Archipelagoes of Melanesian New Guinea.* London: Routledge & Kegan Paul.

Malinowski, Bronislaw. 1948. *Magic, Science and Religion and Other Essays.* Boston: Beacon Press.

Malotki, Ekkehardt. 1983. *Hopi Time: A Linguistic Analysis of the Temporal Concepts of the Hopi Language.* Berlin: Mouton.

Mamdani, Mahmood. 1972. *The Myth of Population Control: Family, Caste, and Class in an Indian Village.* New York: Monthly Review Press.

Marcus, George. 1995. "Ethnography in/of the World System: The Emergence of Multi-Sited Ethnography." *Annual Review of Anthropology* 24:95–117.

Marcus, George, and Michael M. J. Fischer. 1986. *Anthropology as Cultural Critique: An Experimental Moment in the Human Sciences.* Chicago: University of Chicago Press.

Mares, Teresa. 2014. "Another Time of Hunger." In Janet Page-Reeves, ed., *Women Redefining the Experience of Food Insecurity: Life Off the Edge of the Table,* pp. 45–64. Lanham, MD: Lexington Books.

Marks, Jonathan. 1995. *Human Biodiversity: Genes, Race, and History.* New York: Aldine de Gruyter.

Marty, Martin E., and R. Scott Appleby, eds. 1991. *Fundamentalisms Observed.* The Fundamentalism Project, Vol. 1. Chicago: University of Chicago Press.

Marx, Karl. 1867/1990. *Capital: A Critique of Political Economy.* New York: Penguin.

Massey, Douglas, Joaquin Arango, Graeme Hugo, Ali Kouaouci, Adela Pellegrino, and J. Edward Taylor. 1993. "Theories of International Migration: A Review and Appraisal." *Population and Development Review* Vol. 19, No. 3 (Sept. 1993): 431–66.

Mauss, Marcel. 1924/1954. *The Gift: The Form and Reason for Exchange in Archaic Societies.* Trans. W. D. Halls. New York: W. W. Norton.

McCabe, Terrence. 1990. "Turkana Pastoralism: A Case Against the Tragedy of the Commons." *Human Ecology* 18:81–103.

McElhinny, Bonnie. 2003. "Theorizing Gender in Sociolinguistics and Linguistic Anthropology." In Janet Holmes and Miriam Myerhoff, eds., *The Handbook of Language and Gender,* pp. 21–42. Malden, MA: Blackwell.

McFate, Montgomery. 2005. "Does Culture Matter?: The Military Utility of Cultural Knowledge." *Joint Forces Quarterly* 38:42–8.

McGrath, J. W., C. B. Rwabukwali, D. A. Schumann, J. Pearson-Marks, R. Mukasa, B. Namande, S. Nakayiwa, and L. Nakyobe. 1992. "Cultural Determinants of Sexual Risk Behavior Among Baganda Women." *Medical Anthropology Quarterly* 6:153–61.

McIntosh, Peggy. 1997. "White Privilege and Male Privilege: A Personal Account of Coming to See Correspondences Through Work in Women's Studies." In Richard Delgado and Jean Stefancic, eds.,

Critical White Studies: Looking Behind the Mirror, pp. 291–9. Philadelphia: Temple University Press.

McIntosh, Roderick. 2015. "Climate Shock and Awe: Can There Be an 'Ethno-science' of Deep-Time Mande Paleoclimate Memory?" In Jessica Barnes and Michael Dove, eds., *Climate Cultures: Anthropological Perspectives on Climate Change,* pp. 273–88. New Haven, CT: Yale University Press.

McIntyre, Matthew H., and Carolyn Pope Edwards. 2009. "The Early Development of Gender Differences." *Annual Review of Anthropology* 38:83–97.

McKenna, James J. 1996. "Sudden Infant Death Syndrome in Cross-Cultural Perspective: Is Infant-Parent Co-sleeping Protective?" *Annual Review of Anthropology* 25:201–16.

Mead, Margaret. 1928. *Coming of Age in Samoa: A Psychological Study of Primitive Youth for Western Civilization.* New York: William Morrow.

Mead, Margaret. 1930a. *Growing Up in New Guinea: A Comparative Study of Primitive Education.* New York: W. Morrow.

Mead, Margaret. 1930b. *Social Organization of Manu'a.* Honolulu, HI: Bishop Museum Press.

Mead, Margaret. 1938. "The Mountain Arapesh: I. An Importing Culture." *Anthropological Papers of the American Museum of Natural History* 36:139–349.

Meigs, Anna. 1997. "Food as a Cultural Construction." In Carole Counihan and Penny Van Esterik, eds., *Food and Culture: A Reader,* pp. 95–106. New York: Routledge.

Menzies, Gavin. 2002. *1421: The Year China Discovered America.* London: Transworld Publishers.

Merry, Sally Engle. 2003. "Human Rights Law and the Demonization of Culture." *Anthropology News* 44 February: 4–5.

Miller, Daniel. 1987. *Material Culture and Mass Consumption.* Oxford: Basil Blackwell.

Miller, Daniel, ed. 1995. *Acknowledging Consumption: A Review of New Studies.* London: Routledge.

Miller, Daniel. 1998. *A Theory of Shopping.* Ithaca, NY: Cornell University Press.

Mohanty, Chandra Talpade. 1991. "Under Western Eyes: Feminist Scholarship and Colonial Discourses." In Chandra Talpade Mohanty, Ann Russo, and Lourdes Torres, eds., *Third World Women and the Politics of Feminism,* pp. 333–58. Indianapolis: Indiana University Press.

Money, John. 1985. *Destroying Angel: Sex, Fitness, and Food in the Legacy of Degeneracy Theory, Graham Crackers, Kellogg's Corn Flakes, and American Health History.* Buffalo, NY: Prometheus Books.

Moore, Francis, Justin Mankin, and Austin Becker. 2015. "Challenges in Integrating the Climate and Social Sciences for Studies of Climate Change and Adaptation." In Jessica Barnes and Michael R. Dove, eds., *Climate Cultures: Anthropological*

Perspectives on Climate Change, pp. 169–95. New Haven, CT: Yale University Press.

Moran, Mary. 1997. "Warriors or Soldiers? Masculinity and Ritual Tranvestism in the Liberian Civil War." In Louise Lamphere, Helena Ragone, and Patricia Zavella, eds., *Situated Lives: Gender and Culture in Everyday Life,* pp. 440–50. Chicago: University of Chicago Press.

Morgan, Edmund. 1975. *American Slavery, American Freedom.* New York: W. W. Norton.

Morgan, Lewis Henry. 1871. *Systems of Consanguinity and Affinity of the Human Family.* Washington, D.C.: Smithsonian Institution.

Morgan, Lewis Henry. 1877. *Ancient Society: Or, Researches in the Lines of Human Progress from Savagery, Through Barbarism to Civilization.* New York: Henry Holt.

Morris, Rosalind C. 1995. "All Made Up: Performance Theory and the New Anthropology of Sex and Gender." *Annual Review of Anthropology* 24:567–92.

Mullings, Leith. 2005. "Interrogating Racism: Toward an Antiracist Anthropology." *Annual Review of Anthropology* 34:667–93.

Munson, Barbara. 1999. "Not for Sport." *Teaching Tolerance Magazine.* Accessed on July 31, 2010: http://www.tolerance.org/magazine/number-15-spring-1999/not-sport.

Murray, Gerald. 1987. "The Domestication of Wood in Haiti: A Case Study in Applied Evolution." In R. M. Wulff and S. J. Fiske, eds., *Anthropological Praxis: Translating Knowledge into Action,* pp. 223–40. Boulder, CO: Westview Press.

Nadasdy, Paul. 2005. "The Anti-Politics of TEK: The Institutionalization of Co-Management Discourse and Practice." *Anthropologica* 47:215–32.

Nader, Laura. 1990. *Harmony Ideology: Justice and Control in a Zapotec Mountain Village.* Stanford, CA: Stanford University Press.

Nader, Laura. 1995. "Civilization and Its Negotiators." In Pat Caplan, ed., *Understanding Disputes: The Politics of Argument,* pp. 39–63. Oxford: Berg Publishers.

Nader, Laura, ed. 1996. *Naked Science: Anthropological Inquiry Into Boundaries, Power, and Knowledge.* New York: Routledge.

Nader, Laura. 2001. "The Underside of Conflict Management—in Africa and Elsewhere." *IDS Bulletin* 32:19–27.

Nader, Laura, and Terry Kay Rockefeller. 1981. *Little Injustices: Laura Nader Looks at the Law.* Washington, DC: PBS Video (Distributed by Documentary Educational Resources).

Nader, Laura, and Harry F. Todd, eds. 1978. *The Disputing Process—Law in Ten Societies.* New York: Columbia University Press.

Nagengast, Carole, and Michael Kearney. 1990. "Mixtec Ethnicity: Social Identity, Political Consciousness, and Political Activism." *Latin American Research Review* 25:61–92.

Nanda, Serena. 1994. "Hijras: An Alternative Sex and Gender Role in India." In Gilbert Herdt, ed., *Third Sex, Third Gender: Beyond Sexual Dimorphism in Culture and History*, pp. 373–417. New York: Zone Books.

Nanda, Serena. 2000. *Gender Diversity: Crosscultural Variations*. Prospect Heights, IL: Waveland Press.

Nash, June. 1981. "Ethnographic Aspects of the World Capitalist System." *Annual Review of Anthropology* 10:393–423.

Nash, June. 2007. "Consuming Interests: Water, Rum, and Coca-Cola from Ritual Propitiation to Corporate Expropriation in Highland Chiapas." *Cultural Anthropology* 22:621–39.

Nash, Manning. 1958. *Machine Age Maya*. Glencoe, IL: Free Press.

Natcher, David C., Susan Hickey, and Clifford G. Hickey. 2005. "Co-Management: Managing Relationships, Not Resources." *Human Organization* 64:240–50.

National Collegiate Athletic Association (NCAA). 2005. "NCAA Executive Committee Issues Guidelines for Use of Native American Mascots at Championship Events." (Released Friday August 5, 2005). NCAA Press Release Archive. Accessed August 2014: http://fs.ncaa.org/Docs/PressArchive/2005/Announcements/NCAA%2BExecutive%2BCommittee%2BIssues%2BGuidelines%2Bfor%2BUse%2Bof%2BNative%2BAmerican%2BMascots%2Bat%2BChampionship%2BEvents.html.

National Public Radio. 2009. Brian Lehrer interviews Nancy Scheper-Hughes, July 24, 2009. http://www.wnyc.org/shows/bl/ episodes/2009/07/24/segments/137306.

Nederveen Pieterse, J. 2004. *Globalization and Culture: Global Mélange*. Lanham, MD: Rowman and Littlefield.

Norberg, Johan. 2006. "How Globalization Conquers Poverty." Accessed on November 19, 2006: http://www.cato.org/special/symposium/essays/norberg.html.

Nordstrom, Carolyn R. 1988. "Exploring Pluralism: The Many Faces of Ayurveda." *Social Science and Medicine* 27:479–89.

Nyamwaya, D. O. 1993. "Anthropology and HIV/AIDS Prevention in Kenya: New Ways of Cooperation." *AIDS and Society* 4:4, 8.

Oberschall, Anthony. 2000. "The Manipulation of Ethnicity: From Ethnic Cooperation to Violence and War in Yugoslavia." *Ethnic and Racial Studies* 23:982–1001.

O'Hanlon, Michael, and Robert L. Welsch, eds. 2000. *Hunting the Gatherers: Ethnographic Collectors, Agents and Agency in Melanesia, 1870s–1930s*. New York: Berghahn.

Omi, Michael, and Howard Winant, eds. 1996. *Racial Formation in the United States*. 2nd ed. New York: Routledge.

Ong, Aihwa. 1988. "The Production of Possession: Spirits and the Multinational Corporation in Malaysia." *American Ethnologist* 15:28–42.

Orlove, Ben. 2005. "Human Adaptation to Climate Change: A Review of Three Historical Cases and Some General Perspectives." *Environmental Science & Policy* 8:589–600.

Ortner, Sherry B. 1971. "On Key Symbols." *American Anthropologist* 75:1338–46.

Ortner, Sherry B. 1974. "Is Female to Male as Nature Is to Culture?" In Michelle Rosaldo and Louise Lamphere, eds., *Woman, Culture, and Society*, pp. 67–88. Stanford, CA: Stanford University Press.

Ortner, Sherry B. 1989. *High Religion: A Cultural and Political History of Sherpa Buddhism*. Princeton, NJ: Princeton University Press.

Ortner, Sherry B. 1996. *Making Gender: The Politics and Erotics of Culture*. Boston: Beacon Press.

Ortner, Sherry B. 2006. *Anthropology and Social Theory: Culture, Power, and the Acting Subject*. Durham, NC: Duke University Press.

Osburg, John. 2013. *Anxious Wealth: Money and Morality Among China's New Rich*. Stanford, CA: Stanford University Press.

Ottenberg, Simon. 1991. "Review of 'Into the Heart of Africa'." *African Arts* 24:79–82.

Owusu, Maxwell. 1992. "Democracy and Africa: A View from the Village." *Journal of Modern African Studies* 30:369–96.

Owusu, Maxwell. 1996. "Tradition and Transformation: Democracy and the Politics of Popular Power in Ghana." *Journal of Modern African Studies* 34:307–43.

Parent, Anthony S., Jr. 2003. *Foul Means: The Formation of Slave Society in Virginia, 1660–1740*. Chapel Hill: University of North Carolina Press.

Parker, Richard. 1989. "Acquired Immunodeficiency Syndrome in Urban Brazil." *Medical Anthropology Quarterly* 1:155–75.

Parker, R. G. 2009. *Bodies, Pleasures, and Passions: Sexual Culture in Contemporary Brazil*. 2nd ed. Nashville, TN: Vanderbilt University Press.

Parkin, David, and Stanley Ulijaszek, eds. 2007. *Holistic Anthropology: Emergence and Convergence*. New York: Berghahn Books.

Parry, Jonathan, and Maurice Bloch, eds. 1989. *Money and the Morality of Exchange*. Cambridge, UK: Cambridge University Press.

Parsons, Talcott. 1951. *The Social System*. Glencoe, IL: The Free Press.

Partners in Health. 2010. Partners in Health web page. http://www.pih.org/

Patterson, Penny, director. 2003. *Koko and Friends*. Videorecording, produced by the Gorilla Foundation, distributed by Dave West, Utah Film and Video.

Peters, William, producer. 1970. *Eye of the Storm*. Human Relations Film Series. Videocassette. New York: Insight Media.

Peters, William, producer. 2005. *A Class Divided*. PBS Video. (Originally broadcast March 26, 1985, on *Frontline*.)

Pinker, Steven. 1997. *How the Mind Works*. New York: Norton.

Piot, Charles. 1999. *Remotely Global: Village Modernity in West Africa*. Chicago: University of Chicago Press.

Polanyi, Karl. 1944/1975. *The Great Transformation*. New York: Octagon Books.

Price, David. 2002. "Past Wars, Present Dangers, Future Anthropologies." *Anthropology Today* 18: 3–5.

Radcliffe-Brown, Alfred R. 1941. "The Study of Kinship Systems." *Journal of the Royal Anthropological Institute of Great Britain and Ireland* 71(1/2): 1–18.

Radcliffe-Brown, Alfred R. 1952. *Structure and Function in Primitive Society: Essays and Addresses*. Glencoe, IL: Free Press.

Radin, Paul. 1927. *Primitive Man as Philosopher*. New York: D. Appleton.

Ragoné, Helena. 1996. "Chasing the Blood Tie: Surrogate Mothers, Adoptive Mothers and Fathers." *American Ethnologist* 23:352–65.

Rahnema, Majid, and Victoria Bawtree. 1997. *The Post-Development Reader*. London: Zed Press.

Ramos, Alcida Rita. 1990. "Ethnology Brazilian Style." *Cultural Anthropology* 5:452–72.

Ramos, Alcida Rita. 2000. "Anthropologist as Political Actor: Between Activism and Suspicion." *Journal of Latin American Anthropology* 4/5:172–89.

Rasmussen, Susan. 1991. "Modes of Persuasion: Gossip, Song, and Divination in Tuareg Conflict Resolution." *Anthropological Quarterly* 64:30–46.

Rex, John. 1999. "Racism, Institutionalized and Otherwise." In Roger S. Gottlieb (series ed.) and Leonard Harris (volume ed.), *Key Concepts in Critical Theory: Racism*, pp. 141–60. Amherst, NY: Humanity Books.

Rice, Andrew. 2016. "Is Jim Kim Destroying the World Bank—Or Saving It From Itself?" *Foreign Policy*, April 27, 2016. Accessed on January 17, 2017: http://foreignpolicy.com/2016/04/27/is-jim-yong-kim-destroying-the-world-bank-development-finance/.

Richards, Paul. 1996. *Fighting for the Rainforest*. London: James Currey.

Richardson, Jane, and Alfred L. Kroeber. 1940. "Three Centuries of Women's Dress Fashions: A Quantitative Analysis." *University of California Anthropological Records* 5:i–iv, 100–53.

Riches, David. 1986. "The Phenomenon of Violence." In David Riches, ed., *The Anthropology of Violence*, pp. 1–27. Oxford: Basil Blackwell.

Rivers, William H. R. 1906. *The Todas*. London: Macmillan.

Rivoli, Pietra. 2005. *The Travels of a T-Shirt in the Global Economy: An Economist Examines the Markets, Power, and Politics of World Trade*. Hoboken, NJ: John Wiley & Sons.

Robarchek, Clayton A., and Robert Knox Dentan. 1987. "Blood Drunkenness and the Bloodthirsty Semai: Unmaking Another Anthropological Myth." *American Anthropologist* 89:356–65.

Robben, Antonius. 1989. *Sons of the Sea Goddess: Economic Practice and Discursive Conflict in Brazil*. New York: Columbia University Press.

Robbins, Richard. 2001. *Cultural Anthropology: A Problem-Based Approach*. 3rd ed. Itasca, IL: F. E. Peacock.

Rosaldo, Renato. 1989. *Culture and Truth: The Remaking of Social Analysis*. Boston: Beacon Press.

Roscoe, Will. 1994. "How to Become a Berdache: Toward a Unified Analysis of Gender Diversity." In Gilbert Herdt, ed., *Third Sex, Third Gender: Beyond Sexual Dimorphism in Culture and History*, pp. 329–72. New York: Zone Books.

Rowlands, M., and J. P. Warnier. 1988. "Sorcery, Power and the Modern State in Cameroon." *Man* (n s.) 23:118–32.

Sahlins, Marshall. 1972. *Stone Age Economics*. Chicago: Aldine-Atherton.

Sahlins, Marshall. 1976. *Culture and Practical Reason*. Chicago: University of Chicago Press.

Sahlins, Marshall. 1999. "Two or Three Things That I Know About Culture." *Journal of the Royal Anthropological Institute* 5:399–421.

Sahlins, Marshall, and Elman Service, eds. 1960. *Evolution and Culture*. Ann Arbor: University of Michigan Press.

Said, Edward. 1978. *Orientalism*. New York: Pantheon Books.

Sakala, Leah. 2014. "Breaking Down Mass Incarceration in the 2010 Census: State-by-State Incarceration Rates by Race/Ethnicity." Prison Policy Initiative. Accessed on February 17, 2017: https://www.prisonpolicy.org/reports/rates.html.

Sanjek, Roger. 1990. "Vocabulary for Fieldnotes." In Roger Sanjek, ed., *Fieldnotes: The Making of*

Anthropology, pp. 71–91. Ithaca, NY: Cornell University Press.

Sapir, Edward. 1921. *Language: An Introduction to the Study of Speech.* New York: Harcourt, Brace.

Sapir, Edward. 1929. "The Status of Linguistics as a Science." *Language* 5: 207–14.

Sayer, Andrew. 2000. "Moral Economy and Political Economy." *Studies in Political Economy* Spring 2000: 79–103.

Scheper-Hughes, Nancy. 2004. "Parts Unknown: Undercover Ethnography of the Organs-trafficking Underworld." *Ethnography* 5:29–73.

Scheper-Hughes, Nancy, and Loïc Wacquant, eds. 2003. *Commodifying Bodies.* Thousand Oaks, CA: Sage Publications.

Schildkrout, Enid, and Curtis A. Keim. 1998. *The Scramble for Art in Central Africa.* Cambridge, UK: Cambridge University Press.

Scott, James. 2009. *The Art of Not Being Governed: An Anarchist History of Upland Southeast Asia.* New Haven, CT: Yale University Press.

Seligman, Rebecca. 2005. "Distress, Dissociation, and Embodied Experience: Reconsidering the Pathways to Mediumship and Mental Health." *Ethos* 33:71–99.

Sharma, Ursula. 1999. *Caste.* In Frank Parkin (series ed.), *Concepts in the Social Sciences.* Buckingham, UK: Open University Press.

Sheridan, Michael. 2006. "Linguistic Models in Anthropology 101: Give Me the Cup." In P. Rice and D. McCurdy, eds. *Strategies in Teaching Anthropology.* 4th ed., pp. 54–56. Upper Saddle River, NJ: Prentice Hall Professional.

Shore, Bradd. 1996. *Culture in Mind: Cognition, Culture, and the Problem of Meaning.* New York: Oxford University Press.

Shorris, Earl. 1992. *Latinos: A Biography of the People.* New York: W. W. Norton.

Shorris, Earl. 2001. *Latinos: Biography of a People.* New York: W. W. Norton & Company.

Silverblatt, Irene. 1988. "Political Memories and Colonizing Symbols: Santiago and the Mountain Gods of Colonial Peru." In Jonathan Hill, ed., *Rethinking History and Myth: Indigenous South American Perspectives on the Past*, pp. 174–94. Urbana: University of Illinois Press.

Simmons, Ozzie G. 1955. "Popular and Modern Medicine in Mestizo Communities of Coastal Peru and Chile." *Journal of American Folklore* 68:57–71.

Sivo, Ellen. 2005. "The DOs and DON'Ts of College Romance." *The Vermont Cynic*, Nov. 29, 2005. Accessed January 2006: http://media.www .vermontcynic.com/media/storage/paper308/ news/2005/11/29/LifeAndStyle/The-Dos.And .Donts.Of.College.Romance-1115738.shtml.

Sloane, Patricia. 1999. *Islam, Modernity, and Entrepreneurship Among the Malays.* New York: St. Martin's Press.

Small, Meredith. 1998. *Our Babies, Ourselves: How Biology and Culture Shape How We Parent.* New York: Anchor Books.

Smedley, Audrey. 2007a. *The History of the Idea of Race . . . And Why It Matters.* Paper presented at the conference "Race, Human Variation and Disease: Consensus and Frontiers," Warrenton, Virginia, March 14–17, 2007. Accessed on June 11, 2015: http://www.understandingrace .com/resources/ papers_author.html.

Smedley, Audrey. 2007b. *Race in North America: Origin and Evolution of a Worldview.* 3rd ed. Boulder, CO: Westview Press.

Smith, Adam. 1776/1976. *An Inquiry into the Nature and Causes of the Wealth of Nations.* Chicago: University of Chicago Press.

Smith, M. Estellie. 2000. *Trade and Tradeoffs: Using Resources, Making Choices, and Taking Risks.* Long Grove, IL: Waveland Press.

Society for Medical Anthropology. 2014. "What Is Medical Anthropology?" Accessed on June 1, 2014: http://www.medanthro.net/9/comment-page-1/#comment-36.

Spencer, Herbert. 1874.*The Principles of Sociology.* London: Williams and Norgate.

Spiro, Melford E. 1958. *Children of the Kibbutz.* Cambridge, MA: Harvard University Press.

Spittler, Gerd. 1999. "In Praise of the Simple Meal: African and European Food Culture Compared." In Carola Lentz, ed., *Changing Food Habits: Case Studies from Africa, South America, and Europe*, pp. 27–42. Newark, NJ: Harwood Academic Publishers.

Spitulnik, Debra. 1998. "Mediating Unity and Diversity: The Production of Language Ideologies in Zambian Broadcasting." In Bambi B. Shieffelin, Katharyn A. Woolard, and Paul V. Kroskrity, eds., *Language Ideologies: Practice and Theory*, pp. 163–88. New York: Oxford University Press.

Stack, Carol B. 1997. *All Our Kin.* New York: Basic Books.

Starr, Paul. 1982. *The Social Transformation of American Medicine.* New York: Basic Books.

Steward, Julian. 1955. *Theory of Culture Change: The Methodology of Multilinear Evolution.* Urbana, IL: University of Illinois Press.

Stocking, George W., Jr., ed. 1985. *History of Anthropology, Vol. 3: Objects and Others: Essays on Museums and Material Culture.* Madison: University of Wisconsin Press.

Stoffle, Richard, Rebecca Toupal, and Nieves Zedeño. 2003. "Landscape, Nature, and Culture: A Diachronic Model of Human-Nature

Adaptations." In H. Selin, ed., *Nature Across Cultures: Views of Nature and the Environment in Non-Western Cultures*, pp. 97–114. London: Kluwer Academic Publishers.

Stonich, Susan C. 1993. *I Am Destroying the Land! The Political Ecology of Poverty and Environmental Destruction in Honduras.* Boulder, CO: Westview Press.

Strang, Veronica, and Mark Busse, eds. 2011. *Ownership and Appropriation.* New York: Berg.

Strathern, Marilyn. 1996. "Enabling Identity? Biology, Choice and the New Reproductive Technologies." In S. Hall and P. du Gay, eds., *Questions of Cultural Identity*, pp. 37–52. London: Sage.

Strong, Pauline. 1996. "Animated Indians: Critique and Contradiction in Commodified Children's Culture." *Cultural Anthropology* 11:405–24.

Sturtevant, William. 1964. "Studies in Ethnoscience." In A. Kimball Romney and Roy G. D'Andrade, eds., *Transcultural Studies of Cognition*, pp. 99–131. Menasha, WI: AAA.

Tainter, Joseph. 2006. "Archaeology of Overshoot and Collapse." *Annual Review of Anthropology* 35:59–74.

Tannen, Deborah. 1990. *You Just Don't Understand: Men and Women in Conversation.* New York: Morrow.

Tator, Carol, Frances Henry, and Winston Mattis. 1998. *Challenging Racism in the Arts: Case Studies of Controversy and Conflict.* Toronto: University of Toronto Press.

Thomas, Mark. 2008. *Belching Out the Devil: Global Adventures with Coca-Cola.* London: Ebury Publishing.

Thomas, Wesley. 1997. "Navajo Cultural Constructions of Gender and Sexuality." In Sue-Ellen Jacobs, Wesley Thomas, and Sabine Lang, eds., *Two-Spirit People: Native American Gender Identity, Sexuality, and Spirituality*, pp. 156–73. Urbana: University of Illinois Press.

Thomson, Rob, Tamar Murachver, and James Green. 2001. "Where Is the Gender in Gendered Language?" *Psychological Science* 12:171–5.

Tibon, Jorelik. n.d. "What is 'Mo'? Traditional Conservation Sites in the Marshall Islands." Republic of the Marshall Islands Biodiversity Clearinghouse Mechanism. Accessed on February 17, 2017:http://biormi.org/index_navmap.shtml?en/community.html.

Tierney, Patrick. 2002. *Darkness in El Dorado: How Scientists and Journalists Devastated the Amazon.* New York: W. W. Norton.

Toren, Christina. 1996. "Psychological Anthropology." In Alan Barnard and Jonathan Spencer, eds., *Encyclopedia of Social and Cultural Anthropology*, pp. 456–61. London: Routledge.

Trevor-Roper, Hugh R. 1983. "The Invention of Tradition: The Highland Tradition of Scotland."

In Eric Hobsbawn and Terence Ranger, eds., *The Invention of Tradition*, pp. 15–41. Cambridge, UK: Cambridge University Press.

Truman, Harry S. 1949. Inaugural Address, January 20, 1949. Accessed on June 3, 2014: http://www.bartleby.com/124/pres53.html.

Tsing, Anna Lowenhaupt. 2000. "The Global Situation." *Cultural Anthropology* 15:327–60.

Turner, Victor. 1967. *The Forest of Symbols: Aspects of Ndembu Ritual.* Ithaca, NY: Cornell University Press.

Turner, Victor. 1969. *The Ritual Process: Structure and Anti-Structure.* Chicago: Aldine.

Two Bears, Davina R. 2006. "Navajo Archaeologist Is Not an Oxymoron: A Tribal Archaeologist's Experience." *American Indian Quarterly* 30(3–4): 381–7.

Tylor, E. B. 1871. *Primitive Culture: Researches Into the Development of Mythology, Philosophy, Religion, Art, and Custom.* London: John Murray.

Ulijaszek, Stanley J., and Hayley Lofink. 2006. "Obesity in Biocultural Perspective." *Annual Reviews of Anthropology* 35:337–60.

Underhill, Paco. 2005. *Call of the Mall: A Walking Tour Through the Crossroads of Our Shopping Culture.* New York: Simon and Schuster.

United Nations (UN). 2016. "International Migration Report 2015." Department of Economic and Social Affairs. Accessed on February 17, 2017: http://www.un.org/en/development/desa/population/migration/publications/migrationreport/docs/MigrationReport2015_Highlights.pdf.

Valentine, David. 2003. "'The Calculus of Pain': Violence, Anthropological Ethics, and the Category Transgender." *Ethnos* 68:27–48.

Valentine, David. 2007. *Imagining Transgender: An Ethnography of a Category.* Durham, NC: Duke University Press.

van den Berghe, Pierre. 1999. "Ethnicity as Kin Selection: The Biology of Nepotism." In Roger S. Gottlieb (series ed.) and Leonard Harris (volume ed.), *Key Concepts in Critical Theory: Racism*, pp. 50–73. Amherst, NY: Humanity Books.

van Gennep, Arnold. 1960. *The Rites of Passage.* Trans. by Monica B. Vizedom and Gabrielle L. Caffee. Chicago: University of Chicago Press. [Orig. published 1909 in French.]

Veseth, Michael. 2005. *Globaloney: Unraveling the Myths of Globalization.* Lanham, MD: Rowman and Littlefield.

Vincent, Joan. 1978. "Political Anthropology: Manipulative Strategies." *Annual Review of Anthropology* 7:175–94.

Viswesaran, Kamala. 1997. "Histories of Feminist Ethnography." *Annual Review Anthropology* 26:591–621.

Vivanco, Luis A. 2006. *Green Encounters: Shaping and Contesting Environmentalism in Rural Costa Rica.* New York: Berghahn Books.

Vivanco, Luis. 2013. *Reconsidering the Bicycle: An Anthropological Perspective on a New (Old) Thing.* New York: Routledge.

Wackernagel, Mathis, Larry Onisto, Alejandro Callejas Linares, Ina Susana López Falfán, Jesús Méndez García, Ana Isabel Suárez Guerrero, et al. 1997. *The Ecological Footprints of Nations: How Much Nature Do They Use? How Much Nature Do They Have?* Report manuscript. Toronto: International Council for Local Environmental Initiatives.

Wade, Edwin L. 1985. "The Ethnic Art Market in the American Southwest, 1880–1980." In Richard Handler (series ed.) and George W. Stocking, Jr. (volume ed.), *History of Anthropology, Vol. 3: Objects and Others: Essays on Museums and Material Culture,* pp. 167–91. Madison: University of Wisconsin Press.

Wade, Peter. 1997. *Race and Ethnicity in Latin America.* London: Pluto Books.

Wagner, Roy. 1967. *The Curse of Souw: Principles of Daribi Clan Definition and Alliance.* Chicago: University of Chicago Press.

Wagner, Roy. 1969. "Marriage Among the Daribi." In R. M. Glasse and M. J. Meggitt, eds., *Pigs, Pearlshells, and Women: Marriage in the New Guinea Highlands,* pp. 56–76. Englewood Cliffs, NJ: Prentice Hall.

Wagner, Roy. 1975. *The Invention of Culture.* Englewood Cliffs: Prentice-Hall.

Wallace, Anthony F. C. 1956. "Revitalization Movements: Some Theoretical Considerations for Their Comparative Study." *American Anthropologist* 58:264–81.

Wallace, Anthony F. C. 1966. *Religion: An Anthropological View.* New York: Random House.

Wallace, Anthony F. C. 1970. *The Death and Rebirth of the Seneca.* New York: Knopf.

Walsh, Lorena. 2013. Development of Slavery in the 17th-century Chesapeake. Accessed on June 2, 2017: http://www.historyisfun.org/video/development-slavery/.

Warren, Kay. 1998. *Indigenous Movements and Their Critics: Pan-Maya Activism in Guatemala.* Princeton, NJ: Princeton University Press.

Watson-Gegeo, Karen Ann, and Geoffrey White, eds. 1990. *Disentangling: Conflict Discourse in Pacific Societies.* Stanford, CA: Stanford University Press.

Watters, Ethan. 2011. *Crazy Like Us: The Globalization of the American Psyche.* New York: Free Press.

Weiner, Annette. 1992. *Inalienable Possessions: The Paradox of Keeping While Giving.* Berkeley: University of California Press.

Welsch, Robert L. 1983. "Traditional Medicine and Western Medical Options Among the Ningerum of Papua New Guinea." In Lola Romanucci-Ross, Daniel E. Moerman, and Laurence R. Tancredi, eds., *The Anthropology of Medicine: From Culture Toward Medicine,* pp. 32–53. New York: Praeger.

Welsch, Robert L. 2006. "Coaxing the Spirits to Dance." In R. L. Welsch, V.-L. Webb, and S. Haraha, *Coaxing the Spirits to Dance: Art and Society in the Papuan Gulf of New Guinea,* pp. 4–44. Hanover, NH: Hood Museum of Art at Dartmouth College.

Welsch, Robert L. 2013. "Exploring Linguistic Diversity Along the North Coast of New Guinea." In J. Forbes Farmer, ed., *The Social Sciences: Understanding Inquiry and Analysis,* pp. 17–29. Buford, GA: LAD Custom Publishing.

Welsch, Robert L., Luis A. Vivanco, and Augustin Fuentes. 2017. *Anthropology: Asking Questions About Human Origins, Diversity, and Culture.* New York: Oxford University Press.

Werner, Cynthia, and Duran Bell, eds. 2004. *Values and Valuables: From the Sacred to the Symbolic.* Lanham, MD: Rowman Altamira.

Westermark, George D. 1998. "History, Opposition, and Salvation in Agarabi Adventism." *Pacific Studies* 21:51–71.

Weston, Kath. 1993. "Lesbian/Gay Studies in the House of Anthropology." *Annual Review of Anthropology* 22:339–67.

White, Leslie. 1949. *The Science of Culture: A Study of Man and Culture.* New York: Farrar, Strauss.

Whitehead, Neil L. 2004. "Cultures, Conflicts, and the Poetics of Violent Practice." In Neil Whitehead, ed., *Violence,* pp. 3–24. Santa Fe, NM: School of American Research.

Wilk, Richard, and Lisa Cliggett. 2007. *Economies and Cultures: Foundations of Economic Anthropology.* 2nd ed. Boulder, CO: Westview Press.

Wolf, Eric. 1984. *Europe and the People Without History.* Berkeley: University of California Press.

Wolf, Eric. 2001. *Pathways of Power: Building an Anthropology of the Modern World.* Berkeley: University of California Press.

Woolard, Kathryn A. 1998. "Introduction: Language Ideology as a Field of Inquiry." In Bambi B. Shieffelin, Kathryn A. Woolard, and Paul V. Kroskrity, eds., *Language Ideologies: Practice and Theory,* pp. 3–47. New York: Oxford University Press.

Worthman, Carol M. 1995. "Hormones, Sex, and Gender." *Annual Review of Anthropology* 24:593–616.

Wright, Lawrence. 1994. One Drop of Blood. *New Yorker,* July 25, pp. 46–55.

Zagato, Alessandro, ed. 2015. *The Event of Charlie Hebdo: Imaginaries of Freedom and Control.* Oxford: Berghahn.

Credits

Anthropologist as Problem Solver (p. 134): Teresa Mares; **Figure 6.8 (p. 138)**: no known rights holder could be located; **Figure 6.9 (p. 140)**: Bettmann/Getty Images.

CHAPTER 7

Opening image (p. 143): Sim Chi Yin/VII/Redux; **Figure 7.1 (p. 145):** Spontoon Pipe Tomahawk from ANTIQUES ROADSHOW (http://www.pbs.org/wgbh/roadshow/season/18/anaheim-ca/appraisals/spontoon-pipetomahawk-ca-1840--201303A07l) © 1997–2018 WGBH Educational Foundation; **Figure 7.2 (p. 150):** richardmcguire.ca; **Figure 7.3 (p. 152):** AP Photo/Brett Deering, File; **Figure 7.4 (p. 154):** from *Argonauts of the Western Pacific* by Bronislaw Malinowski (1922); **Figure 7.5 (p. 156):** AP Photo/Peter Kramer; **Figure 7.6 (p. 157):** Photo Lot 97 DOE Oceania:Poly: New Zealand: New Zealand Gov't 05097700, National Anthropological Archives, Smithsonian Institution; **Figure 7.7, top (p. 159):** Daderot/Wikipedia; **Figure 7.7, bottom (p. 159):** Photo by James Leynse/Corbis via Getty Images; **Figure 7.8 (p. 161):** AP Photo/Richard Drew; **Anthropologist as Problem Solver (p. 163):** Debby Wong/Shutterstock.

CHAPTER 8

Opening image (p. 167): by Apa Hugo, courtesy of Robert L. Welsch; **Figure 8.1 (p. 169):** © Anthony Bannister/Gallo Images; **Figure 8.2 (p. 174):** Patrick T. Fallon/Bloomberg via Getty Images; **Figure 8.3 (p. 176):** by Apa Hugo, courtesy of Robert L. Welsch; **Figure 8.4 (p. 178):** WOOLAROC MUSEUM, BARTLESVILLE, OKLAHOMA; **Anthropologist as Problem Solver (p. 179):** Courtesy of Maxwell Owusu, photo by Shafica Ahmed; **Figure 8.5 (p. 182):** courtesy of Documentary Educational Resources; **Figure 8.6 (p. 183):** AP Photo; **Figure 8.7 (p. 186):** Photo by Craig Barritt/Getty Images for Electus Digital/WatchLOUD.

CHAPTER 9

Opening image (p. 190): North Wind Picture Archives via AP Images; **Figure 9.1 (p. 193):** Agustín Fuentes, *Core Concepts in Biological Anthropology*, McGraw Hill 2007: 310, Figure 10.4; **Figure 9.2 (p. 196):** from *Pudd'nhead Wilson and Those Extraordinary Twins* by Mark Twain (1894) via HathiTrust; **Figure 9.3 (p. 197):** Bettmann/Getty Images; **Thinking Like an Anthropologist (p. 200):** Courtesy of Robert L. Welsch; **Figure 9.4 (p. 202):** Patti McConville/Alamy Stock Photo; **Figure 9.5 (p. 203):** Pictorial Press Ltd/Alamy Stock Photo;

Figure 9.6 (p. 205): RAVEENDRAN/AFP/Getty Images; **Figure 9.7 (p. 207):** Library of Congress Prints and Photographs Division Washington, D.C. 20540 USA; **Figure 9.8 (p. 210):** Genna Martin/seattlepi.com.

CHAPTER 10

Opening image (p. 213): PASCAL GUYOT/AFP/Getty Images; **Figure 10.1 (p. 215):** © Iris Images/Getty Images; **Figure 10.2 (p. 218):** FABRICE COFFRINI/AFP/Getty Images; **Figure 10.3 (p. 220):** Courtesy of Kirk and Karen Endicott; **Figure 10.4 (p. 223):** Blend Images via AP Images; **Figure 10.5 (p. 225):** Photo by David Victor; **Figure 10.6 (p. 226):** INDRANIL MUKHERJEE/AFP/Getty Images; **Figure 10.7 (p. 228):** HECTOR MATA/AFP/Getty Images; **Thinking Like an Anthropologist (p. 229):** Photo by Jason Kempin/Getty Images for The Point Foundation; **Figure 10.8 (p. 231):** Photo by Arthur Siegel/The LIFE Images Collection/Getty Images.

CHAPTER 11

Opening image (p. 236): Photo by Edgar Negrete/Clasos.com/LatinContent/Getty Images; **Figure 11.2, top (p. 241):** Collection 10: James Willard Schultz Photographs, 1859-1947, Merrill G. Burlingame Special Collections at Montana State University Libraries; **Figure 11.2, bottom (p. 241):** Courtesy of Robert L. Welsch; **Thinking Like an Anthropologist (p. 245):** Trevor Thompson/Alamy Stock Photo; **Figure 11.5 (p. 247):** Courtesy of Robert L. Welsch; **Figure 11.6, top (p. 251):** Photograph Collection, Prints and Photographs Division, Library of Congress, LC-DIG-ppmsca-13196; **Figure 11.6, bottom (p. 251):** GEORGE FREY/AFP/Getty Images.

CHAPTER 12

Opening image (p. 257): AP Photo/BH; **Figure 12.1 (p. 260):** from *The Ghost-Dance Religion and the Sioux Outbreak of 1890* by James Mooney (1896), via Archive.org; **Figure 12.2, top (p. 263):** Photo by Dan Kitwood/Getty Images; **Figure 12.2, bottom (p. 263):** AP Photo/Jessica Kourkounis; **Figure 12.3 (p. 266):** Curtis (Edward S.) Collection, Prints and Photographs Division, Library of Congress, LC-USZ62-47016; **Figure 12.4 (p. 268):** Hood Museum of Art, Dartmouth College: Gift of Peter H. Voulkos; 2001.51.34345; **Figure 12.5 (p. 271):** Hood Museum of Art, Dartmouth College; 29.58.7934; **Figure 12.6 (p. 272):** AP Photo/Chris Clark; **Thinking Like an Anthropologist (p. 273):** Photo by Mario Tama/Getty Images.

CHAPTER 13

Opening image (p. 279): Richard Levine/Alamy Stock Photo; **Figure 13.1 (p. 283):** Hemis/Alamy Stock Photo; **Figure 13.2 (p. 284):** YASUY-OSHI CHIBA/AFP/Getty Images; **Figure 13.3 (p. 287):** AP Photo/Jerome Delay; **Figure 13.4 (p. 288):** Image Source/iStockphoto; **Figure 13.6 (p. 292):** Breastfeeding promotion campaign poster developed by Arkansas Foundation for Medical Care, www.afmc.org, under contract with the Arkansas Department of Human Services, Division of Medical Services. Image copyright 2014 by Getty Images. All rights reserved; **Figure 13.8 (p. 298):** Jochen Tack/Alamy Stock Photo; **Anthropologist as Problem Solver (p. 299):** Nancy Scheper-Hughes.

CHAPTER 14

Opening image (p. 304): With permission of the Royal Ontario Museum © ROM; **Figure 14.1 (p. 309):** Courtesy of Kellen Haak; **Anthropologist as Problem Solver (p. 310):** The Field Museum, GN91326_119d, Photographer John Weinstein; **Figure 14.2 (p. 314):** Courtesy of Luis A. Vivanco; **Figure 14.3 (p. 316):** Hood Museum of Art; **Figure 14.4 (p. 317):** Courtesy of Robert L. Welsch; **Figure 14.5 (p. 319):** Paradigm PR; **Figure 14.6 (p. 320):** Private Collection/The Stapleton Collection/Bridgeman Images; **Figure 14.7 (p. 322):** CREATISTA/Shutterstock.

EPILOGUE

Opening image (p. 326): Tim Sambrook/Alamy Stock Photo.

Index